"This is a brilliant, disturbing book. Modern cities have often been seen as places of extraordinary creativity and creative destruction, but for this very reason they are also often sites of spectacular military and paramilitary violence. These essays unsettle so many taken-for-granted ways of thinking about cities. Their authors crouch and scurry along streets that, for too long, have seemed opaque to our political and intellectual imaginations. There is a tremendous power and urgency to their arguments that should be confronted by anyone concerned at the intimacy of the connections between cities, war, and terrorism."

Derek Gregory, author of *The Colonial Present*

"*Cites, War, and Terrorism* is a rare accomplishment. Bringing together a truly interdisciplinary group of authors, it provides the first, original investigation of the urbanization of modern conflict. In their plural ways and myriad sites, the essays in this book investigate the changing nature of the contemporary battlespace and the implosion of distinctions between inside and outside, civilian and military. Together, they mark the beginning of a new and vital field of analysis – an urban geopolitics – that must concern us all."

David Campbell, author of *Writing Security*

"Acts of war and terror against cities and their inhabitants (both anti-state and state sanctioned) are saturating our contemporary world. Yet urban researchers are in denial of this starkest of contemporary urban realities. Graham brings together the renegade thinkers and researchers who are tracking the ways in which global geopolitics is imploding into the urban world. *Cities, War, and Terrorism* is a stunningly successful synthesis of the subtle interpenetration of global geopolitics and the micro-politics of cities and neighborhoods. It marks the beginning of a new and crucial research domain: that of urban geopolitics. This book must, and will, change the way urban researchers and planners think about and explore city regions. It helps to make sense of the ways in which the historic functions of cities and nation-states (social welfare, education, health, planning) are being overwhelmed by the imperative of 'security' and the politics of fear. Purposely provocative and deeply disturbing."

Leonie Sandercock, author of *Towards Cosmopolis*

D1193146

CITIES, WAR, AND TERRORISM

Studies in Urban and Social Change

Published by Blackwell in association with the *International Journal of Urban and Regional Research*. Series editors: Harvey Molotch, Linda McDowell, Margit Mayer, Chris Pickvance.

The Blackwell Studies in Urban and Social Change aim to advance debates and empirical analyses stimulated by changes in the fortunes of cities and regions across the world. Topics range from monographs on single places to large-scale comparisons across East and West, North and South. The series is explicitly interdisciplinary; the editors judge books by their contribution to intellectual solutions rather than according to disciplinary origin.

Published

Cities, War, and Terrorism
Stephen Graham (ed.)

Cities and Visitors: Regulating Tourists, Markets, and City Space
Lily M. Hoffman, Susan S. Fainstein, and Dennis R. Judd (eds.)

Understanding the City: Contemporary and Future Perspectives
John Eade and Christopher Mele (eds.)

The New Chinese City: Globalization and Market Reform
John R. Logan (ed.)

Cinema and the City: Film and Urban Societies in a Global Context
Mark Shiel and Tony Fitzmaurice (eds.)

The Social Control of Cities? A Comparative Perspective
Sophie Body-Gendrot

Globalizing Cities: A New Spatial Order?
Peter Marcuse and Ronald van Kempen (eds.)

Contemporary Urban Japan: A Sociology of Consumption
John Clammer

Capital Culture: Gender at Work in the City
Linda McDowell

Cities After Socialism: Urban and Regional Change and Conflict in Post-Socialist Societies
Gregory Andrusz, Michael Harloe, and Ivan Szelenyi (eds.)

The People's Home? Social Rented Housing in Europe and America
Michael Harloe

Post-Fordism
Ash Amin (ed.)

Free Markets and Food Riots
John Walton and David Seddon

Urban Poverty and the Underclass: A Reader
Enzo Mingione

Forthcoming

Social Capital in Practice
Talja Blokland and Mike Savage (eds.)

Getting Into Local Power: The Representation of Ethnic Minorities
Romain Garbaye

Cities and Regions in a Global Era
Alan Harding (ed.)

Cities of Europe
Yuri Kazepov (ed.)

Urban South Africa
Alan Mabin and Susan Parnell

Urban Social Movements and the State
Margit Mayer

Social Capital Formation in Immigrant Neighborhoods
Min Zhou

Eurostars and Eurocities
Adrian Favell

CITIES, WAR, AND TERRORISM

TOWARDS AN URBAN GEOPOLITICS

Edited by

Stephen Graham

BLACKWELL PUBLISHING
350 Main Street, Malden, MA 02148-5020, USA
9600 Garsington Road, Oxford OX4 2DQ, UK
550 Swanston Street, Carlton, Victoria 3053, Australia

First published 2004 by Blackwell Publishing Ltd

2   2005

Library of Congress Cataloging-in-Publication Data

Cities, war, and terrorism: towards an urban geopolitics / edited by Stephen Graham.
p. cm.—(Studies in urban and social change)
Includes bibliographical references and index.
ISBN 1-4051-1574-2 (hbk : alk. paper)—ISBN 1-4051-1575-0 (alk. paper)
1. Cities and towns. 2. Urban warfare. 3. Terrorism. I. Graham, Stephen, 1965– II. Series.
HT119.C573 2004
307.76—dc22

                                                                2004004244

ISBN-13: 978-1-4051-1574-2 (hbk : alk. paper)—ISBN-13: 978-1-4051-1575-9 (alk. paper)

A catalogue record for this title is available from the British Library.

Set in 10/12 pt Plantin
by Kolam Information Services Pvt. Ltd, Pondicherry, India
Printed and bound in India
by Gopsons Papers Ltd, Noida

The publisher's policy is to use permanent paper from mills that operate a sustainable forestry policy, and which has been manufactured from pulp processed using acid-free and elementary chlorine-free practices. Furthermore, the publisher ensures that the text paper and cover board used have met acceptable environmental accreditation standards.

For further information on
Blackwell Publishing, visit our website:
www.blackwellpublishing.com

For Mum and Barb

Contents

Part II: Urbicide and the Urbanization of Warfare

Part III: Exposed Cities: Urban Impacts of Terrorism and the "War on Terror"

Plates

Figures

Tables

Notes on Contributors

Zygmunt Bauman is Emeritus Professor of Sociology at the University of Leeds and the University of Warsaw. He was formerly of the University of Warsaw until 1968 and the University of Tel Aviv, and held several visiting professorships, in Australia and elsewhere, before coming to Leeds. He is known throughout the world for works such as *Legislators and Interpreters* (1987), *Modernity and the Holocaust* (1989), *Modernity and Ambivalence* (1991), *and Postmodern Ethics* (1993). He is the author of some 21 books in English and of numerous articles and reviews. He was awarded the Amalfi European Prize in 1990 and the Adorno Prize in 1998. It is difficult to think of higher honors being bestowed on a sociologist, in this case of European and indeed world standing.

Ryan Bishop is Associate Professor in the American Studies Program and the Department of English at the National University of Singapore. Among his publications are works on international sex tourism in Thailand, critical theory, rhetoric, and the history of technology in relation to the university, the military, and aesthetics. He is co-editor of *Postcolonial Urbanism* (with John Phillips and Wei Wei Yeo).

Gregory Clancey received his PhD from the Program in the History and Social Study of Science and Technology at MIT, and currently teaches in the Department of History at the National University of Singapore. He is the co-author of *Major Problems in the History of American Technology* (with M. Roe Smith), and *Historical Perspectives on Science, Technology, and Medicine in East Asia* (with Alan Chan and Loy Hui Chieh). His research centers on constructions of science and nature in modern Japan.

Jon Coaffee is a Lecturer in Urban Regeneration in the Global Urban Research Unit, School of Architecture, Planning and Landscape, University of Newcastle. He is an urban geographer by background, and undertakes research within the broad areas of urban regeneration/governance and militarized urban landscapes. He undertook his doctoral research on the relationship between terrorist risk, insurance, and changes to urban landscapes. This was published in book form as *Terrorism, Risk and the City* (2003). His current work has refined this earlier work, placing it within the context of the post-9/11 world.

Martin Coward is a Lecturer in International Relations at the University of Sussex. His research focuses on political violence, theories of community, and questions of territoriality. His doctoral work comprised an analysis of the relation between urban destruction and the constitution of community in the context of the 1992–5 Bosnian war. Elements of this work can be found in "Community as heterogeneous ensemble: Mostar and multiculturalism," *Alternatives*, Vol. 27, No. 1, 2002.

Matthew Farish is an SSHRC Postdoctoral Fellow in the Munk Centre for International Studies, University of Toronto. He holds a PhD from the University of British Columbia. His research interests range from foreign correspondence to film noir, and he is currently preparing a book manuscript on the geography of militarism in the United States after World War II.

Stephen Graham is Professor of Human Geography at the University of Durham, having moved there from Newcastle University's School of Architecture, Planning and Landscape in spring 2004. His research develops critical perspectives of the changing relations between cities, mobilities, technologies, and social power. He is the co-author of *Telecommunications and the City* and *Splintering Urbanism* (both with Simon Marvin), the editor of the *Cybercities Reader*, and the co-editor of *Managing Cities*.

Simon Guy is Professor of Urban Development in the School of Architecture, Planning and Landscape at the University of Newcastle. His research interests revolve around the social production and consumption of technology and the material environment. He has undertaken research into a wide spectrum of urban design and development issues, including the development of greener buildings, the role of architecture in urban regeneration, and the links between environmental building design and the provision of infrastructure services. This research has been funded by the UK's Economic and Social Research Council, the UK's Engineering and Physical Research Council, and the European Union.

Marc W. Herold is an Associate Professor of Economic Development, International Affairs and Women's Studies at the University of New Hampshire, where he has taught since 1975. His current research interests are on Brazil (survival strategies of poor urban women, the construction of modern business since 1840, steamship rivalry to secure trade routes to Brazil, a case study of economic change of the state of Bahia) and Afghanistan. He is the author of *Blown Away: The Myth – and Reality – of "Precision" Bombing in Afghanistan* (2004). His work on the human costs of the US war upon Afghanistan has been translated into many foreign languages and is cited worldwide.

Alice Hills lectures in Defence Studies for King's College, London at the Joint Services Command and Staff College, where she specializes in urban operations and police–military relations. In 2001 she was awarded the British Academy's Thank-Offering to Britain fellowship for research into urban operations as a potentially critical security issue.

Timothy W. Luke is University Distinguished Professor of Political Science as well as Program Chair for Government and International Affairs in the School of Public and International Affairs at Virginia Polytechnic Institute and State University in Blacksburg, Virginia. His research interests are focused upon issues in political and social theory, international affairs, and environmental politics.

David Lyon is Professor of Sociology at Queen's University, Kingston, Ontario and Director of the Surveillance Project. He teaches in the areas of sociology of technology, sociology of religion, and social theory. Among his most recent books are *Surveillance Society: Monitoring Everyday Life* (2001), *Surveillance as Social Sorting: Privacy, Risk, and Digital Discrimination* (ed., 2003), and *Surveillance after September 11* (2003).

Peter Marcuse, a lawyer and urban planner, is Professor of Urban Planning at Columbia University in New York City. His book *Globalizing Cities: A New Spatial Order of Cities*, co-edited with Ronald van Kempen, deals with the impact of globalization on internal urban structure of a diverse set of cities around the world. *Of States and Cities: On the Partitioning of Urban Space*, similarly co-edited, focuses on the role of states in dealing with the urban consequences of globalization.

Martin Shaw is a sociologist of war and Professor of International Relations and Politics, University of Sussex, and editor of www.theglobalsite.a-c.uk. He is the author of many books on war, the state and global politics, including *War and Genocide* (2003).

Michael Sorkin is the Principal of the Michael Sorkin Studio and Director of the Graduate Program in Urban Design at the City College of New York. His books include *The Next Jerusalem: Sharing the Divided City*, *Starting From Zero: Reconstructing Downtown New York*, and *Some Assembly Required*. The Sorkin Studio is currently working on urban design for Queens Plaza,

New York, a masterplan for CCNY, a plan for the Cleveland waterfront, and a housing project in Vienna.

Robert Warren is a Professor of Urban Affairs and Public Policy at the University of Delaware. His work has focused on urban governance, telecommunications and information technology, and planning theory. He is currently doing further research on the militarization of urban space and on the rhetoric and reality of using surveillance technology for controlling movement and behavior in cities.

Eyal Weizman is an architect based in Tel Aviv and London. After graduating from the Architecture Association in London, he worked with Zvi Hecker in Berlin. He is now in private practice. Among the projects done in partnership with Rafi Segal are the rebuilding of the Ashdod Museum of Art (opened June 2003), a stage set for Itim Theatre Company (premiered at the Lincoln Center in July 2003), and a runner up proposal for the Tel Aviv Museum competition. The exhibition and the catalogue *A Civilian Occupation: The Politics of Israeli Architecture*, which he edited/curated together with Rafi Segal, were banned by the Israeli Association of Architects, but were later shown at the Storefront Gallery for Art and Architecture (New York, February 2003), in Territories at the Kunst-Werke (Berlin, May 2003), and in Witte de With in Rotterdam. The catalogue is now published.

Series Editors' Preface

The Blackwell *Studies in Urban and Social Change* series aims to advance theoretical debates and empirical analyses stimulated by changes in the fortunes of cities and regions across the world. Among topics taken up in past volumes and welcomed for future submissions are:

- Connections between economic restructuring and urban change
- Urban divisions, difference, and diversity
- Convergence and divergence among regions of east and west, north, and south
- Urban and environmental movements
- International migration and capital flows
- Trends in urban political economy
- Patterns of urban-based consumption

The series is explicitly interdisciplinary; the editors judge books by their contribution to intellectual solutions rather than according to disciplinary origin.

Proposals may be submitted to members of the series Editorial Committee:

Harvey Molotch
Linda McDowell
Margit Mayer
Chris Pickvance

Preface

This book is the culmination of a widespread, collective effort. Through its production I have generated considerable debts of gratitude.

First and foremost, I must thank Simon Marvin for his friendship and inspiration over the past twelve years. This book is the result of three years' collaborative work through which Simon and I have tried to unearth some of the links between cities, war, and terrorism. Starting before 9/11, when we began to organize a conference called Cities as Strategic Sites (held in Manchester in November 2002), this collaborative work has been central in the shaping of this book. While Simon's name is not on the cover, and I have carried out the final stages of the editing, Simon has played a massive role in shaping this work in terms of the organization and running of that conference (which brought together first drafts of many of the chapters here), fundraising, sourcing literature, approaching authors, structuring the book, and developing theoretical and analytical discussions.

Second, I owe my colleagues and friends at Newcastle University's School of Architecture, Planning and Landscape an inestimable debt. For eleven years they were the continuing source of remarkable levels of inspiration, friendship, and support. As my research shifted towards the urban aspects of geopolitics I have been able to find enormous inspiration from Newcastle colleagues. While I have now moved a short distance south to Durham, I am glad that my proximity means that I will still be able to play some part in Newcastle University. Particular gratitude is due to Jon Coaffee, David Campbell, Stu Cameron, Andy Gillespie, Simon Guy, Patsy Healey, Ali Madani Ponv, Tim Shaw, Suzanne Speak, Elisabeth Storey, Geoff Vigar, and David Wood.

Third, I would like to thank the British Academy for supporting my research through a Research Readership (2003–5). Without their support this book simply could not have been completed.

Fourth, thanks are due to everyone who helped on the production side of the book. Harvey Molotch, Linda McDowell, Margit Mayer, and Chris Pickvance helped considerably in sharpening the book's focus in the initial stages. Angela Cohen, Jack Messenger, and Brian Johnson did an excellent job on the production of the book.

Finally, this book would not have been possible without the tolerance, and dedication, of the chapter authors, all of whom produced excellent work at short notice. Thanks for being so tolerant to delays and my suggestions for changes. I hope that you feel that the final result does your work justice!

The following authors would like to make acknowledgments for their respective chapters:

Ryan Bishop and Greg Clancey's chapter is republished from R. Bishop, J. Phillips, and Wei Wei (eds.), *Postcolonial Urbanism: Southeast Asian Cities and Global Processes*, London: Routledge, 63–86 ©2003 by Taylor and Francis. Reproduced by permission of Routledge/Taylor & Francis Books, Inc.

Jon Coaffee's chapter is a revised version of a paper entitled "Morphing the counter-terrorist response: Beating the bombers in London's financial heart," published in *Knowledge, Technology and Policy* (Transaction Periodicals), 2003.

Martin Coward would like to thank the University of Sussex for financial assistance in obtaining permissions for the image of Mostar Bridge. Parts of this chapter are based on material from "Community as heterogeneous ensemble: Mostar and multiculturalism," *Alternatives*, Vol. 27, No. 1, 2002, copyright (2002) by Lynne Rienner Publishers. Used with permission. Earlier versions of this paper were presented at *Cities as Strategic Sites: Militarization, Anti-Globalization and Warfare* (a conference at the University of Salford's Centre for Sustainable Urban and Regional Futures) and the University of Sussex. He would like to thank those present on these occasions for their comments. He would also like to thank David Campbell for his comments on an earlier draft of this paper.

Parts of Matthew Farish's chapter are drawn from a longer, less empirical sketch of Cold War urbanism published in *Cultural Geographies*, 10, 3 (2003).

Stephen Graham's chapter "cities as strategic sites" includes some of the text published in an article in *City* 8 (2), 2004.

Stephen Graham's chapter, "Constructing urbicide by bulldozer in the occupied territories," is an updated and adapted version of the essay published as "Lessons in urbicide" in *New Left Review*, 19, Jan./Feb., 63–78. He would like to thank Eyal Weizmann, Bill Cook, Susan Brannon, Micah Ian Wright, and Nir Kafri for kindly agreeing to provide illustrative material for his various chapters in the book.

David Lyon's chapter was originally presented as a paper at the International Sociological Association meetings in Brisbane, July 2002, and a revised version appeared in the *International Journal of Urban and Regional Research*, September 2003. This version is further revised. Some sections appear in Lyon (2003). David Lyon would also like to thank Bart Simon of Concordia University for discussions on the distinction between monitoring and identifying.

The first part of Martin Shaw's chapter was originally published as "Nueva guerras urbanas," *Dos, Dos: Revista Sobre Las Cuidades* (Valladolid, Spain), 2, 1997, pp. 67–75, and he is grateful to the editors of that journal for first stimulating him to write about the issue. This work then appeared in English as "New wars of the city" on his personal website, www.martin-shaw.org.

Stephen Graham
Durham

Introduction: Cities, Warfare, and States of Emergency

Stephen Graham

Across the world people who live in, have abandoned or been expelled from cities can testify to the mounting crises of contemporary urban life. (Schneider and Susser, 2003: 1)

Baghdad burns in real time. The global population accelerates towards the seven billion mark. Protestors rally in the streets – from Karachi to São Paulo to Lagos. The Third World is ravaged by an incurable epidemic. Information is constant. Distance is negligible. Sprawl continues its slow march across vast territories, as the world gets hotter by the day. (Johnson, 2003: 7)

To be sure, a cityscape is not made of flesh. Still, sheared-off buildings are almost as eloquent as body parts (Kabul, Sarajevo, East Mostar, Groznyy, 16 acres of lower Manhattan after September 11, 2001, the refugee camp in Jenin). Look, the photographs say, this is what it's like. This is what war does. War tears, war rends. War rips open, eviscerates. War scorches. War dismembers. War ruins. (Sontag, 2003: 5)

Being chiefly human, cities can be killed. (Spiller, 2000: 6)

Each new conflagration pushes at the limits of the humanly tolerable...All too often, the city's survival hangs in a precious balance. (Lang, 1996: 5)

The Mutuality of War and the City

Cities, warfare, and organized political violence have always been mutual constructions. "The city, the polis, is constitutive of the form of conflict called *war*, just as war is itself constitutive of the political form called the *city*" (Virilio, 2002: 5; original emphasis). War and the city have intimately shaped each other throughout urban and military history. "There is . . . a direct reciprocity between war and cities," writes the geographer Ken Hewitt. "The latter are the more thoroughgoing constructs of collective life, containing the definitive human places. War is the most thoroughgoing or consciously prosecuted occasion of collective violence that destroys places" (1983: 258).

The widespread survival of massive urban fortifications – especially in Asia, Africa, Latin America, and Europe – are a living testament to the fact that, in premodern and pre-nation-state civilizations, city-states were the actual agents, as well as the main targets, of war. In premodern times cities were built for defense as well as being dominant sites of commerce, exchange, and political, religious, and social power. "The city, with its buttressed walls, its ramparts and moats, stood as an outstanding display of ever-threatening aggression" (Mumford, 1961: 44).

The sacking and killing of fortified cities and their inhabitants was the central event in premodern war (Weber, 1958; Gravett, 1990; Corfis and Wolfe, 1995; Kern, 1990). Indeed (often allegorical) stories of such acts make up a good part of the Bible – especially the books of Jeremiah and Lamentations – and other ancient and classical religious and philosophical texts. "Myths of urban ruin grow at our culture's root" (Berman, 1996).

In the sixteenth and seventeenth centuries, as modern nation-states started to emerge in Europe as "bordered power containers," they began seeking a monopoly on political violence (Giddens, 1985b). "The states caught up with the forward gallop of the towns" (Braudel, 1973: 398). The expanding imperial and metropolitan cities that lay at the core of nation-states were no longer organizers of their own armies and defenses, but they maintained political power and reach. Such cities directed violence, control, repression, and the colonial acquisition of territory, raw materials, wealth, and labor power from afar (Driver and Gilbert, 2003).

By the nineteenth and twentieth centuries, industrial cities in the global North had grown in synchrony with the killing powers of technology. They provided the men and material to sustain the massive industrial or "total" wars of the twentieth century. At the same time, their (often female-staffed) industries and neighborhoods emerged as the prime targets for total war. The industrial city thus became "in its entirety a space for war. Within a few years . . . bombing moved from the selective destruction of key sites within cities to extensive attacks on urban areas and, finally, to instantaneous annihilation of entire urban spaces and populations" (Shaw, 2003: 131). Right up to the start of the twenty-first century, then, the capture of strategic and politically important cities remains "the ultimate symbol of conquest and national survival" (Shaw, 2001: 1).

In fact, the deliberate destruction and targeting of cities and their support systems in times of war and crisis is a constant throughout the 8,000 years or so of urban history on our planet. Hewitt, speaking in 1987, pointed out:

Destruction of places, driven by fear and hatred, runs through the whole history of wars, from ancient Troy or Carthage, to Warsaw and Hiroshima in our own century. The miseries, uprootings, and deaths of civilians in besieged cities, especially after defeat, stand amongst the most terrible indictments of the powerful and victorious. In that sense, there is, despite the progress of weapons of devastation, a continuity in the experience of civilians from Euripides' *Trojan Women* or the Lamentations of Jeremiah, to the cries of widowed women and orphaned children in Beirut, Belfast, the villages of Afghanistan, and those of El Salvador. (Hewitt, 1987: 469)

Given the centrality of both urbanization and the prosecution of political violence to modernity, this subtle interpenetration of cities and warfare should be no surprise. "After all, modernity, through most of its career, has been modernity at war" (Pieterse, 2002: 3).

While far from new, acts of war and terror against cities and their inhabitants are saturating our world. For centuries, it has not been feasible to contain cities within defensive walls or effective cordons which protect their citizens from military force (Virilio, 1987). Just as it is no longer adequate to theorize cities as local, bounded sites that are separated off from the rest of the world, so, similarly, political violence is now fueled and sustained by transnational networks that can be global and local at the same time.

"Security" and the Urbanization of War

Security and fear have become the dominant chords in the politics of liberal democracies. (Jayasuriya, 2002: 131)

While they remain major sites of military, economic, and regulatory power, nation-states are becoming increasingly "decentered." Within a context of neoliberal globalization, transnational flows between cities and metropolitan regions, and the growth of transnational governance, are undermining their coherence and meaning. In some cases, modern, developmentalist nation-states have collapsed or "failed" altogether since the end of the Cold War.

As a result, "with regard to violence, as with production, the state no longer holds the preeminent position it used to" (Pieterse 2002: 2). Traditional state vs. state wars, driven by imperial or geopolitical imperatives of maintaining, or expanding, national territories, are now rare events deserving special historical scrutiny. In their place, non-traditional, "asymmetric," "informal," or "new" wars are proliferating (Kaldor, 1999).

Such wars have not reduced the military and security efforts of nation-states. Rather, the risks thrown up by such wars, which tend to transcend national boundaries and territories, now mean that "security" "imposes itself as the basic principle of state activity" (Agamben, 2002: 1). Some even argue that the imperative of "security" is beginning to overwhelm the other, historic functions of nation-states that were built up over the nineteenth and twentieth centuries (such as social welfare, education, health, infrastructure development, economic regulation, and planning). "What used to be one among several decisive measures of public administration until the first half of the twentieth century," writes Italian philosopher Georgio Agamben, "now becomes the sole criterion of political legitimation" (2002: 1).

In the "new" wars of the post-Cold War era – which increasingly straddle the "technology gaps" separating advanced industrial nations from informal fighters – cities are the key sites. Indeed, urban areas are now the "lightning conductors" for the world's political violence. Warfare, like everything else, is being *urbanized*. The great geopolitical contests of cultural change, ethnic conflict, and diasporic social mixing; of economic reregulation and liberalization; of militarization, informatization, resource exploitation, and ecological change are, to a growing extent, boiling down to often violent conflicts in the key strategic sites of our age: contemporary cities (Sassen, 2002b).

As a result, war, "terrorism," and cities are redefining each other in complex, but poorly explored, ways. Such redefinitions are, in turn, bound up with deeper shifts in the ways in which time, space, technology, mobility, and power are constructed and experienced in our societies as a whole (Virilio, 1986).

Warfare Re-Enters the City: The Parallel "Rescaling" of Urbanism and Political Violence

As the bipolar world fades away, we are moving from a world of enemies to one of dangers and risks. (Beck, 1999: 3)

It is now clear that the days of the classical Clauswitzian definition of warfare as a symmetrical engagement between state armies in the open field are over. War has entered the city again – the sphere of the everyday, the private realm of the house...We find ourselves nervous when we use public transport systems or mingle in crowds, due to frequent bomb scares. (Misselwitz and Weizman, 2003: 272)

The last two decades have seen a geopolitical and strategic reshaping of our world based heavily on a proliferation of organized, extremely violent acts against cities, those who live in them, and the support systems that make them work.

The events of September 11, 2001 are, of course, the best known and extensively reported case (see Calhoun, Price, and Timmer, 2002; Booth and Dunne, 2002). But there are many, many others. Catastrophic urban terrorist attacks – fueled by religious or political radicalism, anti-modernism, or resistance to brutal occupation, repression, or perceived biases of globalization – have also targeted urban sites in Madrid, Kitay (Bali), Moscow, Mumbai (Bombay), and Karachi; Jakarta, Casablanca, Delhi, and Islamabad; Riyadh, Mombassa, Kabul, Istanbul, and Nairobi.

Since 9/11, George Bush's "war on terror" – a purported response to those attacks – has inflicted massive onslaughts by US and British forces on Basra, Baghdad, Fallujah, Kandahar, Kabul, and surrounding areas. In the case of Iraq, this has happened despite the fact there was not a shred of evidence to link Saddam Hussein's regime to Al-Qaeda. Far from being routes to simple "regime change" and peaceful reconstruction, however, these attacks have been followed by complex, uneven, guerrilla-style resistance campaigns against occupying ground forces. Such forces have to move down from their GPS targeting from 40,000 ft, or out from behind armored plate, to occupy urban sites, and have thus become immensely more vulnerable to political opponents and bitter local civilians alike.

Nor should we forget the leveling of Groznyy by the Russians in 1996; the sieges of Sarajevo and Mostar in the Balkan wars of the early 1990s; the LA riots of 1992; the US's bloody incursion into Mogadishu in 1993; the continuing suicide bombings in Israeli bars, buses, and malls; Israel's bulldozing of Jenin and Nablus in spring 2002 and its continuing policies of strangulation, immiseration, and demolition against Palestinian cities; or the resource- or drug-fueled guerrilla wars in Freetown, Bogotá, and Monrovia.

Finally, we must not ignore the increasingly violent, temporary urban sieges that now regularly occur around the planet (Warren, this volume; Cockburn and St. Clair, 2000; Negri, 2002). Anti-globalization or anti-state movements "swarm" together around the fortified urban summits of the IMF, the G8, and the WTO, to protest against the inequities of neoliberal globalization. In postmodern, high-tech replays of medieval sieges, temporary walls, battlements, and massive armed force work – often with extreme violence – to try to separate the "inside" from the "outside" on the other side of the street. This happens even though both sets of protagonists are global organizations temporarily settled in local space for ritualized, bloody combat.

More and more, civilian and domestic spaces of urban civil societies emerge, or in many cases *reemerge*, as *geopolitically* charged spaces (Luke, this volume). Both cities and organized violence are "rescaling" together as they are remade through transnational connections, technologies, diasporas, and flows, which tend to transcend and undermine the (always fleeting and violently enforced) stabilities of Cold War blocs or modern nation-states (Dalby, 2000; Giddens, 1985b).

As a result, the world's geopolitical struggles increasingly articulate around violent conflicts over very local, urban, strategic sites (Scheper-Hughes and Bourgois, 2003; Sassen, 2002b). This process parallels, and is closely bound up with, the wider processes of neoliberal globalization. For these, too, are unleashing powerful processes of "creative destruction" which tend to intensify the roles of strategic, subnational spaces and city regions in economic governance and social, cultural, and political change (Brenner and Theodore, 2002).

The "Implosion of Global and National Politics into the Urban World"

The [9/11] attacks on the US and the war against organized terrorism should not keep us from seeing and remembering all the other struggles going on and the larger landscape of rage and hopelessness engulfing more and more people. (Sassen, 2002b: 313)

Far from going away, then, strategies of deliberately attacking the systems and places that support civilian urban life have only become more sophisticated since the mass, total, urban annihilation that characterized the twentieth century. The deliberate devastation of urban living spaces continues apace. Fueling it are multiple, parallel transformations which together characterize the postcolonial, post-Cold War world. Here we must consider a veritable blizzard of factors: the unleashing of previously constrained ethnic hatreds since the end of the Cold War bipolar system; the proliferation of fundamentalist religious and political groups; the militarization of gangs, drug cartels, militia, corrupt political regimes, and law enforcement agencies; the failure of many national and local states; the urbanization of populations and terrain; the growing accessibility of heavy weapons; a crisis of increasing social polarization at all geographical scales; and the growing scarcity of many essential resources (see Turton, 2002; Castells, 1997, 1998).

To this cocktail we must add the destabilizing effects of the US's increasingly aggressive and violent interventions in a widening range of nations and its long-term support for many a repressive, brutal regime; plus the deleterious impacts of neoliberal restructuring and "structural adjustment" programs imposed on many nations by the IMF, WTO, and World Bank in the past two decades (Hoogvelt, 1997). Such programs have added to the sense of crisis in many cities. This is because they have directly resulted in the erosion of social and economic security and the further immiseration of the urban poor (and, increasingly, the urban middle classes) (see Falk, 1999; Lomnitz, 2003; Humphrey, 2003; Schneider and Susser, 2003).

These complex processes of change are interweaving at a time when the scale of urbanization is at an unprecedented global level. During the 1990s the world's urban population grew by 36 percent. By 2003, 900 million people lived in slums. The increasing polarization of cities caused by neo-liberal globalization is providing many conditions that are ripe for extremes of civil and militarized violence (Vidal, 2003; Castells, 1997, 1998).

Neoliberal globalization *itself* operates through a vast scale of violence, exploitation, and criminality (Brennan, 2003; Hardt and Negri, 2000). In fact, in many ways its operation is similar to the "rhizomatic" dynamics of transnational terrorism. "Our own politicians and businesses sail a strikingly similar pirate sea [to the al-Qaeda network]," suggests the archi-tectural writer Keller Easterling, "slipping between legal jurisdictions, lever-aging advantages in the differential value of labor and currency, brandishing national identity one moment and laundering it the next, using lies and disguises to neutralize cultural or political differences" (2002: 189).

Put together, these factors are forcing what the anthropologist Arjun Appadurai has called an "implosion of global and national politics into the urban world" (1996: 152). This has led to a proliferation of bloody, largely urban, wars. Many of these, in turn, have stimulated vast migrations and the construction of city-scale refugee camps to accommodate displaced populations (which stood at a global figure of 50 million by 2002) (see Agier, 2002; Diken and Laustsen, 2003).

Such "new" urban wars "take their energy from macro events and processes ... that link global politics to the micro politics of streets and neighborhoods" (Appadurai, 1996: 152–3):

> In the conditions of ethnic unrest and urban warfare that characterize cities such as Belfast and Los Angeles, Ahmedabad and Sarajevo, Mogadishu and Johannesburg, urban war zones are becoming armed camps, driven wholly by *implosive* forces that fold into neighborhoods the most violent and problem-atic repercussions of wider regional, national, and global processes. (Appa-durai, 1996: 152–3; original emphasis)

To Appadurai, these new urban wars thus represent little less than:

> a new phase in the life of cities, where the concentration of ethnic popula-tions, the availability of heavy weaponry, and the crowded conditions of civic life create futurist forms of warfare ... and where a general desolation of the national and global landscape has transposed many bizarre racial, religious, and linguistic enmities into scenarios of unrelieved urban terror. (Appadurai, 1996: 152–3)

Dialectics of Place Attachment: The City as Site and Symbol for Violent Struggle

Contemporary cities are the battlegrounds on which global powers and stubbornly local meanings and identities meet. (Bauman, 2001: 20)

Cities are often located on the fault-lines between cultures – between modernizing societies and traditional cultures; between individual-based and community based economies; between democracy and more authoritarian regimes; between colonial governments and native populations. (Bollens, 2001: 170)

Appadurai helps us understand why contemporary warfare and terror now largely boil down to contests over the spaces, symbols, meanings, support systems, or power structures of cities and urban places. As throughout the history of war, such struggles are fueled by dichotomized constructions of "us" and an "othered" *them* – the target...the enemy...the hated. "War...mobilizes the highly charged and dangerous dialectic of place attachment," writes Ken Hewitt. This involves "the perceived antithesis of 'our' places or homeland and 'theirs,' an unbridled sentimentalizing of one's own while dehumanizing the enemy's people and land" (1983: 258).

Such binaried views of the world as a "black-and-white" split of territories, ethnicities, religions, political or religious orientations, and identities – of "us" and "them" – are essential to make and sustain political violence. The latest Western rhetoric of a "clash of civilizations" (Huntingdon, 1993), or Al-Qaeda's assertion of the need for "pure," "Islamic" transnational spaces and states, are only two among many of such incendiary propositions.

"Cracking Down on Diaspora": The "Domestic Front" in the "War on Terror"

National borders have ceased being continuous lines on the earth's surface and [have] become non-related sets of lines and points situated within each country. (Andreu, 1997: 58)

The rhetoric of "insides" needing protection from external threats in the form of international organizations is pervasive. (Dalby, 2000: 5)

The reconstruction of national boundaries rel[ies] on linguistic work. (Kaplan, 2003: 85)

In attempting to split an intrinsically mobile, heterogeneous, and urbanizing world into jigsaw-like pieces of territory – which are assumed to have essential and "pure" identities – such views fundamentally and violently challenge the reality of cities and urban life on our planet (Laguerre, 2003). As throughout urban history, in these times of intensifying globalization urban areas are crucial centers of heterogeneous mixing. Increasingly, the differences, tolerances, and hatreds of the globe are inseparably related to, and constituted through, day-to-day encounters, and cosmopolitan accommodations (and frictions) in the streetscapes, schools, city halls, and neighborhoods of cities.

Ironically, 9/11 itself symbolized that this telescoping of the world's political violence into the city (and vice versa) was now inescapable. "If it existed, any comfortable distinction between domestic and international, here and there, us and them, ceased to have meaning after that day" (Hyndman, 2003: 1).

On the one hand, then, the 9/11 attacks can be seen as part of a fundamentalist, transnational war, or Jihad, by radical Islamic movements against pluralistic and heterogeneous mixing in (capitalist) cities (Buck-Morss, 2003). This loosely affiliated network of radical Islamic terror organizations needs to be considered as one of a large number of social movements against what Castells calls the "new global order." Heterogeneous mixing of ethnicities and religious groups holds no place within *umma*, the transnational fundamentalist Islamic space that these movements are struggling to establish (Castells, 2004: 111). Thus, it is notable that cities that have long sustained complex heterogeneities, religious pluralism, and multiple diasporas – New York and Istanbul, for example – have been prime targets for catastrophic terror attacks. Indeed, in their own horrible way, the grim lists of casualties on that bright New York day in September 2001 revealed the multiple diasporas and cosmopolitanisms that now constitute the often hidden social fabric of "global" cities like New York. As Watson writes:

> Global labor migration patterns have . . . brought the world to lower Manhattan to service the corporate office blocks: the dishwashers, messengers, coffee-cart vendors, and office cleaners were Mexican, Bangladeshi, Jamaican, and Palestinian. One of the tragedies of September 11, 2001 was that it took such an extraordinary event to reveal the everyday reality of life at the heart of the global city. (Watson, 2003: 109)

On the other hand, Bush's neoconservative and neo-imperial "war on terror" also problematizes such urban cosmopolitanism. It, too, undermines both the possibility and the legitimacy of city-based democratic pluralism and dissent against the "new global order." In asserting a binaried split between "the civilized and savage throughout the social circuitry," the war on terror rhetoric of the Bush regime, and the policies based on it, have produced a "constant scrutiny of those who bear the sign of 'dormant' terrorist." It has also "activated a policing of points of vulnerability against an enemy who inheres within the space of the US" (Passavant and Dean, 2002; cited in Gregory, 2003).

Mainstream media in the West now talk endlessly of "the enemy within" Western cities (Klaidman et al., 2002). "Terrorism experts" warn "of the 'Islamic threat' in the American underclass, and alerting the public that the ghetto and the prison system could well supply a 'fifth column' to Osama bin Laden and his ilk" (Aidi, 2002: 36).

I would not dispute that small numbers of Western-born Muslims have volunteered for terrorist action on behalf of radical Islamic organizations – the brutal and dehumanizing impacts of Bush's war on terror are perfect recruitment agents for al-Qaeda and Jihad (MacAskill, 2003). Nor would I question the need to take every possible step to prevent those planning terrorist atrocities from carrying out their plans (Molotch and McClain, 2003). The problem is that the polemical, sensationalist, and nationalistic accounts of much mainstream media coverage unhelpfully resort to the simplistic, racist generalizations of whole communities because it makes good copy. These are fueled by a lack of real knowledge of the complex histories and cultures of both the Middle East and the West (and the relations between them). Above all, such discourses "recycle the same unverifiable fictions and vast generalizations to stir up 'America' against the foreign devil" (Said, 2003: 6).

A "domestic front" has thus been drawn in Bush's war on terror. Sally Howell and Andrew Shryock (2003) call this a "cracking down on diaspora." This process involves deepening state surveillance against those seen to harbor "terrorist threats," combined with a radically increased effort to ensure the filtering power of national borders (see Molotch and McLain, 2003; Andreas and Biersteker, 2003). After decades when the business press triumphantly celebrated the "death of distance," or the imperative of opening borders to the "free" movements of neoliberal globalization, post 9/11, "in both political debates and policy practice, borders are very much back in style" (Andreas, 2003: 1). Once again, nations are being (re)imagined as bounded, organized spaces with closely controlled, and filtered, relationships with the supposed terrors of the outside world. In the US, for example, national immigration, border control, and social policy strategies have been remodeled since 9/11 in an:

> attempt to reconstitute the [United States] as a bounded area that can be fortified against outsiders and other global influences. In this imagining of nation, the US ceases to be a constellation of local, national, international, and global relations, experiences, and meanings that coalesce in places like

New York City and Washington, DC; rather, it is increasingly defined by a "security perimeter" and the strict surveillance of borders. (Hyndman, 2003: 2; see Anderson, 2002)

In the process, systematic state repression and mass incarceration have been brought to bear on Arab-American neighborhoods like Dearbon in Detroit. In the UK, meanwhile, 529 Muslims have been arrested and interrogated since 9/11 – with considerable racist and physical abuse – but only five have been convicted of any "terrorist" crime (Barnett and Bright, 2003; Muir, 2003). This sense of Western Muslim communities being "under siege on all sides" has emerged even though both US and British Muslim communities have overwhelmingly expressed their collective revulsion at the 9/11 attacks (Bright, 2003, Howell and Shryock, 2003). It must be said that this clampdown has generated much collective resistance, from Arab-Americans and British Muslims and others alike.

The "hybrid," transnational identities of many neighborhoods and communities in cities, shaped by generations of transnational migration and diasporic mixing, are thus becoming problematized. Inevitably, such places and groups are being "stretched" across the resurgent "them and us" or "home and foreign" binaries that are being imposed. Many people, spaces, and communities in Western cities are thus becoming "'othered' simply because they are perceived to be associated with 'Arab' or 'Muslim terrorists'" (Hall, 2003).

Fear, Insecurity, and the Militarization of Urban Life

Are fear and urbanism at war ? (Swanstrom, 2002)

Notions of community are now organized not only around flag-waving displays of patriotism, but also around collective fears and the ongoing militarization of visual culture and public space. (Giroux, 2003: ix)

As global violence telescopes within and through local places, so new physical, social, and psychological barriers are being constructed and enacted. In many contexts, militarized discourses of "homeland security" are infiltrating, and starting to reshape, previously civil societies, spaces, and policy debates (Kaplan, 2003; Rainham, 2003). In the wake of 9/11, and the other catastrophic terrorist acts of the last few years, the design of buildings, the management of traffic, the physical planning of cities, migration policy, or the design of social policies for ethnically diverse cities and neighborhoods, are being brought within the widening umbrella of "national security."

As globe-spanning, geostrategic concerns blur into very local, urban spaces, all of a sudden it seems normal for Western cities to face a palpable militarization previously more common in cities of the global South. Tanks protect airports. Troops guard rail stations. Surface-to-air missiles sit around office blocks housing meetings of international leaders. Combat air patrols buzz around Manhattan and London. New York street police now carry pocketsize radiation detectors in the hope that they might detect any nuclear "dirty bombs" smuggled into the metropolitan area. US postal sorting depots now have automatic anthrax sniffers. New York's Grand Central Station now has automatic bio-weapons detectors. And in a curious replay of earlier debates about strategic bombing and nuclear war, some commentators in the United States have even argued that the risks of terrorism – and particularly the risk that such attacks will utilize nuclear, chemical, and biological "Weapons of Mass Destruction" – mean that large, central cities should be actively decentralized (Swanstrom, 2002; see Glaeser and Shapiro, 2002; Coaffee, 2003b)

The danger, of course, is that this sense of a proliferating risk of violence against cities is adding to a vicious circle of fear and insecurity that already surrounded crime and social violence in many cities (Friedmann, 2002; Furedi, 1997; Davis, 1990, 1992, 1998; Soja, 2000, ch. 10; Body-Gendrot, 2000). Certainly, this powerful combination means that a particularly anxious state of perpetual fear and emergency now pertains in many cities (Agamben, 1998; Dillon, 2002; Savitch and Ardashev, 2001).

Rather than being completely new, however, the demonization of Islamic groups and neighborhoods is being added to the long-standing demonization of other ethnic minorities in many Western cities (see Soja, 2000). The similarities with earlier xenophobic discourses of urban fear, risk, and disorder are, indeed, striking. The disorder of the Los Angeles riots in 1992, for example, produced a sense of urban emergency and restructuring that seems powerfully resonant in post-9/11 times. Barbara Hooper argues the result was:

> a heightened concern over borders; a situation of struggle over spaces and meanings; a milieu of fear that manifests itself as a ferocious racism and xenophobia, as a concern for the pathology of bodes and cities which are produced as dangerous carriers of the disorder, incubators and contagions in the global epidemic of shrinking Western power. (Hooper, 2000: 368)

In many cases, of course, the risks of war or terror – and terror produced by the war on terror – are palpable and real. The proliferating bombs and dismembered bodies cannot be ignored. But such cultures of fear are, in many cases, being exaggerated and exploited by politicians. Take an example: George Bush's first TV ad for the 2004 US election, in November

2003. This included a clip of the president looking sincerely into the camera and uttering in a low, somber, voice: "It would take one vial, one canister, one crate slipped into this country to bring a day of horror like none we have ever known" (quoted in Dows, 2003).

Such rhetoric, and the deliberate fabrication of scares about uranium from Niger and Iraqi weapons of mass destruction, demonstrate that post-9/11 cultures of fear are being ruthlessly manipulated, even manufactured, for political ends – largely to try to boost politicians' standings. (We should remember that "the tragic events of September 11 transformed a president whose election was the most questioned ever into a president with the highest popularity ever": Zulaika, 2003: 194.) It is also happening to legitimize massive state violence targeting the supposed sources of these risks (so, in the process, realizing the long-standing geopolitical ambitions of nation-states).

Sensationalist local and national media, meanwhile, also stoke and satisfy the demands of an increasingly voyeuristic public to be "drawn into the action" of transnational urban war and terror. In many cases, their coverage is being reduced to little more than nationalistic, jingoistic "24/7" infotainment which continually invokes binaried notions of a "clash of civilizations" (Abrahamian, 2003). This blurs more and more with the fictional depictions of urban disasters and warfare that have long been the staple of Hollywood (Gregory, 2004b).

Urban Dimensions of the "State of Emergency"

Because they require constant reference to a state of exception, measures of security work towards the growing depoliticization of society. In the long run, they are irreconcilable with democracy. (Agamben, 2002: 2)

At what point does [the West's] behavior become as bad in consequence as the thing [Western nation-states] desire to prevent? (Aaronovitch, 2003: 27)

War is the new psychotropic. War precludes our doubts. War preserves our right to pursue overabundance. War closes the circle. It creates anxiety; it cures anxiety. It defines our alienation; it resolves our alienation. (Hart, 2004: 16)

In this "state of emergency" the normal rules of civilian, democratic law are being supplanted or replaced (Agamben, 1998, 2002). In their place come emergency, executive powers, and covert state actions which are justified – when discussed at all – because of the "temporary" imperatives of "national security," the post-9/11 "crisis," or the demands of a globe-spanning "war on terror." At the same time, the laws of war are being reshaped to accommodate routine, state-backed, high-tech violence against cities and essential urban infrastructures (Smith, 2002, Naumann, 2003).

The wars within the war on terror are, in turn, being widely justified through indiscriminate Orientalist categorizations. This language of the "new barbarism" works by separating "the civilized world" – which must be "defended" – from the "dark forces" and the "axis of evil" which are alleged to threaten the health, prosperity, and democracy of the whole "free" world (Tuastad, 2003; Tisdall, 2003). Such dualisms are used to justify the recolonization of the Middle East by Western powers because of the supposedly innate inabilities of the "Arab mind" to support development and stability (El-Affendi, 2003). Thus, such rhetoric conveniently lumps together the residents of whole nations as sources of "terrorism." It legitimizes the use of massive, overwhelming, and often indiscriminate state violence against them and the fragile systems that sustain the lives of the people who live there (Gregory, 2003). This results in "a wild zone of power, barbaric and violent, operating without democratic oversight" (Gregory, 2003: 321).

As the obsessive concern with "security" and preemptive war gathers pace, so any thought of using *non-military* means to address the root causes of instability and informal, terrorist violence – mass poverty, injustice, an all-powerful neoliberal globalism, the gross abuse of power, quasi-imperial and colonial efforts to secure oil and other resources – are pushed further away (Zunes, 2002; Dower, 2002; Thornton, 2003; Mepham, 2002). "Simply put, brutal, hegemonic actions will sooner or later evoke hostile reactions . . . Secure pipelines are obviously more important than human rights in the globalist scheme of things" (Thornton, 2003: 209). Giorgio Agamben wonders whether "the time has come to work towards the *prevention* of disorder and catastrophe, and not merely towards their control" (2002, 2; emphasis added).

Thus, a global vicious circle is now established along the lines so familiar in the Palestinian–Israeli conflict. State-backed terror, atrocity, and crimes against humanity breed informal terrorist atrocity and crimes against humanity. States respond with more of the same while invoking states of emergency and cultures of fear. These, in turn, allow legal restraints to be dispensed with and more state-backed terror . Such state violence goes on to deepen resentment, recruit more volunteers, and exacerbate the intransigence, or the ethic of martyrdom, that sustains the growing ranks of willing suicide bombers (Hage, 2003). Religious fundamentalism and essentialized racism on both sides – Bush's Orientalist, evangelical Christianity; Osama bin Laden's radical Islam – fuel and legitimize further violence.

Such a circle of atrocity actually allows fundamentalist terror organizations to grow, prosper, and bring in ever-larger cohorts of recruits. Bush's war on terror and his unflinching support for Israel's assaults on Palestinian cities could not have been designed by Osama bin Laden himself as a better agent of global polarization, splitting the world in two (MacAskill, 2003). Thus, the rhetoric of the war on terror "not only mirrors bin Laden's ideology. It also ultimately serves the interests of al-Qaeda" (Gregory, 2003: 319). And so the cycle continues...

In a way, then, terrorism and counter-terrorism are umbilically connected. In the end, they tend, tragically, to be self-perpetuating. As Zulaika argues:

> The ultimate catastrophe is that such a categorically ill-defined, perpetually deferred, simple minded Good-versus-Evil war ["against terror"] echoes and recreates the very absolutist mentality and exceptionalist tactics of the insurgent terrorists. By formally adopting the terrorists' own game – one that by definition lacks rules of engagement, definite endings, clear alignments between enemies and friends, or formal arrangements of any sort, military, political, legal, or ethical – the inevitable danger lies in reproducing it endlessly. (Zulaika, 2003: 198)

"A Welcome Blanket of Geopolitical Disguise"

The post-9/11 United States is a classic example of the construction of a "state of emergency." Here, the Bush administration has carefully "invoked a global state of emergency to wage infinite war on an indefinite enemy" (Dillon, 2002: 77). In the process, preexisting legal norms on human rights, civil liberties, the right to trial, assumptions of innocence before the proof of evidence, due process, or the Geneva Convention are now being systematically pushed aside (Giroux, 2003).

This state of emergency is used to justify mass detentions without trial. It legitimizes extra-territorial, city-size detention centers, where those rounded up and accused as "terrorists" – many of whom were simply bystanders in the Afghanistan war – may fall into legal black holes with no rights whatsoever (potentially for the rest of their lives) (An Architektur, 2003; Meek, 2003).[1] And it is used to justify unprovoked military attacks against impoverished, weak nations (in Iraq's case, with no evidence whatsoever linking the regime there with Al-Qaeda).

All these are part and parcel of the construction of a "permawar" against a loosely defined notion of informal violence (i.e., "terrorism") that has been abstracted from any discussion of the geopolitical tensions and processes that fuel it. This "permawar" is being developed in order to pursue US geopolitical priorities that were identified well before 9/11 (Vidal, 2002; see Project for the New American Century, 2000). It is also happening without any notion of when, if ever, this war may be completed or what the signifiers of "victory" might actually be.

All this means that, to many, "the 'war on terror' becomes a war of terror" (Gregory, 2004a: 1). Richard Falk writes that Bush's war on terror is little but a "welcome blanket of geopolitical disguise," which uses the instruments and techniques of the state of emergency to ruthlessly pursue what Bush's neoconservative regime sees as United States' global geopolitical interests (2003, 16; Harvey, 2003a).

Capsularization vs. "Crisis Conviviality"

Crucially, from the point of view of this book, such constructions of states of emergency and fear are changing the very tenor of urban culture and society (Molotch and McClain, 2003). Many urban societies which are already experiencing widespread fragmentation and fortressing are seeing these processes amplified further as people seek to "capsularize" themselves away from people, experiences, and spaces that they perceive as risky, vulnerable, or unpredictable (De Cauter, 2004; see Graham and Marvin, 2001; Ellin, 1997; Gold and Revill, 2000).

As a result, urban public life is being saturated by "intelligent" surveillance systems, checkpoints, "defensive" urban design, and intensifying security (see Lyon, Coaffee, Marcuse, this volume). Such strategies will not completely undermine the role of cities as dense sites of heterogeneous, unpredictable mixing. Cities are far too complex, porous, and multidimensional to be somehow "programmed" by computers and surveillance systems (Graham and Marvin, 2001). But, together, these purported anti-terrorist strategies can "creep," to have a chilling effect on urban and democratic public culture. Very often, anti-terror policies and technologies are used to regulate and undermine wider public dissent and activism. In the UK, for example, anti-terror laws are being used to arrest people protesting peacefully against arms fairs and neoliberal globalization. They have been used since 9/11 to undermine and criminalize legitimate public protest on city streets.

We should also note, however, that in cities such as New York, a counter to this process has been evident. Here it has been possible to observe what Michael Sorkin (this volume) calls a "crisis conviviality." In Manhattan the collective spirit of urban adversity has worked to engender *more* street life, solidarity, and social interaction than was common during the 1980s and 1990s. Strikingly, after the Darwinistic frenzy of the 1990s dot.com boom and the hardline intolerances of the Guiliani era, after the attack, for a while at least, "New Yorkers . . . for the most part rallied around ideals of community, togetherness, solidarity and altruism, as opposed to beggar-thy-neighbor individualism" (Harvey, 2003: 39b).

The current state of emergency is combining with preexisting processes of urban militarization. As part of the growth of neoliberal policy, many states have been militarizing their systems of criminal justice, law enforcement, and public space regulation, bringing the weapons, doctrines, and technologies of war to the streets of cities and the borders of nations (Nunn, 2001; Kraska, 2001; Garland, 2001; Young, 1999). Paradoxically, "amidst privatization and deregulation, one of the few aspects of the capitalist state generally reinforced is the security apparatus" (Dyer-Witheford, 1999: 141).

The massive growth of civilian markets for "security" technologies and services is thus blurring into military–industrial ones (Flusty, 1997; Kraska, 2001; Marcuse, this volume). With the widening debates about "Homeland security" it is even more the case that "conflict and security have become growth industries – the erstwhile war economy [has been] reborn as part of the post-Cold War economy." Instead of the "military–industrial complex," Pieterse talks of an emerging "criminal–industrial complex" or "security–industrial complex," which straddles home-domestic and international-foreign scales (Pieterse, 2002: 3).

The Collective Terror of Banal Events

Everything and everywhere is perceived as a border from which a potentially threatening other can leap. (Hage, 2003: 86)

Permanent anxiety means that the everyday events, malfunctions, or acts of violence in the city – which would previously have been seen as the results of local social problems, individual pathologies, accidents, or bureaucratic failings – are now instinctively assumed to be the results of global acts of unknown, hidden, and "othered" "terrorists" (Sorkin, this volume). The banal sites and events of everyday urban life – especially parked vans, mobility systems, envelopes with white powder, people with packages – are now sources of mass anxiety. As with the Cold War paranoia that so powerfully shaped Western urban culture between the 1950s and 1970s, reminders of terror, or the potential for terror, are all around, linguistically as well as materially (Farish, this volume).

Geographer Cindi Katz calls this the "routinization of terror talk and the increasing ordinariness of its physical markers." She argues that such a process is what she calls "ontological insecurity" – a sociological concept that captures the pervasive crisis in feelings of safety in everyday urban life. Katz also believes the manipulation of these processes by states and the media "smuggle with them an acquiescence to state violence" as part of the war on terror (2004: 1).

Thus, every sign of a breakdown in the ordinary technologized flows of contemporary urban life – electricity cuts, subway accidents, computer collapses – now switches quickly into an immediate search for "terrorist" attackers. A wheel falling off a London tube train prompts immediate speculation about Al-Qaeda adopting new tactics. A few ill subway workers prompts a frantic search for biological or chemical "WMD" in the tunnels beneath city streets. In the US since 9/11, exploitations of the postal system to deliver anthrax, or of the day-to-day street spaces of Washington DC to murder civilians, have instinctively been assumed to be the work of Osama bin Laden, Al-Qaeda, or even Saddam Hussein (Katz, 2004).

Cities as Refuge From High-Tech US Hegemony

Geopolitics is a flat discourse. It largely ignores the vertical dimension and tends to look across rather than to cut through the landscape. This was the cartographic imagination inherited from the military and political spatialities of the modern state. (Weizman, 2002: 3)

The orbital weapons currently in play possess the traditional attributes of the divine: omnivoyance and omnipresence. (Virilio, 2002: 53)

Some people say to me that the Iraqis are not the Vietnamese! They have no jungles of swamps to hide in. I reply, "Let our cities be our swamps and our buildings our jungles." (Tariq Aziz, Iraqi foreign minister, October 2002; quoted in Bellamy, 2003)

As military treatments of "home" and "foreign" cities blur together, so there is increasing evidence that high-tech war is being constructed as "the ultimate disciplinary instrument of the world market" (Dyer-Witheford, 1999: 140; see Sharma and Kumar, 2003). By paving the way for what David Harvey (2003a: ch. 4) calls "accumulation by dispossession" (especially through the privatization of assets in conquered lands), even moderate commentators like Michael Ignatieff admit that the high-tech war on terror is, essentially, a classic, imperialistic strategy at the heart of the United States' drive for a globe-spanning empire (Ignatieff, 2003; see Klein, 2003).

As key instruments of this strategy, US military forces are being re-designed to "fight and decisively win multiple, simultaneous major theatre wars" (Project for the New American Century, 2000; see Harris, 2003). Because both the "homeland" and most colonized and invaded spaces are becoming more and more urban, urban terrain increasingly provides the "battlespace" for the US military in both spheres.

As a result, the war on terror is being supported by a vast military research and development exercise that focuses overwhelmingly on cities

(Gregory, 2004b). This is being undertaken to adapt US and "coalition" forces to the three-dimensional urban terrain that they are having to fight in as part of their globe-spanning humanitarian and military interventions (known as "MOUT" or "Military Operations in Urban Terrain" in the military jargon). As a result, resources devoted to "urban research" in the world's military are starting to match those devoted to "civilian" research about cities. This creates a kind of "shadow" urban research world that remains almost completely ignored by urban social science proper (see www.urbanoperations.org; Hills, Warren, Graham, this volume; Rosenau, 1997; Peters, 1996, 1997; Kitfield, 1998).

The product of all this effort is a profoundly anti-urban military discourse in which urban terrain – particularly the urban terrain in poor, Islamic countries – is portrayed as a great leveler between high-tech US forces and their low-tech adversaries (Gregory, 2004b; Graham, 2004). The complex, congested, and contested terrain below, within, and above cities is seen as a set of physical spaces which limit the effectiveness of high-tech space-targeted bombs, surveillance systems, and automated, "network-centric" weapons. These have been deliberately developed in the last thirty years, under the auspices of the so-called "Revolution in Military Affairs," to ensure that the US remains a preeminent global military power with "full spectrum dominance" over its potential challengers (Gray, 1997). The urbanization of battlespace is therefore seen to reduce the ability of US forces to fight and kill at a distance (always the preferred way because of their "casualty dread" and technological supremacy). As is being revealed in the Iraqi insurgency, urban warfare is also seen to necessitate a much more labor- and casualty-intensive way of fighting than the US is used to these days.

Echoing these points, a leading US military commentator on urban warfare, Ralph Peters, argues that: "in fully urbanized terrain warfare becomes profoundly vertical, reaching up to towers of steel and cement, and downward into sewers, subway lines, road tunnels, communication tunnels, and the like" (1996: 2). This verticality is seen to break down communication. It leads to an increasing problem in distinguishing civilians from combatants. And it undermines the awareness and killing power that high-tech sensors give to US combatants in the urban battlefield.

Like many of his colleagues, Peters' military mind recoils in horror at the prospect of US forces habitually fighting in the majority world's burgeoning megacities and urbanizing corridors (see also Rosenau, 1997; Spiller, 2000). To him, these are spaces where "human waste goes undisposed, the air is appalling, and mankind is rotting" (1996: 2). Here, cities and urbanization represent decay, anarchy, disorder, and the post-Cold War collapse of "failed" nation-states. "Boom cities pay for failed states, post-modern dispersed cities pay for failed states, and failed cities turn into killing grounds and reservoirs for humanity's surplus and discards (guess where we will fight)" (1996: 3).

Peters starkly highlights the key geostrategic role of urban regions within the post-Cold War period: "Who cares about Upper Egypt if Cairo is calm? We do not deal with Indonesia – we deal with Jakarta. In our recent evacuation of Sierra Leone Freetown was all that mattered" (1997: 5). Peters also candidly characterizes the role of the US military within the emerging neoliberal "empire" with the USA as the central military enforcer (although he obviously doesn't use these words) (see Hardt and Negri, 2000): "Our future military expeditions will increasingly defend our foreign investments," continues Peters, "rather than defending [the home nation] against foreign invasions. And we will fight to subdue anarchy and violent 'isms' because disorder is bad for business. All of this activity will focus on cities."

Again in synchrony with his colleagues, Peters sees the deliberate exploitation of urban terrain by opponents of US hegemony to be a likely key feature of future war. Here high-tech military dominance is assumed to directly fuel the urbanization of resistance. "The long-term trend in open-area combat is toward overhead dominance by US forces," observes Peters (1996: 6). "Battlefield awareness may prove so complete, and 'precision' weapons so widely available and effective, that enemy ground-based combat systems will not be able to survive in the deserts, plains, and fields that have seen so many of history's main battles." As a result, he argues the United States' "enemies will be forced into cities and other complex terrain, such as industrial developments and intercity sprawl" (1997: 4).

For Peters and many other US military commentators, it is as though global urbanization is a dastardly plan to thwart the US military gaining the full benefit from the complex, expensive, high-tech weapons that the military–industrial complex has spent so many decades piecing together. Annoyingly, cities, as physical objects, simply *get in the way* of the US military's technophiliac fantasies of trans-global, real-time omnipotence. The fact that "urbanized terrain" is the product of complex economic, demographic, social, and cultural shifts that involve the transformation of whole societies seems to have escaped their gaze (see Graham, this volume).

"Terrorism" and the "War on Terror": Negotiating Bias, Ideology, and Language

"Terrorism" has been made polymorphous. (Gregory, 2003: 319)

Definitions of terrorism are fungible and change according to political necessity. (Brennan, 2003: 174)

From "civilization" to "WMD," words are weapons in the global crusade. (Tisdall, 2003)

Essential to the current war on terror is an extraordinary discourse about "terrorism" (Collins and Glover, 2002). The very word "terrorism" itself – always a byword for vagueness and political bias – is now so ubiquitous and over-used that it has ceased to have much meaning. This reflects the fact that in parts of the Western media and polity, the word has been carefully marshaled to brand all those who commit political violence against the USA and its allies. "Without defined shape, or determinate roots," Derek Gregory writes, the mantle of "terrorism" can thus "be cast over *any* form of resistance to sovereign power" (2003: 219; original emphasis).

Furthermore, in many states the branding of indigenous people or non-violent dissidents as "terrorists" has allowed violent state colonialism and repression to continue and, in many cases, deepen (often with the implicit or explicit support of Western nation-states). The recent war on terror has provided many dubious regimes around the world with a carte blanche to escalate state repression of minority or dissident opinion (New Internationalist, 2002b). In addition, as part of the "cracking down on diaspora" discussed above, many nations have brought repressive legislation against asylum seekers directly into their "anti-terror" strategies.

Meanwhile, a long litany of atrocities, human rights abuses, and politically inspired violence against civilians, committed by the Western nations and their allies, has tended to escape definition as "terrorist" – at least in dominant Western discourses. As a result, it is strikingly clear that "what we think we 'know' about 'terrorism'," as John Collins suggests:

> is the product of specific efforts by specific people to define certain examples of political violence (especially violence committed by those who are opposed to US policies around the world) as illegitimate. In other words, when someone uses the word "terrorism," they are describing the world in a way that works to the advantage of the powerful . . . words and ideas that masquerade as neutral and objective "reality," while actually expressing the narrow interests of a dominant group, are called *ideology*." (2002: 157)

"Terrorist" branding is therefore nothing if not flexible. For example, dominant Western depictions of the French resistors against the Nazis, or the Jewish fighters who struggled against the British for the establishment of the State of Israel – both of whom committed acts of violence against civilians and military alike – romanticize these groups as freedom fighters. At the same time, Palestinian resistors against the Israeli occupation of *their* homeland are overwhelmingly vilified as "terrorists" – even on the occasions when their attacks have concentrated entirely on military targets.

Take another example. When Iraqi civilians and insurgents attacked US occupying forces after "peace" was declared there in May 2003, George Bush quickly branded such guerrilla-style attacks a "terrorist" problem.

This occurred even though a large number of those attacks carefully targeted *military* occupiers ("terrorist" violence against military occupiers of one's nation is, by definition, impossible). Such a branding also ignored the fact that many of the Iraqi fighters – whether loyal to the Ba'athist regime or not – were clearly attacking what they saw as unprovoked aggression, occupation, dispossession, and a willful neglect of the need to maintain order and basic services in Iraq after the fall of the Hussein regime (Medact, 2003). As Derek Gregory (2004b) suggests, it is therefore necessary to speak of a *variety* of wars of resistance against the US–UK occupation of Iraq.

Clearly, some radical Islamic fighters, from both within and outside Iraq, were involved in suicide and bombing attacks. But there is also no doubt that many ordinary Iraqi civilians – even those grateful for the fall of a murderous dictator – were persuaded to take up arms in a less organized way against the occupiers. This was because of the mass slaughter and incarceration of their compatriots in the invasion, and the continuing carnage of everyday urban life that followed. For example, between May 1 and September 30, 2003 in Baghdad alone at least 94 Iraqi civilians were unlawfully killed simply going about their daily lives because of the hyper-aggressive stance of the US military occupiers (Graham, 2004; Human Rights Watch, 2003). In April 2004, at least 300 women and children were killed by US Marines as they laid siege to the city of Fallujah. Tellingly, the US military was *deliberately not even keeping count* of these deaths.

In the same breath, Bush and Blair maintain that the killing (June 2004) of between 15,000 and 25,000 innocent Afghan and Iraqi civilians – not to mention tens of thousands of soldiers and fighters – was necessary to larger acts of national "liberation." Given the above, it is difficult to disagree with Lummis when he argues "air bombardment is the terrorism of the rich" (1994: 304; cited in Herold, this volume).

Such outrageous hypocrisy is fueled and legitimized through language. Fueled by Orientalist depictions of Arab people and their cities, and simple oppositions between "civilization" and "barbarism," these wars "on terror" work by projecting entire countries and cities as "*beyond* the pale of civilization." Such "casting out" of Islamic cities and societies as a whole from any notion of civilization, in turn, allows Arab civilians in these areas to be "placed beyond the privileges and protections of the law so that their lives (and deaths) [are] rendered of no account" (Gregory, 2003: 313).

Thus, ongoing Iraqi and Afghan civilian casualties remain curiously invisible, unworthy, and uncounted (Herold, 2002b; Gregory, 2004a). Meanwhile, the Western media obsessively document the lives, deaths, and even the final words of the people who died on 9/11, or the Western soldiers who have died during the invasion and occupation of the two countries.

Towards an Urban Geopolitics: Introducing
Cities, War, and Terrorism

Of course, all nationalistic and fundamentalist discourses, and appeals to knee-jerk reaction, tend to obfuscate the complex geopolitical nature of the current post-9/11 and post-Cold War world. Such discourses also work to obscure the complex and crucial links that are emerging between cities, warfare, and "terrorism" that are the focus of this book.

While the contributors to this book do use the words "terrorism" and "terror," the overall approach is to strive for balance and equivalence. By "terrorism" we mean "deliberately targeted surprise attacks on arbitrarily chosen civilians, designed to frighten other people" (Keohane, 2002: 77). In other words, "terror is armed or brutal force against those who can be terrorized – i.e., who cannot fight back" (Hewitt, 2003: 9).

This book engages in detail with the urban impacts of such violence. But it also addresses the more formal (and neglected) violence and terror that nation-states pursue when they attack cities and their inhabitants. Thus, the starting point of this book is not to see "terror" in and against cities and their inhabitants as the product solely of informal, non-state violence. Such a biased and limiting view has, unfortunately, dominated much recent urban research on "terrorism" (see, for example, Cutter, Richardson, and Wilbanks, 2003; Savitch and Ardashev, 2001).

Instead, *Cities, War, and Terrorism* adopts a comprehensive approach to organized, political violence in and against cities. It strives to address what Derek Gregory and Alan Pred have called "a multiplicity of terrorisms": state-backed and non-state backed, formal and informal (2003). Such a comprehensive perspective is vital. This is because, even in the contemporary period, from a global point of view, state terror in and against cities and their populations – while often ignored – continues to be even more significant and devastating than informal terror. From the perspective of geography, for example, Ken Hewitt has argued that, while "very few geographers have had anything to say about state terror," the indiscriminate violence of nation-states remains by far "the largest source of harm to people in most countries and worldwide" (2003, 6; see Rummel, 1997).

In fact, as Eduardo Galeano (2001) has stressed, there is actually "much common ground between low- and high-tech terrorism, between the terrorism of religious fanatics and that of market fanatics, that of the hopeless and that of the powerful, that of the psychopath on the loose and that of the cold-blooded uniformed professional" (quoted in Mendieta, 2001). Moreover, it is crucial to see the circular relationships that bind state terror to informal terror; to analyze the umbilical connections which link state-backed terror, in the name of "counter-terrorism," and the terrorism of Al-Qaeda and its ilk. This is crucial because, "usually, where irregular terror is present, so is state terror" (Hewitt, 2003; see Chomsky, 2003).

Cities, War, and Terrorism is the first interdisciplinary, international, critical, and comprehensive analysis of the intersections of war, terrorism, and cities. Its purpose is to demonstrate that both the informal ("terrorist") and the formal (state) violence, war, and terror that characterize the post-Cold War and post-9/11 periods largely *entail systematic and planned targeting of cities and urban places.* To achieve this the book draws on a range of cutting-edge social, urban, cultural, architectural, and military theories and case studies.

While it focuses overwhelmingly on the post-Cold War and post-9/11 periods, the book also addresses the ways in which attacks against cities, urban wars, and atrocities against urban civilians of the last few years are intimately connected – and often strikingly similar – to those that occurred before. As cities emerge as targets, there is also much continuity in the ways in which cultures of urban fear are constructed to impact on debates about urban planning, governance, and social policy. Thus, while the book provides an unrivaled analysis of how cities, warfare, and terrorism are currently remaking each other, it also places the tumultuous events of the early twenty-first century into a broader historical and theoretical context.

Cities, War, and Terrorism is motivated by a response to two parallel failings in social science as a whole: the virtual invisibility of political violence against cities and their inhabitants within critical urban social science, and the almost complete dominance of *national*, rather than *subnational*, spaces and politics within International Relations and Political Science. The purpose of the book is thus to force an interdisciplinary opening in the spaces between these disciplines. To succeed, such an opening will need to place the intersections of war, terrorism, and subnational – specifically urban – spaces at the center, rather than the periphery, of analysis. As documented above, the development of such an "urban geopolitics" is made necessary, indeed imperative, by the parallel rescalings of political violence in today's rapidly urbanizing world. Without it, the analytical domains of both urban studies and international relations will inevitably fail to address the crises of urban terrorism, and the proliferating scope of urban war and state urban terror, that are reshaping the contemporary world.

To achieve this "opening," *Cities, War, and Terrorism* brings together the work of an unprecedented array of thinkers, theorists, writers, and commentators. These are deliberately drawn from an unusually wide range of disciplines. Included here are political science, international relations and sociology; geography, urban planning and architecture; and critical theory, history, and military studies. From their wide variety of perspectives all the writers in this book address one key question: how do urban areas and organized, military conflict shape each other in these post-Cold War, post-9/11 times?

Cities, War, and Terrorism has three parts, each of which begins with a brief introduction by the editor. Part I – Cities, War, and Terrorism in History and Theory – sets the context for the rest of the book. It includes six chapters which together map out in unprecedented detail the conceptual and historical transformations in the strategic and geopolitical dimensions of urbanism that have been such an intrinsic element of the transition from Cold War to post-Cold War contexts.

Part II – Urbicide and the Urbanization of Warfare –includes a range of seven chapters which together analyze the implications of the urbanization of our planet for the prosecution of war and violent struggle. Here, authors present detailed analyses of the ways in which cities and urban areas are increasingly being directly targeted in war; their roles as strategic sites for increasingly militarized anti-globalization battles; and the critical importance of architecture, urbanism, and planning in shaping particular urban military struggles (such as the Balkan wars of the 1990s and the ongoing Israeli–Palestinian war).

A key concept which runs through this second part of the book is that of "urbicide": the deliberate denial, or killing, of the city. While much less recognized than the more familiar "cides" – genocide, homicide, ecocide, domicide, democide – the chapters in Part II together suggest that the deliberate denial or killing of the city, through war or terrorism, is such a common element of contemporary conflict that urbicide is a theoretical and legal concept who's time has come.

Part III – Exposed Cities: Urban Impacts of Terrorism and the "War on Terror" – includes five chapters that delve into the urban impacts of acts of catastrophic terrorism (such as the iconic 9/11 attacks) and the devastating human and urban consequences of the US "coalition's" "war on terrorism" that has followed.

Note

1   This process is also underway with much more stealth in the UK, where 14 foreign men have are being held in Belmarsh Prison in southeast London under emergency anti-terrorist legislation which permits their incarceration until death without trial (see Cohen, 2003).

Part I

Cities, War, and Terrorism in History and Theory

Introduction

As long as people have lived in cities, they have been haunted by fears of urban ruin ... Every city on earth is ground zero in somebody's doomsday book. (Berman, 1996: 175–84)

While at one time war elsewhere guaranteed peace at the center of the empire, now the enemy strikes precisely and more easily at the center ... War abroad no longer guarantees peace at home. (Eco, 2003)

In Part I we bring together six chapters which attempt to theorize, as sociologists Diken and Laustsen put it, "the way in which discipline, control, and terror coexist in today's imaginary and real urban geography" (2002: 291). Each chapter grapples with the changing meaning of urban spaces and the processes, legacies, and meanings of organized violence targeting cities. To do this they analyze the geopolitical tensions between cities as sites of violence and the information flows and networks that shape both contemporary urbanism and contemporary war. They analyze the contested meanings, and memories, of warfare, violence, urban ruins, and modern architectural forms. And they explore the ways in which the mundane and everyday aspects of urban life can be simply perverted to generate acts of terror.

First, the urbanist Stephen Graham offers a scene-setting chapter. Graham stresses that the purposeful annihilation, or at least, the attempted annihilation of cities, has long been a research taboo in urban social science. As an attempt to begin "excavating" what he calls the "dark" side of urban modernity, Graham offers a series of nine short illustrations. These underline that, while it tends to be cloaked by analytical and professional taboos, the deliberate destruction of cities and urban places is utterly intrinsic to both urban modernity more broadly, and to modern urban planning and urbanism more specifically.

In chapter 2 Ryan Bishop and Gregory Clancey – critical theorist and historian, respectively – offer a detailed cultural analysis of the idea of city-as-target. Written before September 11, 2001, their essay seems eerily prescient of the onslaught of urban war and violence that has engulfed the world since then. Bishop and Clancey position political violence against the city and its population within a broader narrative about the vulnerabilities of urban life to decay, collapse, and disaster. They go on to explore in depth why the destruction of cities has become what they call a "show at the periphery" in both intellectual and geographical terms. That is, urban war and disaster has been marginalized within narratives of both urban modernism and urban social science at the same time as the cities of the global South have been assumed to be most prone to natural and human-made catastrophe. The authors finish with a detailed discussion of how planning and national security discourses have reflected the urban annihilations and disasters that have befallen, and continue to threaten, the booming cities of East and Southeast Asia.

As well as shaping the physical landscapes of cities, violence and war linger deep in the more intangible spaces of collective urban memory. In no city in the world are such memories of war and violent ideology as multi-layered and complex as in Berlin. In chapter 3 the architectural sociologist Simon Guy presents a sweeping perspective of these complex emotional landscapes of amnesia and (contested) collective memory. He analyzes the struggles over the meaning and development of Berlin's countless spaces and buildings which are deeply linked to Nazi terror, anti-Semitic genocide, aerial annihilation, Cold War division, and post-Cold War reconstruction. Drawing on Walter Benjamin, Guy looks in detail at three classic examples of such struggle: the Reichstag, the Berlin Wall, and Potsdamer Platz. The result is a powerful analysis which delves deep into the collective memories of the twentieth century's archetypal geopolitical city.

The Cold War city is also the concern of chapter 4. Here, the geographer Matthew Farish presents a pioneering analysis of the urban dimensions to nuclear paranoia in the Cold War United States. Highlighting the ways in which the nuclear vulnerability of US cities combined with deep-seated anti-urbanism among strategic and military planners, Farish shows that postwar efforts to decentralize US metropolitan regions were strongly influenced by notions of nuclear risk reduction. As well as a normative judgment that dense urban agglomerations were somehow "abnormal" among the planning and military communities alike, such concerns were fueled by a wide variety of predictions and simulations of the impact of nuclear Armageddon on urban America.

In chapter 5 the eminent sociologist Zygmunt Bauman offers an elegant essay unraveling some of the links between globalization, urbanization, and war. Highlighting the astonishing scale of demographic growth, and the vast scale of urban poverty on our "full" planet, Bauman points out the ways in which processes of globalization have tended to externalize risks, pollution, waste, and insecurity from affluent developed cities to poor underdeveloped ones. As modernization and urbanization become a near-universal human condition, Bauman stresses that vulnerabilities and violent conflicts are being generalized, too. Drawing on the work of Manuel Castells, he argues that this is happening as power and violence become more "liquid" forms, which operate through transnational networks and flows rather than simple territorial formations. The result is a dynamic and volatile "frontier-land" geopolitics where conflicts and violence erupt flexibly in an ongoing array of "reconnaissance battles," which have little in common with traditional state vs. state wars.

The inherent vulnerabilities of modern cities and societies are also the concern of chapter 6, which is by political scientist Timothy Luke. Drawing on the sociology of technology and the urban anthropology of Marc Augé (who developed the concept of "non-places"), Luke emphasizes the sheer scale, reach, and intensity of the urban "technostructures" that sustain everyday life in modern urbanized societies. These include transport systems, telecommunications and information networks, energy grids, food and logistics systems, e-commerce networks, and so on. While generally taken for granted, Luke notes that these are the essence of urban, liberal modernity. They sustain every aspect of daily life in cities. They provide the very sinews of "globalization." And they are a legacy – indeed, almost an embodiment – of Enlightenment dreams of conquering nature, delivering salvation from want, and sustaining endless "progress" and modernization based on technoscientific discovery.

At the same time, however, Luke stresses that an urban life within these banal everyday technostructures and "big systems" is an inherently vulnerable one. As the events of 9/11 demonstrate, such embedded assets can very easily be turned into weapons of mass destruction and agents of chaos. In some cases, even small shifts in the operation of these systems can bring annihilation and mass death. As Umberto Eco has written, "the true enemy, we have seen, doesn't even need his own technology; he uses those of the people he wants to destroy" (2003).

1

Cities as Strategic Sites: Place Annihilation and Urban Geopolitics

Stephen Graham

Introduction

Biologists have prepared "red books" of extinct or endangered species; ecologists have their "green books" of threatened habitats. Perhaps we need our "black book" of the places destroyed or nearly destroyed by human agencies. Actually it would take many books and street maps packed with remembrances to record the settlements, neighborhoods, and buildings in those places destroyed in recent wars. (Hewitt, 1983: 275)

Arguably, humankind has expended almost as much energy, effort, and thought on the attempted annihilation and killing of cities as it has on their planning, construction, and growth (Berman, 1996). Such attempts at city annihilation require purposive work. They necessitate detailed analysis. Often, they involve "scientific" planning and operational strategy-making of a complexity and sophistication that matches anything ever done to sustain the more familiar acts of "civil" urban planning (Bauman, 1989). Of course, these stories are never celebrated. Usually, they are consciously or unconsciously obscured. But dig a little, and it is not uncommon to find the work of cartographers, geographers, and planners, of architects, engineers, sociologists, anthropologists, psychologists, and statisticians, running through the atrocities and place annihilations of the twentieth (and early twenty-first) centuries like the names of seaside resorts that run through the famous British holiday candy, "rock."

Take the bombing-based annihilation of German and Japanese cities by the Allies in World War II as an (admittedly extreme) example. To "succeed" – and the deaths of over 900,000 Japanese and 600,000 German civilians were seen here as a "success" – vast technoscientific and bureaucratic systems were required (Hewitt, 1983, 1987). The bombing necessitated huge workforces and incredibly complex divisions of labor. It relied on the dehumanization of the residents of "target" cities and the scientific rationalization, and routinization, of the killing process. And it was built on the construction of a euphemistic language to hide the terrible reality on the ground – a reality still rarely exposed – to concentrate instead on generating heroic imagery and discourses about the war in the "air" (Sebald, 2002; Friedrich, 2003; Gray, 1997). People who were made homeless in the incendiary and high explosive attacks, for example, were described as "dehoused" (Davis, 2002).

When analyzed like this, the total bombing of urban Japan and Germany actually had many similarities to the Holocaust, with its much more familiar machinery of spatialized annihilation and industrialized, genocidal killing (Cole, 2003). In a detailed comparison of the two strategies, historians Markusen and Kopf (1985) have argued that, while it may be a deeply uncomfortable thing to realize (for many in Britain and the USA, at any rate), these similarities are so strong that the mass annihilation of cities by bombing in World War II must properly be labeled genocidal.

This example demonstrates powerfully that, in an urbanizing world, cities provide much more than just the *backdrop* and *environment* for war and terror. Rather, their buildings, assets, institutions, industries, and infrastructures; their cultural diversities and symbolic meanings; have long actually *themselves* been the explicit target for a wide range of deliberate, orchestrated attacks.

The starting point for this chapter at the beginning of the twenty-first century, these attacks against cities together constitute what we actually think of *as* "war" and "terrorism." And yet, curiously, the purposive and planned destruction of urban places is scarcely mentioned in urban social research (Bishop and Clancey, this volume). Purposive and planned city killing remains cloaked and veiled by powerful cultural, intellectual, and professional taboos.

In 1983 the geographer Ken Hewitt argued that, from the perspective of urban social science, the "destruction of cities, as of much else, remains *terra incognita*" (Hewitt, 1983: 258). While there has been some progress since, the deliberate annihilation of cities tends still to remain *terra incognita* in urban social science twenty years after Hewitt first made this point. Certainly, the attempted annihilation of Verdun, Ypres, Guernica, Nanking, and Rotterdam; of Coventry, London, Leningrad, Stalingrad, Warsaw, Hamburg, and Dresden; of Tengchong, Tokyo, Hiroshima, Nagasaki, Seoul, Phnom Penh, My Lai, Algiers, Beirut, Sarajevo, Jenin, or Groznyy, are only very rarely discussed in urban course books and textbooks designed for urban planners, geographers, sociologists, or architects. What Mike Davis (2002) calls the "radical contingency of the metropolis" is thus being actively and continually *forgotten*.

Hewitt suggested such neglect was made even more problematic because the shift to "total war" in the twentieth century meant that cities and their populations overwhelmingly became the *actual targets* of war. He noted that World War II, in particular, was "warfare that strove towards, if it did not always achieve, an end of the settled historic places that have been at the heart of civilian life, and an extermination of entire communities" (1987: 446).

For this explicit concentration on the killing of cities in modern war, Hewitt coined the term "place annihilation." "For a social scientist," he stressed that "it is actually imperative to ask just *who* dies and *whose* places are destroyed by violence" within such wars of place annihilation (1987: 464; original emphasis). This is because such strategies are usually far from indiscriminate. Commonly, they involve a great deal of planning, so that the violence and destruction achieve the desired political, social, economic, ecological, and cultural effects on the "target" population and their places.

All of which means that the division between urban planning geared towards urban growth and development, and that which focuses on attempts at place annihilation or attack, is not always clear. It is certainly much more fuzzy than urban planners – with their Enlightenment-tinged self-images of devoting themselves to instilling urban "progress" and "order" – might want to believe. In fact, it is necessary to assume that a continuum exists connecting acts of building and physical restructuring, on the one hand, and acts of all-out organized war and place annihilation on the other.

Such a continuum is complicated, of course, by the fact that much planned urban change *itself* involves war-like levels of violence, destabilization, rupture, forced expulsion, and place annihilation (Berman, 1996). Particularly within the dizzying peaks and troughs of capitalist urbanism, state-led planning often boils down to the legitimized clearance of vast tracts within cities in the name of decay eradication, modernization, improvement, ordering, economic competition, or facilitating technological change and capital accumulation and speculation. As David Harvey argues: "The economically, politically and socially driven processes of creative destruction through abandonment and redevelopment are often every bit as destructive as arbitray acts of war. Much of contemporary Baltimore, with its 40,000 abandoned houses, looks like a war zone to rival Sarajevo" (Harvey, 2003: 26b).

My purpose in this chapter is to illustrate the inseparability of war, terror, place annihilation, and modern urbanism. I do this by revealing a range of "hidden histories" of what I call the "dark side" of urban modernity – the propensity for urban life to be deliberately attacked, destroyed, or annihilated, both in acts of organized war and through the bureaucratic machineries of urban planning and nation-state regimes. To achieve this I offer a series of nine illustrative vignettes or mini case studies.

Architectures of Annihilation: The "War Ideology of the Plan"

In our first vignette, as we have just noted, civilian urban planning, development, modernization, and restructuring often actually involve levels of devastation of cities, ruination, and forced resettlement that match that which occurs in all-out war. Even in supposedly democratic societies, planned urban restructuring often involves autocratic state violence, massive urban destruction, the forced devastation of livelihoods, and even mass death. These are justified through heroic and mythologizing discourses emphasizing modernization, hygiene, or progress. Invariably, the destruction that follows is directed against marginalized places and people that are discursively constructed as backward, unclean, antiquated, or threatening to the dominant order. In both authoritarian and democratic societies, ideologies of urban planning have often actually *deliberately invoked* metaphors of war and militarism to legitimize violent acts of planned transformation (Sandercock, 1998). Anthony Vidler (2001: 38) calls this "the war ideology of the plan."

Thus, place annihilation can be thought of as a kind of hidden – and sometimes not so hidden – planning history. The planned devastation and killing of cities is a dark side of the discipline of urban planning that is rarely acknowledged, let alone analyzed. It is rarely realized, for example, that the analytical and statistical methods so often used in post-World War II civilian planning have also been used – sometimes by the same demographic, economic, and planning "experts" – to spatially organize the apartheid regime in South Africa, maximize the "efficiency" of the systematic fire-bombing of German and Japanese cities, organize the house-by-house demolition of Warsaw in 1945, set up the giant urban-regional process of the Holocaust, or starve many Easter European cities and regions into submission in the mid-1940s. The latter work even involved the founder of Central Place Theory, that seminal economic geographer Walter Christaller – star of any traditional school human geography course. Following the invasion eastward in 1941, he was employed by the Nazis to rethink the economic geography of an "Aryanized" Eastern Europe – a process directly linked to the planned starvation and forced migration of millions of people (see Aly and Heim, 2002; Rössler, 1989; Cole, 2003).

Meanwhile, mock German and Japanese housing units, complete with authentic roofing materials, furniture, interior decorations, and clothing, were erected in Nevada to allow the design and chemical makeup of incendiaries that would later burn Dresden and Tokyo to be carefully customized for their intended targets on a *city by city basis* (Davis, 2002: 65–84). Thousands of operation scientists and urban statisticians pored over every urban bomb blast in Japan and Germany in an effort to improve the "efficiency" of the city killing and urban "dehousing" (Vanderbilt, 2002). To predict the effects of incendiary and "A"-bombs on Japanese cities, a "Japanese village" was also constructed – again in Nevada. This was complete with all sorts of realistic Japanese-style buildings, contents, and infrastructures (Vanderbilt, 2002; Goodman, 2000).

This work goes on and on. More recently, the US and Israeli militaries have cooperated to construct and run a kind of shadow *urban system* of the complete urban neigbourhood, replete with "mosques, hanging laundry and even the odd donkey meandering down dusty streets" (Marsden, 2003: 2). These have been used for joint military exercises to train the marines and soldiers who invaded Baghdad, Basra, Fallujah, and Jenin (Graham, this volume).

It is also scarcely realized that demographers, statisticians, geographers, architects, and planners have been central to Israel's efforts to deepen its control over the three dimensional spaces of the Occupied Territories (Weizman, this volume). Their analyses and prescriptions have helped to shape the annexing of Palestinian land, the construction of walls and "buffer zones," the mass bulldozing of houses and olive groves, the demodernization of Palestinian cities, the ethnic cleansing of selected areas, the construction of carefully located Jewish settlements and access roads, and the appropriation of water and airspace (Weizman, Graham, this volume).

"Planning" and Occupation as War on the Colonized City

One of the achievements of the great wave of modernization that began in the late eighteenth century was to incorporate urbicide into the process of urban development...Its victims, along with their neighborhoods and towns, vanish without a trace. (Berman, 1996: 181)

In our second illustration, many strategies of occupation and colonization have also been based explicitly on the planned destruction and devastation of cities. Of course, colonization is essentially about the subordination, annihilation, or exploitation of one people's culture, life world, and places by another. Urban "planning" in many colonized cities, thus, often amounts to little but the planned devastation and bulldozing of indigenous cities to underpin the strategic and social control of the occupiers or settlers (Said, 2003; Yeoh, 1996; Yiftachel, 1995). Here the "orderly" imprints of Western-style urban planning and property law have long been used as a form of urban warfare (Blomley, 2003). At first, this was done to quell local insurgencies in non-Western, colonized cities. Later, such militarized planning strategies were often imported back to the "homeland" to reshape the great imperial capitals for similar purposes (Misselwitz and Weizman, 2003).

Tellingly, the first special manual on "urban warfare" was produced in 1847 by the French army to show how troops could ruthlessly put down insurrections in Algiers that were then erupting, led by Abdel Kager. This book, *La Guerre des rues et des maisons*, was authored by the leader of the French Forces, Bugeaud (1997). After a bloody seven-year struggle in a classic "asymmetric" urban war – with 100,000 French troops pitched against 10,0000 local resistance fighters – Bugeaud simply destroyed entire neighborhoods in the dense Algiers Casbah. In the process, he committed many atrocities against civilians and fighters alike and imprinted massive avenues through the city to sustain the surveillance, movement, and killing power of the occupying forces. This broke the resistance (for a time, at least) (Misselwitz and Weizman, 2003).

In a process that would be paralleled many times later, these techniques were then used to inform urban planning strategies designed to quell civil and social unrest in the "homeland," imperial centers of the colonizing powers. Bugeaud's doctrines, for example, had a major influence on Baron Haussmann in the 1870s, as he violently imprinted a strategy of massive boulevards and canon-firing arcs on Paris, partly for the sake of improving the state's strategic control of the volatile capital (Misselwitz and Weizman, 2003). In the process "Haussmann draped a facade of theatres, cafès, and shops over boulevards laid out for the benefit of the troops who might be called upon to quell civil disturbance" (Muschamp, 1995: 105).

Thus, the anti-urban rhetoric of ruling elites tended to see both colonized and "home" cities as morally toxic hotbeds of unrest that needed to be "regularized" and disciplined through similar, violent, urban restructuring efforts:

> If strategic urban design previously focused on strengthening the city's peripheral walls and fortifications to keep out the enemy, here, since the enemy was already *inside* the city, the city had to be controlled from within. The city fabric itself, its streets and houses, had to be adapted accordingly... Military control was exercised on the drawing board, according to the rules of design, fashion, and speculative interests. (Misselwitz and Weizman, 2003: 272; emphasis added)

There are sometimes striking continuities between the control strategies adopted in colonial and supposedly "postcolonial" cities. In an episode that sadly would be repeated in the same city some 56 years later by the Israelis (see Graham, this volume), in 1936 the British took 4,200 kilos of explosives to the refugee camp in Jenin and completely leveled a whole quarter of

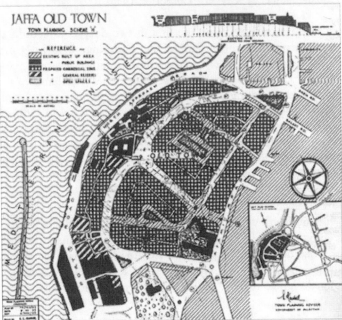

הגרעין הקדום של יפו כפי שצולם בתום שני ימי הפעילות של הצבא הבריטי ב"מבצע עוגן", ומפת
התכנון המחודש של העיר שהכין היועץ הממשלתי הבריטי לתכנון ערים. הן בצילום האוויר והן במפת
התכנון המחודש קל להבחין בשני הנתיבים, שנוצרו כתוצאה מפיצוץ 732 הבתים, המתחברים זה לזה
ויוצרים מתווה של עוגן

Plate 1.1 Operation Anchor: the use of explosives by British forces
to carve boulevards through the Palestinian Casbah in Jaffa in 1936, to
improve their strategic control of the settlement. Source: Missewitz and
Weizman (2003: 275).

the town. This was an act of collective punishment for the continuing resistance to the British occupation of Palestine (Corera, 2002).

As plate 1.1 shows, the old Palestinian Casbah in Jaffa was similarly heavily remodeled by explosives in the same year during what the British called Operation Anchor.[1] This was an attempt by the British occupiers to reduce their vulnerability to snipers in the closely built streets of the old settlement by forcing an anchor-shaped set of broad boulevards through the Casbah (Missewitz and Weizman, 2003). Military discourses which construct cities and built-up areas as threats to order and control remain at the heart of strategic discourse about cities in our post-Cold War world (Graham, Marvin, Weizman, Hills, this volume).

Modernism and Urban War I: Aerial Living as Response to Aerial War

The airplane indicts the city! (Le Corbusier, 1935: 100)

Our third illustration centers on the first of two deep connections that run between modernist urbanism and aerial bombing. For Le Corbusier's famous obsession with loosely spaced modern towers set in parkland – most famously elaborated in his *Ville Radieuse* or "Radiant City" – was not just a celebration of light, air, and the modern house as a "machine for living." It was also a reaction to a widespread obsession in 1930s Europe with the need to completely replan cities so that they presented the smallest possible targets to the massed ranks of heavy bombers then being fielded by the major powers. Corbusier's towers – variants of which had hardened "anti-aircraft" bombproof roofs – were also designed to lift residents above expected gas attacks (Markou, 2002) (see plate 1.2).

Le Corbusier celebrated the modernism of the aircraft machine and its vertical destructive power. "What a gift to be able to sow death with bombs upon sleeping towns," he wrote (1935: 8–9). His response to the "sinister apotheosis" of death and destruction heralded by aerial warfare was the total demolition of the old city, and its replacement by a modern utopia specifically designed to be "capable of emerging victorious from the air war" (1935: 60–1).

Post-9/11 – an event which seemed to underline the extreme *vulnerability* of skyscrapers – it seems painfully ironic that the dreams of that arch celebrator of skyscrapers were, in fact, partly intended to *reduce* the city's exposure to aerial annihilation. The famous modernist architectural theorist Siegfried Gideon – who was strongly influenced by Le Corbusier's views – argued in 1941 that:

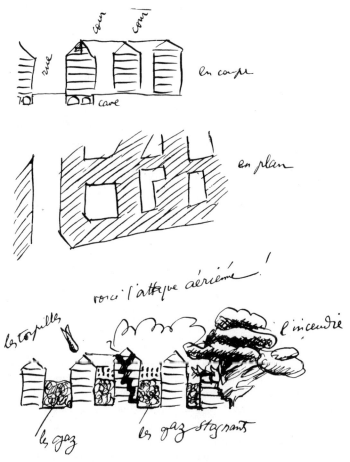

Plate 1.2 Le Corbusier's 1933 *Ville Radieuse* designs for apartment blocks and cities, which minimized the risks of aerial bombing and gas attack. These are contrasted with the supposed vulnerabilities of traditional, dense, urban streetscapes (see plate 5.1). Source: Le Corbusier (1933: 60–1).

The threat of attack from the air demands urban changes. Great cities sprawling open to the sky, their congested areas at the mercy of bombs hurtling down out of space, are invitations to destruction. They are practically indefensible as now constituted, and it is now becoming clear that the best means of defending them is by the construction, on the one hand, of great vertical concentrations which offer a minimum surface to the bomber and, on the other hand, by the laying out of extensive, free, open spaces. (Gideon, 1941: 543)

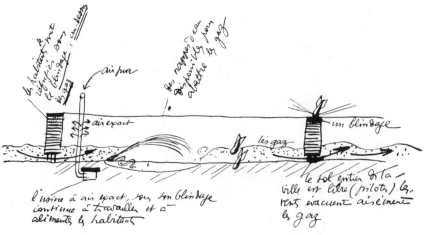

Plate 1.2   *(Contd.)*

Modernism and Urban War II: Aerial Bombing as a "New Chance"

Following World War II, as the scale and scope of place annihilation became clear, preservationists achieved some limited success in rebuilding parts of some cities along old lines. Many ruined buildings – churches especially – were also preserved as war memorials. The British war artist Kenneth Clark even argued "bomb damage itself is picturesque" (Woodward, 2001: 212).

Our fourth illustration, however, centers on the way in which devout modernists saw the unimaginable devastation as an unparalleled opportunity to reconstruct entire cities according to the principles of Le Corbusier and other modernist architects. As part of the "brave new world" of postwar reconstruction, modernist planners and architects seemed in many cases to be almost grateful that the deadly work of the bombers had laid waste to urban landscapes of traditional, closely built streets and buildings (Tiratsoo et al., 2002; Diefendorf, 1993). For example, one pamphlet, published in the UK by John Mansbridge during World War II, expressed gratitude to that modernist icon, the aeroplane (plate 1.3). Not only had it "given us a new vision," but the bombing also offered Britain "a new chance by blasting away the centers of cities." Thus, it continued, modernist reconstruction would now be delivered to sustain "the swift flow of modern traffic for the play of light and air" (Tiratsoo et al., 2002).

Meanwhile, in Germany, the closing stages of World War II saw Third Reich planners preparing to totally disperse the city of Hamburg – which had

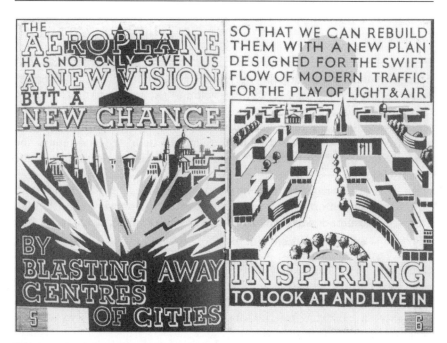

Plate 1.3 Illustrations from John Mansbridge's British World War II pamphlet *Here Comes Tomorrow*, celebrating both the modernism of aircraft and the "new chance" their bombing offered British cities to rebuild along modernist lines. Source: Tiratsoo et al. (2002: 57).

been so devastated by the firestorm raids of 1943 – as a test case in the complete "deurbanization" of German society. When the founder of the Bauhaus, Walter Gropius, returned from exile to Germany in 1947, to advise on postwar reconstruction, he argued that the urban devastation in Germany meant that it was "the best place to start breaking up cities into home towns and to establish small-scale communities, in which the essential importance of the individual could be realized" (cited in Kostof, 1992: 261).

Thus, in a way, the total bombing of total war – an enormous act of *planned* urban devastation in its own right – served as a massive accelerator of modernist urban planning, architecture, and urbanism. The *tabula rasa* that every devoted modernist craved suddenly became the norm rather than the exception, particularly in postwar Europe and Japan. As a result, to use the words of Ken Hewitt (1983: 278), "the ghosts of the architects of urban bombing – (Guilo) Douhet, (Billy) Mitchell, (Sir Hugh) Trenchard, (Frederick) Lindemann – and the praxis of airmen like ("Bomber") Harris and (Curtis) LeMay, still stalk the streets of our cities."

Cold War Urban Geopolitics

In our fifth illustration, Cold War cities were often deliberately remodeled as a function of the perception that they rested at the center of the nuclear cross hairs. As Matthew Farish (2003, this volume) shows, the familiar story of deconcentration and sprawl in postwar US cities was not just fueled by federal subsidies, the Interstate highway program, and "white flight." It was also actively encouraged by military strategists in order to reduce the United States' strategic vulnerability to a massive first nuclear strike by the Soviet Union.

As well as burrowing underground (McCamley, 1998; Vanderbilt, 2002), massive efforts were made to make cities sprawl. In the United States, especially, vast new suburban tracts were projected as domesticated citadels, populated by perfect "nuclear" families living the "American dream," yet also shaped to be resilient in the face of atomic Armageddon (Zarlengo, 1999; McEnaney, 2000). Core cities, meanwhile, were widely portrayed by popular media and planners as inherently risky and unsafe – a politics of fear that mixed tragically with the wider racialization of urban centrality in postwar America and further fueled central city decline (Galison, 2001; Farish, this volume).

At the same time, huge research and development cities – "gunbelt" urban complexes such as Cambridge (Ma.), Palo Alto, and Novosibirsk – were established to furnish the technoscience of Armageddon to the military in ever increasing doses (Castells, 1989; Markusen et al., 1991; Hookway, 1999). In addition, city-sized complexes and bases were established around the world to sustain the global reach of the superpowers' naval, air, and land forces. Some, such as Guantánamo bay, in Cuba, would later become notorious as extra-territorial camps used in the prosecution of post-Cold War strategy (in this case with the incarceration of alleged "terrorists" beyond the reach of domestic and international human rights law) (see An Architektur, 2003).

Planning as "Urbicide": Postwar Urban "Renewal" and the Military–Industrial Complex in the USA

> Building, by its very nature, is an aggressive, even war-like act. (Woods, 1995: 50)

A sixth illustration is the critical influence of such quasi-military urban planning on the huge effort at urban "renewal" in the postwar United States. One of it's arch proponents, Robert Moses – who was mayor of New York City for much of this period – believed that, in modernizing New

York, "when you operate in an overbuilt metropolis you have to hack your way through with a meat ax" (quoted in Berman, 1982: 307).

Following the forced displacement of 50,000 people before a highway was carved through the Bronx, for example, Moses helped set in train a war-like process of disintegration. By the 1970s this "had become spectacular, devouring house after house and block after block, driving hundreds of thousands of people from their homes" (Berman, 1996: 172). Marshal Berman argues the scale of devastation in such programs – if not the human lives lost – means that the Bronx needs to be seen in the same light as the all-out or guerrilla wars of Berlin, Belfast, and Beirut. Along with several other authors – as we shall see in Part II of this book – he even invokes the word "urbicide" – or "the murder of the city" – to describe all these, and many other cases (1996: 175).

Robert Goodman, in his book *After the Planners* (1972), argued that a US-wide drive for such "urban renewal" actually amounted to little more than an exercise in racist (anti-black) state violence on a par with the genocidal attacks on the indigenous North Americans that drove them to the edge of extinction (see Porteous and Smith, 2001: ch. 4).

Importantly, major military research and development bodies like RAND, STC, and MITRE had major inputs into the statistical analyses, operations research strategies, and "rational" planning doctrines that fueled the huge scale of Cold War "urban renewal" and comprehensive redevelopment in the US (Light, 2002). Thus, in many cases, the "sciences" of urban and military strategy became extremely blurred and interwoven during this period. On the one hand, city governments pledged "war" against the "urban crisis" (see Farish, this volume). On the other, the military–industrial complex sought to gain finance and power by re-shaping civil strategic spaces in cities (Beauregard, 2003). The result was that, "by 1970, the military–industrial complex had successfully done what it had set out to do at the start of the decade – expand its market to city planning and management" (Light, 2002).

Although it is rarely discussed, such planning-based urbicide is still extremely widespread around the world. For example, countless informal settlements continue to be bulldozed around the planet in the name of modernization, freeway construction, economic development, "hygiene," and the improvement of a city's image (see, for example, Patel, D'Cruz, and Burra, 2002). In addition, in these times of neoliberal finance-led capitalism, state-sponsored urban "regeneration" is increasingly orchestrating the annihilation of whole districts of the poorer parts of cities. This is being done to engineer vast edifices of construction in order to sustain the hyper-profits for financial industries that come through real-estate speculation; to allow urban "mega projects" to be constructed; and to enable spaces to be cleared for gentrified up-market housing. London Docklands is an extreme and famous example, but there are countless others (Harvey, 2003b).

Urban Ruination and the Politics of "Unbuilding"

It is crucial to stress – in our seventh illustration – that, after decades of urban crises of various sorts, and an entrenchment of global, neoliberal restructuring, the discipline of urban planning is now confronting "the radical contingency of the metropolis" in many guises and many places. The capitalist and post-socialist worlds are littered with shrinking cities, rotting, utopian urban landscapes, and failing infrastructures. Many of these now resemble dystopian sites of ethnic conflict, economic and social collapse, financial meltdown, and physical decay (Olalquiaga, 1995; Buck-Morss, 2000; Humphrey, 2003).

In that paradigmatically modern city, Detroit, for example, much urban planning doctrine and effort now centers on "unbuilding" rather than building (Daskalakis, Waldheim, and Tound, 2001). As in many other US core cities, old industrial European cities, and Asian and Latin American megacities confronting recent financial collapse, the challenge here is not to "plan" for growth, prosperity, and modernization (see, for example, Wilson, 2003). Rather, it is to try to overcome obsolescent structures, abandoned neighborhoods, half-built or half-ruined cityscapes, decayed infrastructures, and war-like levels of gang, ethnic, and drug-related violence and arson (Vergara, 1997, 1999; Roldàn, 2003; Mullings, 2003). Such:

> enclaves of disinvestment reverse normal codes of controlled development; they are pockets of free-fall urban implosion, partaking of a frenzied violence . . . matched only by the half-machine cyborgs of the _Robocop_ science fiction movies. Here the police plead for their own automatic weapons, pleading to be outgunned by teenage gangs. (Shane, 1995: 65)

A Geopolitics of Urban Decay and Cybernetic Play: Urban Annihilation, Entertainment, and Military Strategy

Which brings us, penultimately, to the argument that the neglect of place annihilation in urban social science has also left the connections between today's cities and the obsession with ruined, post-apocalyptic urban landscapes in contemporary popular culture largely unexplored. This is important because cities are unmade and annihilated _discursively_ as well as through bombs, planes, missiles, bulldozers, plans, and terrorist acts.

As suites of electronic media become evermore dominant in mediating the tenor of urban culture, so the depictions of cities offered through them crucially affect collective notions of what cities and urban life actually are, or what they might actually become. Increasingly, in these times of electronic, postmodern culture, cities are widely depicted in films, novels, video games, and Internet sites as places of ruination, fear, and decay, rather than development, order, and "progress." Crucially, this means that the millennia-old "link between civilization and barbarism is reversed: city life turns into a state of nature characterized by the rule of terror, accompanied by omnipresent fear" (Diken and Laustsen, 2002: 291).

As long ago as the mid-1960s, Susan Sontag observed that most sci-fi films, for example, emphasized an "aesthetic of destruction, the peculiar beauties to be found in wreaking havoc, making a mess" (1966: 213). More recently, in an analysis of cyberpunk science fiction, Claire Sponster diagnosed what she called a prevailing "geopolitics of urban decay and cybernetic play" (1992: 253). She was particularly struck by the prevailing landscapes in that genre of "blighted, rubble-strewn, broken-down cityspaces" with their "vast terrains of decay, bleakness, and the detritus of civilization."

Even popular urban simulation games like SimCity™ – which are often used to train urban planners in universities – offer introductions and guides which emphasize the god-like propensities of players to first indulge in orgies of (virtual) city killing. One reads: "Let's start off by destroying Tokyo! Studies show that nine out of ten [virtual city] 'mayors' begin their careers with a frenzy of destruction . . . Simply point at the disaster of you choice and push B to activate it" (see Bleecker, 1994).

Added to this, a swathe of recent post-apocalyptic films has so shaped the collective culture of urbanism that the stock response to the 9/11 catastrophe is "it was just like a scene in a movie!" While the output of such films paused after 9/11, they were soon back in full flow (Maher, 2002). Mike Davis has argued the 9/11 attacks:

> were organized as epic horror cinema with meticulous attention to the *mise-en-scéne*. The hijacked planes were aimed precisely at the vulnerable border between fantasy and reality . . . Thousands of people who turned on their televisions on 9/11 were convinced that the cataclysm was just a broadcast, a hoax. They thought they were watching rushes from the latest Bruce Willis film . . . The "Attack on America," and its sequels, "America Fights Back" and "America Freaks Out," have continued to unspool as a succession of celluloid hallucinations, each of which can be rented from the video shop: *The Siege, Independence Day, Executive Action, Outbreak, The Sum of All Fears*, and so on. (Davis, 2002: 5)

Indeed, the links between virtual, filmic, and televisual representations of city killing and actual urban war are becoming so blurred that they are almost indistinguishable. On the one hand, at least among US forces, the military targeting of cities is, at least in part, being remodeled as a "joy stick war." This operates through "virtual" simulations, computerized killing systems, and a growing distanciation of the operator from the sites of the killing and the killed. In the process, the realities of urban war – at least for some – start to blur seamlessly with the wider cultures of sci-fi, film, video games, and popular entertainment (Thussu and Freedman, 2003).

Take, for example, the unmanned low-altitude "Predator" aircraft that are already being used for extra-judicial assassinations of alleged terrorists (and whoever happens to be close by) in the Yemen, Afghanistan, and Iraq, "piloted" from a virtual reality "cave" in a Florida airbase 8–10,000 miles away. For the US military personnel doing the piloting, this "virtual" work is almost indistinguishable from a "shoot-'em-up" video game (except that the people who die are real). "At the end of the work day," one Predator operator recently boasted during Gulf War II, "you walk back into the rest of life in America" (quoted in Newman, 2003).

On the other hand, as war is increasingly consumed by a voyeuristic public, so digital technologies, in turn, bring the vicarious thrills of urban war direct to the homes of thrill-hungry consumers. In the 2003 Iraq war, for example, US newspaper and media websites offered a wide range of vertical, satellite image-based maps of the city as little more than an array of targets, to be destroyed from the air. As Derek Gregory describes:

> The *New York Times* provided a daily satellite map of Baghdad as a city of targets. On the web, *USA Today*'s interactive map of "Downtown Baghdad" invited its users: "Get a satellite-eye view of Baghdad. Strategic sites and bombing targets are marked, but you can click on any quadrant for a close up." The site also included images of targets "before" and "after" air strikes. The *Washington Post*'s interactives invited the viewer to "roll over the numbers to see what targets were hit on which day; click to read more about the targets. (Gregory, 2004b: 29)

In a perverse twist, corporate media and entertainment industries increasingly provide both computer games and films which virtually simulate recent urban wars to mass participants, *and* the virtual and physical simulations of cities that US forces use to hone their warfare skills for fighting in Kabul, Baghdad, or Freetown. The actual prosecution of wars is merging more and more with electronic entertainment industries. "The US military is preparing for wars that will be fought in the same manner as they are electronically represented, on real-time networks and by live feed videos, on the PC and the TV actually and virtually" (Der Derian, 2002: 61). The "military now mobilizes science fiction writers and other futurologists to plan for the wars of tomorrow just as they consciously recruit video-game playing adolescents to fight the same conflict" (Gray, 1997: 190). As Henry Jenkins (2003) argues, "in a world being torn apart by international conflict, one thing is on everyone's mind as they finish watching the nightly news: "Man, this would make a great game!'"

To exploit this market, the world's media conglomerates now concentrate vast resources on repeating virtualized urban killing for consumers. On the very night that US bombers and missiles first rained their destruction on Baghdad, Sony trademarked the phrase "shock and awe" with the idea of using it as title for a since-abandoned computer game.

Not to be out-done, the US Army, now the world's largest video game developer, spent $8 million in 2002 on producing *America's Army* – a deliberate aid to recruitment. This is a "Net based soldier-simulation game that was, by 2003, amongst the 5 most popular online videogames in the world with 2 million registered users (Turse, 2003). Meanwhile, the Army has also had a major role in *Full Spectrum Warfare* – an urban combat training game produced in 2004 for Microsoft's X-Box system in partnership with Paramount Pictures and Hollywood's Institute for Creative Technologies (ICT). Launched as a commercial urban warfare game, this offers startlingly realistic virtual reality renditions complete with demonic "rogue states," "terrorist leaders," mythical Middle Eastern urban battle spaces ("Zekistan"), and stressful urban warfare simulations where those volunteering to "fight for freedom" face devious, underhand barbarians who exploit the city for their own ends (Turse, 2003). "The mission is to slaughter evil-doers, with something about 'liberty' . . . going on in the background . . . Zekistan conforms to trailer-park perceptions in being some Afghanistan/Iran/Iraq composite" (O'Hagan, 2004: 12).

To close the cycle even more disturbingly, actual weapons systems – for example, the Dragon Runner remote-control urban warfare vehicle – are being designed to mimic the controls of Sony Playstations so that new recruits can quickly make the transition from simulated to real combat.

The result of all this is a "media culture thoroughly capable of preparing children for armed combat" (Turse, 2003). James Der Derian (2001) coined the term "military–industrial–media–entertainment network" to capture the deepening and increasingly insidious connections between the military, defense industries, popular culture, and electronic entertainment. Here, huge software simulations are constructed to recreate any possible urban warfare scenario, complete with vast forces, casualties, the gaze of the media, and three-dimensional, real-time participation by thousands. Hollywood specialists of computer generated films provide extra "realism" in these simulations; their theme park designers, meanwhile, help in the construction of the "real" urban warfare training cities that are dotted across the world. Major "invasions" – such as the Urban Warrior exercise in March 1999 – are even undertaken on major US cities from air, land, and sea to further improve training both for foreign incursions and the control of major domestic urban unrest. Civilians are employed in these exercises to play various parts (Willis, 2003). Such mock invasions have even been proposed as local economic development initiatives for declining city cores.

Finally, we must also remember that the US military are deepening their connections with corporate news media, so that the "information warfare" side of their operations (i.e., propaganda) can be more successful. Just as Al-Qaeda timed the second plane's impact on 9/11 so that the world's news media could beam it live to billions of astonished onlookers, so the "Shock and Awe" strategy at the start of the US bombing of Baghdad was a carefully orchestrated media spectacle. (The world's TV journalists were lined up in a major hotel, a short but safe distance away from the carefully selected – and largely empty – buildings that were pinpointed for GPS-based destruction.) As a psychologist comments, both events were "meant to be right before our eyes" (cited in Konstantin and Hornig, 2001: 126).

Thus, both formal and informal attacks against cities emerge as "rhizo-matic," internationally networked operations orchestrated heavily with global, media representation in mind (see Deleuze and Guatarri, 1987). Both Al-Qaeda and the US military are transnational organizations con-cerned both with symbolic effects and the real devastation of local sites (Zizek, 2003). "This war takes place in the invisible space of the terror imaginary of the US (attacks on buildings and government, germ infection, etc.) and in the visibly impoverished landscape of Afghanistan" (Aretxaga, 2003: 144).

James Lukaszewiski, a US public relations counselor who advises the US military, admits that the links between terrorist organizations and the global media can be equally insidious:

> Media coverage and terrorism are soul mates – virtually inseparable. They feed off each other. They together create a dance of death – the one for political or ideological motives, the other for commercial success. Terrorist activities are high profile, ratings-building events. The news media need to prolong these stories because they build viewership and readership. (Cited in Rampton and Stauber, 2003: 134)

Homeland/Globe: War, "Security," and the Global Geopolitics of Production and Consumption

> Every generation has a taboo and ours is this: that the resources upon which our lives have been built are running out. (Monbiot, 2003)

A final vignette on the inseparability of contemporary war, terror, and urbanism centers on the ways in which the reconstruction of landscapes and consumption habits in the wealthy cities of the global North impact on security, terror, and urbanizing war elsewhere (Le Billon, 2001). A powerful example of these important but poorly researched connections is the growing fashion for large four-wheel drive Sports Utility Vehicles (SUVs) in Western – particularly US – cities.

Given the very high degree of influence of major US oil companies on the Bush regime, there is growing evidence of direct connections between the increasingly profligate use of oil in sprawling US cityscapes, the geopolitical remodeling of US defense forces, and the so-called war on terror through which the US government is achieving a high level of geopolitical control of the world's largest untapped oil reserves in and around the Caspian Basin (Kleveman, 2003; see plate 1.4). 9/11 has thus been ruthlessly exploited. In particular, the attacks provided the "catastrophic and catalyzing event" that was identified by the influential 2000 report *Project for a New American Century* – who's authors included Donald Rumsfeld and Paul Wolfowitz – as necessary to allow the US to justify the invasion of Iraq with any hope of legitimacy (Harvey, 2003a: 15).

While the US strategy is not necessarily about directly controlling Caspian Basin and Iraqi oil resources *per se*, there is little doubt that "it is about ensuring that whoever controls it buys and sells it in US dollars through the New York commodities market" that lies a few hundred meters from "ground zero" in downtown Manhattan (Halevi and Varoufakis, 2003: 66). There is also little doubt that a key objective of the US attack on Iraq was to install a US-friendly oil producing regime there that would eventually displace the Saudis as the main "swing producer," so allowing the United States to regulate the international price of oil in place of OPEC (Gregory, 2004b; Harvey, 2003a; Vidal, 2002: 19).

Three key points are crucial here. First, SUVs were carefully fashioned and marketed after the first Gulf War as quasi-militarized "urban assault luxury vehicles" (Rampton and Stauber, 2003). Clotaire Rapaille, a psychological consultant to major US SUV manufacturers, reveals that his research suggests that Americans want "aggressive cars" that can be thought of as "weapons" or "armored cars for the battlefield." To achieve market share and profitability he argues that the design and marketing of such vehicles – with their names like "Stealth," "Defender," and "Warrior" – needs to tap into, and address, consumers' fears about the risks and dangers inherent in contemporary urban life (cited in Rampton and Stauber, 2003: 138). Depictions of such vehicles in adverts thus turn the discourses of postmodern war into discussions about urban everyday life. "Just try blending in!" yells the UK ad for the Jeep Grand Cherokee "Stealth Limited Edition," released in 2003.

Post-9/11, then, it is now clear that advertisers have been deliberately exploiting widespread fears of catastrophic terrorism to further increase sales of highly profitable SUVs. Rapaille himself has recently been urging the main auto manufacturers to address the fact that "the Homeland is at war" by appealing to buyers' most primitive emotions (Rampton and Stauber, 2003: 139).

Plate 1.4 Satirical World War II-style poster by Micah Ian Wright stressing the links between SUVs, the United States' profligate oil consumption, and the attacks by US forces in the Middle East after 2002 as part of the war on terror. Source: Wright (2003: 96).

Second, the SUV is being enrolled into urban everyday life as a defensive capsule or "portable civilization" – a signifier of safety that, like the gated communities into which they so often drive, is portrayed in advertisements as being immune to the risky and unpredictable urban life "outside" (Garner, 2000). Such vehicles seem to assuage the fear that the urban middle classes feel when moving – or queuing – in traffic in their "home-land" city.

Subliminal processes of urban and cultural militarization are going on here. This was most powerfully illustrated by the transformation of the US Army's "Humvee" assault vehicle into the civilian "Hummer" SUV just after the first Iraq war – an idea that came from the *Terminator* film star (and now California governor) Arnold Schwarzenegger (who promptly received the first one off the production line). During the 2003 Iraq invasion, organizations of US Hummer drivers mobilized publicity campaigns to project their vehicles as patriotic symbols. "When I turn on the TV," gushed one owner, Sam Berstein, "I see wall-to-wall Humvees, and I'm proud. The [US soldiers are] not out there in Audi 4x4s" (cited in Clark, 2004: 12). Andrew Garner writes that:

> For the middle classes, the SUV is interpreted culturally as strong and invincible, yet civilized. In the case of the middle-class alienation from the inner city, the SUV is an urban assault vehicle. The driver is transformed into a trooper, combating an increasingly dangerous world. This sense of security felt when driving the SUV continues when it is not being driven. The SUV's symbols of strength, power, command, and security become an important part of the self-sign ... With the identification of enemies within our borders, this vehicle has become a way of protecting members of the middle class from any threat to their lifestyle. (Garner, 2000: 6)

Third, the fact that SUVs account for over 25 percent of US car sales has very real impacts on the global geopolitics of oil. With their consumption rates of double or triple that of normal cars, this highly lucrative sector clearly adds directly to the power of the neoconservative and ex-oil executive "hawks" in the Bush regime. This is especially so as they have operationalized their perpetual war on terror in ways that are helping the USA to secure access to the huge, low-priced oil reserves that it needs to fuel its ever-growing level of consumption. (In 2003 this stood at 25.5 percent of global oil consumption to sustain a country with less than 5 percent of the world's population.)

Clearly, then, the profligate oil consumption and militarized design of SUVs "takes on additional significance in the light of the role that dependency on foreign oil has played in shaping US relations with countries in the Middle East" (Rampton and Stauber, 2003: 139).

"The economic, cultural and military infrastructure that undergrids US Middle East policy will not be so easily undone," writes Tim Watson. "And without its wholesale reform or dismantling, Islamic terrorists will not so easily disappear" (2003: 110). As with the cosmopolitan nationalities of the dead, then, so the events of 9/11, in their own way, reflect and symbolize the deep connections between urban everyday life and city form and the violence spawned by geopolitical conflict and neo-imperial aggression. Watson writes that he has been haunted since 9/11 by images of the hundreds of vehicles abandoned, never to be recovered, at rail stations by commuters to the twin towers in the states of New York, Connecticut, and New Jersey. For him, "these symbols of mobility" became instead "images of immobility and death. But these forlorn, expensive cars and SUVs also represent a nodal point between the US-domestic economy and a global oil market in which Saudi, Kuwaiti, and Iraqi production is still so important" (Watson, 2003: 110–11).

Conclusion: Looking at Ruins

> The ruins are painful to look at, but will hurt more in the long run if we try not to see. (Berman, 1996: 185)

To conclude, it is strikingly clear that ignoring attempts to deny, destroy, or annihilate cities, or the "dark" side of urban modernity which links cities intimately to organized, political violence, is no longer tenable for urbanists or urban researchers. In this post-9/11 and post-war on terror world, urban researchers and social scientists – like everyone else – are forced to begin to confront their taboos about attempted city killing, place annihilation, and urbicide. International relations theorists, similarly, are forced for the first time to consider urban and subnational spaces as crucial geopolitical sites.

As a result, researchers in both traditions are now starting to colonize, and focus on, the spaces and practices that emerge at the intersections of urbanism, terrorism, and warfare. As the rest of this book demonstrates, there is a growing acknowledgment that violent catastrophe, crafted by humans, is part and parcel of modern urban life. A much needed, specifically *urban* geopolitics is thus slowly emerging.

As an exploratory synthesis, this chapter has developed a particularly broad perspective on the ways in which the purposive destruction and annihilation of cities in war, planning, and virtual play is utterly interwoven with urban modernity. As the gaze of urban social science starts to fall once again on the purposive ruination and annihilation of place, so this synthesis underlines five related challenges. First, the research and professional taboos that cloak the geopolitical and strategic aspects of modern urbanism must be undermined. Second, the "hidden," militarized histories of modern urban planning and urban state terror must be excavated and relentlessly exposed. Third, the characteristics of city spaces that make them the choices *par excellence* of those seeking to commit terrorist acts require detailed analysis. Fourth, the transnational connections between the geopolitics of war and the political economies of production, consumption, technology, and the media require rigorous theorization and analysis. Finally, the usually hidden worlds of "shadow" urban research, through which the world's military perceive, reconstruct, and target urban spaces, must be actively uncovered. As a starting point, readers will find that each of these five challenges is taken up extensively in the rest of this book.

Note

1   As it has been absorbed into the Israeli metropolis of Tel Aviv since 1948, the old city of Jaffa has, in turn, been ruthlessly emptied, resettled, reshaped, and stripped of its original Palestinian cultural meaning as part of Israeli state-building (see Rotbard, 2003b).

2

The City-as-Target, or Perpetuation and Death

Ryan Bishop and Gregory Clancey

Prologue

The last substantial draft of this chapter was finished on September 5, 2001. We'd written it for the *Perpetuating Global Cities* workshop held in Singapore that spring, where the consensus seemed to be that it was interesting, perhaps even worrying, but peculiar. With the events of September 11 we ceased working on it, partly because we were as immersed in the news coverage as everyone else, and because the piece was essentially done, but also because we were now uncertain what to do with a work entitled "The City-as-Target, or Perpetuation and Death." Although the article was not about New York – our one reference to that city spoke of its relative security in comparison to its Asian counterparts – we knew that from now on, it would have to do with New York. One instinct was to rewrite it, or at least write more. Another was to stop writing, and let the piece stand. We decided to stop. If it seems less than perfectly complete, given our current context, and strangely incognizant of the stunning events of autumn 2001, it is both those things. It's a record of what we were thinking in the first week of September 2001. We've now followed it with a brief epilogue, however – our attempt to continue a conversation that had prematurely collapsed in blood and complexity.

Introduction

For a child it is extraordinary to see to what degree a city can be obliterated in a single bombardment. For a kid, a city is like the Alps, it's eternal, like the mountains. One single bombardment and all is razed. These are the traumatizing events which shaped my thinking. (Paul Virilio, quoted in Der Derian, 1998: 16)

As the global city emerges ever more hegemonic, the attention it reaps is not always welcome. Attention is another word for targeting. The city is a target for a range of catastrophes, from natural disasters (such as earthquakes, floods, tornados, hurricanes, tidal waves, and plagues) to those of more obviously human construction (chemical spills, factory explosions, mass transit accidents or derailments), strategic geopolitical targeting (official military aggression to terrorist attacks), large-scale macro-investments (International Monetary Fund or World Bank interventionism, UN development schemes), more modest global investing (by multinational corporations, advertising campaigns, IT networks, real estate speculation, global capital maneuvering, currency markets, satellite imaging of neighborhoods for marketing purposes), planned (il)legal immigration (foreign labor for menial tasks), or unplanned illegal immigration (refugees fleeing war, famines, ethnic cleansing). The list hints at the range of the tropological and intellectual terrain proffered by the city-as-target model. Their densities of population, material goods, and wealth have made cities, from their inception, simultaneously a given culture's goal (future and potential glory realized) and vulnerability (future and potential destruction of the culture's perceived trajectory).

The city is a lure to both settlers and sackers, something to shoot *for* as well as shoot *at*. In the earliest secular work in the Western intellectual tradition, the *Iliad*, Homer evocatively captures the inescapable duality of the city by exploiting the pun in the Greek word *kredemnon*, which means both veil and battlement. When Andromache watches from the walls of Troy as her husband, Hektor, is dragged in death behind Achilles' chariot, she removes her veil. Both she and the city are undone by the failure of the veil/battlement to protect and by its success in attracting undesired attention. This sense of the city as both stronghold and Achilles' heel, as it were – physically manifested in the walled fortress – was best realized in the collective Western imagination with the metonymies of Rome and Carthage.

As the Enlightenment yielded to modernity, however, the memory of Carthage receded. Modernity, especially, avoided the confluence of urbanism and catastrophe. We are not just referring to the imaginary of catastrophe, but to the kind that produces bodies that have to be burned or buried and rubble that has to be cleared. Death on this scale was exceptional, exotic, or merely absent in the official and academic literature of the "The City," especially the dominant stream produced by urban theorists in the late nineteenth and twentieth centuries. "Decay" and related disease-terms were common, but these fell short of depicting large-scale destruction and death. The analogies were medical and therefore hopeful, rather than mordant or funereal. Biblical and classical descriptions/celebrations of urban extinction, in which walled enclosures are entirely wiped out to the last inhabitant, had little counterpart in The City discourse (Mumford, 1961; Hall, 1988; Ellin, 1999). Urbicide has been mainly encountered in politico-military histories whose central characters were not cities but armies and nation-states.

Why could catastrophe not be modern? Beginning with the Bible and then reinforced by the rise of ancient history and archeology in the nineteenth century, the destruction of cities was a theme readily available to academic narratives, in both their religious and secular manifestations. The theme grew increasingly attenuated, however, and eventually petered out. The demarcation between modern and ancient, from the perspective of the nineteenth century, was between the time when whole cities were destroyed and their inhabitants slaughtered, and the time when that no longer happened – when cities instead built glass exhibit halls for each other's steam engines and wallpaper. The hinge was perhaps the Napoleonic War, when urban sacking was sporadic and relatively contained. While Europeans continued to raze African and Asian cities, it now came to be reported under words like "retaken," "pacified," or "civilized."

The destruction of cities became a show at the periphery; in a non-European world read as still ancient and/or subject to rule by Nature (including human natures in need of taming). Earthquakes, the most newsworthy city-destroyers of the period between the beginning of the Enlightenment and World War II, generally happened far from the North Atlantic power grid, in a geography largely coterminous with the orientalized world. The most dramatic destruction of a major European city between Lisbon (1755) and Warsaw (1939) was the earthquake-induced disappearance of Reggio/Calabria in 1907, cities on the southern fringe of a metropole that had moved decisively north and out of the seismic zone in the seventeenth and eighteenth centuries. The United States provided more regular examples – Chicago in flames, followed by San Francisco. Here it was an East–West axis that projected the images of natural disaster against geographies already considered disordered, violent, and overly spontaneous. Media centers consumed urban catastrophe as exotic news, safe from any sense of their own vulnerabilities.

In the natural sciences, the nineteenth-century replacement of "catastrophism" with "uniformatarianism" made sudden disaster an epiphenomenon of natural history, and rendered steady progress in historical time more natural as a result. Where the destruction of Lisbon had given the Enlightenment pause, the destruction of Chicago (1871) or Tokyo (1923) only accelerated the tempo of nascent global capitalism. In the age of trans-city finance, destruction came to be seen as prelude to a reconstruction synonymous with growth or evolution. Disaster was mitigated for an influential few. The rest suffered as before, but their damage was now collateral.

Yet if the perpetuation of The City in modernist discourse was partly conditioned by catastrophe avoidance, the same cannot be true for The City in its post-World War II hypermodern form. That war was, after all, an absolute orgy of city killing. The premeditated murder of very large cities was one of its most salient characteristics, Hiroshima and Dresden being only the iconographic examples. The genealogy of catastrophe visited upon ancient cities was consciously articulated in names bestowed on targeting plans. For example, the assault on Hamburg was called Operation Gomorrah. As in the Old Testament, all cities became potential "cities on the plains," with few fitting another typology found in the Pentateuch: "cities of refuge." The rise of modern architecture and "the architect" as a god figure – and of architectural history as about the future more than the past – was partly due to the opportunities to rebuild urban centers laid flat by (mostly) Allied air forces. The modern bomber, a design icon for the prewar Le Corbusier, became a major technological facilitator of his postwar influence. And this was no irony. The master builders, especially from Haussmann onward, were first master targeters and master destroyers, although their acts of ground-clearing have left far fewer traces in the historical record. The bulldozer was as much a legacy of World War II as penicillin and DDT.

To renew the question, how is it that, in the aftermath of 1940–5, the most sustained period of urban disaster since Tamerlane, and continuing through a period of global targeting for future urban catastrophism on a near-total scale, The City remained a multidisciplinary discourse almost utterly shorn of catastrophic tropes? One reason is The City's heroic status in both capitalist and socialist storytelling. It was not only the actor, but also the stage, scenery, and audience in a drama of irreversible world-historical change. The thunderous collapse into one another of modernization and urbanization was one of the few "emperial" spectacles that collectively bound politicians and intellectuals of all persuasions, at least until the final quarter of the twentieth century. More mundanely, urban planning, architecture, art, and journalism –the professions who most controlled the object of The City – were also most dependant on cities as work sites. The suburb, and all-that-was-not-The-City, was often constructed as their enemy. Death – centered now in the soul – was relocated outside the city gates. Until Stephen Spielberg's portrayal of the liquidation of the Krakow ghetto in the 1993 film *Schindler's List*, even the Holocaust was presented in media images as mainly a suburban phenomenon. The banality of evil that made Auschwitz possible, from certain abstracting perspectives, can seem akin to the banality of postwar Levittown – better to leave The City out of it.

The absence of death within The City reflected the larger economy of death within the academy: its studied absence from some disciplines and compensatory over-representation in others. History (the discipline) has been left largely by default to animate the city of the dead. It is not just that the dead are the historian's actors. He or she is actively interested in what killed them. We are particularly interested if people have *been* killed, although the killed arrange themselves into hierarchies of historical interest. Murder is more historically fascinating than other forms of death, because it is "social, cultural, and political" (the historian's declaration of solidarity with his/her social science colleagues). Those who have been killed by Nature, as in earthquakes, have traditionally not been considered to be "historical actors" by a profession whose stage center remains The State (rarely The City) and which shares only a short border with the natural sciences. Tokyo can burn up with most of its inhabitants, for example, and yet barely register as an event(s) in survey history texts of Japan. Epidemics, likewise, seem to come and go like the common flu. Demicide, the murder by a state of its own citizens, ranks high on the list of killings that would attract progressive historical research, as history overlaps with the law and investigative journalism in its studied instinct for the pursuit of justice. The resulting imbalance in how historians arrange and treat their dead sometimes makes them seem sloppy in the eyes of social scientists. To historians, on the other hand, the utter lack of corpses in social science texts on The City is the problem, the puzzle, needing to be explained.

We don't make these observations for the sake of morbidity, or from anti-urban instincts, but to demonstrate that a history of The City as a site of catastrophe – of urban densities as targets – certainly has been constructible from available evidence, particularly in our own time. The failure of modernism to produce this history – its writing of The City as a site of "processes" and "development" – is thus worth noticing, especially when its own concentric zone models look so much like bull's eyes. Evolutionary models of the urban ecologists could not allow for emergency, in the form of the sudden and unpredictable event, a phenomena-set too closely associated with Fascism, the opposite of Planning. The City was, after all, the site of data gathering and trend setting *par excellence*. The principal "event" was growth, or decay. It was all botany. The power of biological metaphors in city development and planning, whether medical or botanical, rests in their ability to avoid agency and responsibility for the way cities have been grown, despite the rhetoric of planning, just as similar metaphors for the marketplace have elided human control over economic forces and conditions.

The city-as-target, a reading long buried under layers of academic modernism, did find a certain robust expression in popular culture. As Mike Davis and H. Bruce Franklin have recently reminded us, cities have been insistently destroyed, and over a more sustained period, in novels, movies, and comic books (Davis, 1998; Franklin, 1988). At least in the last two art forms, however, destruction on a truly Judeo-Christian scale was arguably held in check through the end of the Cold War, as Hollywood and the American comic industry are relatively optimistic media. No imagery the West produced (until only very recently) could match that of a fire-breathing atomic-born Godzilla dismantling Tokyo *cho* by *cho*. Americans preferred that their giant screen creatures live in the jungle or desert, and merely menace nearby cities. King Kong is defeated by The City, not the other way round. The same would generally hold for most of his Cold War permutations.

Target Practice: Consuming Hiroshima, Hanoi, Phnom Penh . . .

The Arab and Kurd . . . now know what real bombing means in casualties and damage; they now know that within 45 minutes a full-sized village (vide attached photos) can be practically wiped out and a third of its inhabitants killed or injured by four or five machines. (British Wing-Commander Arthur Harris – later Air Marshall Sir Arthur "Bomber" Harris – writing of his participation in the aerial bombing of Iraq in 1924; quoted in Simons, 1994: 214)

Japan offers an ideal target for air operations . . . [Its] towns, built largely of wood and paper, form the greatest aerial targets the world has ever seen . . . Incendiary projectiles would burn the cities to the ground in short order. (US General Billy Mitchell, writing in *Liberty* magazine, January 1932; quoted in Franklin, 1988: 98)

Because of Picasso's artistry, it is widely believed that the first aerial bombing of a concentrated civilian target was the Luftwaffe's raid against Guernica, Spain in 1934. But the colonized world, more specifically North Africa and Asia, experienced even earlier aerial bombardments of concentrated populations, beginning with an ineffective but symbolically important raid on Tripoli in 1911 and including some carried out with deadly effect by the air forces of Spain. Aerial bombing in the twentieth century, of course, continued an age-old tradition of bombardment by land and sea, but in seeking to distance it from historic strategies and practices, its earliest advocates continually suggested its use not against walls or fortifications, but the densities that they contained. The Hague Convention of 1907 prohibited the targeting of civilian populations by airborne weaponry. In colonial territories, however, civilian population didn't necessarily count as a "civilian population."

Italy, France, Spain, and Britain led the way in the use of aerial attacks against colonial populations as a means of "pacification." France, in fact, called its first systemized form of air attack "colonial bombing" and developed a specific plane, *Type Colonial*, for just such a purpose. Anticipating the benefits of contemporary long-range high-tech weapons, Britain called its air targeting of colonial cities "control without occupation." The expansion of such bombing to target cities like London, Berlin, and Paris during World War I constituted an expansion from colonized cities to cosmopolitan ones. In fact, if the "civilizing" of colonial areas occurred through means of urbanization, then it also converted colonial populations into potential aerial targets. The colonial city was the paradigm for the city-as-target that has dominated the military imagination in the twentieth century (Lindqvist, 2001). Although countless cities, towns, and villages across Asia have been consumed (literally) in aerial and naval attack, the histories of their destructions have yet to be consumed (figuratively) through images or even, in many cases, texts. They have, with few exceptions, lacked their Picassos (Van Tijen, n.d.).

To suggest that Hiroshima and Nagasaki were not fully consumed seems at first unreasonable. Did not their very names become metaphors for destruction of the most complete, nearly Carthaginian type? Yet the catastrophism these words evoked was always about the future more than the past – about your own place rather than their place. Marguerite Duras articulated this in Alain Resnais' film *Hiroshima Mon Amour*, in its opening sequence and its sustained meditation on the consistent external construction of the city as a global metaphor for, of all things, "peace." "Hiroshima" came to mean, for many who deployed it, the possibility of the end of the world in its entirety, an event "beyond history." History (and specificity) often stopped with the towering white cloud that symbolized all nuclear explosions from Hiroshima to the final one(s). How many people could ever pick out Hiroshima and Nagasaki's unique death columns from the dozens of mushroom clouds that might merely have been tropical tests? Post-occupied Japan cooperated by reconstituting the victims in universal rather than ethnically specific terms. Whatever the good intentions, moral or geopolitical, the dead of Hiroshima and Nagasaki suffered a second act of disappearance. An image of a little girl, bodily whole and holding her head and arms hopefully aloft, cannot begin to represent what actually happened in both those places. Nor, it seems, is she meant to.

So passionless, disembodied, and consumable was the mushroom cloud image that it became the icon on many American consumer products in the middle to late 1940s, helping flog everything from toothpaste, drive-in movies, and a terrific Count Basie album, to special drinks at bars. Indeed, the US Post Office very nearly issued it as a Hiroshima commemorative stamp in 1995. The stamp was subsequently taken into private production by a group of American veterans angry at its last-minute cancellation, and it is now distributed via the website of Brigadier General (retired) Paul Tibbets, the pilot of the *Enola Gay* and leader of the 509th Composite Group over Hiroshima. According to the same website, the grandson of General Tibbets is a pilot in the present 509th Bomb Wing, recommissioned in 1993 specifically to receive the new B-2 bombers (Tibbets, n.d.). It was the 509th, whose shoulder-patch emblem is the Nagasaki mushroom cloud (archivally correct), which flew B-2s against Belgrade. The "509ers have every intention" boasts their own website, "of equaling, if not surpassing, the past accomplishments of the 509th Bomb Wing" (Office of Public Affairs, 509th Bomb Wing, 1999). The restoration of the 509th, an intentional act of convergence between B-2s and "the story of Hiroshima/Nagasaki" (a story of how the American citizen-army was saved by a *Deus ex machina*, which is also "the story of the Gulf War" projected forward and backward in time) was coincident with the restoration of the *Enola Gay* itself for iconographic exhibition at the American National Air and Space Museum.

How little of Hiroshima and Nagasaki had really been consumed became apparent in 1994, when even "liberal" American media like the *Washington Post* worked (successfully) to prevent items such as half-melted lunchboxes and tricycles from being moved into the immediate proximity of a "restored" *Enola Gay*. At stake was the creation, even indirectly, of embodied victims, for the lunchbox's disfigured surface too neatly evoked the flesh of the child who carried it (Lilenthal and Engelhardt, 1996; Harwit, 1996; Nobile, 1995). Compare "Hiroshima" to "the Holocaust," not in terms of moral equivalence, but economy of images. The Holocaust is all about bodies, violated in every imaginable way. Hiroshima, according to a popular imaginary, is exactly the opposite: a place where bodies simply disappeared ("vaporized"). If not a mushroom cloud, our first image of the city is of a flat and lifeless plain. The most famous Hiroshima "body" might be that of a shadow-figure on a concrete wall, this despite massive documentation by the US Department of Defense that showed burn victims and immediate effects of nuclear radiation. "Vaporization" and even radiation poisoning were bloodless by comparison with the imagined effects of "conventional" aerial bombing. Particularly in the immediate postwar period, they seemed "scientific" – read clean, painless, and uncarnate – ways to die (Lindee, 1994; Lifton and Mitchell, 1995; Hogan, 1996).

Hollywood, despite its remarkable stable of special effects artists, never portrayed the actual bodily horrors of nuclear warfare. Such images exist, however, in the form of often haunting colored drawings by atomic bomb survivors and photographs of horribly disfigured living *hibakusha* (atomic bomb victims), such as the "Hiroshima Maidens" (see the "Nagasaki nightmare" website maintained by the Che Café Collective). Hiroshima also has its Picassos in Iri Maruki and Toshi Maruki, the artist couple whose series of "Hiroshima Murals," completed over a period of three decades, have been described by historian John Dower as displaying "[an] anger, complexity, and humanism...unparalleled in the Japanese artistic tradition; indeed one is hard pressed to find counterparts in the non-Japanese traditions of high art" (1993: 252). Despite their publication outside Japan, these and other images from ground-level Hiroshima and Nagasaki have yet to find a secure place in the "global" (Western) economy of images of modern war-related destruction. The perspective of the bombardier, who sees his urban target only as a map through the clouds, became (and arguably still is) the agreed-upon shared perspective of the postwar war-consuming public (Dower, 1993; Dower and Junkerman, 1986; Japan National Broadcasting Corporation, 1981).

Even in Japan, "Hiroshima and Nagasaki" have often been made to stand for all the bombing victims, while the more numerous dead of Tokyo and other cities have been less visibly memorialized. The proof is in the comparative anonymity of the firebombing of Tokyo, in which more people were killed than in either atomic blast. Yet the firebombing of Tokyo was in no sense conventional – it was not an episode of factory bombing that got out of hand. Rather, the US Army Air Force constructed an authentic Tokyo neighborhood in the western desert and experimented with various incendiary devices before arriving at the perfect formula for a firestorm. The intentional incineration of whole urban populations was invented there and elsewhere, not at Los Alamos. The technology was napalm, which would become (in)famous throughout the world only with the Vietnam War (Remers, 2000; Kerr, 1991; Edoin, 1987; Werrell, 1996; Vanderbilt, 2002).

It was the disembodied, metahistorical reading of Hiroshima that gave aerial bombing depiction its postwar style. Belonging to the realm of "communication" more than atrocity – for the sake of its victims as much as its perpetrators – targeting was invariably depicted from a God's-eye perspective. It took the Vietnam War, uniquely productive of images of death and maiming at ground level, to produce a picture of aerial bombing comparable in its impact to that of the crying Chinese infant alone in the ruins of Shanghai – the little girl running naked down a road was a victim of the same technology that had killed Tokyo. Yet this was, for all its impact, a "rural" scene "explainable" in terms of "collateral damage." This last term would itself have little meaning without the model of Hiroshima, this time as a towering column of intentionality and completeness.

A history of modern urbanization in Indo-China could be written with the B-52 bomber at its center. Political theorist Samuel Huntington made this explicit in coining the phrase "forced-draft urbanization" to describe the twentieth-century airborne version of eighteenth-century enclosure (Huntington, 1968). Thus did Phnom Penh double in size because of American aerial bombing of the countryside around it. When the peasant-victims of Cambodian carpet-bombing eventually took that city, they forcibly emptied it out in the most infamous deurbanization of modern times. Hanoi also emptied out dramatically, but this time under the direct threat of American bombs. Less is remembered of the dramatic urbanizations/deurbanizations of South Vietnam as a result of military action. The American Air Force likely killed more urban residents of the southern cities it was "defending," particularly during the Tet Offensive, than it did in campaigns against the urban North. In most filmic and other popular accounts, the Vietnam battlefield is remembered as countryside and jungle, and its cities as the "normative" sector of a hellishly abnormal geography, or as the liminal space between the chaotic jungle and the "normal" US suburbs. Yet there was nothing normative about urban Indo-China during the period of warfare, and the present shape and character of its cities are very much artifacts of sustained military targeting (Smith, 1998; Gibson, 1986; Littauer and Uphoff, 1972).

Retargeting the City

Mechanical and Electrical Engineers destroy targets. Civil Engineers build them. (Anonymous)

Target 7. To direct or aim on a course. Freq. const. *to;* Hence *targeting vbl. n.* 1961 *Guardian* 24 Oct. 8/4 Being forced to rely on so much inspection that targeting information would be given away to the other side. 1963 *Newsweek* 11 Feb. 23 Planners have recently put forward the notion of city-avoidance, a tacit agreement between potential enemies to arrange their targeting so that missiles are aimed at military objectives rather than civilian populations. 1968 *Economist* 8 June 65/2 A general complaint is that consultants sometimes stick too much to their business precepts, such as "targeting" and do not bend enough to the particular needs of the company. 1976 *National Observer* (US.) 27 Nov. 5/1 NCEC laid out $350,000 for candidates in 1976. That paid for 64 polls in 32 separate congressional districts and for computerized precinct targeting and analysis in more than 40 districts. 1977 *Time* 21 Nov. 24/2 None of these possess as sophisticated a targeting system as the new Soviet model's [*sc.* a T-72 tank]. 1982 *Financial Times* 13 Mar. 14/1 In terms of targeting ability. (*Oxford English Dictionary Online*, 2001)

The above examples of usage for the gerund form of the verb "target" that are found in the Oxford English Dictionary unsurprisingly reiterate the city-as-target applications in this chapter's opening paragraph. Roughly contemporary with the emergence of postcoloniality and the triumph of global urbanism, the OED examples range from military, to business, to political notions of targeting, all relevant to how the current global city functions as both imagined and experienced entity. The convergence of military and marketing designs on urban areas has both political and economic implications, for the technology that makes it possible to so target the city in our current post-Cold War moment results from concerted military-funded research and development that has become the basis for the information technology revolution in the "new economy" of the global order. This same technological revolution remains in military hands, however, and allows us to imagine (and visualize in popular culture and news broadcasts) wholesale urban destruction with ever-greater intimacy. Tripoli, Beirut, Belgrade, Groznyy, Sarajevo, and Baghdad have provided recent generations with images of urban targeting altogether more insistent, clear, and technicolored, yet disturbingly adrift from progressive narratives.

Thus, with the end of the Cold War, The Modern City has begun to be subject to a new kind of catastrophic imaginary, and this despite the immediate post-Cold War claim that the targeted city has lost its bull's eye. The recent intensification and increase in Old Testament-scale images of urban destruction in the convergent realms of journalism, film, military action, telecommunications, government policy-making, computer gaming, and the academic press show no sign of abating, as if the collective sigh of relief of having dodged "the big one" allowed the possibility – and invited the pleasure – of its representation in more "contained" forms. The Post-modern City is now visualized more commonly than before as a site of violent, sudden death writ large and small, a new economy of images that makes the old (modern) one seem tinted and opaque.

This imaginary is still largely absent, however, from current urban planning, theory, and discussion. Current trends in global (read, North American and European) urban planning seek to fuse an eclectic, New Age spirituality (emergent from the unprecedented privilege that results from global exploitation) with notions of "ecology" and "nature" as kindly, corrective, and nurturing – a sort of a cybernetic Bambi-ism. The result is a nostalgic reclamation of community and local color in the face of increasing corporate global homogenization. The fusing of spirituality and nature in constructed urban environments that reclaim "the local" points toward a "Romantic resurgence" by urban theorists and planners (Ellin, 1999: 12–21). This 1990s reaction against the corporatization of cities and the globe (which, ironically, fuels and drives the very technologies these thinkers claim as emancipatory) envisions "tribal groups" at spatial(but not temporal) distances forming communities no longer dependent on topographical proximity, but on the proximity of "shared interests." These interests are produced, circulated by, and consumed on "real time" information technologies, themselves increasingly in the control of fewer and fewer multimedia conglomerates – the very organizations such groups wish to eschew while having that eschewal become instrumental in their built environment. Far from being an element which narrows human and ecological horizons, technological virtualization, from this perspective, has helped actualize a delicate balance of urbanism and spiritual fulfilment in tune with ecosystems.

As we have seen, however, the foundation for this global reharmonization of nature and culture, ecology and city, global and local, is composed of fragile electronic grids that can disappear in the click of a mouse. Silicon Valley residents and the rest of California experienced many brownouts and rolling black outs in 2000 and 2001 as deregulation derailed electrical utilities. The ironies are heavy and manifest. An environmentally driven urban zeitgeist depends on plundering the earth's natural resources, from opening Alaskan nature reserves to drilling, to ensuring the flow of Persian Gulf oil through military action. But, as with the long-distance high-tech weaponry now favored by the US military, and the exorbitant inequity of global trade, the Romantic resurgence in contemporary urban planning operates in a mystified and mystifying discursive and epistemological domain that obliterates the relationship between cause and effect.

The Romantic shift in current global urbanism is simultaneously prospective and retrospective, as is all nostalgia. At the same time that the Romantic impulse emerges as a dominant intellectual mode in global urbanism, with environmental concerns taking a supposedly central role, the city-as-target of human-created disaster, directly or indirectly, is elided from public discourse and the memory of urban trajectories. Human habitats have been, and remain, the total targets of total war in the twentieth century, and, as Paul Virilio reminds us, "scientific arms aim at the volatilization of environmental conditions; what biological warfare accomplished for animal life, ecological warfare did for flora, and nuclear warfare, with its radiation, for the atmosphere" (Virilio, 1996: 38). Cold War satellite technology used for urban planning forgets its military origins just as the aerial photography used to plan cities at the turn of the twentieth century forgot its own links to bombing. Yet cities remain targeted sites well within the military's aerial and prosthetically enhanced visual sights.

The retargeting of the city in the post-Cold War era, bearing the full weight of real-time technology's ramifications, is neatly exemplified in both the 1997 Southeast Asian economic crisis and the Gulf War – two events from the past century's last decade that reveal the vulnerability of urban space, urban dwellers and urban economies locked in the global embrace. The Gulf War marked a return to, or a retargeted application of, "conventional weapons" and "strategic intervention," capable of rendering a city, a nation, and a military immobile. Bombing in the Gulf War took advantage of real-time data transmission, sophisticated information technology systems, and intelligent projectiles to reinvent bombing without Cold War vaporization, Vietnam War sledgehammering, or World War II inaccuracy. This event reopened the city as a viable military target, rendering urban space more vulnerable to airborne attack, if only because it could be "contained." The City was once more a legitimate military option, more so than at any point between 1945 and 1990. Just as the bombing of colonial cities in Africa and Asia pointed toward the later aerial targeting of the metropoles which controlled them, the bombing of Hanoi and Haiphong pointed toward the potential targeting of other urban clusters. Though no new technology or restraint prevented the wholesale destruction of North Vietnamese provincial capitals, the attacks showed that it was possible to avoid the nuclear annihilation embedded in Cold War policies while also avoiding World War II-like practices.

As the Cold War itself has vanished from our collective screens, Cold War technology transfer to the private sector has spilled over into daily life with unintended consequences. The very same real-time technologies that allowed instantaneous data transfer for identifying military targets during the Gulf War were used to target global capital investments and pullouts during the Southeast Asian economic crisis some seven years later. Technologies designed to take snap-second decisions out of human hands in military situations – taking the human element out of the loop – function similarly with currency exchange markets and other global investment strategies. Maximum technological control contributed to maximum economic meltdown, leaving urban centers such as Bangkok, Singapore, Jakarta, and Manila exposed to the vagaries of capital speculation. Investors, or rather their computer programs, suddenly and dramatically lost confidence in the region in a self-fulfilling prophetic spiral of documented real-time loss of confidence, and capital ran for high ground outside Southeast Asian urban investment schemes.

The targeting can, and does, take on more ominous tones if we consider the [first] Gulf War and the Southeast Asian economic crisis as two sides of the same complex geophysical, ideological, and technoscientific coin. The globalization thrust that allows for the real-time surveillance of the earth and its networked nodes also provides the means for homogenizing the earth into a single market. And if a "rogue nation" refuses to play by the end-of-history political/economic rules, it can be (and has been) targeted for punishment, including strategic bombing. Stereoscopy telescopes the horizon (which has been lost in the vanishing point of perspectival painting and cartography) as well as market, economic, social, and urban choices. The global market consumption predicated on and enacted in the name of "choice" works well enough for urban denizens as long as they (and their nation-states) choose correctly.

Just as currently constituted and understood globalization processes emerged from Cold War policies, practices, and technologies, so too did the interconnected fate of global cities. As nodes in the global, ideological grid of surveillance and intercontinental ballistic missile targeting, each global city was potentially *every other* global city. A nuclear attack on one (which implied direct attack on others because of Mutually Assured Destruction policies) meant radiation fallout and environmental devastation generally. Global cities became, and remain, global insofar as they are targeted. It is their status as targets that renders them, *de facto,* "global." The conversion of military technology into the bases of the "new economy" merely shifts the targeting from directly to indirectly geopolitical , while remaining wholly ideological. And as we have seen, this conversion can easily be shifted back to direct military targeting – as the convergence of the Gulf War and Southeast Asian economic crisis attests.

Global cities bear the marks of their global targeting status in myriad ways: civil defense plans, emergency operations, and military infrastructure. Each manifests itself as a procedural tool, ready in the event that the city-as-target finds itself directly in the crosshairs: bunkers/shelters, evacuation plans, and defensive military systems such as "Star Wars." Many of these plans, and the supports necessary to put them into practice, serve double duty. That is, civil defense and evacuation plans can also provide clean up for chemical spills or natural disasters. The imprint of the Cold War can be found everywhere in the great global city, in all of its technologies, in all the distributed systems that link cities in nodes – even in the designs of office workstations meant to expedite communication and decrease hierarchies, as does that other great Cold War technology, the Internet (Hookway, 1999, 61–8; Bishop, Phillips, and Wei Wei, 2004). Cities bear the mark of their status as target at every level of empirical, quotidian life. This has been true for a long time, as the etymology of city planning terminology reveals. The French "boulevard" is a corruption of the Dutch word for an artillery bastion, *bolwerk,* while an esplanade in today's global city forgets its origins as the open space lying before fortifications (Ashworth, 1991: 170). Singapore's most recent investment in the arts is a complex called the Esplanade of Theatres on the Bay. We are constantly reminded of the relationship between city targeting and urban planning, especially when we remember that urban destruction is a prerequisite to urban reconstruction. The Cold War and its New World Order aftermath have simply upped the ante, through increases in the speed of targeting, delivery, and impact.

The Asia-Pacific as Disaster Zone

Indeed, we are today forced to produce the Metropolis and are given no other choice: it is the savage and meager return for all that has been subtly and ceremoniously expropriated from us. (Sanford Kwinter, quoted in Hookway, 1999: 12)

I think no power to your refrigerator, no gas to your stove, you can't get to
work because the bridge is down – the bridge on which you hold your rock
concerts and you all stood with targets on your heads. That needs to disappear at three o'clock in the morning. (Lieutenant General Michael Short,
NATO's top air-war commander during the bombing of Serbia, quoted in
International Herald Tribune, 5/14/99)

Most of the world's earthquakes occur in a belt that extends from the
Mediterranean Sea, across central Asia, through northern India, and
around the Pacific rim: a geography strangely convergent with the map of
world power prior to the rise of Protestantism. Cities in this zone are seen to
have a fundamentally different relationship with their earth than those
outside it. They can theoretically be brought down without warning at
any time, and sometimes are. They thus watch each other's disasters
more closely than they are watched outside the region. Because seismology
has never evolved into a predictive science, there is nothing that cities in the
Eurasia-Pacific earthquake zone can do but fortify themselves and hope for
the best. Yet earthquakes come so infrequently, apocalyptic ones may never
come at all, and good fortification is so expensive (and surveillance intensive) that if the great quake is truly unprecedented in its ferocity the city
may be destroyed despite everything. Such is the gambler's logic that works
against putting too many of one's resources into self-fortification, and
makes every new earthquake disaster an occasion for intense, but temporary, recrimination (Clancey, 2002).

But earthquakes and other potentially city-destroying forms of nature
(typhoons, tsunamis, floods, etc.) are not uniform in their effects on Asia,
despite the West's historic construction of this continent as peculiarly ruled
by superhuman forces. The cities of "Island" Southeast Asia (Indonesia
and the Philippines) are within the Trans-Pacific Earthquake zone, for
example, while those of "Mainland" Southeast Asia are not. Singapore,
despite the occasional tremor telegraphed from Sumatran epicenters, experiences Nature as tamer and less threatening than Amsterdam or Minneapolis do. Of all of the major urban concentrations in the geographies of
Pacific Rim and Asia-Pacific, Singapore is arguably least aware of itself as
existing in a natural environment that might do it harm. No earthquakes,
typhoons, volcanoes, or tsunamis. Singapore experiences Nature not as
threat, but as an absence. The absence of natural resources is what begins
to trace the contours of the city's sense of its own vulnerability.

Singapore's self-image as target is a dense collage of memory, geography,
and political science. There is its identity as a small city-state between two
much larger and resentful neighbors, one of whom controls its water
supply. There is its newness, its perceived artificiality – the unmaskable
fact of its colonial creation and function (more easily masked in Bangkok

and Jakarta) within a region alive with ancient claims and anticolonial mobilizations. It has a Chinese majority far from "home," again between countries that have been accused of persecuting their own Chinese. And marbled through these geopolitical and geolocal awarenesses is the historical memory of what happened after the city fell to the Imperial Japanese Army in 1941.

The *Sook Ching* was a ceremony of concentration and targeting. The majority Chinese population was gathered, examined, and some marked – often arbitrarily – for immediate death. It was a moment of intense emergency, from which some members of the later leadership emerged as accidental survivors. It arguably set in train a whole series of emergencies, including the unexpected emergence of independence in 1965. Emergency – "a moment of anguish" colored with an acute sense of vulnerability, and even regret – is the story the country chooses to tell about its birth, a narrative relatively rare in the annals of nations. This narrative undergirds a continued sense of mobilization and preparedness, which both integrates Singapore into the grid of global cities while subliminally questioning its purported securities. In different forms, however, emergence/emergency are a not uncommon dualism among global cities in the Asia-Pacific disaster zone. None has ever experienced the "security" of New York, nor can they reasonably expect to.

Singapore's emergence as a "virtual" global city comes with protections and maskings. Because the strength of its geography (as a world-class port) is also its greatest weakness (as the Japanese occupation and proximity to a volatile Indonesia and recalcitrant Malaysia reveal), Singapore's full-bore plunge into the "new economy" has the added advantage of deterritorialization. In the contemporary moment, as space yields to time – the world time of real time – Singapore's economy becomes increasingly spectralized, rendering the nation a less appealing target, at least for aggressive occupation. Why would any potential invader want to possess the intelligent island of Singapore? What gain could be had? The infrastructure, like the web, is both here and not here; the city has become not-a-city. Virilio could well have been describing Singapore when he discusses a teleoptical sleight-of-hand that also serves as a protective device: "While the topical *City* was once constructed by the 'gate' and the 'port,' the teleoptical *metacity* is now reconstructed around the 'window' and the teleport, that is to say, around the screen and the time slot" (Virilio, 1997: 62). The screen provides a screen for the city-as-target to hide behind, just as the timeslot allows an opening for space to disappear into real-time teletechnologies' erasure of here and there. As the virtual replaces the material, as the uncarnate replaces the incarnate, a new type of "protection" coincides with the new economy.

The new protection provided by the new economy is just as illusory, of course, as any old protection ever was, a point the 1997 economic crisis made painfully clear. Just as the mind-body split remains a metaphysical desire always dragged down by inescapable embodiment, so too the virtual metacity functions with the "betweenness" of stereoscopy. In this space between the wired and the geopolitical worlds pulse petrochemical plants, a *real* and *really active* port, and other desiderata of the material world we would rather slough off. The ads for the home office, painted on double-decker buses with the slogan "There's no place like home," remind us that a potential *Sook Ching* looms ever on the horizon. Similarly, the Civil Defense ads remind us "there is no place like home" because home cannot ever really be a no-place, a utopia, free from the vagaries of the body and bodies, no matter how neatly or centrally planned.

A mural outside the Civil Defense station near Queenstown makes this point. The mural depicts dedicated Civil Defense workers armored in protective garb from visor to boot clearing some generic toxic spill that never-was but could-be at any moment. The mural, in essence, memorializes a *potential future moment* of the city-as-target that we might not live to memorialize once it actually enters the past. At the same time, the mural is meant to instill confidence and well-being in the people who pass it, so they can go about their business in the virtual, wired, real-time metacity knowing they are protected from the troubles of other, apparently less clean and less safe, industries – hangovers from the old economy. But, as with nuclear fallout shelters, the scene smacks of whistling past the graveyard, and that which is meant to comfort can actually prove discomfiting. The new economic order is just as much a target, if not more so, as any past economic order, if for no other reason than it is almost exclusively the result of targeting technologies.

City Ruins (Targets Past and Future)

Ruin is formal. (Emily Dickinson, *Poem 997*)

It is easier to imagine blowing things sky high than to give up homogenized order as a measure of urban success. (Muschamp, 1995)

When the architectures of cities sported their target status – when they were fortified with walls – masonry, ironically, marked the shift from "barbarism" to "civilization." Nineteenth-century Europe developed a special fondness for the ruins left by cities and empires past. As cities began to shed their walls and camouflage (their potential-target status), artists, historians, writers, urban planners, and a myriad of others found in ruins *memento mori* at individual and collective levels, delineating the deaths of citizens, cities, and states alike. Ruins both humbled and emboldened their viewers. They reminded those who gazed upon their grim visage that no nation or people had defeated the Heraclitian forces of existence, and yet, at the same time, these piles of rubble and graceful dilapidations could also be interpreted as embodying evolutionary theories of science, as purported by Lyell and Darwin. Not only did the earth change, it actually progressed. Ruins, as a result, played a pivotal role in the nineteenth- and twentieth-century European and North American imaginary, and they did so in ways that had direct effects on the understanding of cities as human habitats freed from the devolutionary ways of the targeting past – or so it was believed. In the process, ruins bespoke the present and future as much as they did the past.

If the Civil Defense mural in Singapore memorializes a potential future moment of the city-as-target and ruin, the 1997 Southeast Asian economic crisis has also bestowed on the urban landscape futural ruins resultant from the city-as-targeted by real-time teletechnologies and the flow of global capital. Bangkok flaunts a number of such ruins; high-rise luxury condos abandoned in mid-flight to the heavens; highways to nowhere ending in steel-cable tatters; unfinished office skyscrapers made ghostly despite never having been inhabited. These ruins house squatters from rural areas, suburbanites tossed out of homes they can no longer afford, and criminals and drug addicts seeking addresses that do not appear on maps, not to mention rats and other such urban vermin. Where residents were once threatened with homelessness because they dwelled in the path of upward mobility's crushing progress and would probably no longer be able to afford to live in their neighborhoods, the ruins of the future left behind by the teletechnologies' targeting now threaten them by driving down (rather than up) property prices and imperiling their daily lives. Joining Bangkok in this opulent display of ruins created by opulence's failures are neighborhoods in Jakarta, Manila, and Batam, where development and speculation often ended without fulfilment and only as speculation.

Other futural ruins litter the Southeast Asian city horizon. One example is Singaporean architect Tay Khen Soon's "Tropical City," an imprint of the current Romantic resurgence in urban planning, tinged with nostalgia and "green consciousness." The Tropical City covers its International-style office buildings in vines, foliage, and other indigenous flora, along with running water, in an attempt to take advantage of their properties for functioning in an equatorial climate. Despite a real desire to integrate buildings into the unique tropical setting of Southeast Asia, Tay's designs strike one as resembling camouflage of a sort, as deployed in the Pacific theatre of World War II and later in the Vietnam War. The buildings that populate Tay's Tropical City might easily be in hiding so as not to become ruins due to military targeting by hostile forces. As esteemed local architect Bobby Wong reminds us, the only "green areas" remaining in Singapore belong to the military (Bishop, Phillips, and Wei Wei, 2003b; Kusno, 2000).

Lebbeus Woods argues the current wave of urban planners and architects in the grip of the Romantic resurgence ignore the long-term effects of their building and buildings, not to mention the environmental processes necessary to build in the first place. The delusion operative in "green" building and urban design manifests itself in environmental consciousness as decoration, not to mention marketing tool. But the ruin the "Tropical City" really camouflages is the one that it purports to stave off – the crisis that would result from global warming. That is, the Tropical City camouflages the agency of global cities in the ur-environmental disaster, of which they are both belated victims and perpetrators. As with all of the urban plans swept up in the utopian visions of the Romantic resurgence, the notion of the Tropical City operates with an exceptionally limited view of the interaction between urban planning and ecosystems.

Vines and gardens no more hide the target that is the City than does virtuality. The city's boundaries are always both veil and battlement. The current discourse about global cities and global urbanism emphasizes the positive elements of the various trajectories that make up its complex existence (what one shoots *for*) at the expense of the negative elements (that which is shot *at*), and the dearth of such discursive interaction and critical engagement must come at a cost. The cost might be glimpsed in the futural ruins that haunt our current cityscape.

Epilogue

Having two authors, "The City-as-Target" had two goals, at least. One was to suggest the diversity and relevance of the city-as-target trope, and trace it across a number of normally disconnected domains. Another was to point out how rarely targeting had appeared in modern academic discourse about The City, and how this instinct toward omission had strangely grown as the targeting became more intense and deadly. Because neither of us are urbanists, we actually began the chapter unprepared to encounter the silence about targeting in urban studies literature, particularly urban histories. We set out with the relatively straightforward goals of connecting things we thought belonged together, and beginning to construct a history, along the way, of how they came to be separated. Subsequent events in New York City and Washington, DC showed in dramatic fashion the utter impossibility of separating the economic from the martial in considering the city-as-target model.

The "stunning" nature of what happened in New York was at least partly conditioned by the post-World War II consensus that discourses on death and urban densities do not closely overlap. They were separated above all by discursive styles – for example, the separation of process from event – which worked their mischief in many realms beside the urban one. But urban disasters were also lost to "urban history" by folding them into metanarratives centered on states. It's interesting, and disturbing, that so many American voices have paired the New York bombing with Pearl Harbor – a battle between fleets of warships far from major metropoles – while so few have placed it within the long history of cities whose civilian inhabitants have been mercilessly targeted for obliteration. Pearl Harbor abstracts the tragedy of New York into a national (and nationalist) narrative and away from an urban history (largely unwritten) redolent with terrorized cities from Troy and Carthage to Groznyy. So too the idea that a "Homeland" is under attack, rather than cities, or monuments within cities – that the monuments belong to Homelands rather than to the densities they rise from and help perpetuate – is another move from the specific and locatable to the general and obscuring which seems typical of twentieth/twenty-first century responses to urban death. If the September 11 terrorists were so very specific in their choice of targets, then the post-September 11 counter-targeting has been so very diffuse (involving even categories so large, lofty, and ultimately evanescent as "civilizations") (Herold, this volume).

The assault on New York and Washington was an orchestrated collision of multiple components of a more or less integrated high-technology system – jetliners, skyscrapers, and television cameras/monitors – central to urbanization processes since World War II. The timing of the second plane's impact on the World Trade Center towers was intended to take advantage of real-time technologies that could broadcast the event of death "live" to a global audience, as much as it was an attack on the global power these real-time technologies perpetuate. The catalytic technology at the center of this implosion was a hand tool called the box cutter. The extreme disparity between this weapon (which under "normal" circumstances is the most lowly tool of the global commercial economy) and its effect was hitherto unimaginable to a society whose security seemed to rest on its own technological sophistication. Indeed, it has yet to be fully absorbed, given the immediate turn in the terrorism-related discourse toward increased optoelectronic surveillance, heavier investment in high-tech weaponry, and heightened concern with "weapons of mass destruction." This seems a turn backwards in time, toward a world full of certainties about the relationship between technological capabilities and their effects, between invention and production, launch and strike; that is, a return to the Cold War strategies and technicities central to the urban shaping which our chapter foregrounds. The terrorists of September 11 orchestrated a targeted implosion of a system whose individual components were hitherto considered benign, or at least outside the immediate rubric of violence and war (Luke, this volume). That the general response to this targeting has been an intensification of investment in the very technologies and technicities that conflate the economic, military, and urban spheres reinforces our sense of the density and momentum of the regime we were intent on describing in early September 2001.

3

Shadow Architectures: War, Memories, and Berlin's Futures

Simon Guy

Somewhere else in Berlin there's a huge mound of sand. Okay, so what's the story behind that huge mound of sand? Nothing much – except that once upon a time it used to be the headquarters of the Gestapo, that's all. Until recently, the Wall ran right by it. A bit further away there's a building, now standing with it's eyes closed, that once belonged to the Nazis: the ruins of the Reich Air Ministry. Just imagine, people used to go in and out of the Gestapo building, officials and otherwise. In all likelihood they were just ordinary people. (Armando, 1996: 21)

The history of World War II is still warm in Berlin. Shrapnel-scarred buildings and monuments stand in almost proud defiance amid the glitz of shiny marble and stone that is the new German Capital. (Richison, 2002: 7)

The struggle of man [sic] against power is the struggle of memory against forgetting. (Kundera, 1980: 3)

Introduction

Flying into Berlin for the first time in the winter of 1994, we flew low over the city towards Tempelhof airport – one of the few remaining architectural remnants of the Third Reich and scene of the allied airlift during the Soviet blockade of the city in the grim days following World War II. As I flew towards Berlin these contradictory images flashed through my mind, along-side stories lifted from my *Time Out* travel guide, the pages of recent histories I had been reading in anticipation of my trip, and memories of the many atmospheric films of the city I'd watched and novels I'd read – World War II epics, Berlin Wall escape thrillers, Cold War spy dramas, and off-beat, art-house riddles. As I descended from the plane onto the tarmac at Tempelhof I could not avoid looking at the city through the prism of memories that made up my imagined Berlin.

During this and many subsequent visits to Berlin my efforts to capture and comprehend the mystique of Berlin foundered on the dialectical dilemmas that seemed to revolve around each place I visited. Watching the city being rapidly rebuilt, and following the debates that raged about the future, it proved almost impossible to escape what Brian Ladd has termed the "ghosts of Berlin." Ladd persuasively argues that "memories often cleave to the physical settings of events. That is why buildings and places have so many stories to tell. They give form to a city's history and identity" (1997: 1).

Berlin provides a seminal example of this notion of architecture as what Hitler termed "words of stone," and by exploring some of these highly contested images, perhaps we can also learn something about the symbolic power of the war-torn city as they play out in design and development debates. In doing so I draw loosely on Walter Benjamin's concept of the dialectical image: the idea that, contained within the ruins and decay of the city are archeological remains, and fragments of earlier cultural values and visions, that give us clues as to our past, present, and future. In his "Berlin Chronicle" Benjamin argues that :

> memory is not an instrument for exploring the past but its theatre. It is the medium of past experience, as the ground is the medium in which dead cities lie interred. He who seeks to approach his own buried past must conduct himself like a man digging. (Quoted in Gilloch, 1996: 70)

The dialectical image captures a "moment" of modern ambiguity, the threshold of a new historical era in which the old and the new must be resolved (Roberts, 1982: 182). Benjamin's Berlin essays were written as the Nazis emerged to power and it is hard not to feel his urgency to comprehend his place in this historical moment through his analysis of memory and the city. Graham Gilloch points us to the afterword of Benjamin's essays "Berlin Childhood" in which Theodore Adorno writes of how "the shadows of Hitler's regime fall across all images contained in this text" (cited in Gilloch, 1996: 56). For Benjamin, it was in the ruins of modernity, and the urban forms that express the modern experience, that we can explore and identify the dreams and myths of contemporary culture. Seen this way, our seemingly inexhaustible fascination with the ruins of war-torn cities might be viewed as being driven by our need to understand the present in relation to our sense of both the past and imagined futures. So it seems in Berlin, where the construction frenzy throughout the 1990s made the city the "construction site of Europe" at the same time as huge battles were underway about the meaning of Berlin in the twenty-first century. As Peter Marcuse declared of the constant round of architectural competition and hurried construction that marked the period following the fall of the Berlin Wall:

> The construction of what? Of symbols, of meaning, very consciously... the meaning of each building, each style, each facade, the construction materials, the location and its significance in various historical periods – the Empire, the First World War, the Weimar Republic, post-Second World War, the divided and reunited city – are elaborated. (Marcuse, 1998: 332–3)

Michel Foucault noted that "both architectural and urban planning, both designs and ordinary buildings, offer privileged instances for understanding how power operates" (cited in Wright and Rabinow, 1982). Again, nowhere is this more apparent than in Berlin, where its "troubled past, compounded by a certain fragility of national identity, means that passionate debate greets every issue of preservation or development in the city" (Ladd, 1998: 3).

Berlin, then, encapsulates a terminal meeting point of war and cities, in which the shattering of all the fantasies of a modern urban culture – security, prosperity, and civility – has led to proliferation of, and struggle over, alternative futures. This is not a new phenomenon in Berlin. For as Scheer reminds us:

> Berlin has been, throughout the past century, the focus of countless new ideas in urban design. as the German capital, as a place of monumental will for political ostentation on a global scale, as a city destroyed in World War II, as a testing ground for sociopolitical reform projects, as a city divided by political motivation, as a island city, as a place where previously separated city districts have been reunited, and finally as the capital of a reunified Germany. (Scheer, 2000: 11)

In encountering Berlin we are faced, then, not just with a newly emergent city, but also with a tangled web of memories and memorials. As the artist Armando observed of his life in Berlin, "it's odd, living in a city full of people and walls that are pockmarked with bullet holes" (1996: 24). In Berlin, however hard you try to face the future, you tend to find the past staring back at you. Inspecting a friend's new apartment in a seemingly inconspicuous part of town my friend shows me photos of the building decked out with Nazi flags; a refurbished hotel in which I stay in a remote part of East Berlin turns out to be a former headquarters of the East German secret police, the Stazi; a beautiful nineteenth-century water tower turns out to be a site of Nazi interrogation and torture. Which of the many stories we are told about Berlin do we choose to follow? How do we position ourselves in relation to the past and to the future? Why are we so attracted to and fascinated by these scenes of past terror and destruction in war-torn cities like Berlin? As Armando observes:

> Berlin may not be a beautiful city, but it is exciting. What makes it exciting is
> the occasionally unbearable tension between a seemingly carefree present and
> an oppressive past. Berlin is a city teeming with places and traces. The traces
> of a Reich, frequently overgrown and choked with weeds, are still very much
> in evidence. (Armando, 1996: 12)

Debates about architecture and the future of Berlin all take place in
relation to this "shadow architecture" of "structures which have disappeared
physically but which remain as intangible presences through the awareness
that they once existed" (Feversham and Schmidt, 1999: 132). In revisiting
some of these sites of military memory, and by tracing some of these debates
about remembrance and forgetting, we can recognize some of the many
positions offered to tourists and locals alike by those seeking to shape contemporary Berlin. In this way, by exploring Berlin as "a place of visions, of
experiments, occasionally of contemplation," and by examining the ways in
which it "has repeatedly become a projection screen for a variety of architectural and urban design ideas" (Scheer, 2000: 11), this chapter explores the
dialectical nature of urban images in the shadow of war.

Terminal Experiences and the City of Amnesia

Albert Speer, architect to Hitler, remarked to his postwar interrogators that
"history always emphasizes terminal events," and Berlin following World
War II can certainly be viewed as a terminal city (quoted in Beevor, 2002:
xxxiii). In fact, the erasure of Berlin as a living city was the overt strategy of the
Soviet Army. Anthony Beevor illustrates this by citing a Soviet colonel invoking the "rubble of Stalingrad" as an image of the future of Berlin (2002:
xxxiii). Revisiting the city recently, the historian Eric Hobsbawm found:

> the City in which I spent the two most decisive years of my life lives on only in
> memory. In Berlin the physical past had been wiped out by the bombs of the
> Second World War. On ideological grounds, neither of the two Germanies of
> the Cold War, nor the reunited Germany of the 1990s, were interested in
> restoring it. The capital of the new "Berlin Republic," like the West Berlin of
> the Cold War, a subsidized showcase for the values of wealth and freedom, is
> an architectural artifact. (Hobsbawm, 2002: 43–4)

In 1945 British Air Marshall Arthur Tedder believed that Berlin should be
left in ruins as a reminder of Prussian militarism and the Nazi regime. The
city was dead, he said. One could drive for miles through smoking ruins and
see no buildings fit for habitation. Berlin could never be rebuilt; it could only
serve as an antique memorial for future generations (Monninger, 1991: 17).
This view did not remain popular. Instead, the opportunity to rebuild Berlin

has been seized upon, arguably as a chance to rewrite the past with a very
public focus on world class architecture which has, it is often claimed,
tended to distract debate from consideration and commemoration of
Berlin's history. For Hobsbawm and many other commentators, the redevelopment of Berlin has been characterized by a form of collective, even
purposeful amnesia in which the physical erasure of the city has encouraged
a wider forgetting. According to W. G. Sebald, the destruction of German
cities effected a "lifting of the heavy historical burden of history that went up
in flames between 1942 and 1945 . . . a historical burden ultimately regret-
ted by only a few" (2003: 12–13). For, while books, films, and even music
about Berlin are plentiful, most of them have been written or composed by
outsiders. Brian Ladd has similarly observed that Berliners "love to talk
about their city," but qualifies it with "especially those typical Berliners who
come from somewhere else" (1997: ix).

So, at the heart of the great debate about Berlin that has raged since the
last world war, there is a curious silence. For, while the Berlin of the turn of
the twentieth century has been described by Peter Fritzsche (1996) as a
"city of words" captured in the huge appetite for newspapers that echoed
the dynamism and diversity of metropolitan life, World War II turned
Berlin into what Ladd calls a "haunted city" – a city which words could
no longer describe. Sebold quotes Alfred Döblin, the author of the great
modernist novel of Berlin, *Berlin Alexanderplatz,* on his return from exile in
America. Döblin described people who "walked down the street and past
the dreadful ruins . . . as if nothing had happened and . . . the town had
always looked like that" (Sebald, 2003: 5). For Sebald, this amnesia was
a response to the shock of defeat and the total destruction of what had
briefly seemed an assured and prosperous future. The destruction of an
entire city (in some German cities, within a few hours, by fire), with all its
inhabitants, its domestic pets, its fixtures and fittings of every kind, must
inevitably have led to overload, to paralysis of the capacity to think and feel
in those who succeeded in escaping (Sebald, 2003: 26). Focusing on simple
survival and the slow rebuilding process necessitated forgetfulness:

> People's ability to forget what they do not want to know, to overlook what is
> before their eyes, was seldom put to the test better than in Germany at that
> time. The population decided – out of sheer panic at first – to carry on as if
> nothing had happened. (Sebald, 2003: 41)

This forgetfulness was not limited to ordinary people. Sebald argues that
responses by German writers to the ruin of German cities were an instrument of "individual and collective amnesia . . . a means of obscuring a world
that could no longer be presented in comprehensible terms" (9–10). He
points out that:

> The destruction of all the larger German cities and many of the smaller ones, which one must assume could hardly be over-looked at the time and which marks the face of the country to this day, is reflected in works written after 1945 by a self-imposed silence, an absence also typical of other areas of discourse, from family conversations to historical writings. (Sebald, 2003: 70)

This is the amnesiac space that has been inhabited by those World War II epics, Berlin Wall escape thrillers, Cold War spy dramas, and offbeat, art-house riddles that have so powerfully shaped the postwar image of Berlin. It also opened up the political space that has encouraged huge contestation over the future development of the city and the ways in which Berlin is represented and symbolized.

Potsdamer Platz: Erasure and Entertainment

This collective silence seems to have extended to the architects and planners of contemporary Berlin, where huge projects of reconstruction have come under heavy criticism for their selective amnesia about particular periods of history, usually the Nazi period, and their somewhat uncritical focus on, even celebration of, other periods, often the Weimar Republic. Typical is the showcase example of Potsdamer Platz, situated at the symbolic center of prewar Weimar Berlin. With it's cafés, department stores, show-piece architecture, and Europe's first traffic light, Potsdamer Platz was established as Berlin's Piccadilly Circus or even Times Square, the urban heart of Western modernity. It was left in ruins following World War II. For the whole of the Cold War period it remained a vast, empty wasteland, defined simply by the wall between East and West, cleared to improve the field of vision of the border guards, and known locally as the "death strip."

In a deal that has since drawn accusations of corruption, the land covering the former Potsdamer Platz was sold to Daimler Benz (D-B) – a company many have linked historically to the Nazi regime. D-B, in turn, made a deal with the Sony Corporation to develop the area. A huge architectural competition ensued in which the historical meaning of the area played a large and very controversial role. While the city planners bent over backwards to lay claim to the Potsdamer Platz of the roaring twenties, Sony's architect, Helmut Jahn, made clear his take on the history of the site by declaring their intention to produce a "modern, technical city representing the commercial strength and technical capability of one of the world's most powerful and successful corporations" (*Architectural Review*, January 1999: 44). As documentary filmmaker Marcel Ophuls remarked, "D-B are just car-makers: what do they know of how to make cities? Can they make it so that on spring mornings I could sit at a pavement table and watch the girls go by?" (Quoted in Hatton, 1999: 84).

This debate was not simply played out in the privacy of planning meetings. During the construction of Potsdamer Platz a temporary building was erected, ostensibly to provide the public with information on the project, together with a viewing platform, along with walking tours of the building site. This building, the "Info-Box," proved amazingly popular, providing a new form of architectural tourism in which the investors attempted to enroll visitors with its sense of the future:

> Inside the bright red ten-million mark spacecraft visitors experience a high-tech version of an amusement arcade where everything beeps and flashes and where one can take a virtual ride through the Berlin of 2000 plus. Muzak is everywhere and mixes with the video commentators' statements. Their favorite sentence seems to be: "We are building the city of the future." (Muhs and Wefing, 1998: 161)

As the project moved along at an almost break-neck pace, the unfolding vista astonished many visitors for its scale of ambition and for the roll call of superstar architects that became involved in its construction. There is not space here to recount the unfolding story of the project and the place of design controversies, political disputes, environmental challenges, and alleged financial improprieties in the shaping of the development. More relevant to this chapter is the interpretive role played by the final design in attempting to redefine history, and the way in which it set the tone for much of the rest of Berlin's redevelopment.

More precisely, critics have looked beyond the glitz and expense of the project to its simulation of the past, in particular through its preeminent role as an entertainment and shopping center with pretensions to the celebrated *Cabaret* period of Berlin's Weimar history. Typical is the main square with its glitzy cinema named after Marlene Dietrich, an actress rarely welcome in Berlin after she left for the bright lights of Hollywood. Everywhere there are bright lights, hotels, fast food outlets, and showpiece design. The Sony center is even more entertainment-led, with its multiplex cinemas and shopping malls. In reexamining the historical comparison of Potsdamer Platz and Times Square in New York, Frank Roost find similarities, in that both are "presented as redevelopment projects consistent with their area's pasts...part of the expanding market of urban tourism" (1988: 17). He argues that the projects are, in fact:

> simulations of urbanity and manifestations of the marketing concepts of global entertainment companies. Armed with this strategy of marketing their ersatz city center, the entertainment industry is introducing a new

form of urbanity in Berlin that turns the city center into an object for tourist consumption. (Roost, 1988: 11)

It all seems a long way away from the qualities of haunting and aphasia brilliantly epitomized in Wim Wenders' film *Wings of Desire*, where, in one scene, an elderly man wanders through a devastated postwar Potsdamer Platz muttering to himself: "where has it all gone?" Dreaming of the haunts and friends of his youth, the old man wanders through the wasteland of the Cold War death zone, his rambling interspersed with footage of Potsdamer Platz at its most vibrant, and again by images of the bombing blitz that reduced the area to rubble. As popular as it is, as one wanders round Potsdamer Platz today, it is hard to imagine the vibrancy and cultural diversity of the Weimar period as exhibited in the expressionist painting of Ludwig Kirchner. It is equally difficult to simply recall the bleakness and devastation apparent only a few years ago.

To ascribe success or failure is to miss the point. It is in the erasure of history and its replacement by state-of-the-art twenty-first century entertainment that the dialectics of imagery play out. Not least because a short walk will take you towards a block of what were elite East German housing reserved for those most trusted to gaze out on the West. Here, under an unmarked site, is one of the most controversial places in the city. The journalist Stuart Wolfendale describes his visit:

> We skirted the Potsdamer Platz and walked towards the Bunker. The Führer had ended his life feet away beneath me. Through a temporary wire gate, into what had been the Olympus of the Thousand Year Reich, a worker with a cigarette stuck on his lip waved in cement mixer trucks. Months ago, a bulldozer took the scab off it to reveal frayed blocks of concrete. It is to be covered over again. The authorities very much want it to go away. I would not be surprised if molten concrete has been sent rolling down those dank passages and into the lightless rooms where a nightmare long ago put an end to itself. (Wolfendale, 2000)

Debate has raged about this site, with the argument about avoiding the creation of a Nazi place of pilgrimage – used by the Russians as well as by more contemporary politicians – winning the day. Others are more skeptical of this reasoning, seeing, instead, a failure to deal with the darker side of German history in preference to a wholesale embrace of corporate culture. As Muhs and Wefing say of Potsdamer Platz, "nothing recalls the chaos anymore. New Potsdamer Platz looks like a brand new machine; utility and sobriety are its main features... The architecture negates past and future; it knows nothing but the present" (1998: 165–7).

The Reichstag: Return of the Repressed

There is a more material factor underlying debates about urban development in Berlin. For, while Potsdamer Platz represented a more or less empty space, elsewhere in Berlin the challenge has been more one of redevelopment than of new construction. Why? Because Berlin mostly consisted of nineteenth-century buildings containing relatively little wood, so it did not burn down completely – unlike cities such as Dresden, which were almost entirely obliterated. Despite relentless bomb attacks over many years, Berlin was instead left as a "vast field of smoking ruins" (Confuris, 2000: 215). One such smoking ruin was the Reichstag, which has stood as a self-conscious symbol of German history over the last century. As Wolfgang Thierse, president of the German Bundestag when the Reichstag reopened, states: "the Reichstag is a symbol. But an ambiguous one. It is a symbol for all the ambivalence and ambiguity of German history which we Germans can only accept as such and have to accept in its entirety" (Thierse, 2000: 8)

Like the story of Potsdamer Platz, the history of the Reichstag has already filled many books and much newsprint. Its place in German history is central. Built by Kaiser Wilhelm I in 1884, it was opened with great pomp and ceremony as a home for the fledgling German democracy. As such, it represented for many the struggle of German democracy and, ultimately, the ideals of the Weimar Republic, against authoritarian rule represented firstly by the Kaiser and later by the Nazis. For many years the Kaiser ruled out the addition of an inscription "to the German people" due to its egalitarian sentiment. Eventually, this was inscribed on the western pediment in 1916 in order to raise morale during the Great War.

The Reichstag played a central role in the governance of the Weimar Republic and, for this reason, the Nazis saw it as a symbol of what they wanted to destroy. Hitler never ruled from the Reichstag, although he did, arguably, use it in his ascent to power by exploiting a fire there in 1933, which many argue was started by his supporters, to declare emergency rule, round up communists, and ultimately reassert authoritarian rule. The Reichstag remained unused throughout World War II except for the staging of anti-Jewish exhibitions. It was never seen as a seat of Nazi power. But this did not stop the Russians focusing their final attempts to capture Berlin on the Reichstag and or their use of the building as a symbol of their victory. Indeed, the famous picture of Red Army soldiers raising the Soviet flag on top of the burnt-out Reichstag emerged as the central icon of Soviet victory, even though the photographer, Yevgeny Khaldei, later admitted it was staged some days after the end of the war.

Through the Cold War years the Reichstag merely served as a backdrop to the Wall. Following reunification, a decision was taken to redevelop the

Reichstag as the new home for the unified government. The debates that followed highlighted the contested views of history aroused by ostensibly design considerations. At a 1992 Bundestag-sponsored colloquium to discuss the overhaul of the Reichstag, the building was depicted as a bombastic, war-scarred fossil, the scene of Germany's darkest hours. It was an unwelcome symbol of democracy's failure to grow deep roots under either the monarchy or the Weimar Republic which followed (Wise, 1998: 121).

The finally agreed redevelopment project was preceded in July 1995 by the controversial "wrapping" of the building by the artist Christo, in which a giant silver sheet was placed over the building to create a shiny, ghostly structure. While conservatives feared for the "dignity" of the building, others like Norman Foster saw it as "somehow cathartic. It seemed to unburden the building of its more tragic associations and prepare it for the next phase of its career" (Schulz, 2000: 39).

Again, there is not space here to recount the twists and turns, and the political framing, of the design competition. But two seemingly mundane examples highlight the political contestation. First, graffiti. When Foster was ripping out the legacy of an earlier refurbishment from the building he made a curious discovery: graffiti left by the Soviet soldiers who had fought from room to room to secure the building and the final victory over the Nazis. While much of the graffiti was more often a kind of "I was here" statement, Foster was determined to keep it, alongside elements of the shell-torn interior – to preserve these "wounds" for posterity. For Foster, the Reichstag "bears the imprint of time and events more powerfully than any exhibition" (Foster, 2000: 9) and it was important to celebrate this.

Not all German MPs received this idea warmly. One, a Mr. Zeitlmann, argued: "We punish and penalize graffiti writing on buildings everywhere else in the country. And yet we preserve it here. How come? We should paint over it. At least some of it" (quoted in Traynor, 1999). Foster won the argument, declaring that the Reichstag bears the imprint of time and events more powerfully than any exhibition, representing a "historical palimpsest to be read and understood" (Foster, 2000: 9). Norman Foster recalls the project:

> As we peeled away the plasterboard and asbestos that had lined the interiors of the 1960s rebuilding, the bones of the old Reichstag came to light, along with striking imprints of the past, including nineteenth-century moldings, the scars of war, and the graffiti left by victorious Soviet soldiers in 1945. (Foster, 2000: 9)

There were similar arguments about the cupola on top of the Reichstag (plate 3.1). The original cupola design was aimed to create a "grand impression" (Schulz, 2000: 20) and for this reason Foster's original design left it out, replacing it with a flat roof to minimize any suggestion of

Plate 3.1 The Reichstag during Norman Foster's reconstruction. Photograph: Simon Guy.

grandness and to avoid what he regarded as an "empty historical gesture." He had supporters who saw the dome as an expression of the "reactionary, arrogant behaviors of the past." Others associated it less with authoritarianism and more with a tradition of German democracy that needed to be revived. It was this lobby that prevailed and Foster was forced to come up with a range of designs which were extensively and publicly debated and critiqued. The final design was not simply a like-for-like recreation. Instead, Foster describes his design as a "beacon" highlighting the workings of democracy, while on the inside, double-spiral access ramps allow visitors to look down on the workings of the parliament, emphasizing a political discourse of transparency and openness. Foster claims the cupola has become a "symbol":

> First and foremost, it stands for the German parliament, the Bundestag, which has now taken up permanent residence in the Reichstag. The transparency of the glass cupola communicates the Bundestag's decision to be an institution open to observation and regulation... The image of the new glass cupola incorporates this dual aspect of German unity: recalling its roots in the past on the one hand; and pointing to its new future on the other. (Foster, 2000: 16)

To observe the urban landscape shift over one century through the lens of one building illustrates both the power of bricks and mortar to speak to us and the politically charged struggle over the language and message communicated. In a city as terminally damaged by war as Berlin, such built structures must bear more than physical weight. Rather, as Michael Wise has argued, it is through the symbolic heaviness that "Germans are destined to weigh pride and assertiveness against the competing claim of responsibility for the past" (1988: 158).

The Berlin Wall: Recovery and Resistance

In reopening the debate about how Germans should deal with their own history, W. G. Sebald asks how it is possible to reposition German citizens from a position of aggressor or victim to tell more nuanced stories. How, he asks, should we tell this tale of war? "With a summary of the technical, organizational and political prerequisites for carrying out large-scale air raids? With a scientific account of the previously unknown phenomenon of the firestorms? With a pathological record of typical modes of death, or with behaviorist studies of the instincts of flight and homecoming?" (Sebald, 2003: 33).

Writing about the Berlin Wall, for instance, we could list the number of watchtowers and bunkers, the length of electrified fencing and death strips, or even the weight of the wall. However, simply viewing the wall in terms of its physical scale would miss much of its symbolic role and power. As Feversham and Schmidt declare, "from the very beginning, the Berlin Wall was seen as both symbol and metaphor: Of division, of incarceration, and ultimately of a failed ideology" (1999: 12). Such a physicalist view would also ignore the "emotional resonance that the wall still appears to provoke and how, even a decade after its fall, the Berlin Wall lies in a curious hinterland between memory and actuality" (1999: 10). For:

> Contrary to the static image engraved on the world's imagination, the wall as both symbol and structure was a complex, multi-faceted entity representing many things to many people: for some it was a grossly extended cinema screen on which the projected anxieties of the West flickered and danced; for others, a gallery of graffiti art, a locus of death and tragedy, a ruin, an absence, a memory, a void – the Berlin Wall is, in effect, a text: there is no single reading. (Feversham and Schmidt, 1999: 14)

Despite this ambivalence of reading, the wall came to stand as the symbol of Berlin in the West (plate 3.2). Brian Ladd (1998: 29) argues that the wall supplanted the Berlin airlift as the symbol of Berlin's role as a Cold War victim. Meanwhile, according to Frederick Baker, "for the tourist industry the wall was the defining feature of Berlin. The wall had become the eighth wonder of the world in the West" (2003: 720).

The basic history of the wall is well known. Established in a single day in August 1961 to prevent the exodus of East German professionals to the

Plate 3.2   A section of the Berlin Wall, adorned with protest graffiti, in the late 1990s. Photograph: Simon Guy.

West, and finally dismantled after a torrid history of escape attempts, shootings, and Cold War stand-offs, it was finally opened in November 1989, to widespread jubilation and global television coverage. A frenzied trade in wall souvenirs ensued. Much of this was unofficial, with individuals simply chipping off remnants of the wall to keep as personal mementos or to fuel more commercial ventures. In January 1990 the East German government estimated that the total value of the wall as a consumption commodity was no less than DM800,000,000. It set about marketing it to museums, companies, and rich individuals (Baker, 2003: 723).

But beyond this trade in the material symbols of the collapse of communism, a more reflective debate has emerged as the physical evidence of the wall's existence has rapidly disappeared. For many, the disappearance of the hated wall is to be celebrated. Why, they ask, should we be reminded of this monstrous barrier that ruined so many lives?

Feversham and Schmidt's account of the "Berlin Wall Today," written as a critique of the process of forgetting that accompanied the physical withdrawal of the wall in the 1990s, points to the still "resonant and powerful absence" of the wall, an absence capable of generating "deeply ambivalent memories" (Feversham and Schmidt, 1999: 133). They talk of the "wall inside our heads" that continued to divide Western and Eastern Berliners and the "wall disease" that seemed to result in many instances of mental and physical illness attributed to the effects of the wall long after it demise. For Brian Ladd, the source of this powerful influence lies in the fact that the wall was less a physical barrier than a "controlled sequence of empty, visible spaces"... and a "set of activities – searches, patrols, observation, and identification checks" (1998: 18).

The wall, then, acted to structure all of life in Berlin. It shaped patterns of mobility and surveillance. It even structured the flows of essential resources like energy, water, and waste, as the networks were split and rerouted. Moreover, the experience of the wall varied hugely depending upon one's position and location. Depending on one's perspective, the wall was seen either as an "anti-Fascist protection barrier" or a "wall of shame." Thus:

> The builders of the wall, the citizens of East and West Berlin, the fugitives and the bereaved all interacted with the fortified border in very different ways... this ambiguity of perception is something that is very frequently overlooked. (Feversham and Schmidt, 1999: 10)

For those in the West, the wall acted as a facade, which was often used to daub political slogans and paint graffiti. Famous Western artists like Keith Haring traveled to Berlin specifically to turn the wall into a canvas. This, in turn, resulted in the wall becoming a tourist spectacle, with coach tours to famous sections of the wall becoming commonplace. The most significant piece of the wall now left standing, the East End Gallery, records this activity and translates the wall into a piece of art.

For those in the East, the wall acted as a very real barrier for which mural painting was inconceivable. Beyond the wall lay "freedom," occasionally represented by the sounds of rock concerts, purposely staged by the Western authorities just behind the wall to emphasize the gulf in experience of those on each side. Baker records how, once the original sections of graffiti had been removed and sold, a whole new industry developed in which wall fragments were painted in ways designed to appeal to the Western imagination of the wall (2003: 721).

Feversham and Schmidt's critique of the erasure of collective memories of the wall has many supporters. All around Berlin, numerous attempts are being made to recapture the multiple experiences of the wall. These range from indicating the geographical route of the wall via a copper line engraved in the ground, to preserving sections *in situ*, to artist installations like the East End Gallery, the Checkpoint Charlie museum, crosses and plaques, and books and films.

A German artist now wants to rebuild the entire Berlin Wall for its 45th anniversary in 2006, coinciding with the city holding the football World Cup. Christof Blaesius, an events manager based in Cologne, has been working for three years to raise the €25m he says will be necessary to rebuild a 29-mile plastic copy of the Berlin Wall across the city. Blaesius argues that "the World Cup shows that all nations can communicate and cooperate with each other while the wall separates. Today, there are still several divided nations, such as the Koreas, Israel, and Ireland, and we want to remind people of both the past and the future in a meaningful way. Walls are not just physical, but also exist in your head."[1] Sections of the white plastic replica wall would be lifted to allow traffic to pass underneath. On Potsdamer Platz the wall would be symbolized by gas balloons carrying a floating screen upon which pictures of the original wall would be projected, so that Germany's capital can continue to function. Blaesius intends to invite artists from around the world to decorate the wall, which would stand for the two months of the World Cup.

This process of remembrance must continually negotiate the ambivalence of meanings that are found wherever "buildings, ruins, and voids groan under the burden of painful memories" (Ladd, 1997: 3). Nowhere is this more apparent that in Niederkirchnerstrase, where the excavated cellars of the Gestapo and SS headquarters face Goering's Air Ministry on one side, and a 200-meter listed stretch of the Berlin Wall on the other. The competing symbols of the fall of the two dictatorships have led to huge debate about whether the presence of the wall serves to equate or dilute the crimes of the Nazis. Many have argued for the wall's removal at this highly politicized site.

For Feversham and Schmidt, however, any argument for the removal of the wall would act as a "sanitization of the past." They argue, moreover, that "we cannot choose between more or less acceptable histories (1999: 140). These seemingly intractable tensions sum up the dialectical dilemma facing the reimagining of contemporary Berlin. As Brian Ladd declares, "the wall was built – literally and figuratively – atop the ruin of war, terror and division. The wall – from concrete, to monument, to rubble – gives form to the story of Berlin and of Germany in our time (1998: 12).

Conclusions: The City of Laughter and Forgetting

> People are always shouting that they want to create a better future. It's not true. The future is an apathetic void of no interest to anyone. The past is full of life, eager to irritate us, provoke and insult us, tempt us to destroy or repaint it. The only reason people want to be masters of the future is to change the past. (Kundera, 1980: 22)

Returning to my edition of the *Time Out* guide to Berlin, the cover depicts a building called Tachelaes. This is a ruined department store which was once Jewish owned, partially destroyed in World War II, left vacant during the Cold War, and squatted by artists and anarchists after the Berlin Wall came down (plate 3.3). Since then the building has been the site of struggle between the highly organized residents, fighting to maintain autonomy and the freedom to live an alternative lifestyle, and the city government, who are keen to raise revenues to avoid bankruptcy and regenerate Berlin more commercially. The Tachelaes image would have fitted well into Roland Barthes' semiological collection of "mythologies." The denoted image: a ruined building, typical of any city devastated by war. The connotation: the suffering and survival of Berlin, the dialectical interplay between authoritarianism and democracy, obedience and creativity, privacy and pluralism.

The story of survival is a pervasive myth in Berlin – echoed in the story of the Tachelaes building. It is the story of the power of a city to survive war and to rise from the ashes. W. G. Sebald (2003: 6, 8) illustrates the articulation of this myth of survival and renewal through a postcard bought at Frankfurt station which shows the city before and after – in ruins and then rebuilt. Such postcards can be found in shops all around Berlin, along with a multitude of books demonstrating the rise from ashes of contemporary Berlin. But while mountains of rubble have been transformed into the gleaming capital of Potsdamer Platz and the Reichstag, we might pause to remember Walter Benjamin's image of the digger of history and ask about what still lies buried.

Here we might discover some of the twenty bunkers that remain from World War II which could have provided accommodation for around 30,000 people. These bunkers further illustrate many of the themes I have rehearsed above. For many want them forgotten and even filled in. Politicians prefer not to talk of them for fear of raising the ghosts of the past. Meanwhile, they have been rediscovered by a new generation who have ignored their former history and turned them into nightclubs for rave parties. At the same time, a "Berlin Underground Association" has sprung up to argue for their importance to Berlin's history and for their preservation. This group raises money and generates publicity through guided tours for tourists hungry to revisit the Nazi past and to recreate the atmosphere of World War II.

A similar story could be told of the giant, almost indestructible flak towers built by Hitler to protect Berlin from the blitz. Again, by day there is little government interest in their fate, while Berliners party in them by night. Here, processes of repression, resistance, and remembrance coexist and compete in the rewriting of history and the future of Berlin. As Dietmar and Ingmar Arnold remark, the "history of the underground mirrors the history of the city. Depending upon where one digs up the earth or descends into the depths, one runs into witnesses of the past" (quoted in Bailey, 2002: 108).

Plate 3.3 Buildings as symbols of the suffering and survival of Berlin: the ruined Tachelaes building. Once Jewish owned, this ruined department store was partially destroyed in World War II, left vacant during the Cold War, and squatted by artists and anarchists after the Berlin Wall came down. Photograph: Simon Guy.

In this chapter I have highlighted some of the dialectical images that we stare into when we visit or inhabit Berlin. I could have chosen many other examples. In each case we can observe a dialectic at play. On the one hand, there is the desire to bury the past once and for all. As the Berlin artist Else Blankemaire observes, "that is Berlin. Plasters over the wounds" (quoted in Bailey, 2002: 198). The journalist Stuart Wolfendale puts it similarly:

> What I found so transfixing in 1999 was Berlin's ability to degrade selectively the follies of its former masters. The smells of the Hohenzollerns, the Nazis and the German Stalinists are in the air but their habitats are either corseted relics, revamps for the new democracy, or slippage into the developers' slime. (Wolfendale, 2003)

The other side of these images is reflected in our desire to consume the city of the past. Geoff Dyer has noted our romantic passion for devastated cites. He also notes how the "aftermath of war provides us with instant ruins." On a journey to Berlin he recalled that he was personally:

> actually looking forward to seeing some war damage and so was pleased, on leaving the central district, to come across rocket and bullet-ravaged apartment blocks. No need to apologize for this desire. Antique ruins have held us in thrall for centuries. (Dyer, 2003: 229)

As Fredrick Jameson has famously argued, we are "condemned to seek history by way of our own pop images and simulacra of that history, which itself remains forever out of reach" (1984: 71). This seems to be the case in Berlin and in many other war-torn cities. For example, writing about a visit to contemporary Beirut, Geoff Dyer comments: "not surprisingly, memory – specifically the memory of war – is a subject that much preoccupies artists in Beirut. The fear is that the sight of peace has been followed by a willful amnesia, an over-eagerness to leave the past behind" (2003: 233).

Walter Benjamin's advice to keep digging through the past in order to find the future seems more relevant than ever today. As Rebecca West observed while visiting Yugoslavia in the 1990s, "while part of us craves security and stability, another part craves destruction and conflagration. The ruination of recent war enables us to glimpse the consequences of succumbing to the latter urge without jeopardizing the benefits of abiding by the former" (quoted in Dyer, 2003: 229).

Note

1   See http://www.buzzle.co.uk/editorials/8-13-2003-44166.asp, accessed 6/10/03.

4

Another Anxious Urbanism: Simulating Defense and Disaster in Cold War America

Matthew Farish

Introduction

Late in his 1949 essay *Here is New York*, the critic and author E. B. White observed that, for the first time, American cities were directly threatened by war. The Empire City, in particular, possessed "a certain clear priority," in part "because of the concentration of the city itself." His otherwise exuberant urban homage closed by anticipating the "cold shadow" of bomb-laden planes overhead (White, 1949: 54).

In the wake of the tragedy of September 11, 2001, White's words resurfaced in conversation, in print, and across electronic networks. His uncanny remarks were invoked as part of a small but enthusiastic discussion concerning the future of skyscrapers and urban space. Given that the Russian foes piloting White's planes had been replaced, in a darkly ironic geopolitical shift, by extremists linked to the Afghan resistance against a Soviet "evil empire," his musings were undoubtedly dated. Yet they prompted a wave of reflections that summoned the anxieties of the Cold War – conditions ignored by the numerous American politicians and commentators who repeatedly heralded a novel state of national vulnerability. This amnesia was, moreover, packaged with a plea for reconstructed domestic security initiatives that echoed the excesses of McCarthyism. Such targeting of amorphous, pervasive, and subversive *others* was not only familiar, but it also gave fresh impetus to the careers of certain ardent Cold Warriors.

These comparisons with an earlier era retain virtue insofar as they provide us with cautionary tales concerning technological threats and the militarization of everyday life. Both, in their present manifestations, are products of the atomic age, an epoch inaugurated by the annihilation of two

Japanese cities. Even before the development of frightening tensions with the Soviet Union, many Americans had reflexively remapped the devastation of Hiroshima and Nagasaki over their own metropolitan spaces, an exercise in *anxious urbanism* that became a central component of the Cold War and its geographies. Although the destructive force of atomic energy did not touch American cities during the Cold War, the possibility of this occurrence inspired an array of efforts to prepare both residents and landscapes for the arrival of the bomb.

From the pages of popular magazines and science fiction novels to the models of social science and civil defense exercises, simulations of atomic attack turned "the city" into a "laboratory of conduct" subject to a spatialization of risk and virtue (Osborne and Rose, 1999: 740). This was a process that altered the design and planning of American urban places (Vanderbilt, 2002), but it had even more profound effects on urban *understanding*. As Winfield W. Reifler, the chairman of the Social Science Research Council's Committee on Social Aspects of Atomic Energy, put it in 1947, the "atomic bomb has raised, in fact, the question of the survival of urban culture itself" (in Coale, 1947: viii).

Geographies of Risk

Within Cold War America no partition of space was more explicit than that between city and suburb, a contrast that may not have always been distinct on the ground, but was invoked imaginatively to great effect. The representational discrepancy was powerfully expressed by writers such as George Kennan, better known for his role as the initial architect of American "containment" policy. A 1950 train journey from Washington, DC to Mexico City convinced Kennan that the American metropolis was a homogenous zone of corruption and iniquity. As his train rolled through an anonymous urban landscape during a "sinister dawn," Kennan noted the "desolation of factories and cinder-yards" and the "mute slabs" of skyscrapers. Later, he observed "the grotesque decay" of the St. Louis waterfront – a series of blighted, "indecent skeletons" occupied only by seedy-looking men (quoted in Oakes, 1994: 26–8). Such language was strikingly similar to that used by W. R. Burnett in his classic 1949 noir novel *The Asphalt Jungle*, or, for that matter, a wide range of commentators, including luminaries such as Lewis Mumford, who collectively concluded that postwar cities were declining sites of "social and technological alienation... ringed by expanding centerless suburbs" (Dimendberg, 1997: 69).

For Kennan, the antithesis of the degraded city was the small, independent farm, but by 1950 this image was an anachronism, replaced by the high modernist pastoralism of the postwar suburbs. His diagnosis of urban vice echoed a familiar, much older anti-city refrain, but it also acquired additional potency with the invention of the atomic bomb and postwar geopolitical uncertainty. After Hiroshima, the American city became "the choicest place for the destruction of the new bombs because, like those bombs, [it was] the product of energy in destructive excess" (Conrad, 1994: 297).

Numerous histories of Cold War culture have outlined the role of the suburban "nuclear" family as the emergent locus of normality, an archetype that was nowhere more evident than in the burgeoning civil defense program. Film after film, and pamphlet after pamphlet, depicted the rapid reactions of resourceful families who inhabited Levittown-style dwellings; the Federal Civil Defense Administration's (FCDA) *Home Protection Exercises* (1953) is just one example. Though this information frequently depicted woman as particularly industrious, it did so by encouraging mothers "to imagine themselves as warriors in training," as a central part of a Cold War "civic garrison." And the comforting base of the militarized family was paralleled, at larger scales, by urban and national imaginaries. All three levels were linked by similar ideals of safety, sovereignty, and fortification. These nesting scales were universalizing constructions, insensitive to the complexities of American life (Zarlengo, 1999: 931; Grossman, 2001). The shelter and evacuation programs of the Truman and Eisenhower administration, for instance, were predicated on a middle-class ideal of home and automobile ownership, which encompassed approximately 60 percent of the population in the 1950s (McEnaney, 2000: 7).

On the other hand, "clustered buildings and congested areas of our great cities," according to Hanson Baldwin (1947: 252), were "natural 'area' targets of immense vulnerability" (plate 4.1). To bolster these claims, concentric circles of destruction were inscribed over various urban topographies, whether in *Time* or on a foldout map included in Philip Wylie's civil defense novel *Tomorrow!* (1954). Virtually all of these imaginative cartographies were centered precisely on the urban core – an extraordinary assumption, given the admitted inaccuracy of bombing exercises, but also a strategic decision that created zonal models with profound structural and moral repercussions (plate 4.2).

Whether cities were *primary* targets was not the issue. Not only would such discussions potentially reduce interest in civil defense, there was also no definite understanding of when an attack would come, and where it would occur. This uncertainty resulted in geographies of risk whose gradients, delimited by an overlapping concatenation of multiple "indicators" (Osborne and Rose, 1999: 753), were actually shifting constantly, threatening to spill into or envelop adjoining districts. Frightening, unfamiliar, and profoundly disruptive, the bomb was an uncanny object, but only properly so when given a *geography*, a place of impact. From this

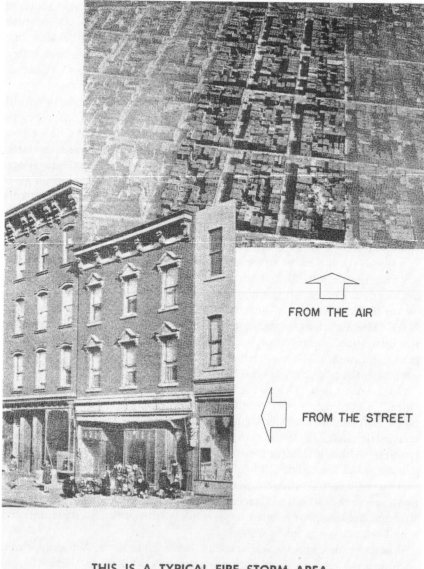

FROM THE AIR

FROM THE STREET

THIS IS A TYPICAL FIRE STORM AREA

Plate 4.1 Congestion and targeting: the Project East River's view of the vulnerabilities of central cities to nuclear attack. Source: Report of the Project East River, part II-B, p. 33.

location in time and space, uncertainty and displacement would spread, upsetting conventions of domesticity, homeliness, and planned order that are the opposite of the city as ruin. Such ambiguity also bolstered calls for the spatial independence of new communities from urban centers.

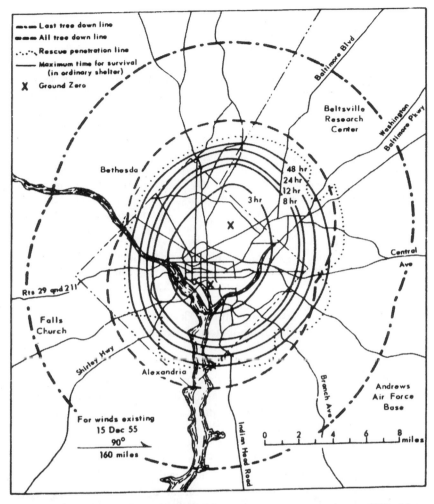

Plate 4.2 "Effect of two high-yield weapons on evacuations of Washington." Source: Bentz, 1956: 38.

Perhaps the most dramatic representations of atomic disaster were produced by periodicals such as *Life, Collier's, Time, Reader's Digest,* and *Newsweek* – magazines at the center of the production of "popular geopolitics" during the early Cold War (see Sharp, 2000). Chilling scenarios unfolded in their pages, in some cases well before the United States had lost the atomic monopoly. The November 19, 1945 issue of *Life* featured a detailed description of a "36-hour war," beginning with the "atomic bombardment" of Washington, DC, followed by the "shower of enemy rockets" on twelve other major cities, and an airborne invasion. *Life*'s dramatization was one-upped by the August 5, 1950 issue of *Collier's*, titled "Hiroshima,

USA," and featuring a cover illustration of an atomic bomb detonating over midtown Manhattan. Inside, accompanied by the lurid, peopleless illustrations of Chesley Bonestell – known for his "views gazing down from a great height upon a city lit by a nuclear fireball" (Weart, 1988: 236), Associate Editor John Lear fictionalized the incident depicted on the cover. Whereas *Life*'s scenario was predicated upon an anonymous enemy, by 1950 this identity was no longer in question. An accompanying note made clear that Lear's account

> may seem highly imaginative. Actually, little of it is invention. Incidents are related in circumstances identical with or extremely close to those which really happened elsewhere in World War II . . . Death and injury were computed by correlating Census Bureau figures on population of particular sections of New York with Atomic Energy Commission and US Strategic Bombing Survey data on the two A-bombs that fell on Japan. Every place and name used is real. [Lear] interviewed officials of the National Security Resources Board, the Atomic Energy Commission, the Defense Department; experts on nuclear physics, engineering, construction, fire and police methods, traffic, and atomic medicine. (Weart, 1988: 11)

While individually intriguing, these dramatizations and others like them all mobilized a similar imagination of disaster (Sontag, 1966; see also Davis, 1998). In addition to the use of abstract yet vivid visual representations, they relied upon the selective deployment of *expertise*, particularly in the form of scientific wisdom. Using a curious blend of graphic and sanitized language, magazines and the authorities they consulted produced "nuclear fear" (Weart, 1988) while simultaneously rationalizing and containing it – a strategy matched by the Cold War civil defense program (Oakes, 1994). But this containment was geographically sensitive. "City people," Richard Gerstell wrote in *How to Survive an Atomic Bomb* (1950: 91), "are the ones who have to guard most against panic."

The composition of urban spaces exacerbated more general suspicions. In a 1953 *Collier's* article, FCDA head Val Peterson claimed Americans were the most "panic-prone" people on earth. War, he noted, was now pervasive: "Every city is a potential battleground, every citizen a target" (21 August 21, 1953: 99–100) (plate 4.3). But in a continuous state of Cold War, constantly maintaining composure was paramount. To determine whether readers were panic-proof, the piece included a quiz based on psychological studies carried out by the RAND Corporation, the Institute of Social Research at the University of Michigan, and other bastions of social scientific rationality. These latter surveys were based, in turn, on the extensive psychological testing of World War II soldiers, a lineage indicating the deep militarization of everyday life during the Cold War. In addition, according to Peterson, women were more likely to panic than men. The

Plate 4.3 US Federal Civil Defense Administration poster, 1952. Source: US National Archives, Still Picture Division, RG 304, Series 304-P, GPO, No. 1052-0-999841; reproduced with permission.

mood required to participate effectively in the struggle against communism was one of masculine level-headedness – precisely the approach sought by defense intellectuals and nuclear strategists.

As the potency of nuclear weapons increased exponentially with the development of the hydrogen bomb, options for survival appeared limited to public shelters deep underground or mass evacuation initiatives. While a *public* shelter system was considered excessively expensive, evacuation posed alternate problems. As Peterson thundered in the pages of *Newsweek*, without clearly defined lines of flight from cities, "we'll have uncontrolled mobs moving about our countryside" (April 5, 1954: 33). Like the racial covenants initially placed on many new suburban developments, the post-disaster infiltration of one community into another was, according to the RAND Corporation's study of psychology and civil defense, a key cause of demoralization and disorganization (Janis, 1951: 189).

Disaster Science and City X

The whole program should not be regarded as an hysterical atomic defense project but rather as a modern adaptation of city growth to social conditions. An important part of this program would seem to be intensive social studies to understand the sociological "make-up" of cities and to determine how natural trends in decentralization may be stimulated. (Lapp, 1948: 54)

Academics and civil defense leaders were particularly concerned with the problem of psychological disarray. Disaster studies became an important interdisciplinary field for numerous research agencies. Recent intellectual innovations such as game theory and behavioral modeling were used to seek out consistency.

However, the work of universities and think-tanks could also be translated into policy, into "an operational model for the 'protection' and surveillance of the emotional well-being of the American public" (Grossman, 2001: 58).

In addition to its glossy leaflets, films, and exhibits designed for the public, and two remarkable tests on a replica "doom town" in the Nevada desert (see Vanderbilt, 2002), the FCDA pursued a wide range of scholarly approaches to atomic cities. Perhaps the most intriguing angle was captured in a 1953 manual ostensibly produced for municipal organizations titled *Civil Defense Urban Analysis*. This book shared much with concurrent attempts that mobilized the tools and discourse of scientific authority to compile and consider pertinent data on strategic environments. In the case of cities, the FCDA recommended an initial collection of information and the presentation of these statistics cartographically. These maps could then be used to determine the area of maximum human and physical damage, and to simulate an attack, resulting in an accurate quantification of destruction. Scenarios such as this one were the foundation of civil defense planning; operational plans and suitable services could be constructed in response. An urban analysis, then, was a practical procedure, and not just a reference tool for occasional consultation.

To determine the "assumed aiming point," the FCDA urged city officials to select separate maps of "industrial plants and population distribution" and place over them acetate transparencies featuring inscribed concentric circles. Shifting this overlay "experimentally" over the various charts, points could be selected and then transferred to a base representation, preferably titled "Target Analysis Map." A line could be drawn between the two locations and the midway position became the aiming point; the size of a bomb required to destroy the areas around both sites could then be calculated. Similar procedures could be conducted for damage and casualties, or for all of the individual functions of a response unit – resulting in a series of specific maps and one "master" grid of the "overall defense pattern." The aiming point, however, was particularly important, the manual stated, because it was a "logical center for the pattern of civil defense ground organization of the community as a whole." Poor targeting or a related error, of course, could undo all of this plotting, but "in practically all cases," damage could still be addressed easily as a result of the maximal specifications accompanying the choice of a management hub (*Civil Defense Urban Analysis*, 9–12, 50). These remarkably *distant* instructions were accompanied by fitting cartographic examples: maps of blast effects that were nothing but contours, and showed no urban detail underneath (plate 4.4).

The FCDA was also interested in more visceral forms of simulation. In a 1954 series of evacuation tests in Spokane, Washington:

National Guardsmen were posted at street corners; emergency civil defense and military vehicles moved on the streets; anti-aircraft and machine gunners fired their weapons from the roof tops of several buildings; jet fighter planes and bombers flew over the area . . . At 10 a.m., to simulate an attack, a bomber dropped leaflets over the city, saying "This might have been an H-bomb." The bomber missed the target area, and the pamphlets fell on an outlying residential district near one of the theoretical evacuation zones. (National Academy of Sciences – National Research Council Archives, Washington, Disaster Research Group Folder)

The results of the contemporaneous Operation Scat, a "drive out" evacuation of a Mobile, Alabama neighborhood, were even more fascinating. There, researchers encountered demographic complexity and inequalities not apparent in Spokane. According to an anonymous report, most of the evacuees "were Negro," without private transportation, and demonstrated an "outstanding . . . conformity to the demands of the (white)

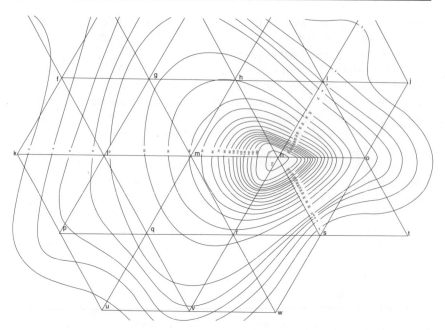

Plate 4.4 "Fatal casualties for city A." Source: US Federal Civil Defense Administration, *Civil Defense Urban Analysis*, Inset facing p. 41, No. 2.

authority." The legitimacy of the report is less important than the indication that actual simulations and their environments were significantly removed from the clean maps of mathematical analysis. As one of the National Research Council's representatives in Mobile noted frankly, almost every conceivable American urban target was populated by "lower-class and lower-middle class people, who in large part represent minority groups" – groups that were seen to be markedly *different* from "community leaders" and "not reached by the usual mass communication media." Another observer gained the impression after speaking with a white policeman that under conditions of disaster racial divides might be partly breached, but only to the extent that black citizens would be picked up by white car-owners "only after all the whites in the area had already been evacuated" (ibid).

In an exemplary study funded and sponsored by Columbia's Bureau of Applied Social Research (BASR), the Ford Foundation, and the Air Force, Fred Iklé argued that speculating on the social effects of bomb destruction was problematic because "rational planning is 'switched off' at the point of the real nuclear attack." After the explosion, Iklé postulated, "irrational thinking takes over: there is nothing but chaos, doom for all humanity, panic, or suicide – and immediate defeat or immediate victory." His dichotomy between rational and irrational time also had a spatial equivalent. Gesturing vaguely to both the Chicago school of sociology and its subsequent Parsonian manifestations, Iklé summoned a functional-ecological model of urban life, arguing that a disaster would upset networks of quantitative "relations," "leaving tangible effects in the form of readjustments and measurable discrepancies" (1958: vii, 7–8).

Iklé's city, in keeping not only with 1950s social science, but also with concurrent geopolitical rhetoric, was an abstraction suited to equilibrium. It would readjust "to destruction somewhat as a living organism responds to injury" – a telling phrase that also suggested the parasitical portrayal of international communism so common in the 1950s. Like the mobile maps of urban destruction, which changed only in accordance to varying urban population statistics, scientific analysis was typically applied to a hypothetical "City X," unless it was necessary to "emphasize certain of the bomb's effects," in which case Washington or New York were typically substituted (Lapp, 1948: 49). The FCDA matched this generic scripting with publications like *Battleground USA* (1957), which outlined the civil defense plans for a "metropolitan target area" whose principle city was "Battleground," an inland port in the state of "E." While obviously intended to appeal to a wide audience, such imagined urban landscapes were nonetheless dependent on particular visions of spatial order, structure, and priority. There was little doubt, for instance, as to which part of City X would suffer the most grievous wounds, or, put differently, which part was most susceptible to infection.

The BASR has been widely credited with promoting a budding postwar quantitative sociology, and beginning in 1950 several of its researchers joined with scholars at the University of Chicago on an Urban Targets Research project sponsored by the Air Force's Human Resources Research Institute (HRRI). While Chicago investigators studied the "sociological and psychological components of intra-urban target analysis," combining the spatial and temporal "patterns" of Chicago to form a "framework for target selection," BASR researchers led by Kingsley Davis considered "inter-urban patterns of target complexes." The data accumulated and models prepared for these studies were valuable for defensive planning, of course, but their appeal was both broader and more flexible – nothing less than the improvement and centralization of information on cities at a *global* scale. According to the BASR contribution to a 1951 HRRI report, the selection of data for inclusion in the "Urban Resources Index," from the dual but compatible standpoints of military intelligence and "economic, political, sociological, and social scientific analyses," would "facilitate systematic comparative analyses for strategic scientific purposes" (BASR Papers, Columbia University, Box 24). Translated, this meant that the index was perfectly designed to suit Cold War operations, since these could hypothetically include any city on earth – as a battleground or a site for strategic bombing.

The most intriguing combination of urbanism, science, and strategy was Project East River, completed for the FCDA by a group of academic institutions known as Associated Universities, Inc. in 1952. East River not only demonstrated the importance of behavioralist social science to the military bureaucracy, but it also echoed the mantra that fear could be channeled through a combination of training, emotion management, and self-surveillance (Grossman, 2001: 59–60). The project's diverse and authoritative cast of "scientists, businessmen, and educators" detected precisely what was wrong with American society, and what could thus doom (Western) civilization: an "apathetic attitude" indicative of "individuals, institutions, and nations that have perished in the past because of the inability or unwillingness to adjust to major environmental changes" (Part 1, n.p.). These environmental changes, the ten-part East River report made clear, were at once national and urban, shifts motivated by both technological "progress" and geopolitical circumstances. And the link to American cities was quite apparent: Part 5 of the report, "Reduction of Urban Vulnerability," began with the assertion: "to keep pace with weapons development, it is essential to make urban targets less remunerative" (1).

In addition, although Project East River was not expected to actually conduct tests, experiments, or exercises to "develop new basic data," and was instead intended as a suitable form for synthesis of prior research and opinion, it did make one partial exception to this imperative: a "selected area study" that formed Appendix V-A of the report. There, East River participants, after deciding that "a typical American city did not exist for our purposes," borrowed from a recent disaster review that had been produced under the aegis of two New York hospitals, the Rockefeller Institute, City and Suburban Homes, Inc., and the New York Life Insurance Company. This collective of risk-related agencies conducted detailed land use and population studies of 47 Manhattan blocks, and then proceeded to simulate the dropping of atomic bombs over this space, varying the location and height of the bombs, as well as the number and position of shelters. The results were predictable and sanitized, facilitating an easy translation from the detailed geographies of New York to "many of the features found in our larger cities" (1a, 6a, 8a).

Dispersal and Decentralization

As the Cold War deepened, many scientists and political commentators began to suggest the United States suffered from excessive urban populations. Atomic disasters would simply affect too many people, and too many industrial sites. The most effective and comprehensive solution to this problem – but also the most contentious and expensive – was a massive program of urban dispersal. Though some aggressive theorists salivated at the prospect of an America speckled by evenly distributed towns of equal population, most agreed that the costs of such a utopia, ironically, would be too damaging to a national war machine dedicated to matching, and besting, the Soviet Union. However, various forms of "limited dispersion" did gain significant currency, particularly with respect to the creation of new urban landscapes, and such principles as remote location of bomb production, placement of war contracts in small cities, creation of new, widely spaced satellite towns, increased highway construction, and control of inner-city rebuilding were all frequently proposed – and implemented. As a result, older, dense, and "geographically bound" cities were considered the most vulnerable. For this reason and others, speculators turned New York and Washington into projected targets far more than they did less dense cities like Los Angeles and Houston (Zarlengo, 1999, 936; Hammond, 1984).

The most powerful early source spurring calls for dispersal was the United States Strategic Bombing Survey's report on Hiroshima and Nagasaki. As *The American City* reported with alarm in August 1946, the two Japanese cities were chosen as targets precisely because of their concentration of activities and population, not to mention Hiroshima's level and open topography, which allowed the effects of the blast to "spread out." As a result, the survey cautioned, given "the similar peril of American cities . . . the value of decentralization is obvious" (5).

The same August 1946 issue of *The American City* also featured an article titled "Planning Cities for the Atomic Age," essentially a summary of the views of noted decentralization advocate and planner Tracy Augur, who had been shaken by the damage visited from the air on dense European cities during the war. In this piece, as well as other contemporaneous publications, Augur consistently laid out the case for the dispersal of cities as a defensive measure against a potential atomic attack. His argument was a simple one: *space* was the best defense against the bomb, and congested, poorly organized, and centralized cities were inviting targets.

Like many advocates of decentralization, Augur was aware of the tremendous fiscal and social costs his campaign seemed to entail, but he deflected these by stressing that the appropriate planning of inevitable *new* construction would not incur any additional expenses. If plotted scientifically, towns of 30,000 to 50,000 residents would not simply girdle an existing urban area, but stand as "semi-independent communities" – clusters, inspired by the British garden city model, that were separated from one another by belts of open or agricultural land (Augur, 1946, 1949). As a result, Augur's hypermodern technocentrism was fused with premodern small-town idealism. This nostalgia was premised, as another proponent of decentralization argued, on the assertion that residents of "small and medium-sized communities lead a much more natural and normal life than those in large cities" (Mitchell, 1948).

Interestingly, the ideal *post*-nuclear community in many science fiction films and novels was either a small town or another type of contained, purposeful settlement such as a college, or the monastery featured in Walter M. Miller, Jr.'s *A Canticle for Leibowitz* (Bartter, 1986). These scenarios shared with those produced by nuclear strategists a belief in *survivability*. Both genres routinely argued that a sufficient number of people would live through a nuclear disaster and rapidly reconstruct American society, and, in most cases, that these would be people "who are closely in touch with the unique spirit of America, and the values of the system of 'free enterprise'." Not one strategist or government planner, Dean MacCannell points out, "has envisaged a post-attack rebuilding by people who never much bene-fited from American society, or quite understood what America was all about, that is, by people who lived at a disadvantage on the margins of society" (1984: 40).

Augur's proposals would not only solve malingering problems of "blight," but they would also provide additional security to the American people, finally guaranteeing "the full benefits of the atomic age." As he put it, "a metropolitan area that is well organized in terms of the amenities of modern urban living and the efficient conduct of modern business will also be an area of decreased vulnerability to atomic bombs and other weapons of mass destruction." For this reason, the value of planned dispersal would not end with the closure of Cold War hostilities. It possessed a logic above and beyond the exigencies of geopolitics and national defense. But there was also a third, related motivation. For Augur, dispersal held "equal value against the type of penetration that has become so common and so effective in modern times and which depends on the fomenting of internal disorder and unrest" (1946: 75; 1949: 110). His advocacy of urban design suited to the atomic age thus moved swiftly and smoothly across scales, linking national defense to the conduct and proximity of individual bodies.

In a 1946 collection titled *Cities are Abnormal*, Warren S. Thompson, describing contemporary cities as particularly vulnerable, suggested an alternative:

> The form best adapted to minimize bomb damage would probably be that of an irregular elongated S. If the community is built in this form, only a small part of the full destructive power of the bomb could be made effective against it; the far greater part would be dissipated into the surrounding open spaces. The exact shape of the curves used should be determined by the best technical advice

available regarding the radius of destruction likely to be achieved by atomic
bombs in the foreseeable future, and by a careful calculation of shapes offering
the most difficult targets to airborne missiles. (Thompson, 1946: 234–5)

As a proposal, Thompson's "S" was not unique, but his comments were
particularly telling with respect to the instrumental *scientization* of urban
spaces, a process that frequently utilized the hard language of physics and
mathematics. Early Cold War America was marked by a series of abstract,
interdisciplinary academic models – "social physics," for instance – that
united the force of physical science with social explanation. Each subject
possessed a repressed spatiality that surfaced explicitly when deployed in
the service of Cold War imperatives. While planners debated the specifics of
atomic physics, scientists became urban visionaries, and both groups
became intimately familiar with geopolitical strategy. Ironically, the coales-
cence of expertise produced "atomic cities" that remained crude – universalizing abstractions dependent on stereotypes and generalizations for their
influence, but powerful and prolific models nonetheless.

Project East River was complemented by a nearly concurrent study on
air defense at MIT. Dubbed Project Charles, the endeavor is now best
known for facilitating the construction of the Lincoln Laboratory, a site
that played the key role in the development of both the SAGE computer
network and the Distant Early Warning (DEW) Line – two of the
most remarkable engineering projects of the early Cold War. Yet the leaders
of Project Charles were concerned with all aspects of air defense, including
the locational pattern of population. Since such patterns were beyond the
purview of most physicists and engineers, three economists – Carl Kaysen,
Paul Samuelson, and James Tobin, all eventually towering figures in their
discipline's postwar pantheon – were enlisted to provide an appendix on
"Economic Aspects of Passive Defense." The result was an astonishing
exposition of neoclassical reasoning, a cold-blooded summary that noted
the logical advantages of urban concentration – but then determined that
this was a moribund equation in the atomic age:

> On any rational calculation, the possibility of enemy attack has radically
> changed, in favor of dispersal, the values to individuals and to society of
> alternative locations of particular installations, whether factories or houses.
> A man who is deciding whether his new house should be build in Manhattan
> or Fairfield, Connecticut should now include an allowance for the distinct
> possibility that in Manhattan both his house and family will be destroyed –
> increasing both the target attractiveness and the danger of fire. (*Problems of Air
> Defense*, VII-I-16)

In urban studies, then, "the city" became a field of inquiry open to an
astonishingly diverse array of writers, many arguing that congested, poorly

organized, and centralized cities were not only inviting targets but also unviable *systems*. Perhaps the most infamous example of such work was the cybernetics pioneer Norbert Wiener's 1950 *Life* plan for radial "life belts" of transportation lines and essential services, separated from downtowns by "safety zones" where most construction would be prohibited. This spatial distinction was essential. As the Detroit planners Donald and Astrid Monson argued in a contemporaneous article in *The American City*, without empty or agricultural interstitial areas, "the very factor which is counted on for defense is lost" (1950: 92).

Since a city, for Wiener and his colleagues, was "primarily a communications center, serving the same purpose as a nerve center in the body," the key to a liveable existence was the ordered planning of informational networks. And Wiener's scheme, *Life* editors noted, would be useful "in any circumstance." During periods of peace, quite incidentally, "it would expand and accelerate the current trend of many city dwellers toward the suburbs" (December 18, 1950: 77–86). Such dual reasoning was identical to that invoked by President Eisenhower's well-known 1956 Interstate Highway Act (Rose, 1990; Jackson, 1985: 249).

For early cybernetics, control was "the never-finished work of regulation which operates to bring deviations from system requirements back in line." Wiener's atomic city was thus not simply an updated version of nineteenth-century urban technical interventions. It also suggested the governance of city life was, in addition to authoritative schemes implemented from above, a problematic of inner subjectivity and individual "participation in the networks of existence" (Osborne and Rose, 1999: 749–50). Moreover, the cybernetic framework was a perfect example of a synoptic worldview that was not contextually dependent.

Conclusion

> The city...had become a bunker of sorts, a Survival City where the reproduction or augmentation of the environment through machinery was viewed not as an emergency measure, but an everyday condition. (Vanderbilt, 2002: 132)

In this chapter I have built upon the claim that Cold War America was characterized by a powerful disillusion for urban life. Central cities, for many commentators, were spaces of blight, repositories of extreme cultures, classes, and races, threatened from above and within. This language may well have been symbolic camouflage for broader fears (Beauregard, 1993: 6). However, this process also operated in reverse: discussions on the status of cities were specifically appropriated and encouraged by the development of Cold War geopolitical uncertainty, and by technology-inspired changes to the theory and practice of warfare. It was precisely the domestic geography of Cold War risks that led to the scientific planning schemes – some more drastic than others – designed to order and manage urban spaces while concurrently maintaining the various symbolic distinctions between city and suburb. While the resemblance was powerful, these schemes were not simply "the suburbs" imagined; they were frequently more rational and ordered than the actual suburban landscapes constructed after World War II. For the Monsons (1950: 92), the suburban growth of the 1940s was "without plan and [was] largely an extension of the amorphous sprawl of the central cities." Planning this spontaneous, inevitable decentralization appeared to be a natural step.

Of course, by the end of the 1950s, support for decentralization initiatives and the technologized sprawl of highway landscapes was beginning to fade, a trend that would deepen during the following decade. Equally, calls for dispersal and evacuation in advance of atomic attack had declined substantially by the end of Eisenhower's presidency in 1960. There were several seasons for the waning of such proposals. Some influential strategists had concluded that cities would be, by and large, secondary to military and other non-urban targets in the event of a nuclear strike. The development of new weaponry, particularly intercontinental ballistic missiles (ICBMs), had furthered the futility of evacuation, despite the vast and extensive warning lines established across the north of the continent.

But perhaps the most intriguing and persuasive reason for the gradual disappearance of explicit discussions of dispersal was that by the late 1950s it had become, through a subtle slippage, largely a "benign discourse over structural changes like suburban high schools and shopping malls" (Mechling and Mechling, 1994: 151). Earlier studies such as Project East River had noted that dispersion policy was "in line with general trends" of postwar urban growth (Part 1: 16). And under conditions of nuclear deterrence, Cold War American cities became "defense weapons" – places not only required to receive an atomic bomb, but also to "*absorb* the hit so that damage minimally spills over to the surrounding areas." The discourse of urban decline and the various distinctions maintained and encouraged between central city and suburb were of very specific strategic value – in funneling money not spent on inner-city improvement to the national arsenal, but also in consistently locating, through a powerful combination of lurid drama and rational science, the locus of atomic danger in the heart of America's cities (MacCannell, 1984: 40, 45). Such circular histories are a telling reminder of the peoples and places literally left behind by the combination of geopolitics and science during the early Cold War. That this history is more fallout than *event* is crucial to understanding our contemporary varieties of anxious urbanism.

5

Living (Occasionally Dying) Together in an Urban World

Zygmunt Bauman

Introduction

This is not an attempt at a synthesis; it is too early for an integrated, not to mention comprehensive, model of the new human condition. Such a model, however carefully constructed, would start ageing well before reaching maturity, since the globalization of the human condition is far from complete and as the globalizing process goes on decomposing one by one all the familiar settings of human life, together with the conceptual frameworks in which we have grown used to grasp them in order to tell their story. None of the descriptions of the mode of planetary togetherness, and of the new dangers with which it is fraught, that are gradually gestalting and will eventually emerge at the other end of a long, messy, and haphazard globalizing process, can pretend to be anything more than a "career report," a story bound to be revised and retold no end.

Wary of the unavoidable immaturity of synthetic models, I confine myself here to signaling rather than mapping three of the arguably most seminal among the globalization-prompted departures in the pattern of planetary cohabitation; and then to the consideration of three, arguably most crucial, consequences of such departures that seem to bear on the changing shape of conflicts, the setting in which the conflicts emerge and are played out, and the strategies of power-and-domination contests.

Departures

The filling up of the planet

The planet is full.

This is, let me make myself clear, not a statement in physical or even human geography. In terms of physical space and the spread of human cohabitation, the planet is anything but full. On the contrary, the total size of the lands sparsely populated or depopulated, viewed as uninhabitable and incapable of supporting human life, seems to be expanding rather than shrinking. As *technological* progress offers (at a rising cost, to be sure) new means of survival in such habitats as were previously deemed unfit for human settlement, it also erodes many habitats' ability to sustain the populations they previously used to accommodate and feed, whereas the *economic* progress renders once-effective modes of making a living unviable and impracticable, thereby adding to the size or the wastelands lying fallow and abandoned.

"The planet is full" is a statement in *sociology and political science*. It refers not to the state of the earth, but to the ways and means of its inhabitants. It signals the disappearance of "no man's lands," territories fit to be defined and/or treated as void of human habitation, devoid of sovereign administration, empty and thus open to colonization and settlement. Such territories, now largely absent, played for a greater part of modern history the crucial role of dumping grounds for human waste turned out in ever rising volumes in the parts of the globe affected by the processes of "modernization."

Production of "human waste," or more correctly wasted humans (the "excessive," "redundant" population that either could not, or was not wished to, be retained and accommodated inside the modernized lands), is an inseparable accompaniment of modernization. It is an inescapable side effect of order building (each order casts some parts of the extant population as "out of place," "unfit," or "undesirable') and of economic progress (that cannot proceed without the devaluation of previously effective modes of "making a living," thereby depriving their practitioners of livelihood). For most of modern history, however, large parts of the globe ("backward," "underdeveloped" parts, when measured by free-market ambitions) stayed wholly or partly unaffected by the modernizing pressures, thus escaping their "overpopulation" effect. Confronted with the modernized sectors of the globe, such ("premodern," "underdeveloped') parts tended to be viewed and treated as lands able to absorb the excess of the "developed countries'" population; as natural destinations for the export of "redundant humans," obvious dumping sites for the human waste of modernization. The disposal of human waste produced in the "modernized" and still "modernizing" parts of the globe was the deepest meaning of colonization and imperialist conquests – both made possible, and in fact inevitable, by the inequality of "development" that is modernization confined to a "privileged" section of the planet. Such inequality allowed the modern part of the globe to seek, and find, *global* solutions to *locally* produced "overpopulation" problems.

This situation could last as long as modernity (that is, a perpetual, compulsive, obsessive, and addictive *modernization*) remained a privilege. Once modernity turned, as was intended and bound to happen, into the universal condition of humankind, the effects of its by now planetary dominion had come home to roost. As the triumphant progress of modernization has reached the furthest lands of the planet, practically the totality of human production and consumption has become money-and-market mediated, and commodification, commercialization, and monetarization of human livelihoods has penetrated every nook and cranny of the globe – global outlets for local problems are no longer available, while all localities (also, most notable, the highly modernized ones) have to bear the consequences of modernity's global triumph, having been faced with the need to seek (in vain, it seems) *local* solutions to *globally* produced problems.

To cut the long story short: the new fullness of the planet means, essentially, an acute crisis of the human waste disposal industry. That industry is fast running short of refuse dumps and the tools of waste recycling at a time when human waste production goes on unabated and, if anything, gains in efficiency.

End of the space era

Again, a caveat is called for. "The end of the space era" does not mean that space "no longer matters," that it has been annihilated or made null and void, as certain openly declared or latent technological determinists, bewitched by the virtual instantaneity of information transfer and the steadily diminishing role assigned to physical distance in action-design and performance, suggest. The *importance* of physical space is indeed waning, but this process is coupled with an abrupt rise in the *significance* attached to the territory, to the place, to locality.

The verdict of "the end of the space era" is a reflection of the new extraterritoriality of power and of the substitution of mobility for engagement as the decisive strategic factor of power struggle. In the emergent global power hierarchy, those least space-bound, least tied to (that is, encumbered by) the place and most free to move, rule. In the "space of flows" where global powers reside and operate, it is the *speed of movement and facility to escape*, not the size of *territorial possessions* (and so responsibilities), that count and decide. Territorial entrenchment, everything that slows down the movement or disallows its contemplation, has turned from an asset into a handicap. It is to be avoided at all cost – and the high and mighty, resourceful enough to afford such cost, do their best to avoid it. New empires are not of this world – not of earthly, geographical world, not of the "space of places."

On the other hand, place has lost its defensive capacity. Holding to the place, however tightly sealed and fortified, is no longer a warrant of security. Borders are eminently permeable. Liquid power respects few if any obstacles; it soaks through the walls however hermetic they are or are deemed to be; it leaks easily through the myriads of cracks, fissures, crevices, however narrow. There is no polyfilla capable to plug the holes and stem the flows. If invented, its sealing capacity would be quickly matched by the new and improved liquidity of free-floating power.

It is under these unprepossessing conditions that the forces barred access to, and cut out from the global flow, the "glebae adscripti" forces, forces tied to the ground, burdened with the territorial sovereignty and with all the local responsibilities such sovereignty entails, that have to seek local solutions to globally produced, and continuously globally modified, problems. The problems are gestated in the "space of flows," but they need to be confronted and tackled in the "space of places" – a task ultimately beyond the capacity of local powers holding local forts (for instance, the perpetual global erosion of livelihood and the unsettling and uprooting of ever new populations by the global spread of free trade are confronted locally as the "problem of immigrants" and "asylum seekers"). The new significance of place is born of, and perpetually fed and reinforced by, that hopelessness. The task cannot be fulfilled, and so it never stops to be a challenge stretching the imagination and prompting ever more zealous, though forever inadequate, efforts to stem the tide.

Divorce of power and politics

About a two-centuries long marriage of power and politics, with the couple happily settled in the household of the modern nation-state and apparently resolved to stay there till death do them part, seems to be now heading towards a divorce, even if no petition has been sent to the courts and no *decree nisi* granted. Partners of the wedlock look in opposite directions: one of them finding the shared domicile too tight for comfort and cumbersome, and the other increasingly frustrated by the first partner's prolonged absences from home. Power develops distaste for politics' embrace, while the lovingly open arms of politics hang in the void, empty.

Having moved to higher floors, power has dismantled the staircase behind itself and placed security guards at the elevator's entry. Politics, left behind in the flat, has been barred access to power's new domicile, with power's new address kept off-directory. Its calls and messages are not certain to reach the addressee and are answered, if at all, by the departed partner's whim. Deprived of power's partnership, its source of strength and confidence, politics must grin and bear it, while trying to make the best of a bad job. It goes on flexing its muscles, or at least pretends that it does – hoping to hide how flabby its muscles have become once power has been lipo-sucked away; or it confines its flurry to the odd jobs with which even the flabbiest of muscles can cope.

Other residents of the former power/politics homestead leave home in droves; bereft of power, politics cannot guard properly the exit and would not wish to guard it even if it could: the quarrelsome residents were too awkward to handle. Indeed, nation/state politics would be pleased to see most of the residents go and settle in their own households. It helps them to do just that through strategies nicknamed "deregulation," "privatization," or "following the principle of subsidiarity" (that is, of gladly and promptly surrendering any such responsibility as its former wards would be willing, or at least would not object, to take over; more often than not, of handing the responsibilities over to them with or without their consent). Most functions that the empowered politics used to appropriate and jealously guard are ceded to market forces and the new domain of "life politics," inside which citizens of the nation-states are encouraged, and expected, to seek biographical solution to problems no one else is eager, or has strength, to confront – let alone to resolve.

The meaning of divorce is the separation of former partners and the end of sharing and cooperation. In the world of globalized interdependence and extraterritorially induced vulnerability, coupled with continuing territoriality of political sovereignty and the transfer of many traditionally political tasks to the areas where the issue of sovereignty does not arise, power is emancipated from the political constraints in which it used to be enclosed by the modern state armed with the institutions of democratic control, whereas the power contents of politics have been depleted, if not evacuated altogether. Power is free to roam the global "space of flows," paying not much more than lip-service to its past political wardens, while disempowered politics can only eye helplessly and haplessly its antics, hoping against hope to drive the graces its way while diverting the blows to other, similarly territorial, sovereigns.

The Consequences

Frontier land

Of all known social landscapes, the global "space of flows" is reminiscent most of the "Wild West" immortalized in Hollywood westerns, or "Frontier land" tales reanimated *ad nauseam* courtesy of the Disney studios.

In a frontier land, there are no rules of conduct that bind the strong and the weak alike and that bind them whether or not those expected to abide by them agree to do so. Neither is there an authority able and willing to impose the observance of such rules. Events follow each other in anything but a consistent, predictable order. In a frontier land, anything may happen, but nothing can be done with any degree of confidence and self-assurance, let alone backed with a reliable anticipation of its consequences. What would indeed occur is anybody's guess, but no one's certainty.

In a frontier land, all boundaries are temporary, and none is impermeable even when uncontested. Boundaries shift, following the peregrinations of their draftsmen. Coalitions are ad hoc and floating, just like the battlefronts circumscribing hostile camps. Friendships and enmities are in flux and always until further notice. Yesterday's allies turn, or are turned, into foes, just as yesterday's sworn enemies join forces with their detractors and are welcomed with open arms.

In a frontier land, freedom of maneuver is the latchkey to success, whereas the commitment to the ground for whatever reason is a recipe for defeat. The outcome of confrontation is decided by the ability to surprise, by the speed with which the blows are delivered and the swiftness with which the deliverers escape the reprisal. Not the territory, but the capacity and freedom to disregard it, are the true stakes of the power struggle.

In a frontier land, all effective powers, the powers that count, adapt their skills, armory, and strategy to the conditions of perpetual and irredeemable uncertainty and improvisation. All such powers thrive when the accident and randomness rule; they would wilt and fade the moment their moves became, or were made, predictable. In the Wild West, one stance that united the cattle barons and the bandits was the shared distaste for the streamlining and routinization of moves that the enforcement of legally prescribed rules would inevitably bring in its wake. Common interest vested in the staving off of the danger of rules and routine underlay their enmity – and allowed that enmity to go on being ever again replayed. The only people interested in the rule of law were the few farmers who, by fencing themselves off, or more correctly *in*, revisited and relived the trials and tribulations suffered by the ancient pioneer settlers, offering themselves as sitting targets and easy prey to the free-roaming nomads.

The difference between power relations in a rule-guided space and those of the frontier land may be grasped with the help of the metaphors of the river and a minefield, suggested by Jurij Lotman. Following the trajectory of the riverbed, waters push their way toward the estuary, eroding, undercutting, dissolving, or bypassing the obstacles on their way – pulverizing the rocks and sweeping off the sands. A minefield holds no lesser powers than rivers do – but unlike rivers, the places of their concentration and condensation and the direction in which they would ultimately erupt cannot be anticipated. One can be pretty sure that the explosions will occur, but one cannot say where and when.

Reconnaissance battles

If the frontlines are not clearly drawn, tend to drift, and are not expected to retain their contours for long, and if the divide between friends and enemies is neither unambiguous nor permanent, if most enemies are in principle potential allies and vice versa (as is the case in a frontier land) – armed confrontations tend to have the character of "reconnaissance battles."

As a rule, reconnaissance battles do not follow, but *precede* the determination of war aims and the designing of war strategy. Their purpose is to find out what alignment of forces and which use of weapons is likely to bring most profits. The logic of instrumental rationality is reversed: in reconnaissance battles, it is the best ends to the given means, rather than the best means to the given ends, that are sought. War plans are eminently "flexible." Available resources seek their most effective uses. The question to be answered is "what can we do with what we have" rather than "what we need to have to do what we want." War aims are revised and often changed, with little if any warning and sometimes beyond recognition, as the armed confrontations proceed.

Clausewitz is remembered for suggesting that wars are the continuation of politics by other means. Reconnaissance battles are, if anything, the continuation of the absence of politics – and filling of "other means" in the place vacated by the policy.

Hopefully, a policy – perhaps even a consistent policy – may eventually emerge at the far end of a long series of trials and errors, hits and misses; this is, at least, as the official *plaidoyer* for the reconnaissance battles goes. One can however surmise, and with good reasons, that the tussles and scuffles of such sort take the urgency out of the task and make the elaboration of policy redundant. This may be even their principal, though latent, aim, given the profusion of means yet to be tried and the dearth of ideas concerning the alternative realities whose feasibility is worth a trial.

Mutually assured vulnerability

In a frontier land, reconnaissance battles are not auxiliary stratagems, the handmaiden of war, as was their role in "classic wars" – regular, predesigned, purposeful, and (at least intentionally) structured combats. Neither are they preliminary steps to something else: to the advance of troops, invasion and conquest of the enemy's territory. They are, rather, the principal, "normal," persistent, quasi-permanent forms the hostilities take. This circumstance makes the affinity of the frontier land with Lotman's "minefield" even closer. If "classic wars" purported to *diminish* the irritating uncertainty caused by the nearness of a strong neighbor with potentially hostile intentions, or better still *eliminate* it altogether, the wars dissipated into a string of reconnaissance battles turn into the *prime cause* of uncertainty. Their immediate effect is a growing precariousness and vulnerability of all the actors, as well as of the actual or potential "collateral casualties" of their actions.

Unraveling the mystery of the earthly, human power, Mikhail Bakhtin began from the description of "cosmic fear" – the human emotion aroused by the inhuman magnificence of the universe; the kind of fear that precedes man-made power and serves it as the foundation, prototype, and inspiration. *Cosmic* fear is, in Bakhtin's words:

> the trepidation felt in the face of the immeasurably great and immeasurably powerful: in the face of the starry heavens, the material mass of the mountains, the sea, and the fear of cosmic upheavals and elemental disasters...The cosmic fear [is] fundamentally not mystical in the strict sense (being a fear in the face of the materially great and the materially indefinable power). (See Bakhtin, 1968; Hirschkop, 1997)

At the core of the "cosmic fear" lies the nonentity of the weak and mortal being faced with the enormity of the everlasting universe; the *vulnerability* of the frail and soft human body that the sight of the "starry heavens" or "the material mass of the mountains" reveals – but also the realization that it is not in human power to comprehend that awesome might which manifests itself in the sheer grandiosity of the universe. That universe's intentions are unknown, its next steps are unpredictable. If there is a preconceived plan or logic in its action, it certainly escapes human understanding. And so the "cosmic fear" is also the horror of the unknown: the terror of *uncertainty*.

Vulnerability and uncertainty are the two qualities of the human condition out of which, as Bakhtin suggests, the "official fear" is molded: the fear of *human* power, of man-made and man-held power. The official fear is construed after the pattern of the inhuman power reflected by (or, rather, emanating from) the "cosmic fear."

If this is what human power is about, and if this is how power extracts the lodes of discipline on which it relies, then the production of official fear is the key to the power's effectiveness. Cosmic fear needs no human mediators, but official fear cannot do without them. Official fear can only be *contrived*. Earthly powers, much like the novelties of consumer markets, must create their own demand. For their grip to hold, their objects must be *made*, and *kept*, vulnerable and insecure.

In an average modern society vulnerability and insecurity of existence and the need to pursue life purposes under conditions of acute and unredeemable uncertainty are assured by the exposure of life pursuits to market forces. Except for creating and protecting the legal conditions of market freedoms, political power has no need to interfere. In demanding the subject's discipline and law observance, it may rest its legitimacy on the promise to mitigate the extent of the already existing vulnerability and uncertainty of its citizens: to limit harms and damages perpetrated by the free play of market forces, to shield the vulnerable against excessively painful blows, and to ensure the uncertain against the risks a free competition necessarily entails. Such legitimation found its ultimate expression in the self-definition of the modern form of government as a "welfare state."

That formula of political power is presently receding into the past. "Welfare state" institutions are progressively dismantled and phased out, while restraints imposed previously on business activities and the free play of market competition and on its consequences are removed. The protective functions of the state are tapered to embrace a small minority of unemployable and invalid persons, though even that minority tends to be reclassified from the issue of social care into the issue of law and order, threat to personal safety, and the source of vulnerability: incapacity to participate in the market game tends to be increasingly criminalized. The state washes its hands of the vulnerability and uncertainty arising from the logic (or illogicality) of the free market, now redefined as a private affair, a matter for the individuals to deal and cope with by the resources in their private possession. As Ulrich Beck (1992) put it, individuals are now expected to seek biographical solutions to systemic contradictions.

These new trends have a side effect: they sap the foundations on which the state power, claiming a crucial role in fighting vulnerability and uncertainty haunting its subjects, increasingly rests in modern times. The widely noted growth of political apathy, loss of political interests and commitments ("no more salvation by society," as Peter Drucker famously put it), and massive retreat of populations from participation in institutional politics all bear evidence to the crumbling of the established foundations of state power.

Having rescinded its previous programmatic interference with market-produced insecurity and having on the contrary proclaimed the perpetuation and intensification of that insecurity to be the mission of all political power caring for the well-being of its subjects, the contemporary state may seek other, non-economic varieties of vulnerability and uncertainty on which to rest its legitimacy. That alternative seems to be located, most spectacularly by the US administration, in the issue of personal safety: threats and fears to human bodies, possessions, and habitats arising from criminal activities, anti-social conduct, of the "underclass," and most recently global terrorism. Unlike the insecurity born of the market, which is if anything all too visible and obvious for comfort, that alternative insecurity which is hoped to restore the state's lost monopoly of redemption must be artificially beefed up, or at least highly dramatized to inspire sufficient "official fear" and at the same time overshadow and relegate to a secondary position the economically generated insecurity about which the state administration can do nothing and wishes to do nothing.

Unlike the case of market-generated threats to livelihood and welfare, the extent of dangers to personal safety must be presented in the darkest of colors, so that the non-materialization of threats can be applauded as an extraordinary event, a result of the exceptional skills, vigilance, care, and good will of state organs. This is the task with which the CIA and FBI are mostly occupied in recent months: warning Americans of imminent attempts on their safety, putting them in a state of constant alert and so building up tension – so that there is tension to be relieved if the ostensibly imminent attempts do not occur and so that all credit for the relief of tension may be by popular consent ascribed to the organs of law and order to which the state administration is progressively reduced. This is how the popular demand for the emaciated version of state power that has successively withdrawn (or has been banished) from most of its past protective functions, is rebuilt on a new foundation – personal vulnerability and personal safety, instead of social vulnerability and social protection.

Far from being an unanticipated, undesirable, and resented outcome of haphazard and uncontrolled developments, the "mutually assured vulnerability" may be a new formula of domination; one consistent policy of global powers in the world conspicuously lacking in visions of alternative and better realities and in policies that may help such visions into being.

6

Everyday Technics as Extraordinary Threats: Urban Technostructures and Non-Places in Terrorist Actions

Timothy W. Luke

Introduction

This chapter reevaluates cities as strategic sites in the twenty-first century during an era of rapid globalization. In particular, it examines how the operational architectures of modern urbanism by their own necessities design, deploy, and dedicate what ironically are tremendous assets for destruction as part and parcel of mobilizing materiel for economic production. These assets are created innocently within a culture of liberal amicality to maintain capitalist relations of exchange. Yet individuals or groups who willingly would work outside of these liberal assumptions with a spirit of illiberal inimicality can leverage them to cause havoc at low cost with return.

This chapter, then, addresses four main concerns. First, it provides an overview of modernization gone awry, in too many ways and places, even as its machinic foundations spin up the convenient technostructures and non-places needed to disrupt its workings. Second, it points to the vulnerabilities of living with big systems, showing how the spatial practices of ordinary high-tech life are a resource-rich terrain for terrorists to exploit. Third, it shows how liberal society assumes amicality in its technostructures to prosper, but the inimicality fostered by its non-places is all opponents need to shatter liberal prosperity and pace. And, fourth, it suggests how no counter-measures against terrorism are likely to succeed, short of undercutting the grievances that spark such antagonistic illiberal reactions.

During the nineteenth and twentieth centuries, the project of modernization pitched the promise of democracy, affluence, equality, and reason against the traditional injustices of rural poverty, aristocratic privilege, and oppressive religion. Those battles, however, were won in many places around the world by the end of the twentieth century (Taylor, 1996). After these victories, harder challenges arise. Defining the risks and then determining the costs and benefits of which rational choices should be made – over and above other rational choices – is much more difficult. In 1959, C. Wright Mills had already asserted how these indefinite ambiguities of permanent risk and incommensurable metrics of value led into "the postmodern" (1959: 178–94).

With the apparent triumph of technology over nature, the secular over the sacred, and affluence over poverty, science, seen as "modernization," is believed to have improved life (Lyotard, 1984). Nonetheless, science "it turns out, is not a technological Second Coming. That its techniques and its rationality are given a central place in a society does not mean men [*sic*] live reasonably and without myth, fraud, and superstition" (Mills, 1959: 168). Therefore, for Mills, at "the *postmodern* climax" of modernity, the promise of continual change, or permanent progress, bogs down, and perhaps even begins to collapse. Postmodernity, therefore, arrives with "the collapse of the expectations of the Enlightenment, that reason and freedom would come to prevail as paramount forces in human history" (1959: 183).

Lyotard also discusses this loss of belief in modernity's grand narratives, which have, in turn, clad Western capitalist society's economic, political, and social practices in fables of reason and freedom since the Enlightenment. A quest for performance and profit appears instead to anchor the essence of today's postmodern conditions (Reich, 1991; Kennedy, 1992); yet economic development "continues to take place without leading to the realization of any of these dreams of emancipation" (Lyotard, 1984: 39). With little trust in old canonical stories of truth, enlightenment, or progress, the global forces of science and technology at work behind big business, now slip into the register of "another language game, in which the goal is no longer truth, but performativity – that is, the best possible input/output equation" (Lyotard, 1984: 46). On another level, these persistent moves toward greater performativity spin up "a new social system beyond classical capitalism," proliferating through "the world space of multinational capital" (Jameson, 1992: 54, 59).

Rather than being a "break," "crisis," or "rupture" in modernity, postmodernization in many ways only accelerates global change within the existing routines for already modernized forms of being (Reich, 1991; Poster, 1995). As the consumption of commodities becomes a way of everyday modern life, postmodernity essentially morphs into "fast capitalism" (Agger, 1989). Its markets reject closed structures, fixed meaning, and rigid order in favor of chaos, incompleteness, and uncertainty (Ó Tuathail, 1999; Thrift, 1998; Rosenau, 1990). Its politics repudiate fixed territories, sacred spaces, and hard boundaries in favor of unstable flows, the non-places used to stage consumer practices, and permeable borders (Diebert, 1997; Augé, 1995; Agnew and Corbridge, 1995). Postmodernity is not a wholly new social order; instead, almost totally commercialized ways of life become generalized on a transnational scale (Luke, 1999; Bourdieu, 1998; Appadurai, 1996). On this terrain, terrorists easily can operate, finding both the tools of assault and their targets for destruction streaming through the non-places of criss-crossed borders and flows of innumerable products.

The Vulnerabilities of Living in Big Systems

Some believe that destroying the World Trade Center and damaging the Pentagon were futile assaults upon the global economy and American military power. In some ways, they are right. World trade has no single true center. And the armed forces of the USA can be controlled from many different points scattered all around the nation, as the wars in Afghanistan and Iraq managed largely in Tampa, Florida since October 2001 easily demonstrate. Nonetheless, iconic buildings are signs, as well as sites, of global wealth, power, and culture. Unleashing chaotic forces against such structures, in today's transnational ways of life, is a uniquely framed stratagem of "shock and awe." Destroying or damaging such significant buildings, then, can be seen as a successful first strike in a sign war tied to propaganda of the deed. Indeed, the attacks of 9/11 were a powerful blow against key nodes in the nation that still dominates the means of communication and relations of signification at the dawn of the twenty-first century – either as a "hyperpower" or as the seat of "Empire"(Hardt and Negri, 2000). The 9/11 strikes were remarkable works of terrorist propaganda, and those who committed them know the global systems of signification will replay those images of destruction forever and a day.

Contemporary life depends upon individuals coping with many risks in a network of such nodes knit into complex, interlinked technostructures (Beck, 1992). Whether it is communication, nutrition and transportation, or finance, housing, and medicine, the ordinary uses of technical artifacts and processes afford terrorists innumerable embedded assets that can be put to destructive purposes. Tremendous lethal capabilities can be created simply by contra-functioning the everyday applications of many technics. Resourceful resistance fighters create weapons from what is at hand. In the global economy of the post-Cold War era, the Internet, 24×7 finance markets, global airlines, agricultural fertilizers, rental trucks, and tourist industries readily can provide much of the organization, intelligence, weaponry, and targets needed for effective terrorist acts. Redirecting a fully fueled wide-body airliner with a normal passenger load, but a kamikaze pilot and cabin crew, does create a strange new type of cruise missile. This system's kinetic energy, chemical fuel, and terrified riders carry immense symbolic impact, which can, as they did on 9/11, forever reconfigure the world's air transport system, New York's skyline, and the exceptionalist myths of American invulnerability. Yet, for global exchange to continue, these same capabilities must remain in place, leaving everyone at some risk as long as airliners fly and gritty geopolitical conflicts anger new suicide pilots.

Protecting against any comparable future attacks, moreover, is a nightmarish defense problem if the generic liberal assumptions of rational, life-enhancing utility presumed by modern technics are pushed outside the daily equations of ordinary technological use. Most large technical systems become extremely uncontrollable dangers if one repurposes their instrumental applications to cause harm rather than create power or profit. The most relevant case in point is the American air transport system. On any given day prior to 9/11, 35,000–40,000 airplanes of various types took off and landed, which included 4,000 commercial flights, at 460 FAA-controlled airports in airline services provided to almost 2 million passengers (*Washington Post*, September 12, 2001: A5). Forewarnings of 9/11 were uncovered years before, as the plots in 1995 to hijack and/or bomb twelve US airliners in Asia and Oceania or later assaults planned for strikes against symbolic sites in Paris, Washington, DC, and other cities clearly demonstrate. Yet little was done, because on any given day, finding less than twenty terrorists among the nearly 2 million passengers on 40,000 planes and 4,000 commercial flights in the USA during 2000–1 was very challenging, even though each one of these flights could be transformed into a terrorist-guided missile.

The *modus operandi* of Al-Qaeda networks, which appear to be behind many acts of domestic and international terrorism over the past decade, displays considerable operational versatility and intellectual adaptability. Still, such tacticians cleverly can seek out new disruptive possibilities in many places. Consequently, the attacks of 9/11 are most likely not going to be repeated in exactly the same way, as the alleged "shoe bomber" and nuclear "dirty bomber" attackers during 2001–2 both suggest. Instead, the next major strike undoubtedly will leverage other embedded assets – like the Bali disco bombings and Saudi apartment bombings of 2002–3 – set within different existing technostructures, to raise havoc.

The option for anonymous resistance nests in networks, sits inside systems, and pulls with processes. It can be simultaneously underground, on the ground, and ungrounded in many different locales. Transnational ethnonational diasporas and horrendously failed states shelter its militants, mobilize its supporters, and nurture its many streams of discontent (Griffin, 2001; Cooley, 2000; Rashid, 2000). Because most mechanisms, structures, and links in world capitalism must be essentially insecure to operate optimally, defense against the insecurities of all who now live amid these linked assemblies in big market-driven systems is neither certain nor final. From the Congo, Somalia, Liberia, and Sierra Leone to Afghanistan, Iraq, Chechnya, and Palestine, there are deodorized wild zones in which stateless formations for organized violence play out their quests for institutional power on both a local and global level (Agnew, 1998; Huntington, 1998; Doty, 1996; Barber, 1995).

Even though the USA and UK have labored to statalize this conflict in both Afghanistan and Iraq by attacking the Taliban and Ba'athist regimes, Washington has now entered into "a state of war" with "stateless warriors" (Halberstam, 2001; Bowden, 2000; Gourevitch, 1999; Kaplan, 1996). This situation has not prevailed in the USA since its "civilizing campaigns" against Native Americans, the Barbary pirates, and Caribbean buccaneers in the eighteenth and nineteenth centuries. Instead of considering 9/11 as a historical oddity, however, the USA needs to ask what strategic failures, political inconsistencies, or economic discontinuities so plague its global roles as the world's last superpower, that such deodorizing developments now are becoming much more endemic (Herod, Ó Tuathail, and Roberts, 1998; Campbell, 1992). Few images underscore as powerfully the postmodernizing qualities of the present moment as what appears to be premodern religious fanaticism mixes with late modern aerospace vehicles to collide into high modernist buildings. Each of these fragments underscores C. Wright Mills' sense of the postmodern as a contradictory condition in which scientific rationality and techniques "are given a central place in society," but this does not mean all can live "reasonably and without myth, fraud, and superstition" (1959: 168).

Finding "the Political" in Liberal Globality

Stateless war machines are quite useful for struggles against contemporary liberal democratic economies and societies. Organizations like Al-Qaeda, Hamas, or Hezbollah, as well as individuals like Ted Kaczynski, Timothy McVeigh, or John Allen Muhammed, do not need to mobilize vast amounts of men, materiel, or machineries to strike their enemies. Schmitt (1996) sees "the political" resting upon who is a "friend" or an "enemy." The amicality of liberal economy and society pre-positions all of the resources – information, energy, matter, and people – terrorists need to wreak tremendous destruction upon elements of everyday life. Merely choosing to brook the demilitarized, depoliticized, and dissocialized assumptions of individual freedom in liberal exchange with an *ad hoc,* or even some standing, declaration of war, allows terrorists to tip the embedded assets of destructive power hidden by the collaborative amorality of commercial exchange. This inimicality in the strategies of terrorists proliferates *sub rosa* until the moment of its expression, making the first, second, or third strike by such enemies extremely difficult to detect and defend against.

Contemporary urban formations, industrial ecologies, and public infrastructures are vast ensembles of artifacts, which have been designed in particular times and places. They carry within their forms and functions specific cultural, economic, and political values that are characteristic of the times and places in which they were propounded. Clearly, these systems now carry the qualities of liberal economies' and societies' systemic depoliticization. Relations of friend and enemy are not forbidden by the specific technicity of liberal society, and trade between antagonistic powers occurs with some frequency. Nonetheless, few modern industrial metabolisms occur within hard and fast envelopes of securitization. The mis-positioning of objects and subjects in technics can occur, and the incidence of malfunction, accidents, and vandalism occasionally bring these realities to mind. Yet politicizing the technics of everyday life through *ad hoc* acts of terrorist violence represents something significantly new for our collective life. It reveals, in fact, just how much artifacts do have a politics, because liberal society itself systematically works to depoliticize everyday life in pursuit of individual freedom and free enterprise. After 9/11, what were fairly fixed standards of trust, conventions of collaboration, and accords of trust have been shot through by suspicion, competition, and mistrust, as every member of "the flying public" sees at any Transportation Security Administration-controlled airport. Formerly apolitical technical operations now are overshadowed by new political calculations.

As Schmitt observes, the root dispositions of liberal society and its commerce, with all of their patterns of insistence upon demilitarization and depoliticization, are what evades politics, the state, and government in order to protect individual freedom, private property, and commercial opportunity. Politics, when it becomes necessary, must be ready and able to require individuals to sacrifice their life in collective struggle against enemies, often with friends, to preserve the collective political formation. Schmitt, however, correctly concludes that:

> Such a demand is in no way justifiable by the individual of liberal thought. No consistent individualism can entrust to someone other than to the individual himself the right to dispose of the physical life of the individual. An individualism in which any one other than the free individual himself were to decide upon the substance and dimension of his freedom would be only an empty phrase. For the individual as such there is no enemy with whom he must enter into a life-and-death struggle if he personally does not want to do so. To compel him to fight against his will is, from the vision point of the private individual, lack of freedom and repression. (Schmitt, 1996: 71 [*sic*])

Political conflicts are pushed down into other "heterogeneous spheres, namely, ethics and economics, intellect and trade, education and property" (Schmitt, 1996: 70).

Consequently, the particular times and places of liberal development usually deprive the state and politics of any specific concrete meaning, leaving the specific technicities of national and international commodity chains setting the tone and tenor of collective life (Walker, 1993; Luke, 1993). One finds that:

> The state turns into society: on the ethical–intellectual side into an ideological humanitarian conception of humanity, and the other into an economic– technical system of production and traffic. The self-understood will to repel the enemy in a given battle situation turns into a rationally constructed social ideal or program, a tendency or an economic calculation. A politically united people becomes, on the one hand, a culturally interested public, and, on the other hand, partially an industrial concern, and its employers, partially a mass of consumers. At the intellectual pole, government and power turns into propaganda and mass manipulation, and at the economic pole, control. (Schmitt, 1996: 72)

The material culture of contemporary liberal capitalist societies is riddled by these depoliticized and demilitarized, but still nonetheless highly polit- ical, qualities.

As the state and society converge in the collectives of commerce, the basic impulse toward market-building and profit-creating stresses amity over enmity in the technics of capitalist everyday life. The liberal individual, for the most part, always presumes there is no enemy with whom he or she encounters in a life or death struggle. Hence, spatiality itself, technics as such, and logistics by and large, all presume not invidious inimicality, but rather an affable amicability, as their root conditions of performance. The tacit consent of the client, consumer, and citizen given to the expert, producer, and bureaucrat is one of accepting the market's allegedly life-extending, life-enhancing, and life-enlarging benefits in exchange for bearing tolerable overhead costs and acceding to expert regulatory author- ity. These contracts of convenience are what underpin the codices of governmentality, empowering specific agencies to propound structures of population, territoriality, and sovereignty in a manner that assures the most convenient disposition of people and things to regulate the conduct of conduct (Foucault, 1991).

Liberal capitalist societies presume, as Schmitt (1996) asserts, virtually null ethical commitments to a universal humanity coupled to an economic– technical system of anarchic production, whose daily traffic constitutes a culturally interested public knit together as producers and consumers of a "gross national product" with industrial concerns as their employers and suppliers. Yet the foundational writ of this order dictates that all assemble together in relative amity to pursue the persona of technified life, individual liberty, and private property. Beyond minimal technical safeguards against accidents, malfunctions, or crimes, to guarantee their freedoms are assured, any repression is unlikely. The industrial ecologies and logistical flows of liberal capitalist life are predicated upon masses of people coexisting amicably rather than competing against enduring inimical threats. Because of their foundational demilitarization and depoliticization, modern technostructures are designed to work together as artifacts and practices of a fashion that both accentuates amicality in market interactions and discounts the prospects of inimicality in the daily running of these systems. And it is precisely these assumptions of amicality and inimicality which terrorists re-jigger through contra-governmental chaos, to impose devastating costs upon the conduct of everyday life.

Cities and Strategies

Mumford's vision of urbanism leads one to recall how cities work as strategic sites, defensive perimeters, and terrorist acts. Materializing power with foundational urban writs as walls, citadels, and markets enabled a new civic order in which "law and order supplemented brute force: to propound a collective action engine." Instead of many little rural villages, like those of Sparta, where:

> such rulers had to back their naked power by covert terrorism, in walled cities the wall itself was worth a whole army in controlling the unruly, keeping rivals under surveillance, and blocking the desperate from escaping. The early cities thus developed something of the same concentration of command one finds in a ship: its inhabitants were "all in the same boat," and learned to trust the captain and execute orders promptly. (Mumford, 1961: 49)

These webs for logistical collaboration, coercive interoperation, and concentrated cohabitation persist in today's urban technostructures, but their imbrication in the chains of commodity production and consumption also takes residents out of old containments to position them in the fluid but fixed channels of transportational, logistical, communicational, and operational non-places (Davis, 2002).

Cities have been from their earliest inception – as walled citadels constructed by monarchical, clerical, and divine authorities – designed as strategic sites (Virilio, 1977). They are the original hardened silos for command, control, communication, and intelligence functions required by aristocratic and/or theocratic war machines intent upon enforcing new spatial practices, like forced labor, territorial domination, and resource expropriation. Such architectures required many new large systems for the provision of their inhabitants, rulers, and visitors. So cities are, as Mumford claims, the durable materialization of a "concrete form of war" (1961: 58). Underneath civilization's pretence that *Stadtluft macht frei* are the realities of *Kriegsschaft und Kriegsnotwendigkeit*.

The random outrages of the still "at large" anthrax letter mailer, or the now imprisoned John Allen Muhammed and John Lee Malvino, in and around Washington, DC during 2001 and 2002, show the ease with which individual inimicality virtually can paralyze numerous urban law enforcement agencies as well as monopolize the attention of the local and national mass media. It takes very little to terrorize a city, a region, or even an entire nation. With the right technology, ranging from a few anthrax-laden pieces of mail to a post-ban .223 rifle and an old Chevy Caprice police cruiser, millions along America's eastern seaboard tripped into low-grade panics during October 2001 and 2002. Mail systems move millions of containers to and from thousands of localities every day as integral parts of technostructures for communication, marketing, transport, and governance. Strip shopping malls, corner gasoline stations, sporting events, bus stops, musical performances, lawns, and schoolyards, in turn, concentrate large numbers of soft targets which stand around with little or no sense of caution against anyone seeking to strike against those deemed inimical to a cause, a faith, or a nation.

Mumford argues that "human life swings between two poles: movement and settlement" (1961: 5). Contemporary terrorist actions play off these phases in human existence: targeting the settled when they least expect violence and exploiting the violent possibilities of continuously anonymous logistical movements. While cities historically rooted their settlement in amicality against inimicality, the machinations of constant mass movements in modern times have pushed the once-ready awareness of "the political" in citizens' minds deep into the background of liberal society's markets as they diffuse, decompose, or displace the state. Terrorist surprise attacks are usually rooted in ruses of amicality, only to be shucked off *ad hoc* to reveal the raw realities of inimicality in riveting episodes of savage violence.

The logistical links connecting cities, the aesthetics of contemporary design, and the growing importance of telematics all combine to create a significant mixture of embedded insecurity in modern urbanism. Rather than providing sites with guaranteed safety and stability, the spatiality of contemporary cities already presumes a high measure of endangerment, instability, and threat, which is unavoidable unless one totally forgoes living within these spaces and systems. What assures security here is mostly "common sense," or a culture of correct use and astute risk management directed at lessening legal liabilities for poor product design, willful abuse, or criminal negligence.

Seeing misused everyday artifacts as prepositioned strategic assets has hitherto been regarded by many as essentially inconceivable or, at least, highly improbable due to modern cultures of military action rooted in statal warfare. Spectacular violence perpetrated by stateless actors, however, alters these equations of techno-strategic action. As the events of September 11 indicate, stateless actors play up otherwise unimaginable acts. Their innovations mobilize assets for attacks that destructively activate the embedded threats of large technical systems, everyday logistics, and civil offensive capabilities.

This operationality is a crucial quality of the contemporary "non-place." As Augé maintains, such sites are essentially materializations of abstract space organized around technofunctionalities and the spatial practices of logistics. Non-places are:

> spaces formed in relation to certain ends (transport, transit, commerce, and leisure), and the relations that individuals have with these spaces. Although the two sets of relations overlap to a large extent, and in any case officially (individuals travel, make purchases, relax), they are still not confused with one another; for non-places mediate a whole mass of relations, with the self and with others, which are only indirectly connected with their purposes. As anthropological places create the organically social, so non-places create solitary contractuality. (Augé, 1995: 94)

The spatial practices of non-places are about moving bodies, goods, machines, and systems: delocalized, individuated, accelerated, networked, homogenized, institutionalized, programmed, and commodified (Virilio, 1995). Non-places are familiar, but often alienating; amical, but easily estranging; accommodating, but barely skimming above the inimical. Augé touts these networks of systems and grids of technostructures, which spin up non-places as "supermodernity" (1995: 93), but such supermodern constructs also are remarkably rich attractors for terrorist action. As the strikes by Al-Qaeda, the anthrax mailer, and Washington snipers show, anything that disrupts or halts such movements in non-places can nearly immobilize entire cities, regions, and nations by triggering suspicions about anyone's amicality and keying searchers for indications of inimicality.

Abstract space is the product and by-product of capitalist relations of production (Lefebvre, 1991). While national variations recur in its concrete materiality, abstract social labor in the systems of markets, technics, and logistics fomented by commodity creation and consumption gradually has occupied absolute and historical spaces with abstract space. Here Lefebvre maintains that:

Capitalism and neo-capitalism have produced abstract space, which includes
the "world of commodities," its "logic" and its worldwide strategies, as well
as the power of money and that of the political state. This space is founded on
the vast network of banks, business centers, and major productive entities, as
also on motorways, airports, and information lattices. Within this space the
town – once the forcing-house of accumulation, fountainhead of wealth, and
center of historical space – has disintegrated. (1991: 53)

Fully enmeshed within governmentality and its triadic assemblies of
population, territoriality, and sovereignty for production, abstract space is
immanently repressive, anti-sensual, and decontextualized. This social
space is an intrinsic product of ongoing commodification which is required
in globalizing spaces of accumulation to link knowledge, technology,
money, and power. Absolute and historical spaces persist, but they are
increasingly displaced substrata or underpinnings of non-places. The systemic command, control, and communication functions of abstract space
function instead:

"objectally," as a set of things/signs and their formal relationships: glass and
stone, concrete and steel, angles and curves, full and empty. Formal and
quantitative, it erases distinctions, as much those which derive from nature
and (historical) time as those which originate in the body (age, sex, ethnicity).
The signification of this ensemble refers back to a sort of super-signification
which escapes meaning's net: the functioning of capitalism, which contrives
to be blatant and covert at one and the same time. The dominant form of
space, that of the centers of wealth and power, endeavors to mold the spaces it
dominates (i.e., peripheral spaces) and it seeks, often by violent means, to
reduce the obstacles and resistances it encounters there. (Lefebvre, 1991: 49)

Terrorism usually is portrayed as an attack on governments, but its
ultimate strategies are (if Lenin is correct about strategy being the art of
making choices about where to apply force) poised mainly against the
operational sites of governmentality, like technostructures, non-places,
and logistics.

Here the smooth interoperations of populations, territory, and the state
are disrupted via contra-governmental interventions, which find and inflict
fearsome "dyspositions" of people and things to disrupt, distend, or disin-
tegrate, as Foucault would say, the conduct of the conduct (Luke, 1996).
Technics are themselves cybernetic systems, governing behaviors and in-
stantiating rules simply by dint of use to generate greater "welfare."
"Misuse" and "dysfunction" lie latent within each technology, and terrorists act in ways that unleash bigger "malfare" functions embedded in any
technology where such irrational action is possible. Interrupting the control
of movement (Virilio, 1977: 30) easily insecuritizes places as well as space
where movements begin, traverse, and end.

Carried to its logical conclusion, the events of 9/11 shift the world from a register of security rooted in Cold War waged between superpower states at the head of vast zone-regimes, to one of hot peace conducted by networks, stateless war machines, and anomic agencies against established states, mass populations, and territorialized structures. Just as the Department of Defense was truly unable to guarantee the security of the USA against a concerted attack by the USSR, the Department of Homeland Security cannot ensure the security of homelands, home populations, or homeplaces against networked assaults.

The terrorism of Al-Qaeda, the anthrax mailer, or the Washington snipers requires supermodern non-places. Here the terrorizer uncovers vulnerabilities in the spatial practices of contemporary society, which iron-ically are the working wherewithal of everyday life. As Lefebvre claims, the spatial practices of society secrete the space its inhabitants occupy and utilize. These connections embrace:

> production and reproduction, and the particular locations and spatial sets characteristic of each social formation. Spatial practice ensures continuity and some degree of cohesion. In terms of social space, and of each member of a given society's relationship to that space, this cohesion implies a guaranteed level of *competence* and a specific level of *performance*. (Lefebvre, 1991: 33)

The technostructures, propounded and presupposed by the secretion of such space, work only if people are accustomed to performing rightly or wrongly in them. Amicable compliance derived from individual compe-tence, and collective performance at particular locations with certain spatial settings, cannot be changed without remaking spatial practices. Yet, remaining as they are, these arrangements put scores of people in fully fueled wide-bodied jets, push millions of pieces of mail through the post, and place thousands of drivers out in the open air to fuel their vehicles. Disrupting ordinary logistical processes with suicide pilots, microbe-infested letters, and sedan-mounted sniper platforms easily cripples the continuity and cohesion of those productive spatial practices. Still, this danger cannot be avoided. The same spatial practices always can be recast to provide unconventional warheads, delivery systems, and soft targets in unanticipated wars by unknown enemies upon unprotected friends.

Responses to the Politics on Non-Places

There are few, if any, satisfactory responses to contemporary forms of terrorism in advanced liberal capitalist economies and societies. Maintain-ing the industrial metabolisms of transnational exchange demands these dangerous materials and machines. They sustain commerce under amical conditions of co-production, but their continuance simply embeds assets for attacks under inimical conditions of destruction. A half-hearted effort to deal with terrorism can essentially, as the Clinton administration did, try to marginalize, ignore, or forget its perpetrators, hoping against hope that each new episode is an extraordinary event, an isolated incident, or an irreproducible outrage (Debrix, 1999). This approach, however, has not worked well, because it remains too mired in the demilitarized, depoliti-cized, and desocialized assumptions of liberalism. Perhaps there will be no more assaults, but hope has proven a feeble defense given that it was President Reagan who first declared "war on terrorism" a generation ago.

Lefebvre is right about the qualities of an everyday spatial code, like liberal amicality, because it is much more than a means of interpreting space and its practices:

> Rather it is a means of living in that space, of understanding it, and of producing it. As such, it brings together verbal signs (words and sentences, along with the meaning invested in them by a significant process) and non-verbal signs (music, sounds, evocations, architectural constructions). (Lefebvre, 1991: 47–8)

Every depository of nuclear material of any type now becomes a preposi-tioned military resource for terrorist action, whether it is leveraged as an element for offensive action where it sits, or when being moved to another site. This fact is also true of all explosive, noxious, or toxic chemical materials, as well as any bacterial and viral agents that could serve as weapons.

Yet the workings of liberal capitalist democracies do not offer many practicable counter-measures. An obvious possibility is radically restructur-ing the industrial ecologies, urban formations, and spatial practices which marshal the energy, material, and people needed to stage terrorist violence (Martin and Schumann, 1998). This is ironically the goal of isolated terrorists like Ted Kaczynski, but dismantling the logistical grids of trans-national corporate capitalism such that all of society would work on the scale of the Unabomber's backwoods shack in Montana or Al-Qaeda training camps in Afghanistan is not a viable option for most average consumers (Luke, 1999).

A second option is the securitization of commerce, deputizing corporate entities to guard those stocks of materiel, instabilities in systems, or resources for mayhem implied by their everyday ways of doing business. Yet this response smacks of excessive repression and regulation in liberal society, and it adds tremendous costs at the corporate bottom line that few companies are willing to pay. The handful of firms making, moving, and managing nuclear materials in the USA are used in providing such services, but even they are largely unproven with regard to their effectiveness in a serious assault after half a century of experience. Airports and airlines have failed to protect their employees and passengers in a number of incidents since the 1960s, which 9/11 only underscored with a vengeance. Hence, the government has intervened politically with the Transportation Security Agency and Patriot Act in 2002.

This response points to a third option: a new level of surveillance, policing, and control unknown since the mass mobilization of 1941–5. The Ashcroft Department of Justice and the Bush administration's Patriot Act unfortunately point toward an odd new *dirigisme* across the USA. By wrapping the cloak of national, municipal, and personal security around the predicates of liberal society, the fetish for individual freedom is dampened by casting state repression as risk management, constant surveillance as insurance, and aggressive policing as collective security. Amicality here is nationalized, class focused, ethnified, and ultimately racialized, creating identifiable foreign, poor, ethnic, and racial others whose enmity is always suspected and amity is never expected (Johnson, 1999; Kaldor, 1999; Luke, 1993). Trust evaporates in a fog of suspicion rather than war.

Such responses turn the "clash of civilizations" into a self-fulfilling prophecy, but it does not guarantee security (Ó Tuathail and Dalby, 1998). Before the Oklahoma City bombing and the Washington sniper attacks, most citizens in liberal capitalist society believed that "no one" or, at least, not "one of us" – that is, an ordinary American white man or black man like Timothy McVeigh or John Allen Muhammed – could have "done what they did." Nonetheless, they did, and even Patriot Act-driven anti-terrorist profiling, which turns every airline ticket holder, suburban gun owner, average motorist, or former serviceman into a ticking terrorist time bomb, cannot prevent new violent events from happening.

A fourth option is, in many respects, the obverse of the first. Instead of reshaping industrial ecologies to deconcentrate, disperse, and decenter dangerous embedded assets for terrorism, new programs of urban renewal and industrial design could perhaps create new systems of containment, stabilization, or control that would separate chemical, nuclear, or biological threats from population centers. By moving away from expectations of caution by amical co-producers to an enforcement of precautions that anticipates all probable inimical collaborators in an industrial ecology, supporting logistical systems would turn into fortifications against terrorist acts.

This move toward safer systems, however, would hyperpoliticize modern economies and societies, forcing every designer, manufacturer, and vendor to ask who is a friend or an enemy at each link of the commodity chain. While such a change is imaginable, it is mostly inconceivable that liberal society would accede to this level of militarized and politicized intervention into everyday personal life. The actuarial mindset of risk management alone probably would balance the number of gasoline tankers, nuclear fuel elements, noxious gases, and toxic material that moves all day, every day, down urban and suburban streets without incident against the one, two, or three that are turned into the instruments of atrocity. These calculations being made, the average consumer undoubtedly could choose to live with the minute prospects of their personal destruction against the immense costs of designing against vast collective endangerment to maintain the integrity of liberal capitalist democratic life.

Ironically, the fifth option for countering terrorism has the greatest possibilities for success but with the least likelihood of being implemented. This measure is, of course, undercutting the illiberal threat to liberal society by removing the source of grievance that drives the terrorists to terrorism. Liberal capitalist democracy is not to blame entirely for the attacks it has suffered, but then so too is it not totally blameless. Its markets mask many everyday forms of abuse in the economies and ecologies of the larger world system. At some point, Osama bin Laden, Timothy McVeigh, David Koresh, Mosvar Barakev, Mohammed Atta, Richard Reed, and John Allen Mohammed were not foundationally opposed to modernity. Hearing and responding to complaints before such enemies exploit the embedded assets of modern technics for terrorist destruction makes sense. Otherwise, anyone ready to repoliticize ordinary technics with twists of enmity can make war upon those with whom they hitherto coexisted amicably (Luke and Ó Tuathail, 1997).

These realities present liberal capitalist democracies – or, indeed, any established state – with difficult choices for defending against terrorist activities. As the events of 9/11, the anthrax attacks of autumn 2001, the Washington, DC sniper attacks of October 2002, and earlier attacks by Al-Qaeda in Africa, Yemen, New York City – or those of Aum Shinri Kyo or the Unabomber in the 1990s – show, it is impossible to defend against all terrorism. The principles of liberalism militate against repression and the commercial impulse behind daily standards of living requires continuing liberalism's industrial metabolisms, but these ways of life maintain inequalities at home and abroad that spark animosities leading to the attacks.

Conclusions

The conditions under which globalization unfolds are transforming the strategic disposition of cities. In many ways, national state formations are losing prominence (Luke, 1999; Walker, 1993). Less able to manage their own national economies, and less effective at controlling the movements of people at their borders, states are uncertain about how to react to intervene in transnational technostructures like the Internet, corporate intranets, global mediascapes, and new biomedical developments. So many nation-states leave the cities inside their boundaries to fend increasingly for themselves against the pressures of globalization. Even Washington after 9/11 is not making good on its solemn promises to the American people to defend them against the nebulous threats of terrorism. Most cities and towns are discovering that "homeland security" is turning into the latest version of "shift-and-shaft federalism" as the Bush administration promises the sky, but then largely blows hot air in funding local-level anti-terrorist defenses.

The "clash of civilizations" (Huntington, 1998) is proving to be a clash at citified sites, as the attacks in Bali, Nairobi, New York City, and Tokyo all have shown. Municipal locations are where non-places are concentrated. Hence, urban zones become highly vulnerable targets, because these sites are where it is easiest for terrorists to operate undetected or unhampered by security forces. Cities are also strategic sites because their large population concentrations anchor many corporate points of sale and service. Urban technostructures cluster together the highly structured technics required to sustain the logistics of everyday life. The flows of ideas, energy, materials, people, and goods pass through thousands of conduits, and the spatial practices intrinsic to their production and reproduction, are what urban civilization hangs upon (Rodrik, 1997). These sites for corporate activities, therefore, must be recognized as strategic sites for municipal defense and civic disruption. The non-places of airports, railway stations, highway interchanges, shipping centers, loading docks, and trucking terminals are technostructured terrains perfectly suited for anonymous movements, undetected mobilizations, and shocking murders. They shape and steer large numbers of targets with nowhere to hide, no place to run, and no way to resist.

Passengers, clients, users, or customers in such technostructures and non-places are hostages ready to be taken, tortured, or executed. The spatial practices of urban space make such realities inherent to such "places." In part, larger cultures of management teach passive compliance rather than active counter-defense; and, in part, accepted traditions of policing choreograph anti-terrorism as one-off arrests, dramatic hostage negotiation, or paramilitary rescue raids. Yet it is not clear that living in non-places is a social contract that should entail aggravating travel hassles punctuated by vicious SWAT unit raids. Still, advocates of globalistic values often reside in big cities, and the greatest signs of globalism's success are the peace and prosperity of the major metropolis (Bourdieu, 1998). For terrorists, successfully striking such sites shatters this peace and prosperity, while securing a maximum level of 24 × 7 media coverage for terrorist successes.

Le Corbusier declared that "houses are machines for living," and cities basically are clusters of the houses made as bigger machines for living. This insight is true, but what makes such houses machines for living are the big systems predicated upon living by, for, and with machines. These same machines, then, can be turned into machines for killing merely by shifting their operational parameters. The high modernist vision of cities as life enhancing is a twentieth-century picture of the city that actually is chrono-centric and wholly anti-ecological. Nothing lives without death preceding and following it, and 9/11 demonstrates how easily these built environments can become machines for killing as well as living.

This chapter has suggested how the non-places in large cities and logistical systems of urban–industrial settings can, and do, provide terrorists with the sites and means for engaging in destructive activities by the refunctioning of ordinary assumptions of technical action. Airports, bus terminals, cargo areas, railway stations, freeways, postal systems, and city streets are conduits for the ordinary traffic of settled urban life. Disrupting these logistical flows, misusing some major technical device, or directing everyday traffic are tactics for terrorists to make otherwise stable systems into dangerous devices. Nonetheless, the pervasiveness and embeddedness of such technostructures raise issues of personal liberty and civic engagement for the future, if their current politicization is fully implemented.

Part II

Urbicide and the Urbanization of Warfare

Introduction

Today, wars are fought not in trenches and fields, but in living rooms, schools, and supermarkets. (Barakat, 1998: 11)

The six chapters in Part II of this book together reflect on the meaning of urbanization, urbanism, and architecture for the prosecution of warfare and the maintenance of contemporary strategic power. In so doing, they delve deep into the way various militaries perceive, construct, and react to the urbanization of our planet. By exploring in depth the ways in which recent and ongoing wars have been shaped by perceptions of urban spaces – in Bosnia, Cambodia, the Occupied Territories, and Iraq – they do much to reveal the ways in which war is being *urbanized.*

At the same time, Part II also has much to say about the concept of urbicide – the deliberate killing, or denial, of the city. While the concept of urbicide has already generated a dispersed literature, this is the first time that a group of authors has collectively engaged with it (see Berman, 1996; Simmons, 2001; Coward, 2002; Safier, 2001; Prodanovic, 2002; Graham, 2003).

Martin Shaw, a sociologist of war, begins the discussion with a historical and sociological account of the connections between urbicide and the more familiar concept of genocide within what he calls the "new wars of the city." Through a historical discussion of a variety of wars (from the Chinese and Cambodian revolutions through to the Yugoslav civil wars) Shaw argues that cities and urban civilian populations are often the victims and targets of such wars, which are commonly driven by a virulent anti-urbanism. However, he suggests that the urbicide that often results can never be simply separated from other strategies of annihilation (genocide, ethnocide, and politicide). Shaw argues also that cities never suffer alone; their misery tends to be bound up with the wider immiseration of whole societies – urban and rural alike. Thus, Shaw suggests, urbicide needs to be seen as an element of wider, genocidal war.

The concept of urbicide also provides the focus for chapter 8, by the political scientist Martin Coward. Coward provides a detailed analysis of the central role played by urbicide within the 1992–5 Bosnian war. In contrast to Martin Shaw, he stresses that urbicidal acts were a distinct feature of that war. To Coward, much of the violence in that war was carefully orchestrated to destroy architectural and urbanistic spaces that were symbols of the relative ethnic heterogeneity and cosmopolitanism of the targeted cities (especially Sarajevo and Mostar). While much violence was genocidal in nature – aiming to extinguish particular ethnic groups through "ethnic cleansing" – the assaults on the collective spaces and symbols of city life were, to Coward, a critical, but neglected, aspect of the Bosnian war. Thus, Coward urges that the deliberate destruction of built environments and cultural heritage – far from being side effects or "collateral damage" – are often the carefully produced products of purposive action. In contrast to Shaw, therefore, Coward argues that urbicidal warfare deserves stronger consideration in legal definitions of war crimes.

In chapter 9 the architect Eyal Weizman provides the first of two essays analyzing the urban dimensions of the Palestinian–Israeli conflict. Weizman focuses on the *developmental* side of Israel's tightening grip on the Occupied Territories. He argues that the Israeli strategy in the Occupied Territories centers on three-dimensional control over the totality of space, infrastructure, the environment, and sub- and above-surface domains. To Weizman, the Israeli state's detailed shaping of massive "security" barriers, bulldozed "buffer zones," fortified new Jewish settlements, new Jewish-only roads, and besieged Palestinian cities, provides a tightening urban matrix of Israeli control. This creates "facts on the ground" which undermine the possibility of a viable or contiguous Palestinian state – an attempt to overcome the effects of the rapid urban and demographic growth that is underway in the territories. Thus, Weizman clearly demonstrates the ways in which the Israeli state is mobilizing planning and architecture as powerful military and geopolitical tools in this most intractable – and most urban – of wars.

In chapter 10 the urbanist Stephen Graham parallels Weizman's analysis by addressing the ways in which the Israeli state seeks to complement its efforts at *construction* (new settlements, barriers, and roads) with the *destruction* and forced *demodernization* of the urban and infrastructural assets of the Palestinians. Like Coward, Graham invokes the concept of urbicide to interpret the increasing centrality of premeditated urban destruction to the Israeli–Palestinian conflict. In particular, Graham analyzes Operation Defensive Shield – the Israeli Defense Force's unprecedented incursions into the Gaza strip and West Bank in the spring of 2002 (which have continued, in various guises, ever since, notably in Rafah in Spring 2004).

As an example of urbicide, Graham focuses in detail on the events preceding the Battle of Jenin, which ultimately led to the bulldozing of the center of the Jenin refugee camp between April 3–16, 2002. While this operation was justified by the Sharon government as a means of destroying the "terrorist infrastructure" that sustained the devastating suicide bomb campaign in Israeli cities, Graham argues it was, in fact, emblematic of a much broader campaign of deliberate urbicide. Extensive evidence exists to show that the Israeli forces did everything they could to demodernize Palestinian urban society.

In chapter 11 our attention turns to the blurring of urban military, law-enforcement, and surveillance practices across the contemporary world. Planning academic Robert Warren provides a groundbreaking review of the ways in which the "war on terrorism" is serving to blur the line separating civilian law enforcement efforts to control and curtain urban anti-globalization protests and full-scale military urban operations. Warren argues that set-piece anti-globalization battles like Seattle (1999) and Genoa (2001) provide a kind of transnational "spatial chess" where "pop-up armies" engage with protestors. He suggests also that, post 9/11,

the meetings of global economic decision-makers have been removed from
city centers to remote, ultra-secure, retreats. Nonetheless, Warren identifies
a worrying erosion of the freedom to protest against the inequities of
neoliberal globalization, or even to simply assemble crowds in urban
spaces, justified through the discourses of the war on terror.

Chapter 12 adds the perspectives of a military urban researcher. Alice
Hills is one of a growing number of professional military urban researchers
who are employed to support the efforts of Western armed forces to adjust
their doctrines, strategies, and technologies to confront the urbanization of
the terrain within which they are being asked to enter combat, occupation,
and humanitarian missions. Hills analyzes in detail the ways in which
Western military doctrine, tactics, and technologies are being reorganized
to face the urbanization of terrain. She develops an instrumental (rather
than a social scientific) focus on urban military tactics. In so doing,
she reviews some recent experiences, as the casualty-averse militaries of
industrial, Northern nation-states have attempted to invade, control,
or subdue various types of urban insurrection and resistance (Chechnya,
Kosovo, Afghanistan, Iraq, the Occupied Territories). Finally, Hills outlines in detail the ways in which cities are "special" from a Western military
point of view. She concludes that the tendency among Western
military strategists to seek expensive technical fixes to operational military
problems will not necessarily make military "urban operations" any easier
or more "successful" – even from the point of view of the military.

7

New Wars of the City: Relationships of "Urbicide" and "Genocide"

Martin Shaw

Introduction

This is a chapter of two halves: in the first part, I explore the historical role of cities in warfare as a means of framing the contemporary targeting of cities in war and political violence, and the emergence of "urbicide." In the second part, I show how the targeting of urban populations is not separate from other kinds of violence. Targeting urbanity has gone hand in hand with campaigns against ethnic groups and indeed against rural, peasant populations. This insight leads into a general argument about the classification and understanding of political violence and its relationship to war. I argue that "urbicide" (like "ethnocide," "politicide," and other "cides" that have been identified) is not a separate phenomenon from genocide, but one of its forms. From this I make a final move: genocide itself is not separate from war, but a specific form of war that must be understood together with it.

War and the City: Historical Perspectives

War is commonly understood as a phenomenon of one form of spatial organization, the territorial nation-state. And yet the state was not always nation-based, and control of *urban* space has often been pivotal to the survival of states. In the origins of the modern *polis*, city and state were one. War in Greek civilization was a struggle of city-states, and although warfare often took place outside the city, the urban center itself was the ultimate prize. The Roman Empire, based on the greatest city-state of all, built fortified cities as centers of its far-flung power, bulwarks of civilization, defended against barbarian hordes. The sack of Rome itself symbolized its defeat and the descent into fractured political authority and social precariousness.

For more than a thousand years afterwards, state power remained fragmentary and its borders uncertain, and the city retained a special role: in medieval Europe a fortified space, the ruler's only certain territory. The city was the redoubt that the ruler could be reasonably sure of defending when more remote territories were invaded, under the control of rebellious lords, or plagued by robbers and bandits. The siege remained the ultimate moment of war, when the center fell.

Modernity transformed the relationship of cities and states. States became "bordered power containers" (Giddens, 1985b) within which rule was consolidated by "surveillance." Borders became demarcations of violence: now the state's whole territory would be defended. The state was defined by nation, not city, and its whole population, even in border regions, became part of the national "defense." So although cities grew in wealth and population, their special military significance changed. Modern cities surpassed historic fortified boundaries; fortifications fell into irrelevance or decay. New industrial cities grew from insignificant villages. The gap between city and country remained, but it was no longer a military border.

Cities did not lose all military significance. Capitals still remained political and administrative if not military centers of power, and their capture remained the ultimate symbol of conquest and national survival. The successive falls of Paris, for example, in the Franco-Prussian and the two world wars, epitomized France's repeated humiliations by Germany. The fall of Madrid was a decisive defeat for Spain's Republic in the Civil War. The defense of Stalingrad, in contrast, was a powerful symbol of Soviet defiance.

Industrial cities were also of great strategic significance as engines of industrialized war. But cities were no longer built for military defense; increasingly, they were militarily indefensible. Fortifications were mostly not fixed structures, and where they were – as in the Maginot Line – they were not around cities. Cities were increasingly open to attack: the new techniques of total warfare brought special dangers. The tank, developed for use in the open battlefields of the Western front, was an instrument of indiscriminate destruction in urban settings, although its mobility could be hampered in narrow streets. The warplane, which first flew over the trenches in 1914–18, was recognized as an instrument of urban mass terror long before its emblematic use at Guernica (1937). The full potential for urban killing was demonstrated in the misnamed "strategic bombing" of Dresden, Hamburg, and Tokyo. The atomic bomb completed this new vulnerability of the city: whole conurbations and populations were destroyed instantaneously at Hiroshima and Nagasaki.

At the same time, new and vile forms of urban life were developed in the Nazi genocide: the Jewish ghettos were grotesque caricatures of city life; the extermination camps, special cities of death. The relationship between "deliberate" genocide and "strategic" mass murder is interesting. With a single bomb, any city could become an instant Auschwitz. In the nuclear age, the city was no longer so important as the industrial engine or political motor of war, but urban areas remained strategic targets as NATO and the Warsaw Pact developed computerized maps of doom. With the intercontinental missile, the capacity to simultaneously destroy *all* major centers of urban life became a symbol of the degeneration of war. Nuclear war was no longer simply genocidal, but produced "mutually assured destruction" or "exterminism" (Thompson, 1982), which threatened human life as such. In response, peace movements persuaded councils to declare cities across the world "nuclear-free zones."

Fortunately, the nuclear threat to cities has remained hypothetical since 1945, but cities have remained highly vulnerable to the more specialized aerial attack of new computer-targeted weaponry. US cruise missiles and bombers with conventional payloads have "selectively" interpolated military destruction into urban life in places like Baghdad and Belgrade. Although eschewing the comprehensive destruction of, for example, the Russian assault on Groznyy, they have nevertheless killed thousands of civilians and damaged the infrastructure on which urban life depends.

The Guerrilla Threat to the City

Guerrilla war has posed a parallel threat to cities. Although romanticized as a "revolution in the revolution" (Debray 1967), it involved a reaction against the classic urban–democratic model of revolution, in which middle- and working-class city-dwellers challenged authoritarian and aristocratic rulers. The socialist and communist traditions initially represented extensions of this model: St. Petersburg (1917) and Barcelona (1936) followed the pattern that originated in Paris (1789). Urban revolt provided leadership to peasant uprisings. However, in China and elsewhere, Stalinized communist parties renounced this model in favor of guerrilla struggle, in which a militarized party mobilized peasant support to surround the cities, entering them as conquerors. This authoritarian form of revolutionary change was hostile to the plural, creative dynamics of modern city life.

The anti-urban bias of resulting communist regimes was evident in some of their most destructive phases. In Mao's Cultural Revolution of the 1960s, urban "intellectuals" – artists, teachers, officials – were targeted by orchestrated mass violence, and often punished by being deported to the countryside where their bodies and in some cases minds were broken by crude physical labor. The Cambodian Khmer Rouge carried this anti-urbanism to even viler extremes, deporting the entire population of cities and exterminating them in an anti-urban genocide. The city was seen as a source of moral pollution, to be "cleansed" by contact with the peasantry: the critique of urban "decadence" had much in common with Nazi hatred of Berlin's cosmopolitan urban culture.

In the North, however, with the lifting of the nuclear threat, the city has ceased to be a symbolic place of death, and represents life: the pluralism, diversity, and creativity of modern civilization. Military bases are typically located in rural areas, leaving the city as a demilitarized zone. Although militaries consume the scientific and technical knowledge produced in urban universities, these functions are almost hidden in institutions with a civilian ethos. In "post-military" Western society (Shaw, 1991), educated youth mostly escape military service even where (as in Germany) this still exists. In professional armies, ordinary recruits no longer come from urban elites, although they may be urban workers. However, the Western officer of the future may be an urbanized "soldier–scholar" (Moskos, Williams, and Segal, 2000).

Urban culture is still saturated with military symbols, but the cult of heroic forces has given way to the fascination of the high-tech weapon in a commercialized "armament culture" (Luckham, 1984). In "spectator sport" militarism (Mann, 1988), the modern urban dweller participates in mediated violence, as a consumer of images. Viewers know that real violence still occurs in wars (Shaw, 1996), but they expect that their own sons and brothers will not be killed. Governments calculate their strategic options on the basis of "risk-transfer militarism" (Shaw, 2003), transferring death risks from urban dwellers in the West to urbanites as well as peasants in peripheral regions.

Anti-Urbanism in the New Wars

While the city becomes demilitarized, new forms of violence within and against the city have made it the focus of the "new wars" of the 1990s (Kaldor, 1999). This gives a political flavor to the wider urban phenomena of gang violence and criminality. Thus, violence between supporters of the African National Congress and Inkatha in the Zulu areas of Natal, which reached its peak during South Africa's transition to democracy, mobilized young, unemployed urban men. However, much violence of the "township wars" was actually in rural areas, where supporters of the ethnically based Inkatha targeted the more urban, multi-ethnic, civic–nationalist ANC.

An anti-urban element is a common characteristic of "new wars," even where they mobilize urban discontents. Ethnic–nationalist political movements often draw on rural and small-town hatred of the city. They are often led by intellectuals like the leader of the Serbian genocide in Bosnia, Radovan Karadzic, who shared but remained uncomfortable with urban cosmopolitanism. Their support is often strongest in relatively isolated rural areas like the "Krajina" stronghold of Serbian nationalism in Croatia and the Herzegovinan fiefdom of Croatian nationalism in Bosnia-Herzegovina.

Pluralist, non-ethnic democratic politics is nearly always strongest in larger urban areas and rooted in their character. Education, intermarriage, and cultural and media diversity led far more people in Sarajevo than in rural areas to identify themselves non-ethnically, as Bosnians or Yugoslavs rather than Muslims, Serbs, or Croats, in the last Yugoslav census. As the power of nationalist authoritarianism has waned, it has done so first in the large urban areas – both Croatia's Franjo Tudjman and Serbia's Slobodan Milosevic annulled democratic local elections in their capital cities won by the opposition, to hang on to power.

The common misunderstanding of genocide as the destruction of one ethnic group by another was clearly brought into question by the anti-urban dimension of the genocide in Cambodia, but the mistake has been repeated in analyses of Yugoslavia. These, like the Nazi war against the Jews, were explicitly genocidal wars, in which civilian groups were as much the enemy as opposing states or armies. But there were in fact two sides to the genocides: in "ethnic cleansing" (a term which originates with Serbian nationalists and should not be used as a neutral description), populations were forcibly expelled from their homes, land, villages, and towns, on grounds of their ethnicity. But genocidists also aimed to destroy plural, multi-ethnic urban communities, which equally offended against their ethnic–national ideals. Sarajevo – historically a center of all the major religions, of cohabitation and tolerance, of education, intellectual and artistic life, of high intermarriage and Yugoslav identity – was anathema to the Serbian and Croatian nationalists. The two sides of genocide came together as "ethnic cleansers" saw educated urban elites, within "enemy" ethnic communities, as their first target in each town and village they conquered. Teachers, officials, and other "intellectuals" were selected for deportation and killing.

While the Bosnian war can be considered a war of the city, in the sense that the viability of plural, democratic urban life was a key issue, it was also a war within the city. Even where, as in Yugoslavia, the central protagonists were state forces, a key role was played by private gangs. Raiding parties, led by notorious urban criminals like Arkan, were the front-runners of genocide. In both Croatia and Bosnia, these "unofficial" warriors often initiated the indiscriminate killing, burning, and rape of conquered communities.

Everywhere in the Yugoslav wars, indeed, private gain was in the forefront of genocide. Nationalist killing gangs were urban looters on a big scale, "weekend warriors" returning home with someone else's TV or video recorder. Individuals and families annexed the farms and houses of dispossessed neighbors, just as the nationalist movements annexed whole towns and villages. On the borders between territories, refugees and aid convoys were robbed; it was common for people to be charged extortionate fees to flee to safer areas.

The industrial city fell into decay as a functioning economic unit: industries ceased to operate. Only tiny fractions of prewar economic output and employment were maintained. Urban economies were damaged more than those of many safer rural areas, where subsistence and local market farming remained. Even cities that were saved from destruction or genocidal occupation fell apart, therefore, under economic pressures from the wars. There was large-scale emigration, especially of younger, more educated urbanites, who were replaced by refugees "cleansed" from small towns and villages.

These experiences of new urban warfare close to the heart of Europe have been repeated, often in even worse forms, throughout the Caucasus, and in large parts of Africa. Sarajevo, for all its human and physical degradations, continued to function as an urban community. The same cannot so easily be said of Mogadishu, where modern urban life more or less disintegrated and the gangs and warlords reigned supreme.

Violence Against the Peasantry

This discussion has shown that, throughout history, the city has been at the center of warfare. The concentration of human populations in larger settlements provided resources for rulers and would-be rulers to wage war. At the same time, however, it provided highly vulnerable targets for warfare. In the modern city, the balance has shifted overwhelmingly in favor of vulnerability. Huge populations, whose lives are more dependent than ever before on sophisticated technical systems, are easy targets for the killing power and physical destructiveness of advanced military technology (Luke, this volume). Moreover, what the city represents is also at stake.

In these senses, contemporary wars are wars of the city, threatened by social forces which deny the vital impulses of modern urban civilization. It is tempting, therefore, to emphasize this element as a distinctive phenomenon, "urbicide." I shall return to this concept and its relationship to others in the following section. However, I want to underline the important historical counterpoints to such a line of argument. Very simply, attacks on urban centers and urban values have only ever been *one* dimension of each phase of warfare. For every city besieged in premodern wars, many fields and farms were also devastated. If plural urban centers constitute a particular provocation to contemporary nationalists, so too do populations of the "enemy" ethnic groups. Anti-urbanism has never been a unique or predominant goal of warfare, but has always been an element in a larger enterprise – in which other aims have usually been in the forefront.

To concretize this argument, we have only to match anti-peasant and anti-rural campaigns, often within the same episodes of violence or by the same perpetrators, to anti-urban cases. For urban rulers, the peasantry has always been an object of mistrust. Rulers of historic empires frequently saw the danger of rebellion among peasant populations. In modern invasions, peasant populations have often been brutally targeted with concentrated violence, rape, and pillage. The Japanese armies that perpetrated the Rape of Nanking, China's capital, also systematically razed the countryside, destroyed villages, and slaughtered peasants. (Their response to Mao's idea of the peasantry as the "sea" in which the communists swam was the chilling order, "drain the sea.") The Nazi forces that invaded the Soviet Union and flattened its cities also torched village after village to deny the basis of Soviet resistance. American forces bombed Hanoi, but they also napalmed the countryside, obliterating villages and forcing their inhabitants into "strategic hamlets."

We should also consider the targeted anti-peasant violence by the same totalitarian regimes that epitomize anti-urbanism. Soviet power began, of course, in the time of Lenin and Trotsky, with a struggle to prevail against the mass of the Russian peasantry, during the Civil War. It turned simultaneously against the pluralism and diversity of the urban working-class parties and unions, and as centralized bureaucratic power was consolidated, against the intelligentsia too. Stalin then turned back on the peasantry in his infamous "liquidation of the kulaks" of 1929–30, the "terror famine" and the forced collectivization that killed millions and wrecked Soviet agriculture later in the decade. (Conquest, 1986).

In China, where the anti-urban bias of communism has been widely recognized, there were equally destructive anti-peasant policies. Mao Zedong's own terror famine, the Great Leap Forward of 1959–61, is only now becoming as well known as the anti-urban terror of the later Cultural Revolution. Although this was possibly the largest single episode of mass death in the twentieth century, with as many as 30 million or even 40 million victims, it was less well known precisely because of the greater ease, for a totalitarian regime, of hiding rural than urban suffering (Becker, 1996). In Cambodia, the Khmer Rouge did not just empty the cities: in their attempt to remake the people they also systematically relocated the rural population and wiped out the kin networks and traditions of the peasants. Peasant ways of life and beliefs were just as much a target as urban ways and beliefs. The party aimed to destroy *all* preexisting social organization and values (Kiernan, 1996). Further complicating these stories is the fact that national and ethnic identities were also targeted. Obviously, the Japanese and German invasions were directed, respectively, against the Chinese and Slav peoples. And for Stalin, the terror famine was also about destroying Ukrainian national identity; Mao's campaign was also aimed against Tibetan national consciousness; Pol Pot specifically targeted the Vietnamese minority.

Urbicide in Context

How then do we understand the significance of anti-urbanism in the context of such complex, multiple targeting in war and genocide? This question takes us directly into the conceptual minefield that is the current state of classification and understanding of political violence. Martin Coward (in this volume) deals with this question by proposing that "there is a certain kinship between urbicide and genocide." This idea of affinity suggests two overlapping or related, but ultimately discrete, phenomena. They suggest a definition of urbicide that emphasizes its distinctiveness from genocide: it "entails the destruction of buildings and urban fabric as elements of urbanity. Buildings are destroyed because they are the condition of possibility of urbanity. Since urbanity is constituted by heterogeneity, urbicide comprises the destruction of the conditions of possibility of heterogeneity."

This definition de-emphasizes the central feature of anti-urbanism in sieges like that of Sarajevo: violence directed at the population as such, in order to destroy their resistance and to undermine the multicultural centers of the independent Bosnian state. I propose, in contrast, that we understand both the destruction of buildings and the targeting of urbanity as *elements* of genocidal war, alongside the attack on Bosnian statehood and on opposing ethnic national identities. *All* of these are explained by the aim of Serbian nationalists to create an ethnically defined state in much of Bosnia, and their determination to destroy the power and ability to resist of the enemy state and enemy population. Thus, urbicide was part of the *war* that also involved *genocide*.

How then do we understand the relationships between these? Martin Coward (this volume) suggests that:

> the meaning of "genocide" is played out in *each* and *every* death, *each and every time*. Since genocide is enacted in each and every death it expresses a relation between what is destroyed and the meaning of destruction that is other than the simple death of the individual. It is integral to our understand-

ing of "genocide" that we recognize what "it" is that is destroyed, and the meaning of the destruction. In genocide "it" is a member of a national or ethnic group and the destruction has the meaning of the eradication of this group.

However, if we define anti-urbanism in terms of its targeting of urban *communities*, rather than separating (rather artificially) the "destruction of urban fabric" from the destruction of people and social relations, then the "it" that is destroyed in urbicide is *not* so distinct from that destroyed in genocide. On the contrary, to the extent that the Serbian forces aimed simultaneously to destroy *both* the plural, cosmopolitan *and* the "ethnic" Bosnian-Muslim characters of Sarajevo, it is very difficult to separate urbicide and genocide (in the conventional understanding of the latter). It is not so much a question of affinity as of intimate interconnection between these aims, both in Serbian policy and ideology, on the one hand, and in Sarajevan experience, on the other. The perpetrators combine the two ideas in a single policy and course of action; the victims experience the two more or less simultaneously. Who was to say, when someone was shot by a sniper, or a mosque was destroyed by bombardment, whether this represented urbicide or genocide, or both together?

This argument draws our attention to two central features of war and political violence: first, perpetrators often have *multiple* targets, and secondly, victims often experience violence and killing as relatively *indiscriminate* rather than as the heavily categorized violence of perpetrator ideologies (and legal or academic classification). Military campaigns target organized state and military enemies, but they also often target various civilian groups as enemies. When campaigns are translated into action, they often go beyond the pseudo-rationality of political–ideological targeting. So in any given war or campaign a number of different things may be going on simultaneously. People who are tortured, wounded, or killed by armed violence, or who see their homes, towns, and symbolic buildings destroyed, do not necessarily know precisely, still less care, which of the goals of political and military leaders is being worked out in their suffering. For them, the violence is often "senseless."

The aim of social theory must be, therefore, to grasp the unities of the relationships and processes of violence and destruction, rather than to counterpose different dimensions of these actions/experiences as categorical opposites. This task requires both a general theoretical reunification of the theory of war and genocide, and specific historical understandings of the relationships in particular episodes. In the remainder of this chapter I shall make some proposals, based on my argument in *War and Genocide* (Shaw, 2003).

War, Genocide, and Their Many "Cides"

The major theoretical problem of the burgeoning academic study of genocide is its categorical separation of genocide from war. This separation goes back to the origins of the international legal definition of genocide, in the 1948 Convention. The victors of World War II wished to define the heinous crimes of the principal losers (Nazi Germany and Imperial Japan) in targeting civilian populations as such. Genocide was thus defined as certain kinds of "acts committed with intent to destroy, in whole or in part, a national, ethnical, racial, or religious group, as such." The acts included not only "Killing members of the group," or "Causing serious bodily or mental harm," but also "Deliberately inflicting on the group conditions of life calculated to bring about its physical destruction," "Imposing measures intended to prevent births within the group," and "Forcibly transferring children of the group to another group" (Roberts and Guelff, 2000: 180–4).

Genocide as a legal concept was an extension of the previous prohibitions on the killing of civilians in war, and the recognition that these had been breached in ever more systematic ways. Genocide was one of the three main categories of crime in war that were prosecuted at Nuremberg, alongside "crimes against humanity" and "war crimes," and this has remained the pattern in the cases brought before the International Criminal Tribunal for Former Yugoslavia. However, the concept of genocide as the destruction of a civilian social group *as such* opened the way to separating genocide from war. This suited the World War II Allies, who wished to emphasize the difference between the killing of civilians through bombing (Dresden, Hiroshima) and the genocide of peoples (Auschwitz). However, as the world war has receded from memory, at the beginning of the twenty-first century there is an even more powerful impetus to separate even its paradigmatic genocide, the Nazi Holocaust, from the war itself. "Holocaust" and "genocide" studies are mushrooming as fields distinct from, and largely unconnected to, war studies.

These tendencies involve considerable distortion of the historical context in which the idea of genocide emerged. The Nazis' campaign against the Jews was waged alongside, and as part of, their wars against the Slav peoples of Poland and the Soviet Union, as well as their more conventional wars against their state enemies. These were, from the start, not separate events, but fully intertwined campaigns: the entrapment of Jewry in the ghettos was part of the larger forced dispersal of the Polish population following the 1939 invasion. The organized, large-scale murder of Jews began in the invasion of the USSR alongside the killings of communists, prisoners of war, and other civilians. Only in the second half of the war was the industrial extermination of Jews, Gypsies, and others carried out in the camp system, fed by railway from all over occupied Europe.

The international legal concept was sophisticated in that it saw the intentional *destruction* of a target group *as such* as the aim of genocide, and recognized that variable extents of actual killing or other physical destruction would accompany this. However, the phrase "in whole or in part" allowed great ambiguity and did not clarify the relationship between killing and genocide. The international concept was also flawed from its inception in specifying "national, ethnical, racial, or religious groups." As critics pointed out during the drafting, this excluded political groups (and social classes), prime targets of Soviet mass murder (the USSR was of course a major contributor to the drafting process) (Kuper, 1981; Schabas, 2000). Certainly, from a theoretical point of view, there is no principled reason to define the destruction of one kind of social group as a supreme crime and of another as not.

This is a central flaw in the legal idea of genocide and means that for social scientific use, the concept must be substantially adapted. One strategy is to develop a more elaborate scheme of classification, in which the notion of genocide as a specific type of mass killing is complemented by many other categories of violence. An example is the table developed by Michael Mann (2004) to classify the "extent of cleansing and violence in intergroup relations." He cross-tabulates extents of "cleansing" and violence, ranging from the absence of both (multiculturalism and toleration) to genocide as the most extreme form of both, combining "premeditated mass killing" with "total cleansing." In his schema, certain types of action are classified as types of *murderous cleansing*: e.g., *ethnocide* is "total cleansing" accompanied by "unpremeditated mass deaths," while *politicide* and *classicide* are forms of "partial cleansing" accompanied by "premeditated mass killing."

Mann's table, which altogether has 18 boxes, is an interesting way of separating out different levels and types of violence and expulsion. However, it has three major problems. First, the central role it gives to "cleansing" as a social scientific category is troubling because it legitimates the ideal of racial or ethnic purification. Second, it presents violence as a question of the relations *between* social groups, rather than as something perpetrated by organized, armed bodies against largely unarmed civilian populations. (Mann wishes to emphasize the wider social participation in genocides: but this definition obscures the central role of organized political power.) Third, Mann's restriction of genocide to total expulsion combined with premeditated killing legitimates the idea of genocide as a maximum case, separated both from "unintentional" mass death among ethnic groups and the destruction of other types of groups such as social classes.

Mann's definitions are in accord with the international legal concept of genocide in separating the destruction of ethnic from political and class groups, as separate categories. (They would clearly permit the addition of *urbicide* as a distinctive type, too.) However, although his categories clearly incorporate, *ad hoc*, the links between war and "murderous cleansing" – " 'Callous' war, civil war & class war & revolutionary projects" and "Exemplary & civil war repression, systematic reprisals" are two of his categories – this classification obscures some crucial relationships. It presents the "cides" – genocide, ethnocide, politicide, and classicide – all as forms of "cleansing" rather than of war.

Mann's classification thus has several weaknesses. It presents the *expulsion* rather than the *destruction* of a social group as the common characteristic of these various types of political violence. It makes it difficult to see processes of simultaneous destruction of *different* kinds of social group (ethnic, class, urban, etc.) in a common frame. It makes it difficult to see various "levels" of destruction as part of the same kind of process, and it makes it more difficult to see how closely the destruction of *social groups* is related to the destruction of *armed enemies* in violent conflicts. And it separates types of political violence against civilians from war, although the forms of violence under discussion are generally perpetrated in the context of war or by heavily militarized regimes (Shaw, 2003: table 2.2).

The theoretical alternative that is proposed here is to go back to the understanding of genocide as an extension of the wider illegitimate violence against civilians in war. My approach adopts the core meaning of genocide in the UN definition, viz. the *destruction* of social groups by organized, armed actors, centrally involving *killing* and other physical and mental harm, but rejects the inappropriate secondary specification of the types of social groups (as "national, ethnical, racial, or religious"). In these terms, then, the destruction of classes, political groups, and plural urban populations are as much genocide as is the destruction of ethnic groups. Indeed, since these groups are often targeted together, as we have seen in the cases of the Serbians, the Nazis, and the Khmer Rouge, it is essential for social understanding to explore the processes that lead to this common victimization. It is also crucial to explore the relations between these different dimensions in the experience of victims.

Genocide differs from war in general in that war is, ideal-typically, the conflict of two (or more) organized, armed groups; genocide is an illegitimate form of war in which an organized, armed group defines a largely unarmed civilian population as its *enemy*, to be *destroyed* by force. The link between the two is the tendency for war to degenerate from the contest of armed groups, by the extension of violence to the civilian population linked to the armed enemy. *Degenerate war* is the use of armed force against a civilian population as the extension of military struggle (e.g., the Allied bombing of civilians in order to pressurize the Axis powers into surrender). It will be evident how narrow is the dividing line between this kind of war on civilians and genocide, where a civilian population (e.g., the Jews) is the enemy as such. (For full definitions, see Shaw, 2003: table 2.3.)

The matter is confused by the fact that genocide usually occurs in the context of war: so that, overall, the Nazis' campaign in 1939–45 and the Serbians' in 1991–5 could accurately be described as *genocidal war*, combining war against armed enemies with genocide of civilian groups. Civilian groups (Jews, Muslims, urban populations) were enemies in their own right, to be murderously "cleansed"; but they were also linked to organized armed enemies. To grasp either the war or the genocide, we need to understand the two as parts of the same process.

Conclusion

This chapter has argued that, while historically cities have always been implicated in wars and specific anti-urban violence has been a feature of recent warfare, it does not make sense to separate urbicide (or other "cides") from genocide, or genocide from war, in genocidal war. The argument about urbicide has thus led into a general argument about the nature of genocide and its relationships to war. We can only understand any of these types as the way in which intentional violent *actions* by the perpetrators combined with the *experiences* of victims in the process of particular episodes. Urbicide is a form of genocide, the fundamentally illegitimate form of modern war in which a civilian population as such is targeted for destruction by armed force.

8

Urbicide in Bosnia

Martin Coward

Introduction: Ethnonationalism and the Violent Destruction of Bosnia

The 1992–5 Bosnian war was characterized by a sustained assault on the civilian population of Bosnia, their culture(s), and their urban environment(s). This intentional violence against the civilian population of Bosnia captured, and defined, the political imagination of those who observed, or intervened in, the conflict. Indeed, the emergence of "ethnic cleansing" onto the agenda of international politics during this conflict represented a recognition that the violence witnessed in the former Yugoslavia was directed primarily at civilian populations. Some of those observing, or involved in, the conflict, contended that so-called "ethnic cleansing" comprised an instance of genocide perpetrated, largely, though not exclusively, by the Bosnian Serbs upon Bosnian Muslims, or Bosniacs (Sells, 1996: 10).[1] Despite the politically contested nature of the definition of the violence against the civilians of Bosnia – whether or not one refers to it as ethnic cleansing, or as genocide – a dynamic can be seen in the violence (Campbell, 1998a: 109–10; 2002: 154–7).

Raphael Lemkin defined genocide as "coordinated plan of different actions aiming at the destruction of essential foundations of national groups, with the aim of annihilating the groups themselves" (Lemkin, 1944: 79). The 1948 Genocide convention defines genocide as "intent to destroy, in whole or in part, a national, ethnical, racial, or religious group" (Andreopoulos, 1984: 229–33; see Shaw, this volume). "Ethnic cleansing" is characterized by this genocidal logic insofar as it represents an attempt to erase from a given territory national/ethnical/racial/religious groups that, through their existence, contest the claims of ethnonationalists to territorial self-determination on the basis of ethnic/national homogeneity. That is, insofar as ethnonationalists can erase plural identities from territory then they can claim it as their own. The Bosnian war was thus constituted by a genocidal violence – (euphemistically) defined by those who intervened in, or observed, the conflict as "ethnic cleansing" – that comprised the removal or erasure of all heterogeneous identities.

Ethnonationalism is predicated on such political violence. Its program of the erasure of heterogeneous identities demands violence due to the heterogeneity of existence. This was particularly the case in Bosnia, a country with an evident historical record of heterogeneity and plurality. As Robert Hayden notes:

> Heterogeneity was concentrated in the central part of the territory of Yugoslavia [in particular] the republic of Bosnia-Herzegovina [and those areas bordering it] . . . In these parts of Yugoslavia, the idea that the Yugoslav peoples could not live peacefully together was empirical nonsense. It was perhaps because these regions constituted living disproof of [ethno]nationalist ideologies that [they] have been the major theatres of . . . war. (Hayden, 1996: 788)

Hayden cites the degree of "intermarriage" in Bosnia, and the number of citizens preferring to classify themselves as Yugoslav rather than by ethnic origin, as evidence of this heterogeneity in Bosnia (Hayden, 1996: 788–90).

Ethnonationalism works specifically, then, to destroy (and thus deny) heterogeneity, in order to advance a claim for national self-determination predicated on ethnic homogeneity. The dynamic of ethnonationalism is threefold: political discourses legitimate the notion that heterogeneity is both threatening and unnatural, elaborate grievances felt by an ethnic group purportedly as a consequence of this heterogeneity, and deny a history of heterogeneous coexistence; political violence is mobilized to destroy heterogeneity and legitimate claims to territorial self-determination; ethnic homogeneity is consolidated and the notion of ethnic separateness is thus naturalized.

This dynamic is readily observable in the violence against the civilian population of Bosnia. However, violence was not only directed against the population of Bosnia, but also against their culture(s) and urban environment(s). While the violence against people captured the political imagination of those who intervened in, or observed, the conflict, it was only one aspect of the ethnonationalist dynamic. Ethnic cleansers have a genocidal impulse to destroy the record of coexistence with other ethnic/national groups. In Bosnia it was necessary, therefore, to deconstruct a heterogeneous and plural culture in order to destroy all record of coexistence (Riedlmayer, 1994: 16). This plural/heterogeneous culture was not just represented in mixed marriages, neighbors of different ethnic origin, or those who declared themselves Yugoslavs rather than Bosnian-Serb/

Croat/Muslim. It was also represented in the material cultures within which everyday lives were lived.

That this is the case can be seen in the manner in which ethnonationalists targeted the cultural symbols of Bosnia. These symbols were not merely symbols of specific ethnic groups, but also of a heterogeneous Bosnian culture: a culture that spoke not just of the presence of a specific ethnic group, but of historical coexistence (plurality/heterogeneity) being the norm in Bosnia. This destruction of culture can be seen in a number of events, including (though not restricted to) the destruction of the National Library (plate 8.1) and Oriental Institute in Sarajevo, the shelling of the National Museum in Sarajevo, the destruction of the Stari Most (or Old Bridge) in Mostar (plate 8.2), and the widespread destruction of mosques and churches across Bosnia (Riedlmayer, 1994, 16–19; Coward, 2002: 29–33).[2] Insofar as these symbolic buildings remained standing, they belied the ethnonationalist notion that ethnic/national groups could not (and thus should not) live together. This destruction was, therefore, an integral part of the dynamic of political violence in the 1992–5 Bosnian war.

However, it is not only symbolic buildings or significant elements of Bosnian cultural heritage that were targeted for destruction. The urban fabric of Bosnia came under a relentless assault. As Nicholas Adams (1993)

Plate 8.1 The National Library, Sarajevo, Bosnia-Herzegovina, July 1997. The library was targeted by Bosnian-Serb gunners on August 25, 1992. Some 1.5 million volumes were destroyed (see Reidlmayer, 2002: 19). Image © Martin Coward.

Plate 8.2 The Old Bridge (Stari Most) in Mostar, Bosnia-Herzegovina. The Old Bridge was shelled first by Bosnian-Serb troops and then by Bosnian-Croat troops (who finally destroyed it at around 10.15 a.m. on November 9, 1993). An ultimately unsuccessful attempt was made to protect the damaged bridge by hanging tires around the stonework. Image © Nigel Chandler/Corbis. Used with permission.

notes, along with "mosques, churches [and] synagogues," "markets, museums, libraries, cafes, in short, the places where people gather to live out their collective life, have been the focus of... attacks."

Early in the conflict a number of architects had noted the widespread, and yet intentional, destruction of the urban environment. They referred to this destruction as "urbicide" (see *Warchitecture*, 1993; *Mostar '92 – Urbicid*, 1992). It appeared to these writers that a phenomenon was emerging that was not properly accounted for in the prevalent modes of analysis of the 1992–5 Bosnian war. Insofar as the violent logics of genocide/ethnic cleansing dominated the political imaginaries of those who sought either to intervene or understand the conflict, the problematics that shaped both understandings of the war itself and concomitant attempts to provide humanitarian assistance or negotiate settlements were predicated upon images and events concerning the destruction of human life, the displacement of individuals or groups, or the misery that human hatred can bring about. In short, understandings of, and interventions into, the Bosnian war were refracted through an anthropocentric political imaginary that concentrated on the death of civilians and the destruction of the symbols they held dear (mosques, monuments, cultural heritage).

The rubble of the Bosnian urban environment has been similarly seen through the lens of anthropocentrism. The destruction of the urban fabric of Bosnia has been interpreted as a phenomenon contingent to, and thus dependent upon, the violence perpetrated against the people of Bosnia. Thus the rubble of Bosnia is an element of genocide or war, rather than a phenomenon in its own right (Shaw, this volume). And yet we should be wary of "thinking in terms of 'collateral damage,' incidental to the general mayhem of warfare" (Riedlmayer, 1995). The urban fabric of Bosnia was targeted deliberately, a fact attested to by the manner in which the violence against the architecture of Bosnia was disproportionate to the task of killing the people of Bosnia.

"It is the expected thing to say that people come first," notes Adams. "And they do, but the survival of architecture and urban life are important to the survival of people" (Adams, 1993: 390). The widespread destruction of urban fabric is the destruction of a *common, shared* space. Insofar as the dynamic of ethnic cleansing is that of the carving out of separate, ethnically homogeneous and self-determining territorial entities, it comprises a denial of common space through a destruction of that which attests to a record of sharing spaces – the heterogeneity of cultural heritage and the intermingling of civilian bodies. And yet the fundamental question for Bosnia is that of sharing a common space. Insofar as this is the demand made upon all those who observe, intervene in, or live in Bosnia, it can only be achieved if a common, shared space exists. And thus the question of the destruction of urban environments, or urbicide, cannot be allowed to be subordinated to questions of ethnic cleansing/genocide.

In this chapter, therefore, I will address the widespread destruction or urbicide to which Bosnian towns and cities were subjected. I will outline a conceptual understanding of urbicide and the role of such destruction in the politics of ethnonationalism. It will be shown that the urban destruction that characterized this conflict cannot be understood according to extant explanations. This necessitates the introduction of the concept of urbicide. Urbicide will be defined as the destruction of the urban insofar as it is the arena in which an encounter with difference occurs. I will then argue that, in Bosnia, urbicide was part of the ethnonationalist program to eradicate difference in order to create and naturalize the idea of separate, antagonistic, sovereign territorial entities.

Urban Destruction and its Interpreters

Given the scope of the destruction of urban environments during the 1992–5 Bosnian war, there have been a number of attempts to understand this violence and its place within the dynamics of this conflict. Within these responses to the destruction of urban fabric in Bosnia, it is possible to identify three common (though not self-consciously defined) interpretive themes. According to these interpretations, urban destruction can be understood as (a) collateral damage or military necessity, (b) the destruction of cultural heritage, or (c) a metaphor for certain concepts or values. I will briefly outline these three interpretations. I will show that these interpretations fail to grasp the meaning of the wholesale destruction of the urban environment and thus necessitate the introduction of a concept that grasps what is at stake in such violence. Urbicide represents precisely such a concept. This examination of conventional interpretations of urban destruction will, therefore, set out the need for an outline of the conceptual contours and political logic of urbicide. (On the notion of a "political logic" see Coward, 2002: 35–7.)

Collateral damage and military necessity

Perhaps the most conventional interpretation of the devastation of the urban environment in Bosnia conceives of the destruction as either collateral damage or as the result of militarily necessary actions. "Collateral damage" refers to "incidental casualties and...property damage" that result from military action (Rogers, 1996: 15). Collateral damage "occurs when attacks targeted at military objectives cause civilian casualties and damage to civilian objects" (Fischer, 1999). Of principle importance in understanding the idea of collateral damage is that it is an unintended (or incidental) consequence of military action. Even where a military action is clearly seen to risk such destruction, in order for any resultant destruction to be classified as collateral damage it must be assumed that the resultant destruction was, despite the risk, unintended.

The destruction of buildings in Bosnia could thus be seen as incidental to the military action undertaken in the 1992–5 war. According to such an interpretation, bridges, mosques, and churches, houses, public buildings, and so on, would have been unintentionally destroyed in the course of legitimate military actions. Given the nature of the combat in the Bosnian war (a large part of which was in urban environments), it could be argued that military action risked, but did not intend, the incidental destruction of the urban fabric. This argument would depend upon the idea that the military actions in which such incidental damage occurred were seeking legitimate military gains and, while risking urban devastation, did not intend this to occur.

Such an idea introduces into the interpretation of urban destruction the idea of military necessity. "Military necessity" can be broadly defined as "those measures which are indispensable for securing the ends of the war,

and which are lawful according to the modern laws and usages of war"
(Lieber, quoted in Rogers, 1996: 4).[3] In the case of the 1992–5 Bosnian
war, it could be argued that certain buildings were lawfully destroyed
in order to achieve certain military ends. The clearest case in which such
an argument might apply is in relation to bridges.

Bridges are often destroyed in military conflict and are commonly taken
to constitute a military (as opposed to civilian) object. A bridge, it is argued,
comprises a link in logistics networks. In order to weaken the enemy, or
achieve the objectives of war, it is legitimate to attack the logistical structure
that supports an opponent's war effort. The destruction of a building
(a bridge) that might only seem to have incidental military use, can,
therefore, be justified as militarily necessary.

Such an argument was prominent during the NATO bombardment of
Serbia in 1999. In April 1999, at the beginning of its military action against
Serbia, NATO destroyed a number of bridges, including road and rail
bridges across the Danube in both Novi Sad and Belgrade. Air Commodore Wilby justified the destruction as militarily necessary, noting that
"bridges . . . have been selected because they are major lines of communication and . . . affect resupply of . . . troops [the Serbian military or the MUP
(Serbian special police units)] . . . So . . . I would say . . . that all our targets
have been justifiably . . . military targets" (NATO, April 6). The destruction
of bridges and other buildings in Bosnia could, similarly, be justified
according to the logic of military necessity. That is, the argument could
be used that the buildings destroyed represented elements in logistical
networks, and, hence, militarily legitimate targets.

Neither of these interpretations seems very satisfactory, however, in the
context of the 1992–5 Bosnian war. Though they may offer superficial
justification for the destruction of *certain* buildings, they do not adequately
account for the widespread destruction of urban fabric. The argument that
this destruction comprises collateral damage sustained in the pursuit of
legitimate military objectives can be easily refuted through the findings of
the *Information Reports on War Damage to the Cultural Heritage in Croatia and
Bosnia-Herzegovina*, delivered to the Council of Europe's Committee on
Culture and Education by the Parliamentary Assembly Sub-Committee on
Architectural and Artistic Heritage. In respect of the destruction of the
Oriental Institute in Sarajevo, for example, the fourth *Information Report*
notes: "it is fair to presuppose that the shelling was carried out to plan: the
Institute was directly targeted" (Council of Europe, 1994). In relation to
the destruction of the minarets of mosques in Bosnia, the first *Information
Report* notes: "It may have been inevitable that mosques in a military 'front'
zone would be hit, but it is highly doubtful that a minaret can be brought
down with a single large caliber shell, which implies a certain amount of
deliberate targeting on these structures" (Council of Europe, 1993). That

the urban fabric of Bosnia was deliberately and not incidentally targeted is confirmed by the conclusion of the fourth *Information Report*: "the small historic core of Mostar...was clearly targeted by the heaviest guns available to the HVO [Bosnian Croat army/paramilitaries]" (Council of Europe, 1994).

If the destruction of the urban fabric of Bosnia cannot be understood as collateral damage, can it be seen as militarily necessary? This argument is even easier to refute than that of collateral damage. For the destruction of all of these buildings to have been militarily necessary they would have had to have played some form of role in the logistics networks of the various armies in Bosnia. There are instances in which such arguments may be credible. For example, the destruction of the central post office in Sarajevo, or the modern road bridges over the Neretva in Mostar, could be seen as attacks on legitimate military targets.

However, the destruction of urban fabric is more widespread than these key buildings. Buildings of no military significance were regularly and deliberately shelled. Moreover, the shelling covered a wide variety of buildings: housing, public institutions, cultural monuments, utility buildings, open spaces. In *Just and Unjust Wars* Waltzer talks about strategy as "a language of justification"(Waltzer, 1992: 13). We could see military necessity in a similar light. Claims that the destruction of a target was militarily necessary are *post hoc* narratives that seek to justify the destruction. In cases such as Sarajevo's central post office or the Neretva road bridges, such narratives are convincing, since they can align themselves with the commonly understood meanings of what constitutes a military object or a military objective. However, in the case of the destruction of the urban fabric in which so much damage was done to buildings that could serve no such purposes, such narratives do not really serve to justify or explain the destruction of the urban fabric.

The destruction of cultural heritage

The second of the three interpretations of the destruction of urban fabric that I want to examine arises in relation to the destruction of the cultural heritage of Bosnia-Herzegovina. Accounts of the destruction of cultural heritage see it as an element of ethnic cleansing, or the attempt to remake "Bosnia-Herzegovina as a series of small, pure ethnic states" (Council of Europe, 1994). Cultural heritage is destroyed because it represents heterogeneous identities and thus what must be destroyed in order to achieve the aim of ethnic purity in a particular territory.

Andras Riedlmayer's work provides a particularly cogent example of an interpretation of urban destruction through the framework of extant

162

Martin Coward

understandings concerning the protection of cultural heritage. Riedlmayer argues that although our attention focuses on the people of Bosnia, "we should also take a look at the rubble." This rubble, he argues, "signifies more than the ordinary atrocities of war... Rubble in Bosnia and Herzegovina signifies nationalist extremists hard at work to eliminate not only the human beings and living cities, but also the memory of the past" (Riedlmayer, 1994: 16). This elimination of the memory of the past, argues Riedlmayer, is an integral element of ethnic cleansing. Riedlmayer argues that though "we are... told that 'ancient hatreds' are what fuel the destruction... this is not true": the museums, libraries, mosques, churches, and monuments "speak eloquently of centuries of pluralism... in Bosnia... It is this evidence of a successfully shared past that the nationalists seek to destroy" (Riedlmayer, 1994: 16). It is the nature of the ethnonationalist project, the project that gave birth to ethnic cleansing, that drives this destruction.

Ethnonationalism seeks to naturalize the idea that the so-called "ethnic" groups in Bosnia are fated to live separate existences. The myth of "ancient hatreds" installs the idea that ethnic groups were always distinct and in antagonistic relationships. Ethnonationalist ideas of separation and ethnic purity are the logical outcome of the acceptance of this idea. However, such ideas are simply the myths on which the ethnonationalist edifice is built. Indeed, as I have noted, Bosnia has a long history of pluralism and coexistence between these supposedly distinct and incompatible ethnic groups (Hayden, 1996: 788–90). The urban environment in cities such as Sarajevo and Mostar are testament to the pluralism/heterogeneity of Bosnia. The coexistence of Ottoman, Austro-Hungarian, and vernacular buildings is a constant reminder that the nationalist project of ethnic separateness is a present-day fiction belied by the past. Thus, to paraphrase Riedlmayer, ethnonationalists sought to destroy evidence of a successfully shared past in order to legitimize a contemporary goal of ethnic separateness.

This account seems to get closer to the theme of the destruction of the shared spaces of Bosnia-Herzegovina than the interpretation of destruction as the result of either collateral damage or military necessity. Indeed, this account understands the destruction of certain buildings as part of the logic of ethnonationalism that has at its heart the destruction of the conditions of possibility of pluralism, key among which is the evidence of coexistence provided by the built environment of Bosnia.

However, this account suffers from its focus upon the symbolic cultural heritage of Bosnia. In other words it focuses only upon the buildings whose loss is judged to be a cultural loss. This means that the buildings for which concern is shown are those that were striking examples of a particular cultural influence upon the pluralist history of Bosnia. Ancient mosques, National Library buildings, and 400-year-old bridges are the subject of this account, as it is these that are the symbolic reminders of the pluralist culture of Bosnia. However, the destruction of the urban environment is more widespread than these symbolic buildings. Indeed, it encompasses buildings that have no distinctive cultural value, or are of indistinct cultural provenance (the bland modernism of the Unis Co. tower blocks in Sarajevo are an example; see plate 8.3).[4] These buildings could not really be said to represent the cultural heritage of Bosnia. And thus the interpretation of urban destruction as an attack on cultural heritage provides only a partial (though striking) account of the destruction of the urban environment in Bosnia.

Plate 8.3 The Unis Co. buildings, next to the Holiday Inn in Sarajevo, Bosnia-Herzegovina, July 1997. These buildings also provide the front cover picture for Silber and Little's *The Death of Yugoslavia* (1995). Image © Martin Coward.

Signs of Balkanization

The third and final interpretation of urban destruction that I want to examine does not treat the ruins in themselves as material symbols of a culture, but, rather, as signs evocative of ideas and values (concepts). This interpretation is, therefore, a *semiotic* understanding that treats the destruction of buildings as a sign that refers to a concept.[5] This interpretation also focuses on the destruction of symbolic instances of cultural heritage and is best seen in responses to the destruction of the Stari Most – or Old Bridge – in Mostar.

For observers of the 1992–5 Bosnian war, the ruined Stari Most (and the rubble of Bosnia in general) signified in graphic fashion the *Balkanization* of Bosnia. According to Der Derian, "Balkanization is generally understood to be the break up of larger political units into smaller, mutually hostile states which are exploited or manipulated by more powerful neighbors" (Der Derian, 1992: 146–50). The destruction of the Stari Most gave such an idea exemplary form. That is, the destruction of the last remaining bridge between the two halves of Mostar was performed by a group manipulated by Croatian President Franjo Tudjman and effectively sealed the creation of two mutually hostile entities (east and west Mostar).

The division of Bosnia into ever smaller, homogenous ethnic territories was clearly represented in the gulf opened up between the two banks of the Neretva River by the destruction of the Stari Most. However, the Balkanization that this sign represented had an additional stratum of meaning. The destruction of the elegant Ottoman bridge not only signified the violent social and political fragmentation of Bosnia-Herzegovina, but also the supposedly "Balkan" character of the violence by which this fragmentation was being achieved. That is, this destruction confirmed the stereotypes that observers held of those who were executing this Balkanization.[6] In this way the fallen Stari Most came to represent the savagery and barbarity of the Bosnian war: the failure of (European) civilization to extend into the Balkans. This idea framed the political imagination of those observing the conflict. Talk of "ancient animosities" was given new life by this supposed sign of ferocious barbarity. Leaders of Western, "civilized" nations threw their hands up in despair, reasoning that intervention was futile insofar as the inhabitants of Bosnia did not seem (given such acts of destruction) to share even the basic values of civilization. It was therefore argued that the various factions at war in Bosnia should be left to fight this conflict out among themselves.[7]

The problem with this interpretation of the rubble of Bosnia is that the destruction is not treated as an event worthy of attention in its own right. Rather, the rubble is appropriated as a sign connotative of a more general concept. While urban destruction may serve as the sign for several concepts, noting this does not get us any closer to understanding the meaning of the destruction of urban fabric. Which is to say that the destruction of shared space may become the sign that frames certain political imaginaries in relation to this war. However, we deny ourselves crucial political possibilities if we simply accept those significatory stories, since we accept that this destruction is interesting only insofar as it connotes the dissolution of political communities or the savagery of this fragmentation.

Urbicide

The partial and flawed nature of the three interpretations of the destruction of urban fabric in Bosnia reviewed above suggests that the destruction of urban fabric in Bosnia should be treated as a conceptual problematic in its own right. In a publication entitled *Mostar '92 – Urbicid* (1992) a group of Bosnian architects highlighted the need for addressing urban destruction as a conceptual problematic in its own right.[8]

It is necessary, therefore, to inquire into the meaning of the term "urbicide" (the Anglicization of the Serbo-Croat *Urbicid*). Urbicide derives its meaning from the collocation of "urban" with the epithet "-cide." Taken literally, urbicide refers to the "killing," "slaughter," or "slaying" of that which is subsumed under the term "urban" (OED). At stake in the meaning of "urbicide," therefore, is what is to be understood in the concept of "the urban," what it is that is destroyed in this act of "killing the urban." "Urban," derived from the Latin *urbanus*, refers to that which is "characteristic of, occurring or taking place, in a city or town" (OED). The experience of city life, or "following the pursuits [and] having the ideas or sentiments . . . characteristic of town or city life" comprises urbanity (OED). It is important to note the way in which urbanity derives its meaning through an opposition with a rural way of life.[9] Examination of this opposition will reveal the principal distinguishing feature of urbanity.

According to the opposition urban–rural, the city represents modern progress, while rural life is taken to exemplify the constraints of tradition that modernity is supposed to sweep away. Durkheim, for example, claims that "nowhere have the traditions less sway over minds. Indeed . . . cities are the uncontested homes of progress; it is in them that ideas, fashions, customs, new needs are elaborated and then spread over the rest of the country . . . No ground is more favorable to evolutions of all sorts" (Durkheim, 1933: 296). This urban–rural opposition echoes with early sociological attempts to grasp the phenomenon of modernity. Such attempts oppose the supposed organic unity of traditional, premodern societies to the heterogeneity that is associated with capitalist modernity. Tönnie's

concepts of *Gemeinschaft* and *Gesellschaft*, for example, exemplify this opposition (Karp, Stone, and Yoels, 1991: 8–12). Where *Gemeinschaft* represents premodern social order, *Gesellschaft* represents the modern,
specifically capitalist, social order. *Gemeinschaft* represents a homogeneous
feudal order "bound by shared values and . . . traditions," *Gesellschaft* refers
to a social order characterized by "heterogeneity of values and traditions"
(Karp, Stone, and Yoels, 1991: 9).

This idea of *heterogeneity* is also at stake in the concept of the urban, or
urbanity. In "Urbanism as a way of life," Louis Wirth argues that it is the
size, density, and heterogeneity of the populations of cities that constitute
"those elements of urbanism which mark it as a distinctive mode of life"
(Wirth, 1996: 190). Despite naming three factors that characterize urbanity, it is heterogeneity that is its principal aspect according to Wirth. Indeed,
the size of an urban population is pertinent insofar as it leads to a greater
number of different identities and associations and thus heterogeneity of
tradition and belief. Moreover, density of the urban population is important
insofar as it is gives rise to a greater frequency of encounters between these
heterogeneous traditions and beliefs. *Heterogeneity*, then, can be said to be
the defining characteristic of urbanity.

Thus, if we identify urbanity as entailing, principally, heterogeneous
existence, we can say that the destruction of urban life is the destruction
of heterogeneity. The destruction of urban fabric is, therefore, the destruction of the conditions of possibility of heterogeneity. What is at stake in
urbicide – the destruction of the buildings which establish common/shared
spaces in which plural communities live their lives – is thus the destruction
of the conditions of possibility of heterogeneity.

Before moving on to examine the political consequences of this destruction of the conditions of possibility of heterogeneity, it is necessary
to delineate the manner in which urbicide consists of two distinct phases.
It is in this respect that there is a certain kinship between urbicide and
genocide. In defining genocide, Raphael Lemkin argued that this "practice
of extermination of national and ethnic groups" can be understood as
consisting of two distinct phases. First, the "destruction of the national pattern of the oppressed group" and second, "imposition of the national
pattern of the oppressor" (Lemkin, 1944: 79).

It is the manner in which genocide is directed at the destruction of a
national group that is its defining feature. This defining feature led Lemkin
to conclude that in genocide, violence "is directed against the national
group as an entity, and the actions involved are directed against individuals,
not in their individual capacity, but as members of the national group"
(Lemkin, 1944: 79).

The concept of "genocide" thus entails *an understanding of destruction in
relation to that which is destroyed*. It is implicit in our understanding of killing

as part of the logic of genocide that we do not simply see the killing of *each* individual as a *means* to the end of extermination. In fact it is not *extermination* – however (in)complete this may be – which defines genocide.[10] Rather, what we understand to be the meaning of "genocide" is played out in *each and every* death, *each and every time*. Since genocide is enacted in each and every death it expresses a relation between what is destroyed and the meaning of destruction that is other than the simple death of the individual. It is integral to our understanding of "genocide" that we recognize what "it" is that is destroyed, and the meaning of the destruction. In genocide "it" is a member of a national or ethnic group and the destruction has the meaning of the eradication of this group.

It is precisely here that the simultaneous kinship and difference between urbicide and genocide can be noted. Like genocide, urbicide derives its meaning from the relationship between the destruction and what "it" is that is destroyed. However, what "it" is that is destroyed is distinct from that which is destroyed in genocide.

If we draw on the previous definition of urbicide, it is possible to outline the relationship of destruction to that which is destroyed that gives urbicide its specific conceptual logic. Put simply, urbicide entails the destruction of buildings and urban fabric as elements of urbanity. Buildings are destroyed because they are the condition of possibility of urbanity. Since urbanity is constituted by heterogeneity, urbicide comprises the destruction of the conditions of possibility of heterogeneity. Moreover, this destruction is, like genocide a two-phase affair. First, the conditions of possibility of heterogeneity are destroyed, followed by the imposition of homogeneity.

Having thus outlined the conceptual contours of urbicide, namely that it comprises a destruction of the buildings as the conditions of possibility of heterogeneity in order to establish homogeneity, it is necessary to set out the political consequences of my argument.

From Agonism to Antagonism: The Politics of Urbicide

In order to understand the politics of urbicide in Bosnia it is necessary to understand what is at stake in this destruction. If the above outline of urbicide is correct, buildings were destroyed in the 1992–5 Bosnian war insofar as they were elements of urbanity. Insofar as heterogeneity is the defining feature of urbanity, urbicide comprises the destruction of buildings as the conditions of possibility for such heterogeneity. It is possible, therefore, to say that it is heterogeneity that is at stake in urbicide, in the destruction of each and every building. I would like, therefore, to turn my attention to the stakes of urbicide: heterogeneity.

The heterogeneity at stake in urbicide might better be described as an "agonism." The common, shared spaces of urban environments are the condition of possibility for the agonistic coexistence of identities. The concept of agonism is developed by William Connolly in his discussion of "agonistic democracy." "Agonistic democracy," according to Connolly, "affirms the indispensability of identity to life, disturbs the dogmatization of identity, and folds care for... diversity... into the strife and interdependence of identity/difference" (Connolly, 1991: x).

For Connolly, agonism refers to the manner in which existence is a network of relations between identity and difference. Identities never exist in isolation from a constitutive otherness, or alterity, against which identity is defined. Self, according to Connolly, is constituted in relation to the non-self by constituting limits at which the self ends and the other begins. In this sense, however, such identity is constantly contested by alterity. Difference threatens to undo efforts at self-identity or presence, by contesting the boundaries of the self, the points at which self is differentiated from its other(s). This contestation constitutes existence as a continual performance of identity in relations to its other(s). Insofar as this performance takes place in the context of difference (many performances of self in relations to many others), existence is heterogeneous.

Insofar as existence is characterized by agonistic heterogeneity it is characterized, to borrow from Foucault, by "reciprocal incitation and struggle... a permanent provocation" (Foucault, 1982: 222). That is, alterity provokes identity into defining its boundaries, as it is only through the definition of the borders of identity/difference that identity can perform itself. Moreover, these borders are constantly contested by alterity and must be reperformed in order to maintain the presence of identity. Tone Bringa notes that everyday Bosnian life prior to the 1992–5 war was an agonistic existence in which identities of any kind were formed in relation to the continual provocation of difference (Bringa, 1995).

It is this provocation that ethnonationalism seeks to eradicate. Ethnonationalism seeks to establish identities free of any relation to difference: ethnically pure, homogenous identities that do not have to exist in a relationship of provocation with their others. Indeed, ethnonationalism denies the existence of a relationship between itself and others. This denial is the basis on which ethnonationalism exists, since to admit of such a relationship would be to admit to a heterogeneity (or plurality) that would radically contest the program of ethnic separateness and purity that ethnonationalism represents.

Urbicide thus comprises a denial of the agonistic heterogeneity that characterizes urbanity. It is this denial that comprises the principle political aim of ethnonationalism. The destruction of urban fabric transforms agonistic heterogeneity into the *antagonism of separate ethnicities*. That is, urban destruction transforms the agonistic provocation (and interdependence between identity and difference) into the stalemate of antagonism. Antagonism has the appearance of a stalemate between opposing parties that, were they not in a confrontation, would be able to exist without each other. It is this appearance of separateness that ethnonationalists intend to create through urbicide.

Urbicide carves out the urban environment into enclaves in order to deny the agonism of urbanity. In so doing, urbicide creates antagonistic enclaves. Urbicide is thus a crucial element in the self-justifying logic of ethnonationalism. According to this circular logic, the product of urbicide (antagonistic enclaves) is the justification for the act of urbicide (the creation of ethnically homogeneous territorial entities). The antagonistic enclaves that give ethnic separateness the appearance of being natural, are the "mystical foundation of authority," or justification, for the ethnic homogenizations of ethnonationalism of which urbicide is a central aspect.[11] The event of urbicide (the denial of agonism) is thus founded on its result (antagonistically separate enclaves) in a self-referring cycle.

As I noted above, urbicide transforms agonism into antagonism in two phases. In the first phase, agonism is destroyed through the widespread destruction of urban fabric. In the second phase, ethnic homogeneity is established through the constitution of remaining urban elements as separate from, and antagonistically related to, any alterity. In particular, two distinct types of urbicidal logic occur. First, there is the razing of cities and towns (or areas within those urban environments) such that (the possibility of) alterity is eliminated. Second, there is the division of cities and towns such that agonism can be transformed into antagonism.

Urbicide is thus responsible for the emergence of either dead zones or zones of separation. In Mostar, for example, a zone of separation was created along the confrontation line, a wide straight boulevard, that served to carve the city into two antagonistic enclaves and give the impression of ethnic separateness (Plunz, Baratloo, and Conrad, 1998: 62–9). Furthermore, in towns across Bosnia, ethnonationalists destroyed the houses of those they had displaced with dynamite or by burning. This action (which continued after the end of the war) eradicated the traces of alterity from the ethnonationalists' statelets (International Crisis Group, 1997).

Concluding Remarks

The politics of urbicide can thus be summarized as follows. Urbicide is the destruction of urban fabric insofar as it comprises the conditions of possibility of urbanity. Urbanity is characterized by an agonistic heterogeneity in which identity is constituted in relation to difference. Urbicide, in destroying the conditions of possibility of urbanity, denies such heterogeneity. This denial is accomplished by transforming agonism into antagonism and thus giving the impression of having dissipated the relationship of identity to difference. Only in this way can the ethnonationalists who practice urbicide create the fiction of ethnic separateness/purity on which their statelets are founded.

Notes

1 "Bosniac" is more adequate in describing those who were the victims of the genocidal violence of the Bosnian Serb Army and militias than the somewhat mistaken designation of "Muslim." "Bosniac" can be defined, following Sells, as "all residents of the internationally recognized sovereign nation of Bosnia-Herzegovina, regardless of their religious affiliation, who consider themselves Bosnian, that is, who remain loyal to a Bosnian state built on the principles of civic society and religious pluralism" (Sells, 1996: xiv). Just as the Jews were not the only victims of the Holocaust, so those who could be identified as Muslim were not the only victims of the Bosnian Serbs. Indeed, in most discourses "Muslim" is deployed as a catch-all category for all those who found themselves to be opposed to, victims of, or excluded from, the Bosnian-Serb ethnonationalist program. See also in this regard Bringa's comments on the evolution of *Bosnjac* identity (Bringa, 1995: 34–6).
2 The destruction of the Stari Most was one of the most prominent images of the 1992–5 Bosnian war. This Ottoman bridge was deliberately shelled until it collapsed on November 9, 1993 (see Coward, 2002: 29–33).
3 The laws and usages of war of concern for the argument in this chapter are principally, though not entirely, contained in the 1949 Geneva Conventions (and their 1977 Additional Protocols) and the 1954 Hague Convention for the Protection of Cultural Property (see Roberts and Guelff, 2000: 195–405, 419–512).
4 See *Warchitecture* (1993) for further examples of the modernist/vernacular/everyday buildings destroyed in the shelling of Sarajevo.
5 For an account of semiology – the scholarly study that defines the *semiotic* – see Culler (1986: 90–106).
6 Regarding the manner in which "Balkan" stereotypes define perceptions of the character of various Yugoslavs, see Bakic-Hayden and Hayden (1992) and Todorova (1997).
7 This view can be seen in the words of a spokesperson for the American Republican leadership, who stated: "I see no reason to send young men over there to lose their lives over something we can do nothing about. These people have been fighting for centuries." ("The Silent Opposition", *New York Times*, November 27, 1995; quoted in Campbell, 1998a: 52).
8 Extracts of this publication were published as "Mostar '92 – Urbicide" (1993).

9   This opposition is explicit in Louis Wirth's definition of the urban experience; cf.: "The city and the country may be regarded as two poles in reference to one or the other of which all human settlements tend to arrange themselves" (Wirth, 1996: 190).

10 Indeed, "although Lemkin's conception included the physical extermination of targeted groups, this was, in his view, only the *most extreme* technique of genocide" (Orentlicher, 1999; my emphasis).

11 On the "mystical foundation of authority" see Derrida (1992). I would like to thank David Campbell for pointing out the manner in which the enclave serves as the ground on which ethnonationalism, and thus urbicide, is predicated.

9

Strategic Points, Flexible Lines, Tense Surfaces, and Political Volumes: Ariel Sharon and the Geometry of Occupation

Eyal Weizman

The wording of the 2003 Middle East peace initiative, the "roadmap," managed – perhaps unwittingly but clearly all the same – to equate the transformation of the built environment with acts of organized violence. Israel is to stop planning, constructing, and populating, and then it is to dismantle settlements built by independent groups in breach of its own laws. The Palestinian authority is to prevent shooting, shelling, and suicide attacks carried out by armed organizations, dismantling their infrastructures and arresting their masterminds in the process. Although the document does not make it clear if it sees the activities of each side as comparable (or merely trapped in a cyclical sequence of causes and effects), never before was the work of architects and planners so clearly equated with those of terrorists.

Indeed, the human and political rights of Palestinians are violated not only by the frequent blows of the Israeli military, but also by a much slower and steadier process in which the totality of the environment in which they live is configured around them as an ever-tightening knot. In this process the transformation of the territories occupied by Israel since 1967 became a parallel conflict carried out with pencil lines on the drafting tables of military and civilian planners and architects. It developed as an "urban war" in which urbanity provided not only the arena of war but also its very weapons and ammunition. Just like a gun or a tank, mundane building matters have been used by the Israeli state to apply its strategic and political agenda. The figure of Ariel Sharon is central to this process. The use of apparently "temporary" security architecture to create permanent "facts on the ground"; the rejection of borderlines as the limits of state territory; the preference for ever-flexible internal frontiers: above all, this is the spatial legacy of Ariel Sharon.

This chapter attempts to understand the way in which Ariel Sharon imagines territory and practices space. It is an attempt to look at his long-lasting physical oeuvre, the one in which both Israelis and Palestinians must struggle to live, as one architect tries to understand the work of another.

Surface

Israel's pre-1967 borders were seen by the military as indefensible. Israeli military strategy, conscious of the strategic inferiorities of Israel's borders, was based on an oxymoron coined in 1959 by Yigal Allon, a Labour politician and a retired military commander: "preemptive attack." This principle conceived an extensive use of Israel's superior air power as a volumetric compensation for its planar inferiority. The 1967 war implemented Yigal Allon's strategy to the letter. With complete control of the skies, the Israeli Defense Force (IDF) was free to progress across the surface, stopping and redeploying along clear, natural barriers.

In the process, the geopolitical balance of the Middle East was radically transformed. Israel tripled the territory under its control. The new lines, stretched now along the Jordan River and the Suez Canal, were seen as the "natural border" of a promised land. This fitted well with a newly developed phantasmagorical attitude of the Israeli state. An unparalleled period of economic prosperity commenced, due, at least in part, to cheap labor drawn from the newly occupied Palestinian population of more than a million people. Gradually, however, the "Occupied Territories" grew too large within the national imagination. This creeping agoraphobia meant that the unfamiliar territories had to be studied, mapped, and domesticated from within. Their edges had to be fortified against the prospect of counter-aggression from the "outside."

Lines

Under the government of Golda Meir, two Labourites – Haim Bar-Lev and Yigal Allon – were put in charge of fortifying the edges of the Occupied Territories on two different fronts. Allon, then the minister of agriculture, devised and implemented the Allon Plan. This marked out the locations of a series of agricultural outposts along the western bank of the Jordan River. It created a security border with Jordan while consciously aiming to settle spaces only sparsely populated by Palestinians.

The Bar-Lev Line was the military counterpart of the Allon Plan. It was an immense technical undertaking that demanded the shuffling of huge quantities of sand from across the desert to the bank of the Suez Canal. This sand was piled up to form a formidable artificial landscape composed of hardened sand ramparts above ground. A parallel system of deep bunkers and communication trenches was also constructed below the Line. Thirty-five fortified positions (*Ma'ozim*) were spread out along the length of the canal at 10-kilometer intervals. These overlooked the Egyptian positions across the water line from a mere 300 meters.

Points

Ariel Sharon served between 1969 and July 1973 as the IDF's chief of southern command. It was during this time that he – always an overtly political general – broke with traditional military ranks, as well as with his Labour–Zionist upbringing, and affiliated himself with the political right. Sharon was also the only general who dared challenge the logic of defense spelled out by the Bar-Lev Line. He argued, in a series of heated meetings with the General Staff, that the army "cannot win a defensive battle on an outer line." Instead, he proposed that the IDF should "fight a defensive battle the way it should be fought – not on forward line but in depth" (Sharon and Chanoff, 2001).

To do this he proposed, and partially implemented, a dynamic system of point-based defense in depth. This was composed of a series of strong points (*Ta'ozim*). These were spread out on elevated ground within the terrain on a series of mountain summits that dominated the canal plain. Between the *Ta'ozim* and the canal Sharon proposed to run mobile patrols, constantly and unpredictably on the move. Then, at the first opportunity, Sharon was dismissed by Bar-Lev, his plan only partially implemented.

The principle of a linear defense is to prohibit (or inhibit) the enemy from gaining any foothold beyond it. General Erwin Rommel, commander of the *Wehrmacht* defenses along the Atlantic in 1944, asserted the core of this principle when he argued that the only chance to stop an Allied invasion force was to beat them at the water's edge. But as the Germans knew full well, after their experience with the supposedly impregnable Todt Line, when the line is breached, even at one location, it is – much like a leaking glass of water – rendered immediately useless.

By contrast, defense based on a "network of points in depth" relies on a matrix of interlocking strong points connected by physical and electromagnetic links: roads and electronic communications. Each point can connect and communicate with any other, and each point overlooks, and, whenever necessary, covers the other with firepower. This creates an interlocking, fortified surface. When the defensive matrix is attacked it can become flexible and adapt to the fall of any number of points by forming new connections across the matrix.

The geography of nodes in a matrix cannot be conventionally measured in distance. "Distance" between nodes is not a measurable absolute but a relative figure that is defined by the speed and reliability of the connection – that is, how fast and how secure can one travel between given points. The network defense is a spatial trap that allows the defenders a high level of mobility while acting to paralyze any possibility for enemy movement. Jeff Halper explains how effective this strategy was in Vietnam, where "small forces of Viet Cong were able to pin down some half-million American soldiers possessing overwhelming firepower" (Halper, 2001).

Breaking the Line

On October 6, 1973, the line that had stood up to two years of Egyptian artillery fire throughout the war of attrition, succumbed to water at the outset of the Yom Kippur war. Egyptian high-pressure water cannons used the water of the Suez Canal to dissolve the hardened sand and melt the formidable artificial landscape into pools of mud. Some 100,000 Egyptian troops were ferried onto the eastern bank, making their way a few kilometers into the Sinai. Then, without encountering much resistance, but scared of entering the fortified depth of Israeli defenses constructed by Ariel Sharon, they stopped and dug themselves in, guns facing east.

Sharon, now a division commander, was the first to succeed in breaking a gap through the new Egyptian lines. He established a bridgehead across the canal over which the Israeli army flowed into the rear of the Egyptians. Cutting off their supply lines, Sharon's forces encircled the entire 3rd Egyptian Army. The counter-crossing of the canal created a bizarre stalemate, with the two armies switched sides across the water line. Such was the power of linear defense that it was crossed twice, in both directions, during a war lasting less than three weeks.

The Yom Kippur war ended in unprecedented public outrage. The heads of the General Staff and of the Labour party rolled, but Ariel Sharon was publicly perceived as the man who saved the nation. The debate around the construction and fall of the canal's fortification, and the trauma of the canal campaign, became deeply etched in the Israeli national consciousness. These events were endlessly replayed and refought, in slow-motion mode, this time on the hills of the West Bank.

Strategic Points

In May 1977 the Likud came to power for the first time in the history of the state. Ariel Sharon was appointed minister of agriculture and took over the ministerial committee in charge of settlement policy. Seizing this opportunity, Sharon started to devise a new location strategy for settlements in order to turn the West Bank into a defensible frontier that would consolidate Israeli control of the Occupied Territories. Having successfully demonstrated the shortcomings of the Bar-Lev Line, Sharon now moved against the second of the Labour defensive lines – the Allon Plan. Seeking to implement the lessons of the Sinai campaign, Sharon claimed that "a thin line of settlements along the Jordan would not provide a viable defense unless the high terrain behind it was also fortified." Consequently, he proposed to establish "other settlements on the high terrain... [and] several east–west roads along strategic axes, together with the settlements necessary to guard them" (Sharon and Chanoff, 2001).

Labour had traditionally conducted its state-building policies almost entirely through the construction of settlements. Before the creation of the state it used the "tower and stockade" cooperative settlements to mark and defend Israel's future borders (Rotbard, 2003a). After Israel's creation in 1948, Prime Minister David Ben Gurion laid out the so-called "organic wall" composed of a string of development towns inhabited by immigrant communities – mainly Jews from the Arab states, along the state's new borders (Efrat, 2003). But after the 1967 war, Labour was indecisive about what policy to take with regard to the new territories and was unable to reinvigorate its past pioneering energies. Thus, the government pursued its settlement policies with far less enthusiasm and vigor.

Instead, it was Sharon, the Labourite turned Likudnik, and Gush Emunim, the national religious and messianic organization, who managed to revitalize the pioneering ethos of Zionism. They saw, in the depth of the West Bank, a sacred territory and a defensible frontier – a border without a line, across whose depth a matrix of settlements could be constructed. The "artificially created" Green Line, Israel's internationally recognized 1949 border, was deeply repressed, and the borders became fluid and elastic again, pulled out to incorporate every new settlement. The open frontier replaced the rigidity of the line and blurred the distinctions between a political "inside" and "outside." This, in turn, blurred the difference between "the political space of the state and the cultural space of the nation" – a difference "hidden by the hyphenated concept of 'nation-state'" (Kemp, 2000).

In a famous syllogism, Lenin once described strategy as "the choice of points where force is to be applied." Points have neither dimension nor size; they are mere coordinates on the X/Y-axis of the plain and on the Z-axis of latitude. In Israel, the settlement "location strategy" is based upon a close reading of the terrain. Decisions are made with the precision of acupuncture regarding where effort should be concentrated. The fact that in Hebrew the term a "point on the ground," and sometimes simply "a point" (*Nekuda*), means "settlement" is indicative of a planning culture that considers the positioning of a settlement less in terms of its essence than in terms of its strategic location. Because settlements are autonomous and separate points on a matrix, a reliable communication had to be established between them.

In 1982, a few months before the Israeli invasion of Lebanon, Sharon, then minister of defense, published his *Masterplan for Jewish Settlements in the West Bank Through the Year 2010* – later known as the Sharon Plan (figure 9.1). In it he outlined the location of more than a hundred settlement points, placed on strategic summits. He also marked the paths for a new network of high-volume, interconnected traffic arteries, connecting the settlements with the Israeli heartland. In the formation of continuous Jewish habitation Sharon's plan saw a way towards the wholesale annexation of the areas vital for Israel's security. These areas he marked onto the map attached to his plan in the shape of the letter H. The "H-Plan" contained two parallel north–south strips of land: one along the Green Line containing the West Bank from the west, and another along the Jordan valley, accepting the presence of the Allon Plan to contain the territory from the east.

These two strips separated the Palestinian cities, which are organized along the central spine of the West Bank's mountain ridge, from both Israel proper and from the kingdom of Jordan. Between these north–south strips Sharon marked a few east–west traffic arteries – the main one connecting through Jerusalem, thus closing a (very) approximate H. The rest – some 40 percent of the West Bank, separate enclaves around Palestinian cities and towns – were to revert to some yet undefined form of Palestinian self-management.

The new Israeli settlements, relying on their own weapons, ammunition, and military contingency plans, were to form a network of "civilian fortifications" integrated into the IDF's overall system of defense, serving strategic imperatives by overlooking main traffic arteries and road junctions in their region. The role of settlements as observation and control points promoted a particular layout for their urbanity (plate 9.1). The layout of a mountain settlement is concentric; its roads are stretched in rings following the topographical lines closing a complete circuit around the summit. The outward-facing arrangement of homes orients the view of its inhabitants towards the surrounding landscape in which "national interests" – main roads, junctions, and Palestinian urban areas – compose a picturesque panorama. The essence of this geometric order is to produce

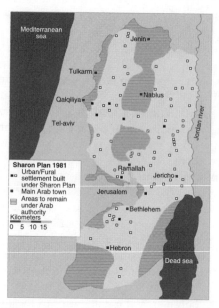

Figure 9.1 The Sharon Plan, 1982. Source: Eyal Weizman.

Plate 9.1 Jewish settlement of Eli, Ramallah Region. Photograph: Eyal Weizman, 2001.

"panoptic fortresses" – optical devices on an urban scale, laid out to generate observation, spatially and temporally, all round. (Weizman, 2002; Segal and Weizman, 2003).

The high ground, on which settlements were located, thus offers the strategic assets of self-protection and a wider view. But beyond being employed militarily, the urban layout of vision also serves an aesthetic agenda: it allows for contemplation over a pastoral landscape evocative of history, one in which biblical scenarios could be imagined and participated in, at least visually. All this feeds the national mythic imagination, giving settlers the sense of foundational authority based on long historical continuity.

In the early 1980s another of the construction frenzies that are indicative of Ariel Sharon's closeness to executive power had begun. The "biblical" heartland of the West Bank became overlaid by the two symbiotic and synergetic instruments of security: the settlement observation point and the serpentine road network. The latter was the prime device for serving the former ; the former overlooked and protected the latter.

Sharon realized the double potential of emerging messianic–religious impulses: to settle a mythological landscape, and to facilitate the desire of the middle classes to push outside of the congested centers of Israeli cities to populate his matrix of points with civilian communities. Unlike Labour's agricultural settlements of the Kibbutz and the Moshav, the new "community settlements" were, in effect, dormitory suburbs of closely-knit social groups composed mainly of national–religious–professional middle classes.

Architecture was thus conscripted to establish the state's control of its territories and help make uniform communities. Uniformity of architectural taste was imposed through the repetition of a small variety of single and double family house-and-garden structures. Beyond responding to middle-class suburban aesthetics, the adorning of settlement homes with red roofs, served a further military agenda – identifying these sites from afar as Israeli.

The fact that the inhabitants had to seek work outside the settlements made them rely on the roads to connect them with the employment centers in the metropolitan areas around Tel Aviv and Jerusalem, within Israel proper. This was similar to the way that the American suburbs developed as an offspring of pacified World War II construction technology, and especially around the system of interstate highways, developed to serve the integrated industry of the American war economy. Israeli suburbia made perfect use of the system laid out for mobile defense in depth. The massive system of fifty highways, together with a modern matrix of infrastructure, became effective instruments of development – merging the needs of a sprawling suburbia with national security and political ambitions to push ever more Israelis into the West Bank.

Sharon and the engineers, already experts in military defense works, and now building for civilian communities, thus had to become urban planners. Sharon "got tremendous satisfaction seeing how everything was moving forward, how drawings on a map were every day becoming more of a reality on the ground" (Sharon and Chanoff, 2001).

Sharon's planning decisions, however, were not made according to professional criteria of economical sustainability, ecology, or efficiency of services. Instead, they were guided by a strategic agenda focused on spatial manipulation. Planning under Sharon shed any pretence of facilitating the social and economic improvement of an abstract "public." Rather, it manifested itself fully as the executive arm of the strategic and geopolitical agenda of the Israeli state.

Architecture and planning were thus used as the continuation of war by other means. Just like the tank, the gun, and the bulldozer (see Graham, this volume), building matter and infrastructure were used to achieve tactical and strategic aims. This was an "urban war" in which urbanity provided not the theatre of war but its very weapons and ammunition. It was a war in which a civilian population was drafted, knowingly or not, to supervise vital national interests as armed, plain-clothes security personnel.

But the geopolitical reality of the 1980s and 1990s – after the terms of the 1978 peace agreement with Egypt were fulfilled, after the drying out of military assistance to the Arab states with the collapse of the Soviet bloc, and after the first *intifadah* began in 1987 – presented new dangers to the strategy. The challenges that the state faced arose less from a conventional attack by Arab armor from the "outside" and more from a disgruntled and restless Palestinian population located "inside" the Occupied Territories.

The centers and headquarters of popular resistance were deep within Palestinian towns and cities, especially the winding and impenetrable fabric of the refugee camps. In the eyes of the state these over-dense and under-serviced urban environments became the "habitat of terror." The rapid urbanization of the West Bank during the relatively prosperous 1980s was seen by the Israeli security establishment as the "*jihad* of building" (Graham, 2002; this volume).

Palestinian urban growth, fueled by a rapidly increased population, "illegally" sprawled beyond the "blue lines" that the IDF's "Civil Administration" traced around them as planning boundaries. Cities swallowed towns, and towns, villages, creating an ever-thickening fabric of large continuously built blocks along the main Palestinian traffic arteries. This was especially pronounced along Route 60 – historically, the most important Palestinian route, the one stringing all major Palestinian cities along the north–south mountain ridge. Urbanity became a Palestinian "weapon" of retaliation, threatening to undermine the "other" urbanity of the settlements that was being produced to maintain Israeli territorial control.

The way to contain these urban threats, from the perspective of Ariel Sharon's planners, was to use the weapon of counter-urbanity – or more precisely, sub-urbanity. From the 1980s onwards, Sharon used settlements as an antidote to uncontrolled Palestinian population growth. He placed them as wedges that disturbed the consolidation of large, Palestinian metropolitan centers – those most likely to form the cultural, demographic, and political basis of a viable territorial entity.

Beyond their status as forward positions in the defense of the state from invasion, the settlements were therefore used to allow the state to exercise the task of civilian control. A continuous fabric of homes, industrial zones, and roads were knitted together to act as wedges separating the different Palestinian population centers.

Sometimes the objective of making the settlement act as a wedge was achieved by its very layout. For example, in the case of the settlement-city of Ariel – the largest settlement in Samaria, coincidentally named after Ariel Sharon – the design was stretched into a long, thin form. This was done in order to partially envelop the Palestinian city of Salfit and to cut it away from the villages which made up its regional hinterland economy (Lein and Weizman, 2002).

The small red-roofed single-family home replaced the tank as the smallest fighting unit. District regional and municipal plans replaced the strategic sand table. Homes, like armored divisions, were used in formation across a dynamic theatre of operations to occupy strategic hills, to encircle an enemy, or cut communication lines.

The location strategy employed for the West Bank was based on yet another basic military principle: the axiom that the party to move faster across a battlefield is the one to win the battle. It acted to make a dromological separation – a differentiation between the speeds by which Israelis and Palestinians could move across the terrain. Traffic arteries are *de facto* separated across national lines: the six-lane bypass roads on which military vehicles and civilian vans can rush between settlements contrast starkly with the narrow, informal dust-roads connecting Palestinian towns and villages. This slowing down of the Palestinian population is what Israeli journalist Amira Hass has called "the theft of time." The architectural research group *Multiplicity* demonstrated that it takes an Israeli driver 90 minutes to cross the West Bank from north to south. The same journey takes a Palestinian driver 8 hours. This assumes that the roads are actually open to Palestinian traffic and that they are not enduring one of the many closures that the IDF enforce (Boeri, 2003).

Jeff Halper (2001) calls the contemporary consequence of this strategic texture in the West Bank "the matrix of control." Within this matrix the inhabitation of nodal points acts as on/off valves regulating movement according to identity. This replaces the necessity for Israeli forces to be directly present within Palestinian cities. The fixing of the Palestinian population as relatively stationary, and its separation into isolated, immobile islands, makes it much easier to manage and control.

The Battle for the Hilltops

Ariel Sharon, fearing the reversal of his spatial practices, was reluctant to implement his 1982 plan gradually. He believed it was important "to secure a presence first and only then build the settlements up."

Sharon therefore acted to lay out the entire skeleton of the project, seeding the area with small outposts, some hardly more than footholds, composed of tents or mobile homes. He knew that each of these outposts, once established as a "fact on the ground," would become a fully grown settlement. (Lein and Weizman, 2002)(see plate 9.2). Defining his policy regarding the West Bank barrier in advance, Sharon advised settlers not to build fences around settlements, but rather to build fences around the Palestinians: "if you put up a fence, you put a limit to your expansion."

At the beginning of 1983, after the Kahan inquiry into the 1982 massacre at Sabra and Shatila refugee camps in Beirut had found Sharon indirectly responsible, he was forced out of government. His influence on the settlement project was thereafter exercised through an active role in the political

Plate 9.2 The outpost of Mitzpe Dani, Jordan Valley Region. Photograph: Daniel Bauer for Peace Now, 1999.

opposition. In this light, the current scenes, in the context of the "road-map," of removal and repositioning of the "illegal outposts" – small, ad hoc settlement "seeds" put up by independent groups in breach of Israeli law – thus need to be understood in the context of Sharon's skeleton strategy.

Soon after it took power in 1992, the Yitzhak Rabin government stopped issuing permits for the construction of new settlements. In response, Ariel Sharon, leading the ferocious opposition to the 1993 Oslo accords, an-nounced the "battle for the hilltops." He urged young, ideological and religious settlers to "move, run and grab as many hilltops as possible." In order to stop any further territorial concessions, Sharon thus wanted to replace the suburban culture of the settlements with a renewed frontier mentality.

In the decade since then, these settlers have established over 100 "temporary" outposts on the remaining strategic hilltops beyond the boundaries of settlements, with a total population not exceeding 1,000 (Etkes, 2003). Their aim is to secure the areas in a way that allows them to challenge any proposal for territorial compromise, or at least change the trajectory of any proposed border – if one has to be set – to Israel's permanent advantage.

The apparent naivety of the forms of outposts hides the fact that, with their potential for immediacy, mobility, and flexibility, these outposts are the perfect instruments of colonization. The prefabricated homes allow for quick, overnight deployment on the backs of trucks or (when a road is not available) even by helicopter. The prefabricated rigidity of the single elem-ent allows for an immediate urbanism, based on patterns of quick repetition and distribution. The seed of mobile homes may then be free to transform and develop into a "mature" settlement as conditions allow.

The government's acts of "dismantling" today are as revealing about the precision of the settlement location strategy as any past decisions regarding the establishment of new settlements. Most outposts spring up again im-mediately after being removed. Evacuation on the backs of trucks very often means relocation, sometimes even to a more strategic position.

Flexible Line

Points and lines are synergistic systems – the distribution of settlement points across the surface of the West Bank called for a complex set of lines both to connect them (roads) and to protect them (barriers). The latter are concretized by a series of long and interlocking mechanisms: barbed wire, ditches, dykes, and checkpoints.

The new West Bank barrier is a complex set of fortifications measuring between 35 and 100 meters in width, designed to separate the Jewish settlements and their supportive infrastructure from the Palestinian population (plate 9.3).

The main component of the barrier is a touch-sensitive, "smart," 3-meter high electronic fence, placed on 150 centimeter-deep concrete foundations (to prevent digging under it), topped with barbed wire (to prevent climbing over it), day and night video cameras, and even small radars. Stretched along the east side of the fence (facing the bulk of the West Bank) are a patrol road, a 3-meter deep trench, and two barbed-wire fences. West of it (towards Israel proper) are a trace road – where footprints of intruders are registered – a patrol road suitable for armored vehicles, and some more barbed-wire fences. At some places, when the barrier nears a Palestinian town, the tactically required see-through/shoot-through fence solidifies into an 8-meter high bullet-proof wall. Watchtowers with firing posts are placed at intervals of a few hundred meters along the barrier.

Seven control gates for Israelis and nine for Palestinians are planned in the barrier in order to allow people in and out of the enclosed area. Some twenty-six "agricultural gates" will serve Palestinian farmers whose lands are on the other side.

The project was born on November 2000, in the wake of the collapse of Labour's political project at Camp David, and a little more than a month after the second *intifadah* began. Prime minister Ehud Barak decided that, if the political borders between Israel and a Palestinian state could not be agreed upon, he would set them out unilaterally. Barak approved a plan to establish a linear barrier, roughly corresponding with the Green Line,

Plate 9.3 The West Bank Barrier, Tul Qarem Region. Photograph: Eyal Weizman, 2003.

composed of a series of ditches and dykes designed to prevent the passage of motor vehicles into Israel. Labour, propagating this idea of unilateral separation along a fortified line, has since lost two elections.

Ariel Sharon insisted – up until the day he appeared to have changed his mind – that "the idea [to build the barrier] is populist." However, on April 14, 2002, two days before the battle for Jenin was concluded and with all other major Palestinian cities firmly in his hands (Graham, this volume), Sharon "surrendered" to the demands of the Labour ministers in his unity government, as well as to growing public pressures. Amid fear of suicide attacks carried out by infiltrators from the West Bank, and awareness that not a single attack had been carried out from fenced-off Gaza, Sharon demanded a "security fence" and announced the coalition government's decision to establish the barrier.

If the direction and path of a line is the sum total of the force field of pressures that is applied to it, the barrier can offer the clearest diagram of the principle of political and social pressure molded into form. The path taken by the barrier line reflects a momentary balance of all the vectors of influences on it. As the path of the barrier "snakes" southwards, it goes through a process in which political pressures on either side of the proposed structure start echoing each other. In a principle of "positive feedback" these pressures generate ever more radical twists and turns, pushing the barrier ever deeper east of the Green Line into the occupied West Bank.

As the barrier neared their region, settlement councils started applying political pressure for the path to "loop around" and absorb them into the western (Israeli) "inside." The settlers initially resisted the idea of a barrier that would cut off parts of the West Bank from Israel proper. But once they realized they could not stop its construction, they opted, instead, to try to influence its route. A particularly loud outcry came from the settlement of Alfei-Menashe – a relatively wealthy suburban community. In the first design for the northern path for the barrier, authorized in June 2002, this settlement was left "outside." The local panic about being "abandoned," mediated through right-wing ministers, managed to force a revision of the path and the stretching out of a long loop to incorporate the settlement back "inside." As a result, the Palestinian towns of Qalqiliya and Habla, a few hundred meters apart as the crow flies, found themselves surrounded on all sides by the barrier's extension, and the connection between them now stretched into a corridor 20 kilometers long.

The path of the barrier was complicated by another series of external influences. Following pressure by government ministers from religious parties, the path of the barrier was stretched a few hundred meters southwards to include an old archeological site believed to be the biblical-era tomb of Rachel. Ten other archeological sites, including one complete Egyptian city, were discovered during the digging works along another part of the barrier and in some cases the path was changed to bring them back "inside." The desire to match the path of the barrier with subsurface interests meant the incorporation of the water extraction points of the mountain aquifer. The desire to serve Israel's aerial interests meant the appropriation of areas located below the landing paths of international flights.

It seems that the only consideration absent from the vectors of push and pull are those relating to the human rights and daily life of the Palestinian residents of the area. Along the whole length of the built and proposed paths, Palestinian villagers will be cut away from their farmland and water sources. The human rights organization B'tselem estimates that the barrier will negatively affect the livelihood of at least 210,000 Palestinians, and irreversibly damage the economic prospects of a Palestinian state (Lein, 2003).

The central phase of the barrier path, under planning and revision in late 2003, is more strategically and politically sensitive than the built-up northern part. In this phase the barrier is supposed to mediate through the densely populated regions close to the metropolitan region of Tel Aviv. There the largest numbers of settlers are located, built densities are high, and settlement real estate is relatively expensive. Israeli per-capita gross domestic product (GDP) is twenty times larger than that of Palestinians; the economic disparity between the two groups is higher then between any two other neighboring populations worldwide. In the central region, where upper-middle class suburbs crowd against impoverished villages, the economic contrast is even more extreme. It was construction in that zone that generated international public attention. European leaders demanded cancellation of the project. Tony Blair proposed delaying it. And American officials proposed physical reroutings of the map, and even reduced loan guarantees as a penalty for the barrier's construction.

Temporary Permanence

The Israeli government maintains that the principle that guides the path of the barrier involves "temporary and urgent security considerations," not political ones. They also insist that the barrier is not and will not become a permanent border. Barriers are indeed different to borders in that they do not separate an "inside" and an "outside" of a sovereignty-based political and legal system, but merely act as contingency apparatuses to prohibit movement across a territory. Throughout Israeli history, though, the state has always preferred to use temporary security arrangements as a way to create permanent political "facts on the ground." The claim for the "temporariness" of the barrier means that it must be seen as an instrument of contingency in a temporary state of emergency (Agamben, 2002). But it is precisely the transient nature of Israeli unilateral actions across the frontier of the West Bank that renders them most effective in terms of the occupation. The occupation perpetuates itself through ever-new seemingly "temporary" facts on the ground. It is the "temporality" of conflict that allows the occupation to continue permanently (Azoulay and Ophir, 2002).

Islands

"The more forces there are in the vicinity of a line, the more complex is its path." With these words the modernist painter Wassily Kandinsky set the basis for the formal organization of lines across a canvas in his book *Points and Line to Plane.* "When the force field around a line contains intense contradictions, the line can no longer maintain its graphic coherence and shreds into fragments and discontinuous vectors."

Ariel Sharon recently made public his intention to extend the barrier from being only in front (west) of Palestinian-populated areas of the West Bank to being also behind (east) of them and run through the Jordan valley, thus fully encircling and completely surrounding the Palestinian areas. Under this outline, more than half of the total territory of the West Bank will remain under Israeli control – namely, the two strategic north/south strips of the Jordan valley in the east and the meandering strip next to the Green Line in the west. They would be connected via Jerusalem and other east–west arteries. The resulting layout will repeat almost exactly the "H" pattern envisaged in Sharon's 1982 plan. Instead of a promise for separation embodied within this border-like device, the barrier will complete a project of containment. Not only will the Palestinians be surrounded on the surface of the land, but Sharon will keep effective sovereignty on the mountain aquifer below their feet and on the airspace above their heads. Thus, Israeli control will wrap the Palestinians figuratively and physically from all directions.

The Palestinian state will effectively become a series of landlocked territorial islands, completely surrounded lest they expand, within a Zionist body politic that will cover all the territory between the Mediterranean and the Jordan river. The archipelago of isolated territories around the Palestinian cities that remain, initially under IDF control, will gradually turn into what will become the "Palestinian state within its temporary borders" – the one the current peace process states as its objective. The Green Line, which the Palestinian government would like to see as its border with Israel, is 350 kilometers long, but the total length of barriers projected to be constructed between Israel and the Palestinians stretches to more than 1,200 kilometers.

In this geographic arrangement, the Palestinians are simultaneously inside and outside. They are landlocked inside a complete territorial envelopment, without any border save the very long and fragmented one to Israel. But – recalling the apartheid-era South African Bantustans – they are also outside the Israeli state system.

Enclaves/Exclaves

Within both Israeli and Palestinian parts of the West Bank, there will be islands or enclaves belonging to the other zone. A few hundred thousands Palestinians will be left within the Israeli side, while almost the same number of Israelis, in remote settlements and military installations, will remain in pockets of "special security zones" within the Palestinian areas.

To protect these settlements and reassure their inhabitants, a sequence of fortifications identical to those composing the primary barrier is being laid out in enclosed circuits around them. The barrier thus ceases to be a single continuous line: like splintered worms taking on renewed life, it has started curling around isolated settlements and along the roads connecting them.

This is a condition of double enclosure. Settlements are fenced in for self-protection while Palestinian towns are enclosed from outside to prohibit "security threats" from leaking out. With this arrangement, the traditional perception of political space as a contiguous territorial surface, clearly delimited by continuous borders, is no longer relevant. If the relation between the length of a border and the surface of the territory is an indication of the amount of "security" present, then the folds of the barrier line and its separate shreds place "security" measures deep throughout the terrain. In a process that is analogous to the way in which the fjords, islands, and lakes along the Norwegian coast create a whole zone across which water meets rock, the barrier's folds and twists create an ever-present high-friction zone where civilian populations are pressed against "security" apparatuses.

With this fragmented geography in mind, Sharon has finally merged the two extremes that defined Israel's relation to its edge. Trying to articulate defense in depth with a line, he has simultaneously created the line of a "border" and the deep conflict space of the "frontier." The paradox in the fact that it is finally Ariel Sharon that set the borders of the state can thus be resolved. The barrier is not a defeat of his geostrategy, based on the historical rejection of the setting of a permanent border. For in its convoluted path, the one inscribed in the logic of his strategic thinking, the barrier is the direct and logical consequence of his free frontier mentality, which seeks to blur the borders of the state, rather than fix them.

The territorial concessions embedded in the "road map" plan are based on nothing but an acknowledgment of the Palestinian demographic advantage. Sharon is aware that, considering current population growth, there will be a Palestinian majority in the combined territories of Israel/Palestine by 2020. He has thus acted to cut out the Palestinian demographic centers from the legal and effective responsibility of the Israeli state. However, the consolidation of lines so convoluted and discontinuous into such expensive material presence will not end the occupation. Rather, they will offer the means to indirectly consolidate occupation. Israel will go on being a borderless society, left in a perpetual state of fermentation and uncertainty in its identity, with the inconsistent behavior and self-destructive impulses that define its own "borderline disorder" (Efrat, 2002).

A Political Volume

When the barrier is completed, and the temporary–permanent security measures outline the border of a permanent "Palestinian state in temporary borders" scattered on landlocked sovereign islands, yet another territorial paradox will have to be resolved. The fragmentation of jurisdiction across the surface will not be compatible with Sharon's public pledges that – with the implementation of the "road map" – he will carve out a "contiguous area of territory in the West Bank that would allow the Palestinians to travel from Jenin [the northernmost city in the West Bank] to Hebron [the southernmost] without passing any Israeli roadblocks."

When Sharon announced this, bewildered reporters objected, and pointed out that the proposed path of the barrier will enclose these cities and set them apart in separate territorial envelopment. Asked how the contradiction between contiguity and fragmentation could be resolved, Sharon responded, probably with one of his famous winks, that this will be accomplished by "a combination of tunnels and bridges." This type of "continuity" was first realized by Sharon in 1996. As minister of national infrastructure under Benjamin Netanyahu, he inaugurated the first apparatus of vertical separation – the "tunnel road" – which demonstrated that continuity, and separation, could be achieved not on the surface but in volume.

The tunnel road connects Jerusalem with the southern settlements of Gush Etzion and further, with the Jewish neighborhoods of Hebron. To accomplish this it performs a double contortion: spanning, as a bridge, a Palestinian cultivated valley, and then diving into a tunnel under a Palestinian suburb of Bethlehem.

The Israeli writer Meron Benvenisti describes the road as the crashing of three dimensions into six: three Israeli and three Palestinian. Both the valley that the road spans and the city it dives under are, according to the Oslo agreement, areas under limited Palestinian sovereignty. Thus the physical separation of traffic arrangements is mirrored by a political one – the city above is under Palestinian limited sovereignty while the road below it is under full Israeli sovereignty. By introducing the vertical dimension, in similar schemes of over- and under-passes, linkage could be achieved between the different territorial islands.

The last territorial paradox of the frontier could thus be resolved. Israeli/ Palestinian roads and infrastructure would connect settlements/Palestinian towns while they span over or under Palestinian/Israeli lands. Consequently, and hand-in-hand with the planned completion of the barrier, plans are under way to transform Route 60 – the main north–south traffic artery connecting all major Palestinian cities – into an elevated construction placed on stilts allowing for Israeli east–west routes (those making the H plan) to pass undisturbed underneath it. At the point where these roads cross, sovereignty will be divided along the up/down axis of the vertical dimension.

In the West Bank, bridges are no longer merely devices engineered to overcome natural boundaries or connect impossible points. Rather, they become the boundary itself. Indeed, a new way of imagining territory has been developed for the West Bank. The region is no longer seen as a two-dimensional surface of a single territory, but as a large "hollow" three-dimensional surface, within which the West Bank can be physically partitioned into two separate but overlapping national geographies. Within this volume, separate security corridors, infrastructure, over-ground bridges and underground tunnels are woven into an Escher-like space.

With the technologies and infrastructure required for the physical segregation of Israelis from Palestinians along complex volumetric borders, it seems as if this most complex geopolitical problem of the Middle East has gone through a scale-shift and taken on architectural dimensions. The West Bank appears to have been reassembled in the shape of a complex building with its closed-off enclaves as walled spaces and its bypasses as exclusive security corridors. The barrier is but the surface component in an occupation that will continue underneath and above the surface – in the effective Israeli control of the water aquifers under Palestinian areas and in Israeli sovereignty over the airways and electromagnetic fields that will allow constant Israeli air force control above the territory. The volumetric technologies of separation might well be geometrically creative and "interesting" in planning terms. But, in essence, they are the very familiar and traditional, absolute and hermetic borders, here disguised within the Trojan horse of spatial radicalism.

The attempt to imagine a spatial–technical design solution to the conflict – one based on different paths of partition achieved by barriers, tunnels, and bridges – has thus reached its most extreme and dystopian logical conclusion and end result. This conclusion is too complex to offer security (unless the entire resources of the state are constantly drafted to maintain and service its length). It is too intrusive and aggressive to offer the appearance of a just solution. And it is too expensive to be economically viable in the long run.

Could the politics of borders and partition be replaced by a more viable alternative – based on inclusion, democracy, and human rights?

10

Constructing Urbicide by Bulldozer in the Occupied Territories

Stephen Graham

Introduction: "Asymmetric Urbicide" and the Circle of Atrocity

Israel, having ceased to care about the children of the Palestinians, should not be surprised when they come washed in hatred and blow themselves up in the centers of Israeli escapism. (Avraham Burg, Israeli Labour Party, 2003; quoted in Urquhart, 2003)

Whilst the Palestinian suicide bomber is rightly condemned for killing and maiming civilians with his or her homemade nail bomb, Israel's supreme court upholds the use of the flechette shell, with which Israel kills and maims civilians in the Gaza strip, one of the most densely populated places in the world. These shells, shot from tanks, are packed with thousands of tiny steel darts that spray in a "kill radius" some 300 meters long and 90 meters wide. Israeli flechette or Palestinian nail bomb: what is the difference again? (Clark, 2004: 34)

At 2.15 p.m. on October 4, 2003 – the eve of the Jewish Yom Kippur – Hanadi Jaradat walked into the Maxim restaurant near the southern border of the city of Haifa, on Israel's northern coast. The restaurant was packed with both Jewish and Arab Israelis in festive mood. In an instant, 19 people were killed and over 50 more horribly injured when she detonated the explosive belt strapped around her waist (Toolis, 2003).

Jaradat's assault, organized through Islamic Jihad, was one of a long string of Palestinian suicide attacks targeting Israeli civilians as part of the second "Al-Aqsa" *intifadah*. Between September 2000 and October 21, 2003 these attacks killed 376 Israeli civilians and had major effects on the economies of Israeli cities (see Human Rights Watch, 2002a). Such suicide attacks have been fueled by the desperation of the Palestinians' situation, and the much worse rate of fatalities, injuries, and devastation that Palestinian civilians have suffered at the hands of the Israeli Defense Forces in the second *intifadah* (2,194 deaths in the same period).[1] Suicide attacks have also been supported by a deepening ethic of martyrdom in the resistance movement, particularly since 2001 (Hage, 2003).

In suicide attacks Palestinian use one of the few weapons that they have: the continuing ability, despite tightening restrictions and lengthening fences, to move their bodies into close proximity to people they assume to be Israelis. In so doing they wreak carnage and havoc on contemporary Israel's sites of everyday urban modernity. The chosen targets – cafés, restaurants, bars, buses, bus stops, pool halls, and shopping centers – are selected carefully. In a highly urbanized country such as Israel, they are, by definition, unavoidably crowded places (Stein, 2003). Israeli responses to the attacks have, in turn, stressed that the symbolic urban places of Israeli nationhood – especially coffee houses – are under direct attack. "This is a war about the morning's coffee and croissant," wrote Adi Shveet in the newspaper *Ha'aretz* in March 2002. "It is about the beer in the evening. About our very lives."

Dig a little deeper and Hanadi Jaradat's case demonstrates that the Palestinian–Israeli struggle now involves what I have called *asymmetric urbicide* (Graham, 2002d). This term is used to describe the fact that, in an intensely urbanized context, the overwhelming effort of both sides in the war is now directed to try to deny the rights of the "enemy" to their respective, city-based, lives. Both sides are attacking the spaces of everyday urban life with weapons that are carefully designed to disrupt and destroy these "soft targets" (see Reporters Without Borders, 2003).

The means of attempting this, of course, could not contrast more strongly – hence the "asymmetric" part of the term. Crucially, this denotes that the levels of violence sustained by both sides are in no way equivalent. Occasional Palestinian violence is totally dwarfed by the vast scale, and continuous nature, of Israeli violence and repression against Palestinians. It is also crucial to stress that Palestinian violence is a violence of resistance against half a century of brutal and intensifying occupation (Gregory, 2003).

On one side of asymmetric urbicide, then, explosives and bodily proximity are being used to try to deny Israelis their relatively prosperous, Western-style, urban modernity. On the other, the Israeli state is now waging a systematic and extremely violent war against Palestinian towns and cities *per se*. As we shall see, every part of Israel's massive, US-supported, military might – from fighter bombers, satellite surveillance, and attack helicopters through tanks, snipers, and bulldozers – is being harnessed to try to forcibly demodernize Palestinian urban society through what Mansour has termed the Israeli Defense Force's "besieging cartography" (2001, 86–7; cited in

Gregory, 2003: 311). Crucially, this strategy of deliberate urban *destruction* is closely integrated with Israel's efforts at carefully planned *construction* of place and space in the Occupied Territories (analyzed in chapter 9 by Eyal Weizman) (see Reuveney, 2003; Yiftachel, 1995).

Hanadi Jaradat's attack was an attempt to avenge just one small act in this state-led, high-tech strategy of urbicide. She made the decision to mount the attack because her two brothers – Fardi and Salah – were both assassinated outside her home in Jenin by undercover Israeli soldiers in the spring of 2003. This was but one of countless other assaults on the daily life, infrastructure, living spaces, and support systems of Palestinian cities that have occurred since the start of Israel's unprecedented campaign – labeled Operation Defensive Shield – which has devastated Palestinian cities and destroyed countless Palestinian lives since it started in April 2002.

Such actions undermine the repeated claims by the Israeli leader, Ariel Sharon, that Israel's aim, both in Operation Defensive Shield and since, has been purely to destroy the "terrorist infrastructure" behind Palestinian suicide attacks. The evidence suggests, rather, that Sharon's real purpose has been to take advantage of the favorable strategic context of the US-led, post-9/11 "war on terrorism" – which allowed him to link Palestinian resistance to Al-Qaeda – to destroy the urban infrastructural and cultural foundations of the proto-Palestinian state (Kimmerling, 2003; Carey, 2001; Gregory, 2003).

Learning from the Israeli defeat in Lebanon in the 1980s, the actual target seems to have been, as the IDF analyst Dov Tamari (2001: 43) has put it, "the social infrastructure, the welfare infrastructure, out of which combatants have grown and on which their families rely." Sharon's is thus a deliberate strategy to compel Palestinians to immiseration and poverty. By May 2002, 70 percent of Palestinians were living below the poverty line of $2 a day and 30 percent of Palestinian children were chronically malnourished. By the end of May 2002 the UN was feeding half a million Palestinians to keep them from starving (Whitaker, 2002: 5).

Hanadi Jaradat's attack therefore captures the way in which ever more violent and extreme efforts by Israel to assault Palestinian urban society simply add to long-standing Palestinian hatred and despair. These have been caused both by the repressive and extremely violent occupation of their homelands, and their bloody expulsion from Israel proper since the founding of the Israeli state in 1948.

The result of this situation, of course, is an interminable circle of atrocity. Intensifying state terror, brutalization, killing, repression and occupation, targeting the everyday civilian life of Palestinians, begets a deepened response of suicidal martyrdom (which now involves women as well as men – see Victor, 2003). This is fueled, in turn, by a proliferating range of radical Islamic resistance organizations. Meir Hadina of Tel Aviv University now argues that "martyrdom is now central to the al-Aqsa *intifadah*. It has created a balance of power between Palestinians and Israel and it will not be easily removed from the Palestinian political agenda" (quoted in Toolis, 2003; see Hage, 2003). Also fueling both sides are deeply rooted racist discourses. These dehumanize the respective "enemy" and facilitate the ongoing bloodletting against military and civilian targets alike.

Depressingly, such atrocities are currently worsening. When they happen, suicide attacks are exploited by Sharon's government to support more annexation of Palestinian land, more state atrocities, more ethnic cleansing, and more air strikes, tank raids, mass incarcerations, curfews, checkpoints, extrajudicial executions, assassinations, barriers, and collective punishments. All these are justified as part of the drive for "security," as Sharon shamelessly exploits the opportunity provided by Bush's post-9/11 war on terror to ratchet up Israel's state terror (Kimmerling, 2003). Thus, as usual, the Jaradat family home was demolished by Israeli forces as a collective punishment for Hanadi's suicide attack.

In this chapter I explore Israel's strategy of state-led urbicide in detail. (For discussions of the impacts of the suicide attacks on Israeli cities, see Human Rights Watch, 2002a; Hage, 2003; Savitch and Ardashev, 2001). Using the battle of Jenin in April 2002 as a central anchor in the narrative, I analyze a range of debates among Israeli military, political, and academic elites which problematize the very existence of Palestinian urbanization and urban settlements and legitimize their devastation and immiseration. I show that these discourses have directly shaped Israeli military strategies that have been carefully designed to directly assault the urban infrastructures and living space of Palestinian cities. Finally, I also demonstrate that such Israeli strategies – which pit high-tech military forces against fighters who exploit closely built Arab urban settlements – are being directly imported into US practice as the US military addresses the Islamic cities that it sees as its main targets in its global war on terror – most notably, in Iraq.

Understanding Urbicide by Bulldozer

The weapon that has dominated the destruction of Palestinian buildings, infrastructure, and cities, both in Operation Defensive Shield and ever since,[2] is the D-9 armored Caterpillar bulldozer (McGreal, 2002) (see plate 10.1). Weighing 60 tons and "built or retrofitted with steel armor plates, tiny bullet-proof cabin windows, special blades and buckets optimized for concrete demolition, and a powerful asphalt-ripper in the rear," the D-9 has been deliberately designed to plough through Palestinian built-up areas with impunity (Zeitoun, 2002). An Israeli chief of staff claimed in 2000 that "the Caterpillar D-9 [armored] bulldozer is a strategic

Plate 10.1 A series of video capture images showing a D-9 bulldozer claw being used to destroy a Palestinian road and water network in Bethlehem as part of Operation Defensive Shield, April 2002. Photographer: a Palestinian activist who wishes to remain anonymous.

weapon here" (Harel, 2000; see Stein, 2002). In 2003 the IDF announced that remote-control D-9s were in operation to minimize the risk to drivers as Palestinian buildings were demolished (Rabinovitz, 2003).

The deliberate bulldozing of whole districts of cities by Israeli Defense Forces in spring 2002 is an intensification of an old policy. Bulldozing has been used as a weapon of collective and individual punishment and intimidation, and as a means of shaping the geopolitical configuration of territory, since Israel's independence in 1948 (Weizman, this volume). Between 1967 and 2002 alone, over 7,000 Palestinian homes were bulldozed or demolished in the Occupied Territories (Gordon, 2002). Over 4,000 Palestinian houses were demolished between 2000 and 2003 (Sales, 2003) (see plate 10.2). Up until the late 1990s, this was generally legitimized because the houses in question were deemed by Israeli authorities to have been "built without a permit." Given that biased planning ensures that almost all applications for a permit are refused, this "illegality" was (and remains) easily constructed.

In placing the intensified demolition of houses and built spaces by IDF bulldozers in context, three key points deserve elaboration.

Geopolitics and the bulldozer

First, such bulldozing is far from random. It is closely integrated into what Eyal Weizman (2002; this volume) calls the "politics of verticality": the three-dimensional orchestration of territorial configurations to maintain and deepen Israel's geopolitical advantage. Thus, the mass bulldozing of housing and city spaces is a critical element of the implementation of Israel's wider territorial strategy. As Achille Mbembe demonstrates, the intersections of three-dimensional urban battlespace and what he calls "verticalized sovereignty" – the verticalized aerial power of the Israeli state – involve a complex and multi-faceted set of processes. On the one hand, Israel's high-tech, US-supplied weapons mean that the "killing of Palestinians becomes precisely targeted" (although many civilians still die as "collateral damage"). On the other hand:

> Such precision is combined with the tactics of medieval siege warfare adapted to the networked sprawl of urban refugee camps. An orchestrated and systematic sabotage of the enemy's societal and urban infrastructure networks complements the appropriation of land, water, and airspace resources. Critical to these techniques of disabling the enemy is *bulldozing*. (Mbembe, 2003: 29; original emphasis)

Such bulldozing overwhelmingly occurs in strategic areas. It backs up the wider use of settlements and access roads to undermine any contiguity in

Plate 10.2 The banality of urbicide: Israeli Defense Force soldiers preparing to blow up a Palestinian home in the Tul Quarem refugee camp in the West Bank, 2002. Photographer: Nir Kafri, 2003.

Palestinian territory (Weizman, this volume). Jad Isaac, director general of the Applied Research Institute of Jerusalem, argues that "it is important to see where the [bulldozed] houses are located and why. It's not arbitrary. These sites are meticulously selected. They are for the bypass roads or new zoning for the settlements, to increase Israeli control" (cited in Smith, 2001).

House and city demolitions are also linked to a broader strategy of the annihilation of landscape – purportedly to reduce the vulnerabilities of the new archipelagos of Jewish settlements and highways to Palestinian attack (Selwyn, 2001). "What is most striking in Palestine now is the violence wrought against the land, the terrain," writes Christian Salmon (2002) of the *Autodafe* writers' collective. He continues:

> Houses are destroyed, olive trees uprooted, orange groves laid waste... to improve... visibility... The bulldozer one runs across at every roadside seems as much a part of the strategy in the ongoing war as the tank. Never has such an inoffensive machine struck me as being more of a harbinger of silent violence. The brutality of war. Geography, it is said, determines war. In Palestine it is war that has achieved the upper hand over geography.

This bulldozing of landscape in the name of "security" was further intensified with the construction, from June 2002, of a massive 360-kilometer fence, with a cleared 2-kilometer "buffer zone," which will eventually completely encircle the West Bank (Bedell, 2003). This is being built on land up to 20 miles *inside* the Green Line – land that is forcibly annexed from Palestinians (Weizman, this volume).

Urbicide as forced demodernization

Second, urbicide by bulldozer is not just about the demolition of homes and urban living spaces. House demolitions have long been paralleled by intensive infrastructural destruction, as Israeli forces work to prevent or systematically undermine the modernization of Palestinian urban society and the development of economic, technological, cultural, or bureaucratic institutions (see Hamzah and May, 2003). In May 2001, Israeli Labour Minister Ben Azri called for the explicit destruction of Palestinian roads, water systems, electricity systems, and cultural facilities as a deliberate aim of geopolitical strategy – a way, as he put it, of "converting the life of Palestinians into hell" (Arabic News, May 6, 2001). Israel has largely done this in a strategy that, once again, directly parallels the construction of intensifying infrastructural mobilities, and technological modernities, for Jewish settlers (with their militarized highways, fortified cars, dedicated energy grids, and favorable access to groundwater and sewerage systems).

The Israelis made dramatic efforts during the 2002 invasion of the West Bank cities of Nablus, Ramallah, Hebron, Bethlehem, Jenin, and other cities to undermine the already slow modernization of these cities (which now house the vast majority of the Palestinian people). What Derek Gregory (2003: 317) calls *"the bare essentials of a dignified human life"* (original emphasis) in an urbanized society were comprehensively targeted and systematically destroyed. Water tanks were riddled with bullets. Electronic communications were bombed and jammed. Roads were dug up and ruined. The water pipes beneath them were clawed up and broken by the attachment on the rear of D-9s (plate 10.1). Electricity transformers were destroyed. Computers were smashed, their hard disks stolen. Any cultural or bureaucratic symbol of the proto-Palestinian state was ransacked. Financial damage to infrastructure from the first major offensive alone has been estimated by donors at US$361 million (Giacaman and Husseini, 2002).

Amira Hass, writing in the Israeli newspaper *Ha'aretz* in April 2002, emphasizes the deliberate destruction of the bureaucratic and informational infrastructure of proto-Palestinian and non-governmental organizations in the Israeli attacks:

> It's a scene that is repeating itself in hundreds of Palestinian offices taken over by IDF troops in the West Bank: smashed, burned, and broken computer terminals heaped in piles and thrown in yards, server cable cut, hard disks missing, disks and diskettes scattered and broken, printers and scanners broken and missing, laptops gone, telephone exchanges that disappeared or were vandalized, and paper files burned, torn, scattered, or defaced – if not taken... This was not a whim, or crazed vengeance. Let's not deceive ourselves – this was not a mission to search and destroy the terrorist infrastructure. (Hass, 2002)

In addition, during the April attacks, hospitals were bombed and medical equipment was looted and wrecked. Ambulances were prevented from entering the war zones, condemning many to a slow, avoidable death, as their blood, literally, seeped away. In some cases those medical staff getting through were deliberately attacked. At least three were killed.[3] Even by the end of April 2002 it was "safe to say that the infrastructure of life itself and of any future Palestinian state...had been devastated" (Schemann, 2002).

Sharon *"the bulldozer"*

Finally, it is important to stress that the Israeli prime minister, Ariel Sharon – who has long been nicknamed the "Bulldozer" – has a particularly long and personal association with its use as a weapon of war and intimidation as part of a broad and long-standing assault on the Palestinians (plate 10.3) (see Kimmerling, 2003). In 1953, for example, forces commanded by Sharon leveled homes in the West Bank village of Kibya, killing 69 Palestinians, in retaliation for the murder of a Jewish woman and her two children.

Intrinsic to the adoption of such tactics is a stereotyped cultural judgment of the critical role of the house within Palestinian society and culture. Sharon revealed his personal philosophy behind urbicide by bulldozer in an interview in the *Ha'aretz* newspaper on January 26, 2001. In answer to a question about how he would respond to the persistent Palestinian shooting into the new Jewish settlements that had recently been implanted in the Palestinian neighborhood of Beit Jela at Gilo, south of Jerusalem, he replied: "I would eliminate the first row of houses in Beit Jela." "And," asked the journalist, "if the shooting persisted?"

> I would eliminate the second row of houses, and so on. I know the Arabs. They are not impressed by helicopters and missiles. For them, there is nothing more important than their house. So, under me, you will not see a child shot next to his father [as was the case with Mohammed Al-Dorra]. It is better to level the entire village with bulldozers, row after row. (Jansen, 2001: 2)

Plate 10.3 Bill Cook's satirical cartoon depicting Ariel Sharon, the "Bulldozer." Source: www.counterpunch.orh May 2002, used with permission.

Legitimizing Urbicide Through Language

The battle for language becomes the battle for land. (Barghouti, 2003: 34)

Operation Defensive Shield marked a major shift from the systematic demolition of houses and occasionally streets, infrastructures, and villages, towards wholesale urbicide as a cornerstone of Israeli policy. Complementing ongoing "pepper-potted" demolitions, Israeli forces switched in the middle of the invasion to embark on the systematic and carefully planned destruction of entire districts within settlements for political and military reasons, a policy that has continued since, notably with the massive demolitions in Rafah in spring 2004.

This shift has been more than a material and political phenomenon. Crucially, it has also been made through *language*. In other words, it has been constructed *discursively*. In fact, three interwoven discourses among political, military, and academic elite within Israeli society can be identified which have provide the legitimization and justification for this shift from ongoing sporadic demolition to wholesale urbicide.

An existential threat to Zionist Israel

First, Israel's shift to deliberate urbicide by bulldozer is the end result of a deepening antagonism among Israel's right-wing military and political elites against the natural demographic and urban growth of the Palestinian people (Zureik, 2003). This discourse portrays rapid and spontaneous Palestinian urbanization and demographic growth, within both Israel and the Occupied Territories, as the Palestinian's major long-term strategic "weapon" in shifting the demographic, geopolitical, and military balance against Israel. It suggests that this growth is overwhelming efforts by Israel to support the in-migration of Jews into both Israel itself and the new settlements.

Sharon and his military leaders have often suggested that Palestinian urbanization and demographic growth – largely unplanned and poorly serviced by infrastructure – is now undermining the long-term viability of the Zionist state itself. Statistical fuel for discourses of existential threat comes from a range of demographic projections and analyses. For nowhere else in the world are two populations with such contrasting demographic and fertility profiles found so juxtaposed and intermingled. Israeli Jews born in Europe are barely replacing their population (at 2.13 babies per family); Palestinians in Gaza have the highest demographic growth in the world (7.73 babies per family) (Fargues, 2000).

Projecting these discrepancies, Arnon Soffer (2001), a leading Israeli right-wing demographer who has completed many geopolitical analyses for the Israeli government, has predicted that the overall population of the land west of the Jordan river (i.e., Israel and the Occupied Territories) will rise from 9.7 million in 2001 to 15.2 million by 2020. Within this pattern, the Palestinian population of the area (which was 4.8 million in 2000) will grow by 3.5 percent per annum to reach around 8.8 million. The area's Jewish population, meanwhile – which was 4.9 million in 2000 – will grow by 1–2 percent a year to reach around 6.4 million by 2020.

Thus, Soffer believes that between 2000 and 2020, Jews will move from constituting 50.5 percent of the overall population to the west of the Jordan river to only 42 percent. Soffer, who has had enormous influence on right-wing political and military thinking, argues that these trends threaten nothing less than "the disappearance of the Jewish-Zionist state . . . unless preventative measures are not taken" (2001: 9). Soffer elaborates what he sees as this "existential threat" to Zionist Israel by arguing that:

> The process of urbanization around Israel's borders will result in a large Arab population, suffering from poverty and hunger, surrounding the Jewish state. These areas are likely to become fertile ground for the evolvement of radical Islamic movements . . . In the Arab zone the urbanization process takes on a wild nature, stemming from the absence of planning policy and, in particular, a lack of supervision and enforcement of construction law. Everyone builds as he [*sic*] sees fit, and the result is hundreds of illegal villages spreading in all directions. (Soffer, 2001: 2, 47)

Evasive "cancer" within the (greater) Israeli body-as-state

A second, related, discourse is based on the construction and naturalization of the metaphor that Palestinian urbanization is an evasive cancer undermining the order, progress, and existence of the purported organic "body" of the modern State of Israel. Such ideas, which tend to be filled with what Mourid Barghouti (2003: 359) has called "apartheid hate-language," have a long history in ultra-Zionist or ultra-Orthodox circles in Israel.

One of the most important advocates of such body-as-state ideology is Efraim Eitam. Eitam is a retired IDF brigadier general, an ex-commander of the IDF army in Southern Lebanon, and an ultra-right wing representative of the Jewish settlers' National Religious Party. Between October 2002 and June 2004, Eitam was a member of Sharon's ruling coalition. A leading figure within national–ultra-Orthodox political circles, he was made minister without portfolio by Sharon on April 6, 2002.[4] This was done as the IDF consolidated its hold over West Bank cities following the first part of Operation Defensive Shield. This created the opportunity for Sharon to bring in a group of hardliners, while marginalizing more conciliatory figures like Shimon Peres.

Eitam argues that, ultimately, Israel should strive to force or "persuade" all Arabs and Palestinians to leave Israel and the Occupied Territories – to be accommodated in Jordan and the Sinai (Egypt). His position is that the Occupied Territories are "a human, demographic and social time bomb" waiting to "explode" upon the Israeli state (quoted in Hasen, 2002). Constructing the state of Israel as a corporeal, ordered body – a tactic common is nationalistic discourse – such allegations make it relatively simple to portray an essentialized and racist construction of the Palestinian "other" as a cancerous, evasive, and multiplying threat which demands extreme Israeli military responses. Eitam has even explicitly used the German concept of *Lebensraum* (living space) – a cornerstone of the Holocaust – to underpin his arguments (Simon, 2002).

In February 2002 Eitam spoke at a major international military conference, attended by the author, in Haifa, Israel (Eitam, 2002). With around 30 urban warfare specialists from the IDF and US and British forces in attendance, this event addressed the links between war and cities in the twenty-first century. In his presentation Eitam argued that Israel faced what he calls a "Jihad of buildings." The spontaneous construction of Palestinian housing and refugee camps within both Israel and the Occupied Territories, was, he argued, a "cancerous tumor destroying the ordered host" of the Israeli state. "Even today, within fast-growing Arab cities within Israel like Galilee," he argued,

> a *de facto* [Palestinian] autonomy is being created, which could in practice turn Israel into the bubble of Tel Aviv, into a kind of pipe state – a country between the Jerusalem–Tel Aviv–Haifa road. Therefore I say that the State of Israel today faces an elusive threat, and elusive threats by their nature resemble a cancer. Cancer is a type of illness in which most people who die from it because they were diagnosed too late. By the time you grasp the size of the threat, it is already too late to deal with it. (Hasen, 2002: 6)

Eitam continued: "we are dealing with the use of urban areas as weapon, the building is a weapon." Places like Galilee, with its 40,000 "illegally" build Palestinian houses constructed within Israel, were, he said, "like a cancer that will destroy the ordered host" of the modern, developed (Greater) Israeli state (i.e., the State of Israel and the Occupied Territories). Elaborating, he argued that:

> Uncontrolled spontaneous urbanization is a threat of war! The attacks against us are not physical but are on the order of the system. It's an evasive threat – not conventional or terroristic. This is very important in the context of the global War on Terrorism. It is destructive not through direct damage but

through its evasive characteristics which eventually kill the order of the host state. As of today we have the evasive tumor which sits within the order of the Israeli system. This is a cancerous threat; the cancer cell multiplies. We see a mosque appearing there, a mass of buildings here. We thus see order destroyed. (Eitam, 2002: 6)

Challenges to Israeli military omnipotence and surveillance

Paralleling these discursive appeals to urbicide and ethnic cleansing, a third discourse has emerged, largely from military strategists. This asserts that the urbanization of Palestinian terrain strongly undermines Israeli military omnipotence, and hence geopolitical power, in the region.

This profoundly Orientalist discourse concentrates on the nature of cities and urban settlements as fighting terrain (see Rabinovitz, 2002; Tuastad, 2003). Here, Palestinian cities are portrayed as essentially unknowable, closed, and unoccupiable spaces, which challenge the three-dimensional panoptic gaze of the IDF's high-technology surveillance systems and lie beyond the reach of many key weapons systems, such as tanks. Here, whole cities are rendered as "terrorist nests" that challenge Israel's military advantage in the new geopolitical situation. Military tactics, including raids into the Occupied Territories, and the bombing of refugee camps by F-16 fighters and gunship helicopters, become a means of demonstrating the reassertion of omnipotence, despite the inevitable carnage that results among Palestinian civilians. Following IDF raids into the Khan Yunis refugee camp of Gaza in early October 2002, for example, Herb Keinon, celebrating the "success" of an operation which killed 16 Palestinian civilians, wrote tellingly that the raid was designed to demonstrate that "no area – even the most rabidly pro-Hamas or pro-Islamic Jihad stronghold in Gaza – is outside the IDF's reach" (*Guardian*, 2002)

Above all, this third discourse asserts that the new urban battlefield renders untenable the military doctrines used by the IDF to fight traditional state-vs.-state wars since independence in 1948 – of open tank engagements, mass fighter-bombing attacks, and the avoidance of cities. Operation Defensive Shield thus represented a major strategic U-turn for the IDF, who's doctrine since 1948 – in common with the prevailing military thinking of the post-World War II period – was that "entering cities should be avoided, as this offered no benefits whatsoever. Thus, cities and population centers should be bypassed" (Tamari, 2001: 35).

Efraim Eitam, meanwhile, argues that buildings and cities are not just "weapons" of geopolitical occupation; their massive influence on the effectiveness of orthodox military tactics means that they should be considered as weapons of war. He argues that, as the defeat of the IDF in Beirut in the 1980s demonstrated, "in the low-intensity fighting [beyond the old state vs. state paradigm] there is a paradox. The weak evasive side addresses the asymmetries of military power by using the building and city as a weapon" (Eitam, 2002).

In the new, urbanized Israeli–Palestinian war, fighters cannot be separated from civilians and often blend into the civilian population after fighting ceases. Standoff weapons from tanks and aircraft are often ineffective and threaten major public relations problems when they kill large numbers of civilians (as in Gaza on October 17, 2002). Surveillance at a distance via satellite systems has reduced power.

Combat in Palestinian cities, as we saw with the deaths of 13 Israeli soldiers in the battle of Jenin on April 9, 2002, also exposes Israeli soldiers to the risks of snipers, ambushes, booby traps, and homemade bombs (which have even destroyed 60-ton Merkava tanks on several occasions in Gaza). Urbanized places can thus dramatically negate the superiority of high-tech Israeli over low-tech Palestinian forces.

Such a fear of built and urbanized spaces reaches very high levels among Israeli military leaders and commanders, who have been deeply influenced by the prevailing IDF doctrine of city avoidance and the need to develop integrated land and air operations in open territory. Interviews with IDF personnel involved in the current strategies of bulldozing settlements, orchards, and "buffer zones" around checkpoints, and Jewish-only settlements, access roads, and borders, reveal a striking discursive obsession with uncluttered, unbuilt geographical territories (that lend themselves to surveillance, Jewish occupation, and both traditional and high-tech practices of military control) (Weizman, this volume).

In 1998, for example, David Bar El, deputy head of Israel's Civil Administration at the time, said: "If we don't keep this territory clean, at the end of the day there will be irreversible facts on the ground that will reduce our 'maneuvering space'" (cited in Smith, 2001). In this equation, tellingly, a simple binary and racialized territorialization is constructed. Jewish and IDF-surveilled land is discursively constructed as "clean." Palestinian occupation and inhabitation, by implication, emerges as "unclean" – something noxious to be metaphorically, and literally, swept away, ordered, and sanitized.

The Battle of Jenin: "I Made Them a Stadium in the Middle of the Camp!"

These discourses in general, and Eitam's in particular, played major roles in shaping the development of the strategic planning that led to Operation Defensive Shield. Along with a whole variety of think-tanks, analyses, and invocations from geopolitical academics and military leaders, Eitam sought, in late 2001, to change the IDF's tactics so that they could support effective urban operations and, when necessary, work to challenge the very existence of Palestinian cities (see Tamari, 2001).

Crucially, Eitam headed a group of retired senior Israeli generals who developed a plan for the current Israeli invasion of the Occupied Territories. This was presented to Sharon on January 31, 2002 as a deliberate attempt to stimulate a major attack on both those making suicide bombs and what Eitam once again called the "elusive threat" of wider, city-based Palestinian resistance. As the *New Internationalist* argued (2002a): "Eitam's description of what should be done is very close to what Ariel Sharon's government is actually doing in Operation Defensive Shield."

The brutal effects of these discourses, and the military tactics legitimized by them, were starkly revealed in Jenin refugee camp between April 3–16, 2002. Here occurred the most extreme act of Israeli state violence against Palestinian cities since the start of the Al-Aqsa *intifadah* in September 2000 (Baroud, 2002). Israeli Defense Forces systematically bulldozed a 160 × 250 meter area in the center of the Jenin refugee camp in the northern West Bank of the Occupied Territories (see plate 10.4). The battle was the most

Plate 10.4 Aerial photograph of the destruction of the Hart-Al-Hawashin district in the center of the Jenin refugee camp caused by Israeli bulldozers. Used by permission from Public Relations Branch, Israeli Defense Forces.

fierce and deadly of those sparked by Operation Defensive Shield. This was because, for both sides, Jenin held a special symbolic significance. To the Israeli right, it was the main "terrorist nest" from which suicide bombers emerged (note the dehumanizing language) (Eitam, 2002). To Palestinians, Jenin was the main center of resistance to Israel's brutal and murderous occupation of their homeland (Baroud, 2002).

A United Nations (2002) report estimated that at least 52 Palestinians were killed in the battle of Jenin. Around half of these were civilians. Unconfirmed reports tell of much higher casualty rates that were covered up because Israeli forces were able to remove bodies during the 3-day period before the media were allowed to enter the camp (Reinhart, 2002; Baroud, 2002).

In their detailed investigation of the Jenin battle, Human Rights Watch (2002b) found that several civilians, including a disabled man, were crushed to death in their homes because Israeli forces failed to allow relatives time to help them escape. Many civilians were also used as human shields by advancing Israeli forces. As a result of the demolition, 140 multi-family housing blocks were completely destroyed, 1,500 were damaged, and 4,000 people from the resident population of 14,000 were made homeless.

After the start of the invasion of this settlement, on April 3, armored D-9 bulldozers focused on tearing new streets from west to east, to allow Israeli tanks to operate and demolish houses where gunfire was emerging. Reports of this stage of the battle tell of Israeli soldiers carefully marking houses for demolition with blue markers from detailed maps. James Nachtwey (2002), one of the first journalists to enter the camp after the first battle subsided, observed the scene soon afterwards:

> The street is a new one, carved by a huge bulldozer out of what was once a narrow alley. It leads to a place where gunmen and tanks forged a new, terrifying chapter in the long wars of the Middle East. The alley was just three feet wide before the Israeli army sent its heavily armored Caterpillar D-9 down what is now a rutted track.

Reconnaissance drones and balloon-lifted video cameras gave IDF strategists an excellent real-time view, both of the newly created tank "streets" that were quickly ripped through the closely built urban fabric of the camp, and of the route of infantry teams who blasted their way through walls to avoid booby traps and ambushes in existing streets.

However, the bulldozing intensified dramatically after the IDF lost 13 soldiers in an ambush on April 9, 2002. The Israeli approach quickly shifted to the indiscriminate machine-gunning of every visible window and the wholesale and systematic destruction of a 250 × 160 meter area at the core of the camp's Hart-Al-Hawashin district – an area that had long been discursively constructed as the "cobra's head" of suicide attack planning by the IDF public relations branch. The retired IDF Brigadier General Gideon Avidor (2002) reflects that "as a result of this ambush we [the IDF] stopped playing nice and polite."

Revealing insights into the mindset of those operating the D-9s in the middle of this second phase of the battle come from a remarkable interview with one of the bulldozer drivers. The intimate connections between the discursive geopolitical constructions analyzed above, and the brutal realities of the invasion, here become startlingly clear. Published in *Yediot Aharonot*, Israel's biggest tabloid newspaper, on May 31, 2002, Colonel Bukhis – a middle-aged IDF reservist – spoke at length about his experience as an operator of one of the dozen D-9 bulldozers employed in Jenin. He described in detail how, in a frenzied period of 75 hours' non-stop demolition, he completed much of the leveling of the center of the camp. He recalled that:

> Before we went in I asked some guys to teach me [how to operate a D-9]. They taught me how to drive forward and make a flat surface...For three days I just erased and erased...I kept drinking whisky to fight off fatigue. I made them a stadium in the middle of the camp! I didn't see dead bodies under the blade of the D-9...But if there were any I don't care. I found joy with every house that came down because I knew that they didn't mind dying but they cared about their homes. If you knocked down their house you buried 40 or 50 people for generations... [After it was finished] I begged for more work: "Let me finish another house!" I wanted to destroy everything. To level everything...It's not that I wanted to kill. Just the houses. Believe me, we demolished too little. (Quoted in Yeheskeli, 2002)

Conclusion: Jenin and the "Palestinianization" of Iraq

Orientalism is abroad again, revivified and hideously emboldened. (Gregory, 2003: 307)

To conclude, it is very clear that Israel's shift to urbicide by bulldozer – far from being some simple Israeli response to the horrors of suicide bombing – reveals a deeply founded Israeli denial of the inevitability and necessity of Palestinian urbanization. It represents a collective denial of the existential rights of Palestinians to urban living space and to the fruits of urban and infrastructural modernization of the kind that Israelis themselves have long enjoyed.

Moreover, this chapter has demonstrated that urbicide by bulldozer is the culmination of the brutal reaction by many Israeli politicians, analysts, and military planners to the fact that many Palestinian fighters seek refuge within a built environment who's very existence challenges Israel's high-tech military omnipotence.

Finally, there is little doubt that wholesale urbicide by bulldozer is part of a concerted effort by the Israeli state to shift the long-term demographic balance of the region in their favor. There is now clear evidence that Israel's underlying motive is to support a "silent transfer" of "ethnically cleansed" Palestinians out of the Occupied Territories because life there has become so utterly unbearable (see Zureik, 2003).

At a deeper level, the systematic leveling of Palestinian urban districts by the Israelis is the end result of a widespread series of increasingly patho-logical, Orientalist discourses. These demonize Palestinian urban and demographic growth. They project all Palestinian urban spaces as intrinsic-ally barbarian, irrational, terroristic, and beyond the pale of civilization. Such discourses, moreover, do geopolitical work. Through them, whole cities are constructed as a "danger to the social order, where the [Zionist] social [order] is understood as a (naturally healthy) body." Consequently, these medicalized and racialized discourses of "cancers" and "bodies" "impute guilt, prescribe punishments, and incite violence" (Campbell, 1998b: 75, 85).

As Derek Gregory (2003: 311) has argued, these demonizing and Orien-talist discourses within Israel work by "casting out" ordinary Palestinian civilians and their places so that they are "placed beyond the privileges and protections of the law so that their lives (and deaths) [are] rendered of no account." Israeli discourses projecting Palestinian cities as dark, impene-trable spaces full of dehumanized, terroristic subjects, go on to sustain massive Israeli violence against both the everyday urban life of Palestinians and the systems which sustain this life. In forcibly creating a kind of chaotic urban hell, perversely, this violence produces what the discourses depict: an urban world "outside of the modern, figuratively as well as physically" (Gregory, 2003: 313).

Tragically, it seems inevitable that urbicide by bulldozer will simply breed depths of despair and hatred that will lead to more Palestinians putting themselves forward for suicide missions. Thus, the circle of atrocity and asymmetric urbicide look set to continue, particularly when combined with the asphyxiating power of Israeli *construction* on Palestinian urban life (Weizman, this volume).

This realization is leading to growing Israeli resistance against Sharon's strategy. Since spring 2002, over 500 Israeli conscripts have refused to serve in the IDF in the Occupied Territories because of its strategies. In October 2003 Sharon's approach was even criticized by Moshe Ya'alon, the chief of the Israeli army. He argued that the strategy was "contrary to Israel's strategic interests" because "it increases hatred for Israel and strengthens the terror organizations" (quoted in McGreal, 2003). Israeli air force pilots are also starting to refuse to carry out revenge attacks, which inevitably lead to mass civilian deaths in Palestinian cities and refugee camps (which are among the world's densest cities).

However, if Jenin was the most extreme example yet of Israeli urbicide by bulldozer, it, and the broader Israeli strategy, also have far wider geopolitical significance. Even by November 2002 – as US forces built up to the invasion of Iraq – it became clear that US forces believed that "the road to Baghdad [lay] through Jenin" (Hugler, 2003). "As the US's ability to detect and strike targets from remote distances grows," wrote Richard Hart Sinnreich of the *Washington Post*, shortly after the first Jenin battle, "so also does an enemy's incentive to respond by locating his military forces in cities, where concealment and protection are easier. In an urbanizing world... scenes such as those in Jenin are likely to become the rule in war rather than the exception " (Sinnreich, 2002).

In fact, it is increasingly apparent that the battle of Jenin was actually planned, prosecuted, and evaluated in very close partnership with specialists in US Military Operations on Urban Terrain (MOUT). Keen to address the closely built-up, labyrinthine Islamic cities that would inevitable be the focus of their ongoing global war on terrorism (Kabul, Kandahar, Basra, Baghdad, Fallujah...), the US military, given their intimate connections with all parts of the IDF, have sought to make the most of the Jenin battle as a learning experiment. The Israeli architect Eyal Weizman has personal testimonies from several Israeli reservists who fought in the battle. These demonstrate "that American military personnel were in Jenin at the time of the battle. Dressed in IDF uniform and walking without weapons, they were observers examining military tactics and methods of combat in the dense fabric of the Arab town" (Misselwitz and Weizman, 2003: 278).

More strategically, an article in the US *Army Times* suggested, on May 31, 2002, that "while Israeli forces were engaged in what many termed a brutal – some even say criminal – campaign to crush Palestinian militants and terrorist cells in West Bank towns, US military officials were in Israel seeing what they could learn from that urban fight" (Lowe, 2002). This article confirmed that a number of visits of urban war specialists occurred between the US and Israel between April and May 2002. "The Marine Corps has taken a close look at the Jenin fight," reported the *Army Times* (Lowe, 2002). US Marine Lt. Col Dave Booth – who oversees US Marine–IDF exchanges on urban warfare – reported in another article in the *Marine Corps Times* in May 2002 that the US Marines wanted "to learn from the Israeli experience in urban warfare and the recent massive search-and-destroy operations for Palestinian insurgents in the West Bank" (quoted in Karkouti, 2002). Joint training exercises in Israeli-built mock

"Islamic cities" in the Negev desert were combined with a widespread exchange system so that US forces could learn how to fight against armed resistors in built-up areas. This exchange also resulted in the Israelis providing US forces with nine D-9 bulldozers for use in Iraq.

Of course, as it transpired, the battle to initially take Iraq's cities, rather than being "a new Stalingrad," was relatively short. It has been followed, however, by a long, drawn-out, urban guerrilla war. In this, evidence of the influence of hardline Israeli tactics used in Operation Defensive Shield has grown with US casualties. By December 2003 a "Palestinianization" of Iraq was clearly underway with a high-tech Western military force brutally suppressing resistance within a highly urban Islamic space. On December 6, 2003 Eb Blanche wrote: "many of the tactics employed by US forces," in response to the widening attacks against their occupation, "bear striking similarities to those used by the Israelis against Palestinian militants in the West Bank and Gaza Strip." These included "a greater use of air power, surface-to-surface missiles, round the clock surveillance by unmanned aerial vehicles of suspected guerrilla centers, large-scale search-and-seize operations, cracking down on a sullen, increasingly hostile civilian population" (Blanche, 2003).

While the D-9 bulldozers were initially used to clear mine fields and trench systems in the US invasion, they later began to be used, or threatened to be used, in acts of collective punishment against those resisting, or seen to be aiding resistance, against the occupation. On December 3, in Kirkuk, for example, US forces drove a D-9 up to the home of a suspected, absent, insurgent and threatened his family with the demolition of the house unless he was handed over (Blanche, 2003). From October 2003, the olive and date groves of Iraqi farmers who allegedly failed to inform US occupiers about the location of resistance fighters were bulldozed by D-9s as collective punishment (Marsden, 2003).

By early 2004, US forces began wrapping razor wire around villages seen as centers of particularly intense Iraqi resistance. (Guarded checkpoints allowed people through only when English-only ID cards were shown.) The relatives of suspected guerrilla fighters were being imprisoned (Filkins, 2003). Buildings seen to offer good vantage points for attacks against US forces were being systematically bulldozed (again by D-9s). Major urban sieges were being undertaken (including the one in Fallujah, in April 2004, where US forces killed over 400 Iraqi civilians). And preemptive air and assassination raids were being launched against suspected fighters and their assembly points, under the direct training of Israeli specialists, some of whom had actually visited Iraq. "It's bonkers, insane!" a former US intelligence official was quoted as saying in the *Guardian*. "We're already being compared to Sharon in the Arab world, and we've just confirmed it by bringing in the Israelis and setting up assassination teams" (Borger, 2003: 1).

To cap it all, once again, racist, Orientalist, and dehumanizing depictions and clichés were being widely used by US forces, both to describe Iraqi people and to legitimize such brutal attacks, intimidation, and punishment. "You have to understand the Arab mind," suggested Captain Todd Brown, one company commander with the US Fourth Infantry Division in Baghdad in early December 2003. "The only thing they understand is force – force, pride, and saving face" (quoted in Filkins, 2003). Tragically, such mentalities and tactics can, surely, only lead one way: to a deepening cycle of atrocity in Iraq that starkly mimics that in Israel–Palestine.

Notes

1 Both figures are available at http://www.btselem.org/English/Statistics/Al_Aqsa_Fatalities_Tables.asp; accessed November 5, 2003.
2 For example, on March 16, 2003, an IDF D-9 ran over and killed Rachel Corrie, a 23-year-old US peace protestor. In October 2003 they were used to bulldoze 200 homes in Rafah.
3 Operation Defensive Shield followed earlier efforts by Israel to destroy the developing infrastructure of the Palestinians, much of which was financed, since the Oslo accords, by aid from Europe and the United Nations.
4 On October 22, 2002, Eitam, just appointed the new infrastructure minister in Sharon's coalition, banned olive picking at the height of the Palestinian harvest. This was done with the justification that IDF troops could not protect Palestinians from armed Jewish settlers stealing their yields. On the same day, Eitam, arguing that he needed to control what he called the "water intifada," made Palestinian boreholes for drinking water and irrigation illegal in the Occupied Territories. Since these rulings, many Palestinian olive groves have been destroyed by settlers keen to expand their settlements. In March 2003 Efraim Eitam was appointed Sharon's minister of housing and construction. In June 2004, he resigned from Sharon's coalition as a protest against Sharon's plan to dismantle some Israeli settlements.

11

City Streets – The War Zones of Globalization: Democracy and Military Operations on Urban Terrain in the Early Twenty-First Century

Robert Warren

Introduction

The city has become the site of two contradictory but intersecting phenomena that have critical importance for democratic practice in the early twenty-first century. The militarization of urban space under conditions other than war is one. The second is the use of cities as mobilization sites by tens of thousands of people coming together to challenge policies being made to regulate globalization by transnational organizations.

In the first case, urban space is increasingly viewed by those wielding state power as a terrain on which militarized operations are necessary to contain crowd violence and prevent and respond to terrorist attacks. The use of military tactics and weaponry by police as well as armed forces in cities has become so extensive that many citizens now accept this as a "natural" part of urban life. Growing amounts of a city's land, underground infrastructure, air space, and water surfaces are closed to citizens, urban space is zoned with different levels of monitoring and control by police and military, and some people are barred from freely moving among cities.

The second phenomenon emerged in the late 1990s when massive numbers of civilians, part of a loosely organized international coalition of counter-hegemonic groups, started to assemble in various cities to oppose what they perceive as the migration of control over their lives and economic well-being from local and national democratic institutions to an opaque network of transnational entities. To such anti-globalization protestors, organizations like the IMF, the G8, and the World Bank are seeking, under the banner of globalization, to impose policies that favor capital and corporate elites over ordinary people. These mobilizations, occurring in cities around the world, have produced increasingly similar and intense state responses that use military resources to control or suppress them.

A literal game of intra- and inter-city "spatial chess" has evolved in which:

- entities committed to the project of globalization, such as the WTO, World Bank, IMF, the G8, the EU, and the World Economic Forum, move among cities to hold well-publicized summit meetings for several days;
- coalitions of citizen groups seek to gain political voice by demonstrating in the same cities at the same times to call for alternative global policies; and
- police and military personnel and armaments are assembled into "pop-up armies" to turn the meeting sites and their periphery into virtual fortresses intended to insulate summit participants from protesters. (Warren, 2002)

In this game of spatial chess, the city is the site of contests over democratic practice on two scales. Within the cities, local residents have their freedom and rights abrogated through the periodic imposition of military control over sections and zones of the city during summit meetings and, in the longer run, face living under general conditions of quasi-martial law. On a macro-level, cities are the location of the world-scale confrontation between transnational organizations and networks of oppositional groups over issues of rights, equity, and democratic control in the regulation of globalization. The elimination of public spheres within cities – spaces in which citizens are free to mobilize politically – compromises a basic and necessary dimension of democratic governance on both a local and global scale.

These developments have been shaped by the confluence of innovations in military doctrine, massive citizen mobilizations, and the post-September 11, 2001 "war on terrorism." Significant revisions in military doctrine concerning operations on urbanized terrain began three decades ago to meet anticipated needs for deploying troops in cities for non-combat missions as well as warfare. New tenets were formulated with the expectation that they would be primarily applied by advanced industrial nations within developing parts of the world. The resulting Military Operations on Urbanized Terrain (MOUT) doctrine, however, has also became a template for suppressing and controlling citizen mobilizations in European and North American cities.

The war on terrorism, declared, defined, and led by the United States after the horrific destruction of the World Trade Center, is not the cause but provides a justification for deepening and expanding an already existing pattern of militarizing urban space. If it were to end tomorrow and citizen mobilizations continued, states would also continue their strategy of transforming cities from civil to militarized environments in support of transnational hegemonic actors.

In the sections that follow the initial focus will be on changes in military doctrine and their relevance to conflicts in cities over globalization. The patterns and consequences of the movement of transnational entities among cities for policy meetings, the citizen mobilizations that challenge them, and state responses, will then be examined. Finally, the effects of the war on terrorism on this preexisting pattern will be considered and the collective significance of these phenomena for the viability of cities as basic units of democratic governance will be discussed.

Military Operations on Urbanized Terrain (MOUT)

Urban warfare has been a consistent phenomenon in human society (Ashworth, 1991). Instances like the capture of Troy by deception have mythic status. Others, such as the mushroom cloud that contained the vaporized remains of people and structures in Hiroshima, have been defining points in the world's history (Bishop and Clancey, this volume). However, a continuing succession of intense, short-term, and debilitating formal and irregular armed conflicts in cities has been far more characteristic of urban conditions over time. This is paradoxical because military theory, from its beginnings, has warned that warfare in urban centers should be avoided.

Sun Tzu's fourth-century BC advice in *The Art of War* was that attacking cities was the worst of policies and should be undertaken "only when there is no alternative" (1963: 78). This assessment is still accepted doctrine, based on well-documented evidence. Military operations in densely built-up environments have high casualty costs, reduce the advantages that numerically and technologically superior forces have in more open space, and generate undesirable "collateral damage" (Legault, 2000; Glenn, Steeb, and Matsumura, 2001).

The maneuverability and tactical use of weapons are limited by mazes of unfamiliar streets. Multi-storied buildings interfere with electronic transmissions, causing the breakdown of communications and command structures. Upper stories, roofs, and underground infrastructure provide an enemy with cover. For military protagonists, urban warfare creates dilemmas concerning "collateral damage" because of the presence of large numbers of non-combatants on site. Symbolically charged elements of the built environment must also usually be keep intact. There are also problems of maintaining public and political support for combat in distant urban places when the mass media report high casualties.

In spite of these factors, it is now recognized that military operations on urbanized terrain are inevitable and require new strategies (Hills, this volume). One of the first documents reflecting this in the US military was the Department of the Army's 1979 Field Manual, *Military Operations on Urbanized Terrain*. Building MOUT doctrine, however, has particularly accelerated in the last decade for several reasons. One is demographic. Currently, half of the world's population is in urban areas. This is projected to increase to 70 percent in the next quarter century, a process that will create additional and diverse demands for military operations in cities, largely in developing countries. This is based on the assumption that the creation of more, and larger, centers of political and economic power, with dense urban terrain favored by irregular and guerrilla fighters, will be accompanied by more volatile conditions (Press, 1999).

The dissolution of the Soviet Union and the resulting US status as the world's only dominant military power is a second factor. Violent group conflicts, regional wars, the emergence of "rogue" nations, radical political and religious non-state terrorist networks, and the diffusion of weapons of mass destruction outside international control, followed the breakdown of the US–Russian global balance (Collins and Horowitz, 2000; Desch, 2001: 9). In this context, US forces have engaged in a number of overseas urban combat and non-combat missions to protect what are perceived as its national interest. At the same time, there are strong pressures on the US and other industrialized nations to involve their armed forces in humanitarian, peacekeeping, and policing operations in other countries that are characterized as "Military Operations Other Than War" or "MOOTW" (Department of the Army, 2002: 1–3).

Continuing evidence of the high military costs and negative political effects of urban engagements were additional incentives for new urban doctrine. The 1993 experience of US troops in Mogadishu, Somalia, and Russian efforts to occupy and control Groznyy, Chechnya, in 1994, are frequently used as examples of "combat in hell" scenarios in military writings (Glenn, 2001). In these "asymmetric" encounters, the urban environment, the presence of non-combatants, and inadequate operational doctrine created great problems for vastly superior forces. In turn, the mass media's reporting of the events reduced homeland public support for both undertakings and led to greater emphasis on the controlling of media reporting as a critical element of MOUT doctrine (Oakley, 2001; Thomas, 1999).

New Military Urban Strategies and Tactics

By 2000, a US-dominated discourse, reflected in meetings, military journals, and formal documents, had generated broad agreement on tenets for reconfiguring and equipping the military to carry out both domestic and overseas urban missions. The proceedings of RAND Corporation conferences convened in 1998, 1999, and 2000 (Glenn et al., 1998; Glenn, 2000, 2001) provide an overview of the basic thinking and the assumptions involved. The RAND book *Corralling the Trojan Horse* (Glenn, Steeb, and Matsumura, 2001) summarizes current MOUT doctrinal strategies that are relevant to this discussion.

Intelligence, surveillance, and *reconnaissance enhancement* include the development of technologies to prevent buildings, underground passageways, and other elements of the built environment from obscuring the location of adversaries, hazardous materials, and non-combatants by generating three-dimensional maps and images of the interior of structures and of movements within them. *Denial of access* strategies are designed to prevent entry into urban areas or limit penetration of both combatants and non-combatants. In the latter case, non-lethal obstacles are called for, such as vehicle barriers, superlubricants, and quick-hardening foams. *Nodal operations* have the goal of selecting key spatial nodes within a city, rather than the whole metropolitan area, to be directly controlled and also recognizes that critical nodes for securing a city may be outside the urban area itself.

Non-combatant control is intended to influence civilian "attitudes and behaviors" to the benefit of the military. Requiring identification tags and limiting movement to specific routes, the use of non-lethal "calmatives" or incapacitators to temporarily disable people in crowds, and psychological operations (PSYOP) and deception are among the range of methods identified. Creating positive media coverage is of high importance. As Edwards puts it, the marginal return from influencing the media may be greater than the return on increased firepower (2000: xiv). Finally, *selective dominance* involves the ability to control areas without physically occupying them and includes a "sector and seal" component to constrain the movements of adversaries and to segregate non-combatants from areas in which they would interfere with military operations.

It was, as noted, initially assumed that the primary application of MOUT doctrine would be outside America and other industrialized nations. By the late 1990s, however, events like the 1992 Los Angeles racial violence and the bombings of the World Trade Center (1993), Murrah Federal Office Building in Oklahoma City (1995), and Atlanta Olympics (1996) made the need for domestic military operations in "Homeland Defense" a well-established theme in US military writings (Miller, 2001: 580; Desch,

2001: 10). According to Iklé, for example, the threat of chemical, biological, and nuclear weapons attacks requires that the military "develop, deploy, and operate a wide range of measures" to secure the US homeland because only they have the capabilities (1999: 1). Buckley concluded that applying MOUT doctrine to US cities will "prove invaluable when we have to conduct urban operations in the streets of America" (2000: 340, 345).

Spatial Chess and Pop-Up Armies

The cities of Seattle (1999) and Genoa (2001) have gained iconic status as sites of citizen mobilizations. Seattle was not the first place where massive street protests occurred against international financial and trade policies. Larger numbers of people gathered in Birmingham, UK and Cologne during G8 meetings in 1998 and 1999, as part of the Jubilee 2000 network that was calling for debt relief for poor countries (Independent Catholic News, 2003). In Seattle, however, a broader agenda, innovations in the use of communication technology, and the unanticipated intensity of the demonstrations, resulted in several days of escalating conflict between some protesters and the police. In turn this interfered with the planned summit. It disrupted daily life in the center of the city. And it generated extensive coverage by the mass media of the violence.

The World Trade Organization, with governmental delegates from 135 nations, met in Seattle in November 1999 to negotiate global trade policies related to agriculture, labor standards, and the environment. In the absence of any institutional means of making policy input, some 50,000 people, representing a wide range of groups from many countries, assembled in Seattle. They called for a more equitable global economy and demanded changes in an organization that was perceived to be undemocratic, opaque, and unaccountable in its favoring of the interests of multinational corporations and advanced industrial nations, to the detriment of the environment and most citizens of the world (Cockburn and St. Clair, 2000; Klein, 2002).

When it became clear that the police were unable to contain protesting groups from clustering where they chose, blocking the movement of some WTO participants, and doing damage to business property, the city made the downtown center and the area around the meeting site a zone closed to protest activity. They also imposed a curfew. National Guard troops were called in to support the police, turning downtown Seattle into a "militarized zone" with the Guards and police "side-by-side doing the same jobs" (plate 11.1; De Mause, 2000). Reflecting Homeland Defense doctrine assumptions of state and local capacity limitations, and the risk of terrorist acts during mass mobilizations, the Department of Defense sent over 160

Plate 11.1 A temporary militarized urban space: the "Battle of Seattle," 1999. Photograph: Kevin O'Sullivan, AP/Wide World Photos, reproduced with permission.

regular army personnel to Seattle to provide expertise and coordination in the case of a terrorist attack during the WTO meeting (CNN.com, 1999).

Mass media coverage focused extensively on damage to property and battles with police by self-identified anarchists. This provided credibility to official statements that forceful control of demonstrations was necessary because, no matter how non-violent the vast majority of participants, there would be a few "radicals" intent on provoking the police and destroying symbols of corporate capitalism (Fairness and Accuracy in Reporting, 1999). The message distributed from Seattle to the world by the media was not about international trade agreements. Rather, it was that masses of protesters, with superior organization and tactics, could overwhelm a police force, shut down the center of a major city, and disrupt the activities of the flagship organization representing hegemonic interests in the regulation of globalization.

The Seattle experience spawned two models that influenced subsequent citizen and state conflicts related to transnational summit meetings. First, it provided a decentralized, non-hierarchical, high-tech Internet and cell phone-driven template and momentum for further massive protests (Klein, 2002; Rheingold, 2002). For states staging further meetings for the agents of hegemonic globalization, it served as a model for counter-responses, increasingly based on MOUT doctrine, to prevent future Seattle-like "victories" for political protesters.

In the next year-and-a-half both of these models were adopted and elaborated on. They confronted each other in a succession of cities: Washington, DC and Prague (IMF and World Bank, April and September 2000); Melbourne and Davos, Switzerland (World Economic Forum, September, 2000 and January 2001); Quebec City (Summit of the Americas, April 2001); Gothenburg, Sweden (EU, July 2001). The July 2001 G8 summit in Genoa was the culmination of this pre-war on terrorism phase.

At least 100,000 demonstrators from more than 700 organizations gathered in Genoa (BBC News, 2001). The Italian state assembled 15,000 police, armed with both lethal and non-lethal weapons, and military personnel to control demonstrators. Air and naval weaponry were added to the deployment, including surface-to-air missiles at the Genoa airport, jet fighters and helicopters patrolling the city's closed airspace, and warships guarding the port area. The cost of the security was reported at $110 million. The elaborate military defense system, as well as the intense level of control within the city, were justified on the basis of a threat, reported to the press by officials, that Osama bin Laden would try to assassinate US President Bush during the summit. Suggesting a PSYOP-touch, the source of this intelligence, as identified in the media, was the head of the Russian Federal Bodyguard Service (CNN.com, 2001).

France, Germany, and Spain coordinated control of their borders to prevent known "troublemakers" from entering Italy. A tightly sealed "Red Zone" was created in the center of the city where the G8 meetings were located and most participants were staying. Only authorized access was allowed and citizens who lived or worked in the zone were required to come and go through a small number of official checkpoints. Many stores and restaurants in the zone had major drops in levels of business (Bevanger, 2001).

Numerous clashes occurred between protesters and security forces. There was property damage that, along with the violence, was attributed largely to anarchists by authorities and the media. One protestor was shot dead and more than 100 others and 30 police were injured. Many charges of brutality and unprovoked violence, as well as harassment of independent reporting organizations, were made against the police. The national chief of police acknowledged that some excessive force might have resulted from "the conditions of urban warfare" in Genoa (*Guardian Unlimited*, 2001). Subsequent official inquiries produced evidence of the police fabricating provocations to justify attacks on demonstrators (BBC News, 2003b; Fairness and Accuracy in Reporting, 2003).

By the time of the Genoa summit, a matured model had evolved of state-sponsored pop-up armies, created to serve transnational entities for short periods of time. The strategies and tactics utilized to prevent or control citizen mobilizations clearly reflected MOUT doctrine for the militarization of urban space in other-than-war conditions. Citizen groups using the streets, in the absence of institutional means to exercise a political voice, had become the *de facto* adversaries of the police and military. Although the scenarios varied from city to city, the basic elements of the model included multinational involvement in the denial of access to cities through coordinated border control; physically isolating the visiting elites from demonstrators by zoning and barricading areas, and limiting and requiring authorization for citizen movement within cities; utilizing non-lethal and, if necessary, lethal weapons; preemptive arrests; harassing independent media; deploying military personnel and air and naval defense systems; and conflating political protesters with violent anarchists and terrorists to deligitimize them, rationalize the use of military force to protect transnational elites, and justify the multi-million dollar security expenditures required.

Post-9/11: A Continuing Pattern

The destruction of the World Trade Center and the ensuing "war on terrorism" have affected military operations in urban space in a number of important ways, including the blurring of war and other-than-war conditions and the further merging of police and military roles, tactics, and weaponry (McCulloch, 2003). The militarization of urban space through the use of pop-up armies had begun well before 9/11and has continued to evolve within its preexisting dynamics.

In March of 2002, during the EU summit in Barcelona, for example, a citizen mobilization of tens of thousands faced some 8,500 police and troops along with aircraft, anti-aircraft missiles, and warships in and around the city to deal with "any terrorist threats or anti-global protests." Barriers around the summit conference building made it a virtual bunker (Nash, 2002). Normally free border crossings from France under the EU Schengen Convention were suspended by Spain and controls were placed on air routes to "keep out anti-globalization protesters suspected of planning violence" (*Guardian Unlimited*, 2002).

A different spatial strategy was adopted for the 2002 G8 meeting in Canada. Prime Minister Jean Chrétien, the host, vowed that the violence and disorder of protesters in Genoa would not be tolerated (Sanger, 2002). The intent was to keep demonstrations totally removed from the summit site – Kananaskis, Alberta, a small, remote luxury resort. Police, the military, and advanced armaments were used to turn Kananaskis into an impenetrable fortress and create a militarized zone that included Calgary, the major city in the region, 70 kilometers away. Calgary served as the summit's base camp where demonstrators and the media would be contained. The city's police, the Royal Canadian Mounted Police, and the military spent close to a year planning the greatest security operation in the country's history to protect the G8 summit for 30 hours at a cost of over $300 million (Girard, 2002a).

The only direct access to Kananaskis was a heavily guarded two-lane road. The heads of governments traveled the distance in total security – boarding a helicopter immediately after landing at Calgary's airport and flying to the resort (Cornwell, 2002). A 6.5 square kilometer perimeter of wilderness around Kananaskis was patrolled by thousands of police and troops (Girard, 2002b). A no-fly zone was established and patrolled by jet fighters, helicopters, and a drone aircraft equipped for surveillance. Ground-to-air missiles were set up around the resort (Careless, 2003).

Demonstrators and the media were confined to Calgary. Many protest groups were denied permits to encamp in public space in Calgary and a variety of other steps were taken by Calgary, the Province of Alberta, and national government to discourage anyone seeking to challenge G8 policies. Court hours were extended and jail facilities were made available in Calgary to process and hold arrested protesters. To do this, existing prisoners were transferred to other locations. Some persons suspected of being potential demonstrators were barred from entering Canada (Rubinstein, 2002).

Two thousand journalists covering the summit had little choice but to spend their time in an elaborate government-provided media center in downtown Calgary's convention facility. There they were provided with bits of news on giant TV screens and periodic opportunities to engage in closed-circuit video interaction with G8 leaders and spokespersons in Kananaskis. A few reporters were allowed to travel to the resort on a special bus. Once there, however, they received only briefings and had no access to official meetings (Sanger, 2002; Weston, 2002).

A number of disruptions of normal civilian life occurred. Vacationers were excluded from around the summit site and highway travelers in a much larger area were subject to delays by security measures (G8 Summit Security, 2002; Habegger and O'Reilly, 2002). In central Calgary some downtown office workers required special identification cards for entry. Major hotels had security checks. And businesses encouraged personnel to work at home if possible during the summit. Barricades were put up around several public buildings and mailboxes were sealed to prevent bombs being placed in them (Monchuk and Graveland, 2002). A substantial proportion of Calgary police were assigned to summit security, raising concern among some about normal law enforcement in the rest of the city. Police from a number of other cities were also deployed in Calgary (Rubinstein, 2002).

No protesters were able to get close to Kananaskis. Several groups, reported numbering between 2,000 and 4,000, did stage demonstrations in Calgary that were characterized as being in "stark contrast" to the Genoa summit (Warn, 2002). As a counter-spatial strategy, some oppositional groups in Canada organized demonstrations in other cities to call for G8 policy changes. Small demonstrations did occur in Ottawa, Toronto, and Vancouver (Girard, 2002b).

France organized the next G8 summit in 2003 and also adopted a strategy of denying protesters access to the meeting site. Although this was achieved, variations from Canada in the urban geography and political environment resulted in a different outcome. Significant negative spatial spillovers occurred to cities in an adjacent country, involving security forces from three nations.

Evian, the summit location – an upscale resort on Lake Geneva at the Swiss border – was effectively sealed off during the summit by at least 15,000 French police and troops. Security personnel outnumbered local residents by two-to-one. Controls were imposed on the movement and activity of Evian residents that disrupted normal life in the town (Bumiller, 2003). Four security zones were set up in and around Evian. Barricades surrounded the meeting area. Roads and railways into the city were closed. Demonstrations were barred within 10 kilometers of the town (BBC News, 2003a). Airspace and portions of Lake Geneva were sealed off. Anti-aircraft missiles were installed. And combat planes, helicopter gunships, and naval patrol craft were all deployed (BBC News 2003a; SchNEWS, 2003a).

In urban spatial terms, Geneva is the major international travel link to Evian and Lausanne the closest large Swiss city. Some G8 staff and non-member leaders attending were housed in Geneva and Lausanne and required secured cross-border transportation. Denied access to Evian, the tens of thousand of people from hundreds of groups that had mobilized to oppose G8 policies aggregated in Geneva, Lausanne, and Annemasse, France.

Anti-G8 demonstrations were mounted in both Swiss cities. Geneva was, as anticipated by the Swiss government, the major flash point. Protesters and police clashed in the streets, there was property damage, and harassment of the demonstrators and independent media base sites in the city similar to the pattern in Genoa. At one point, a 9-hour battle raged between protesters and Swiss police and troops (BBC News 2003b). One thousand German police, who, by prior agreement, were waiting in reserve at the Geneva airport, were mobilized to help control the demonstrators (Sciolino, 2003). As one observer put it, the French innovation in summit security was to host the event and export the damage to Switzerland (Higgins, 2003).

The Militarization of Entertainment and Second-Level Meeting Spaces

The war on terrorism has provided support for the preexisting use of the police and military to restrict urban space as a site of democratic practice in general. In addition, the consistent "official" and media conflation of terrorism with any large urban assembly of people, as well as mass protests, has further normalized the use of MOUT doctrine as the guide to "protect" an increasing array of sports, entertainment, and less-than-summit level globalization events from violence and terrorists.

The Genoa and Kananaskis models of military control, with high civil rights and financial costs, are now standard for mega-sports and entertainment activities. An assumption justifying this, often implicit and seldom challenged in the PSYOP environment of the war on terrorism, is that all citizens attending such events are potential terrorists and must be monitored and controlled. Although anti-terrorist planning for the February 2002 Winter Olympics in Salt Lake City started well before 9/11, it was greatly expanded with the destruction of the Twin Towers and became an initial showcase for the US's war on terrorism (Dao, 2001). Security costs were estimated at over $300 million. At least 2,000 armed National Guard and other troops and 9,000 local, state, and national law enforcement officers were deployed. A barricaded tourist entertainment and Olympia award site was located in the center of the city, with vehicles barred and surveillance checkpoints for citizens going in. A zone for political demonstrations was located well away from any significant flow of people. Air space was controlled by helicopters and military fighter and surveillance planes (Leiser, 2002). These arrangements were touted as the model for future world-class sports events (Squatriglia, 2002).

World Cup football matches held in Japan and Korea in 2002 had police and military security for each of the many cities where games were scheduled (Belson, 2002; Struck, 2002a). A projection has been made that the 2004 summer Olympics in Athens will have 45,000 security personnel in comparison to 9,000 in Atlanta in 1996 (Vecsey, 2003). No-fly zones, barricades around the arena, banning of private vehicles from the immediate area, and airport-type monitoring of all ticket holders entering the stadium have become the norm for the annual American football Super Bowl game that moves among cities (Thornton, 2003). The film industry's annual Academy Award ceremonies in Hollywood in 2002 and 2003 involved the barricading of the award site, the closure of streets and local subway stations, security checks of people coming in, helicopter patrols, and a no-fly zone (Lyman, 2002; Lehmann, 2003). Concern over a terrorist attack during New Year's Eve celebrations in Sydney, Australia, to ring in

2003, caused the deployment of a record number of police, closing main streets and subjecting individuals to bag checks. Vehicles in traffic exclusion zones were searched, police monitored events from roof tops, and helicopters patrolled the air space over the area (Shepherd, 2003).

Militarized protection is also being provided for a range of less-than-summit meetings devoted to fostering hegemonic developments in globalization. During NATO's 2002 annual security meeting in Munich, focusing on terrorism, all protests in the center of the city were made illegal by the city council. Close to 1,000 protesters were arrested or held in preventative detention and suspected demonstrators were prevented from entering Germany. Munich's mayor threatened community organizations with cuts in their municipal subsidies if they offered any kind of support to groups demonstrating against NATO (Statewatch News online, 2002).

In 2003, Sacramento, California hosted a three-day international meeting sponsored by the US Department of Agriculture on agricultural science and technology. Extensive security arrangements were made because protests were expected from citizen groups opposed to genetic modification. This involved months of planning and visits by local officials to cities where "large-scale civil disobedience" had occurred (Enkoji, 2003). The meeting site was "turned into a virtual armed camp" (Bailey and Rubin, 2003) to ensure there would be no repeat of the 1999 WTO disruptions in Seattle (Calvan, 2003). There were oppositional activities that, in most cases, involved no more than 100 protesters who were monitored by a greater number of city and state police.

The British government, also in 2003, assembled 2,000 officers from local and national policing agencies to prevent protest groups from interfering with a London meeting of the Defense Systems and Equipment International Exhibition, Europe's largest meeting of arms dealers. One million pounds of public money was spent to control citizen groups attempting to protest the sale of weapons of mass destruction. The police were given what amounted to blanket authority under the UK's Terrorism Act of 2000 to stop and search demonstrators (SchNEWS, 2003b; Statewatch News online, 2003).

Bunyan (2002) finds a wider pattern of conflating protest with terrorism by EU decision-makers reflected in policies that make EU members responsible for monitoring, reporting on, and inhibiting the cross-border travel of people with a record of participating in public demonstrations. This power to act preemptively against individuals, based on ascribed political intention rather than action, he argues is turning the "war on terrorism" into a "war on freedom and democracy."

Fairness and Accuracy in Reporting (FAIR) analyzed mass media coverage of summits and found reporting consistently characterized "lawful political assembly as a terrorist threat" and civilians as "violent activists."

FAIR concluded that such a spin "risks creating a climate where law enforcement agencies feel able to exercise force against demonstrators with impunity" (Fairness and Accuracy in Reporting, 2002). This effect is indistinguishable from what Edwards, writing for a military audience and drawing upon MOUT doctrine, refers to as "perception management." The means he proposes for this is the aggressive use of the media to disseminate "proof of criminal or hostile actions by the enemy" to "help demonize them in the eye of the public" (2000: 97). The result of this PSYOP tactic, McCulloch (2003: 5) observes, is a shift in responding to public protests from arresting lawbreakers to the use of "overwhelming force to overcome and defeat groups of people conceived as enemies." Thus, the increasing ability of the state to define protesters as *de facto* enemies allows the blurring of other-than-war conditions with warfare during mass mobilizations.

Weaponry and Civilian Collateral Damage

MOUT doctrine's Rules of Engagement ostensibly place importance on limiting collateral damage to civilian populations and emphasize the use of non-lethal weapons. However, the evidence indicates that, in the rhetoric of the war on terrorism, categorizations of "lethal" and "non-lethal" have become blurred both in meaning and use. The type of advanced non-lethal weapons that are being developed for the military constitute overwhelming force. Further, MOUT doctrine is quite clear in stipulating that lethal weapons are always justified when necessary. The current use of air-launched missiles by Israel to kill specific persons in the Palestinian Territories suggests that assertions of strike precision can eliminate past constraints on applying lethal weapons in densely populated cities (Graham, this volume).

A MOUT doctrine priority is the development of non-lethal weapons to go beyond the already widely used tear gas, pepper spray, rubber bullets, and concussion grenades. In 1997 this resulted in the creation of the US Joint Directorate for Non-Lethal Weapons, under the command of the Marine Corps. As Grossman (2002) puts it, the importance of countering large demonstrations without using lethal weapons has led the Pentagon to spend "more and more research-and-development dollars on weapons that stun, scare, entangle, or nauseate – anything but kill." Although public information about the weapons in place or under development is becoming less accessible (MacKenzie, 2002), they range from sticky forms, calmative chemicals, directed energy, acoustical, and electromagnetic pulse weapons, to genetically engineered anti-material agents (Borin, 2002; Wright, 1999; Morales, 2001).

Examples include "electrocuting water cannon" that carry a "debilitat-ing" shock through a water jet treated with additives (Smith, 2003); a Plasma-Taser, able to fire an aerosol spray that "creates a conductive channel for a shock current" that immobilizes a person (Hambling, 2003); malodorants that are so nauseating people are forced to leave an area (Grossman, 2002); a microwave beam that heats people's skins and causes a feeling of severe pain and confusion (Hecht, 2001); and anti-depressants and opiates in gas form that can incapacitate crowds (Wright, 1999).

Confidence that this new generation of non-lethal weapons will actually be non-lethal is open to serious question based on growing recognition that the older, low-tech versions are far from predictable in their effects on people. One recent study concluded that there is a high level of inaccuracy in the trajectory and force of such weapons when fired (Kendig, 2001). Another report indicates that, after a decade of extensive use, police departments in the US are abandoning "non-lethal" beanbag ammunition because they are finding they can be "dangerously inaccurate and deadlier than manufacturers claimed" (Leonard, 2002).

In quite practical cases, an elderly woman in Harlem had the New York City police break her apartment door down early in the morning and throw a concussion grenade in before entering. The action was based on an erroneous report the apartment was occupied by a drug dealer and filled with guns. The grenade, intended to disorient people with a loud noise and flash, resulted in the woman's death, apparently from a preexisting heart condition (Rashbaum, 2003). In 2002, in Moscow, Russian anti-terrorism forces killed 50 Chechen terrorists who had taken over a major theatre and were holding an audience of hundreds as hostages. However, the "calma-tive gas" that was pumped into the theatre and immediately incapacitated the terrorists also killed approximately 130 of the Moscow citizens being held as hostages (Mullins, 2002).

The preference within MOUT doctrine for non-lethal weapons against non-combatants in other-than-war conditions does not exclude lethal options. The use of "precision" lethal weapons in cities outside its direct control has become common practice by Israel. On a number of occasions, Israeli helicopters have fired missiles into buildings and automobiles moving in traffic in highly urbanized areas in the Palestinian Territory with the expressed intent of killing specific individuals identified as terror-ists. No formal or public judicial decisions preceded the action. The fact that this tactic still results in human and material collateral damage has not inhibited its use (Bennet, 2003; Myre, 2003a, 2003b).

Given the extent to which armed planes and helicopters have become part of the weaponry protecting transnational summits and mega-events, and the expanding definition of "terrorist," it is not difficult to imagine situations in which air-to-ground "precision" missiles will be used to strike at vehicles or even individuals in densely urbanized areas believed to have terrorist intentions.

Conclusions

The militarization of urban spaces in North America and Europe in other-than-war conditions is a frequent and expanding occurrence and affects governance on two scales. It undermines both democratic control over a city by its residents, and the critical ability of localities to provide the public space in which citizens can mobilize to express political voice on global issues when no democratic institutional means are available.

This discussion has focused on the transformation of cities from civil to military environments. It has utilized MOUT doctrine and the conflict over the conditions of globalization as the primary lens for doing so. Limited attention, by intent, was given to the extent, vitality, innovation, and adaptive capacity of the array of citizen groups that comprise a network able to mobilize tens and hundreds of thousands of people to engage in counter-hegemonic actions in cities over the world (see Cockburn and St. Clair, 2000; Klein, 2002; Opel and Pompper, 2003; Notes from Nowhere, 2003).

The war on terrorism is also a critical area of inquiry that has not been dealt with in detail (see Introduction, this volume). However, as was indicated at the beginning of this chapter, if the war on terrorism was to end tomorrow, the well established use of military doctrine and personnel to prevent and control mass citizen political expression would continue. Consequently, much more urban research is needed which explores the games of spatial chess and the pop-up armies that characterize citizen mobilizations to contest global regulation.

A key issue to be further explored is the extent to which the short-term encampment of the leaderships of transnational entities is privileged over the normal socioeconomic and political life in the cities hosting meetings, through the imposition of military controls. A related question is the degree to which the militarization of space within urban areas is becoming a permanent marshal law-like condition made to seem "natural" by "psychological operations" (PSYOP) tactics in which the state and media conflate protest and terrorism. What part does the stream of messages that the risk of terrorist attacks is high and continuous for every city and town, and that any person is a potential terrorist, play in turning a city's airport, harbor, and symbolic public buildings into enclaves in which civil rights are suspended?

Other research challenges relate to the identification and measurement of the extent to which the roles, methods, and weaponry of the police and military are merging. Are advanced, incapacitating "non-lethal" weapons created for the military being used on, or being prepared for, citizens participating in political mobilizations? Will missile-equipped helicopters and drone aircraft become part of police departments' standard weaponry for "emergency" use? How do the rapidly growing international networks of police and military cooperation facilitate state control over the movement of civilians among and within cities?

Success or failure of mobilizations in Seattle, Kananaskis, Genoa, Evian, or other summits cannot be viewed individually or collectively apart from the status of cities as basic units of governance and the larger context of local and global struggles to maintain and create democratic practice. The locations of conflict vary greatly from world cities to remote, luxury resorts. However, despite the diversity of sites, state responses are similar and increasingly involve MOUT-based tactics, information and resource sharing among nations and cities, and coordinated actions across multiple locations. Little research has been done to chart these developments and even less has assessed the degree to which there is resistance to them by local officials and citizen groups to protect local governance as an institution.

As this discussion indicates, there is substantial evidence that far more systematic research is needed to identify the dynamic tendencies, and cumulative effects, of the phenomena associated with the militarization of urban space and on ways to incorporate the findings into the general body of urban and spatial analysis and theorization. What is at stake is not simply urban scholarship but the future of democratic practice and the city as its basic site.

12

Continuity and Discontinuity: The Grammar of Urban Military Operations

Alice Hills

Introduction

Urban military operations deserve attention because they are the most complex of all military operations. They engage with key emergent issues and trends in the post-Cold War world, and they serve as a reminder that, when searching for the meaningful purposes and roles that contemporary security articulates, the West runs the risk of paying insufficient attention to the continuities of military force. In particular, urban operations challenge the West's faith in the transformational potential of sophisticated technology, and they defy liberal assumptions that the nature of military force has in some way changed. This chapter discusses the strategic logic – a "grammar" in Clausewitz's writing – of urban war in order to explore such issues.

Although there is no coherent paradigm for urban military operations that can be based on principles independent of specific operations, a hypothesis of why the characteristics and physical constraints of cities consistently affect military operations as they do is now possible. A coherent set of facts and variables is identifiable, which suggests that an urban field is also recognizable, and that a set of relationships between positions characterized by their own logic and practices can be established. This provides insight into the function and purpose of military force in an urbanizing world, and to the role of cities as contested strategic sites. It also suggests how military power may be used in the future.

The discussion presented here is divided into three sections. The first revisits the relationship between urbanization and warfare, and asks whether urban military operations are a distinct or unique type of action, or whether they are special because cities have a critical effect on the military operations taking place within them. The second section discusses the transformational potential of technology for urban military operations, while the third contrasts the technical possibilities with the historically proven grammar of urban military operations. A balance between continuity and discontinuity is proposed in the final section.

Urbanization and Military Operations

The shift from a predominantly rural world to an urban one has been rapid and its military implications are not yet fully understood. Even so there have been military operations on urban terrain for as long as cities have existed, so it is legitimate to ask why have analysts only recently rediscovered them. Do they deserve special attention? Have they failed to receive it because it is more useful to classify operations as counter-terrorism, counter-insurgency (COIN), or peacekeeping? The status of doctrine is accorded only to what is seen as important or significant, so it is revealing that UK urban operations does not have a single, well-defined doctrine, whereas COIN and peacekeeping do. Or is it because there have been few examples of sustained urban combat since 1945? NATO, after all, ignored urban fighting during the Cold War; it assumed that war would occur on the north German plain, but never paid special attention to defending the urbanized Rhine–Ruhr region (Dzirkals, Kellen, and Mendershausen, 1976: 53). On the other hand, the Cold War period saw significant urban warfare in Palestine (1945–9), for example, Algeria (1954–62), Lebanon (1982), and Northern Ireland (from 1969 onwards). More recently, American operations in Panama, Somalia, Haiti, and Iraq included strong urban elements, while the Russian Army fought three ferocious battles in Groznyy (1994–6, 1999–2000).

Much has undoubtedly changed since the end of the Cold War, and today's security threats are generally thought by western militaries to be more diverse, less predictable, and probably less challenging in terms of conventional warfare. At the same time the range of military operations has expanded, as is acknowledged by the increasingly common use of the term urban operations. War fighting remains the archetypal urban military operation, but it is comparatively rare; policing and peace enforcement are more usual. Urban operations accordingly cover the range of operations typically occurring in cities, towns, or villages. They are, in the words of the authoritative US· *Doctrine for Joint Urban Operations*, military actions that are planned and conducted on "a topographical complex and its adjacent natural terrain, where manmade construction or the density of non-combatants are the dominant features" (Joint Staff, 2002: 1-1).

Linked to this expansion is the notion that war itself has somehow changed as a result of what US defense secretary Rumsfeld described (on September 10, 2001) as the transformation "from a bipolar Cold War world where threats were visible and predictable to one in which they arise from multiple sources – most of which are difficult to anticipate" (Rumsfeld, 2001). The idea of transformation is not new, but it has become the USA's defense objective – and the US leads military and technological developments in urban operations. In the mid-1980s, US proponents of military reform emphasized that transformation required new technologies, innovative concepts, and organizational adaptation, if significant improvements in military effectiveness were to be achieved. Since then the objective of "skipping a generation" of military procurement, of developing new military capabilities against uncertain threats by exploiting information technology, has gained momentum. The aftermath of September 11, 2001 made this vision of war even more attractive to the US government. Unprecedented military developments, such as the integration of ground–air communications during the war in Afghanistan later that year (see Herold, this volume), made President Bush's "new kind of war" appear a realistic prospect (see Herold, this volume). Its attractions were further enhanced by the success with which tactical air strikes blended with tanks, infantry, and artillery to maintain the tempo of the US attack on Baghdad in 2003.

Even so, the significance of such developments for urban military operations is as yet unclear. After all, the Iraqi Air Force never flew, the Republican Guard melted away, and the nightmare scenario of sustained and large-scale street fighting in Baghdad did not materialize. Further, the coalition's military success did not translate into a counter-insurgency campaign capable of dealing with the guerrilla forces that emerged in the summer of 2003. By December 3, 2003, the number of US post-"war" fatalities (303) massively exceeded the number killed during the war (139) as the guerrilla war intensified following George Bush's declaration of the end of "formal" hostilities on May 1, 2003 (see plates 12.1 and 12.2).

In the absence of successful, sustained, and intensive urban military operations involving Western forces, the military consensus that such operations are costly, vicious, and best avoided holds. The fundamental question discussed here therefore concerns the extent to which trends, such as transformation and new threats, can affect conventional forces operating in cities. Or, to rephrase the question, whether the tactics and techniques of modern warfare can adapt to the historically proven characteristics and constraints of urban war.

Cities are special

Cities are militarily challenging – but so are jungles and mountains. Each natural environment requires special doctrine, special training, and specially adapted equipment. It is therefore necessary to ask whether urban

Plate 12.1   Royal Marines enter a town during Operation Telic, the British part of the invasion of southern Iraq, 2003. Photograph: UK Ministry of Defence. Used with permission.

operations are a distinct type of action, or whether they are special because cities have a critical effect on the operations taking place within them.

Many professional soldiers believe that urban operations do not deserve special attention, arguing that although they require specialized training

Plate 12.2 A British security checkpoint, to guard against paramilitaries during Operation Telic, the British part of the invasion of southern Iraq, 2003. Photograph: UK Ministry of Defence. Used with permission.

they represent a subclass of tactics (the tactical level of operations is where wars are fought). During the Cold War, urban military operations were regarded as a minor class of operations and, some would argue, they are no more special now. They include a wide range of activities, but most of the tactics and procedures used are the same as in any other operation; command and control requires the same preparation. Applying generic concepts and doctrine and broad operational options should, according to this understanding, be sufficient.

Nonetheless, it is also agreed that many aspects of operating militarily in cities are unique. Close or dismounted combat is invariably attritional. Logistics takes on special importance because the consumption of food, water, and ammunition is typically higher, while supply is especially difficult. Yet many would still argue that cities do not require their own category of operations because the emphasis is on the role performed, rather than the environment, especially in low-level operations such as peacekeeping. Even in mid-intensity operations, which may require more specialized forces, a unique set of guidance is rarely needed. This approach is not unreasonable. Today's uncertainties and shortages mean that a premium is placed on developing a flexible force structure capable of dealing with the unexpected. In British forces this is reinforced by generalist traditions.

Even in Belfast and Londonderry the emphasis was on the counter-terrorist role, rather than the environment in which it occurs. It is true that the British Army prided itself on its street skills in Northern Ireland, but this reflected its culture of generalist professionalism rather than specialized training; expert soldiering covering most eventualities was the key. However, the major danger of this approach is that it dismisses the single most important feature of urban military operations, which is that they are urban. Cities represent a man-made environment that interacts with armies in a way that jungles do not, and urban operations are special because that environment explicitly shapes them.

Of all the environments in which the military operate, the urban environment is the most complex and challenging, as cities influence the conduct of the operations taking place within them to a greater extent than any other type of terrain. There are many reasons for this, of which four are fundamental: physical terrain, the intellectual and professional limitations of approaches designed for war fighting in open areas, the premodern nature of urban fighting, and the presence of non-combatants. The impact of post-Cold War urbanization on conventional military operations must be assessed against four fundamental factors.

First, the physical characteristics and constraints of cities are special. Cities represent a complex blend of horizontal, vertical, interior, and external forms, superimposed on natural relief. Ground maneuver becomes multidimensional. Structural density requires precise small-unit location capabilities within a three-dimensional puzzle. Such terrain provides cover, concealment, and sustainment but it also limits observation distances, engagement ranges, weapons effectiveness, and mobility. Electronic interference and interrupted lines of sight typically reduce the value of overhead sensing systems and Global Positioning Systems (GPS), complicating communications and targeting. Industrial hazards abound and the flammable nature of building materials, combined with the widespread use of propane or natural gas, creates a fire risk. Poor or non-existent sanitation often threatens health.

Second, urban operations emphasize the intellectual and operational limitations of current military thought, decision-making, and logistics, all of which are designed for (and work best in) open areas. Linked to this is a consistent underestimation of the preparations necessary for successful postwar operations. As a result, doctrinal and organizational vulnerabilities remain even as technologies are reexamined, relevant lessons are listed, and internal resource battles are fought.

The controversy surrounding the type of forces needed to fight in cities is indicative of this. The debate concerning the composition of US forces in the 2003 invasion of Iraq ("Operation Iraqi Freedom") makes it evident that today's forces represent the legacy of previous decades, balanced by contemporary political concerns. Transformation's advocates (who include defense secretary Donald Rumsfeld) argue in favor of lighter land forces equipped with better technology and new doctrines, together with innovative plans for greater reliance on Special Forces and "precision"-guided munitions. From a military perspective, this approach worked in Afghanistan (although see Herold, this volume) and could facilitate success in many cities, which are generally thought to require agile forces, backed up by armor, close air support, and good intelligence. On the other hand, urban military operations are notoriously manpower intensive, the key technology in the 2003 battle for Baghdad was conventional armor, and the US Army is fighting to avoid the deep cuts in force structure transformation demands. The extent to which technology can substitute for large numbers of ground forces is unclear (unmanned vehicles may not be able to provide persistent surveillance), and ground forces cannot afford to shed their armored protection (Koch, 2003). Further, most of today's units have general utility, and few armies have developed a cadre of specialists capable of operating effectively in cities without a preliminary training period. Similar considerations apply to the military administration of postwar societies, as the Pentagon's miscalculation of the difficulties of stabilizing Iraq in the summer of 2003 show.

Third, as reference to Iraq suggests, the technical challenges of urban operations are complex but they are only part of the equation. It is natural to argue that developments such as multitasking capabilities that integrate sensors, information operations, and human intelligence can contribute to success, but it is too easy to rely on technology. Despite the speed with which US forces took Baghdad in 2003, urban war has probably changed less than most other forms of war. It remains a brutal and exhausting matter involving significant "collateral damage" and military and civilian casualties, and is the closest the West comes to pre-industrial forms of conflict. The traditional core capability of aggressive dismounted combat – the Hunter-Killer philosophy of "What I find, I can kill" – remains essential. Even the technology employed today is similar to that used during the urban fighting of the 1980s (especially where strict rules of engagement (ROE) prohibited the stronger side from fielding advanced tanks and artillery), though technological, social, and political changes caused other elements to become more significant (Edwards, 2000). "Precision" munitions were invaluable during Operation Iraqi Freedom (although see Herold, this volume), but the US Marines advancing into Baghdad also carried wire cutters, ladders, Kevlar gloves, and mirrors to look round corners. Important elements of urban operations that previous studies identified as critical (intelligence, air power, technology, surprise, and combined arms and joint operations) are arguably no more decisive today than they were in previous wars.

Contemporary military forces may even look to the past for tactical advantage. The capture by the Israel Defense Force (IDF) of the densely populated Palestinian refugee camps in Nablus, Jenin, and Tulkarm in early 2002, for example, was credited by the *Jerusalem Post* of March 9, 2002 to an IDF commander's rediscovery of "mouse holing" (Canadian forces are usually credited with the tactical innovation of blowing holes through adjacent buildings, which was taught in drill schools from 1942 onwards)(Graham, this volume). Paratroopers and Special Forces from the Israeli Home Front Command used electric-powered carbide disks, sledge-hammers, and small explosives to punch their way through the cinder block walls of the camps, so avoiding snipers and booby traps in the narrow alleyways.

Lastly, cities are rarely empty, and, intentionally or accidentally, non-combatants shape the battlespace. Political leaders state that "terrorists" are their target, or a regime's military capability, rather than a city's inhabit-ants, but urban operations take place within, against, and by means of civilians: helicopter gunships kill Islamic militant leaders in crowded Gaza, while Palestinian teenagers bomb crowded cafes (Graham, this volume); US forces barter "security for us in return for electricity for you," while insurgents target Iraq's water, oil, and power infrastructure (Ministry of Defence, 2003: 14; Abdelhadi, 2003). Securing a city means controlling its population, which cannot be compared to open-area oper-ations and is notoriously difficult. The presence of civilians also encourages the media and non-governmental and intergovernmental organizations to pay critical attention to what the military do. In practice this challenges liberal values because non-combatants represent a vulnerability in Western attitudes that can be exploited by opposing forces, as short-term tactical advantage usually lies with the side having least regard for casualties. Iraqi suicide bombers were prepared to die in order to kill American troops manning roadblocks outside Najaf, and Americans were prepared to kill civilians in order to ensure their own safety.

Urban operations are thus distinctive, difficult, and best avoided. Yet the choice of whether to become involved in cities may not be the West's to make. Many Western military operations already occur in populated areas. The port facilities and airfields its expeditionary forces need are located in cities, too. More significantly, cities are destination points for criminals and extremists, and have long been used as sanctuaries or bases by terrorists, insurgents and those resisting Western military operations. The West's technological advantages may even encourage its adversaries to resort to prolonged lower-level conflicts in cities. As a result, the West may be forced into operating cities because its adversaries choose that it should. Not surprisingly, the West looks to technology's transformational potential to manage the known problems. The general understanding that urban war is a primarily tactical challenge, regardless of whether or not the city concerned is or is not a strategic site, strengthens this tendency.

Transformation and Technology

Exploring urban war in relation to technology is important for two reasons: the way a military force makes war hinges on its technological advantages, but at the same time the way in which technology is used depends on how the nature of war is understood. It is not an issue that technology can improve military operational capabilities. The real debate concerns the extent to which sophisticated technology has the potential to change the nature of urban war and ensure operational success. Technology promises dramatic improvements to overcome the disadvantages of urban terrain, offset the scale of cities, replace men with machines, lessen the dangers of friendly casualties, and control non-combatants. Most contemporary technological developments address tactical issues and are targeted to achieve solutions to existing problems, such as the heavy weight of personal equipment. But a true technological transformation of Western forces (based on the exploitation of digital and space technology and organizational adaptations) could move urban military operations from traditional platform warfare to a "network-centric" way of fighting. If delivered, such promises could change the way war is conducted by Western militaries. Commanders could achieve selective dominance without physically occupying a city, while synchronized high-resolution intelligence and enhanced "precision" munitions could enable them to isolate the enemy or separate combatants from non-combatants (Glenn, 2001: 23). Transformation could project and sustain power in distant theatres, deny enemies sanctuary, and allow Western forces to fight on their own terms. If transformation aspirations can be made reality then urban war may be fought very differently in 2025.

Transitional war

In November 2001 Secretary Rumsfeld argued that the combination of new and existing capabilities seen during the war in Afghanistan holds the key to a transformational leap in warfare (*Financial Times*, November 18, 2001; see Herold, this volume). Eighteen months later, Cordesman concluded that American success in the initial invasion of Baghdad means it is no longer necessary to fight urban war on traditional terms (Cordesman, 2003: 174). This may prove to be the case, yet a note of caution is necessary. Many familiar problems were evident in Afghanistan and Iraq – and neither were "virtual" wars won by technicians. For all their sophisticated surveillance equipment, US forces had little idea of the strength and firepower of their adversaries. A Joint Surveillance Target Attack Radar System (JSTARS) would not necessarily solve the problem. Neither would a small elite of Special Forces soldiers whose purpose is to find and fix the enemy and allow "precision" weapons to do the killing. "Precision" strikes promise empty battlefields, but precision works best against massed targets in the open; it is much less effective against the overhead cover and background clutter of cities. And it is noticeable that, while the Pentagon spoke of pinpoint hit-and-run raids amid intense air attack and aerial surveillance, military operations remained reliant on the use of overwhelming force (Herold, this volume).

Nonetheless, events in Afghanistan and Iraq suggest trends likely to influence future urban military operations and these deserve note. Operations in Afghanistan relied on lightly armed conventional infantry with helicopters, thus refocusing attention on ground forces and the development of small agile units. They clarified the utility of information, surveillance, and reconnaissance (ISR) assets, long-range strike weapons and platforms, and the data-link capabilities needed to tie them all together (Burger and Koch, 2002). Operation Iraqi Freedom built on these developments, though the US chose not to use its advantages to their destructive limits in Iraq because of scruples about casualties and collateral damage.

Technically speaking, airpower alone could have devastated Baghdad, but this would have destroyed residual US claims to legitimacy. Instead, the US used new combinations of aircraft and tanks, and a nuanced use of low-cost technology that represents the continuance of trends seen first during the 1991 Gulf War and Operation Allied Force in Kosovo. This produced a new level of "jointness", in which air and land forces worked together to make close air support in cities a reality. Special Forces and intelligence personnel on the ground were used to provide real-time and near-real-time targeting-quality data, either through laser designators or by sending GPS coordinates through radios or laptops to aircraft flying overhead. But such trends produce no evidence to suggest that the mechanics of urban war have changed or that the ability of even small insurgent-like forces to defeat a superior or experienced force may be dismissed. Tanks, artillery, and radios were key technologies in the battle for Baghdad, and military professionalism was arguably the critical factor. This does not equate to transformation, or a fundamental adaptation. It suggests, rather, a rebalancing of existing approaches or resources, or the perfection of old forms of war.

The transformational potential of technological developments in cities is consequently contestable. On the one hand, technology is a key driver of incremental change in other operations: why should urban operations be different? The Gulf War of 1991, for example, introduced "precision"-

guided munitions that seemingly changed the balance between air and land forces. The use of "smart" munitions in the NATO bombing campaign against Serbia in 1999 appeared to show that it was possible to win a war by airpower alone. And in Afghanistan the use of complex communications systems, which included both the new Global Hawk unmanned reconnaissance aircraft and existing Predator unmanned aerial vehicles, meant that President Bush was able to observe the battlefield almost in real time while sitting in the White House.

Furthermore, it is generally accepted within Western militaries that the use of technology to equip soldiers and improve their protection and mobility in cities is a priority. Future improvements in areas such as information technology, robotics, digitization, and non-lethal weapons could, theoretically, provide the foundations for a new approach to urban operations. Information technology could create accurate positioning systems and sensor webs capable of overcoming line-of-sight problems, and could facilitate information superiority. Unmanned ground systems could perform reconnaissance duties, provide logistical support, or even conduct assaults. Effective "non-lethal" weapons (NLW) could reduce non-combatant casualties (although see Warren, this volume). But such developments are aspirational rather than mature, no new core competencies are evident, and digital and space technology has not made old competencies irrelevant. Most of the technological fixes on which hopes are currently pinned are immature or, while conveying advantage, encourage an over-reliance on equipment.

It is not known whether a combination of overhead sensors and "precision" munitions can ensure success for Western forces against an intelligent enemy located in cities. New methods of deploying sensors may prove critical, but it is unclear whether sensors developed for use in complex terrain are automatically useful in cities; steep valleys and cave complexes may have effects comparable to those of buildings, but most do not contain numerous non-combatants. In other words, technology is not synonymous with capabilities, and even successful technological solutions must still be translated into doctrinal, legal, organizational, and training programs before they can make a lasting difference to operations. Most developments are in aid of existing roles and functions, and are unlikely to fundamentally change operations. Not even digitalization, which is seen as the key to integrating and managing core and enabling capabilities (such as firepower and sustainability), does this. Successful digitalization could actually drive determined adversaries into cities, where digitalization confers less advantage. Information, surveillance, and reconnaissance (ISR) systems, for example, are not optimized for cities and there are limitations on the granularity of information they can process; ISR cannot see inside buildings or detect underground activities. Despite the ambitious language, the emphasis of all such programs is on improving the urban capabilities of current (that is, legacy) forces, which have been designed for operations in open environments.

More importantly, low technology remains as important as high. Artillery, for example, will continue to play a major role. It can provide direct-fire support within cities and can be used to isolate or prevent isolation outside them. It is very useful for reducing strong points and has a major psychological impact on defenders; it can also compensate for poor-quality infantry, untrained staffs, and disjointed units. Mortars, meanwhile, will remain the most used indirect-fire weapon for years to come; their high angle of fire allows rounds to reach street-level without being masked by surrounding structures. Mortars can provide obscuration, neutralization, suppression, or illumination fires; they either kill the enemy or allow infantry to close and kill them. Rocket propelled grenades (RPGs) will no doubt retain their dominance, too. Each of the Chechen 7- or 8-man teams in Groznyy included one or two RPG gunners for use against personnel, armor, and structures. And flamethrowers and snipers were used as often in Groznyy in 1995 as in Aachen or Berlin in 1945. In other words, the most useful weapons on urban terrain probably remain the flamethrowers and tank demolition guns that were withdrawn from many Western forces some years ago.

Urban Grammar

Despite major technological developments, the characteristics and physical constraints of urban operations have remained remarkably consistent over the past 60 years. There is nothing in recent military operations to suggest that these are easier than in the past or that urban war has been redefined. If anything, conventional wisdom is confirmed by, for example, the weeks it took UK forces to make significant inroads into the southern Iraqi city of Basra in 2003, by the inability of coalition forces to provide security in the face of widespread criminality and resistance in Basra and Baghdad, and by the Israeli Defense Force's experience of dealing with Palestinian fighters during 2002. Israel has air superiority over the entire region, and most of the Palestinian Authority's strategic assets are dependent on Israel (Weizman, this volume), yet Israel has still to destroy its adversaries. Palestinian fighters lack any form of central organization or coordination, but accounts of IDF assaults, such as that on Yasser Arafat's compound in Ramallah in March 2002, sound remarkably familiar. A giant bulldozer broke through into the compound, followed by an armored personnel carrier that disgorged 30 soldiers. They scrambled into position, inching along with their backs to the breached wall. One by one they stepped through the rubble; moving into the building, they kicked down doors as they went, shooting inside rooms and hurling stun grenades. Noise levels were terrifying as tanks blasted buildings, throwing up clouds of white dust (*Daily Telegraph*, 2002).

Not surprisingly, advantage in urban war is sought from technological advances, thus reflecting – and reinforcing – the belief that urban military operations are a matter of tactics rather than strategy. In consequence the strategic context of urban military operations is neglected even though the political complexity of the Palestinian question, for example, is widely acknowledged. In a similar vein, it is significant that, although coalition forces got to within 60 miles of Baghdad in 1991, the 1990s did not see sustained or systematic attention to the military–strategic implications of cities. If anything, the knowledge that urban military operations are best avoided effectively sanctioned the belief that they could be avoided or, at worst, treated as a primarily tactical challenge. As a result there is no urban paradigm that can be applied to Western military operations. There is no coherent theory that can be based on principles independent of specific operations. Nevertheless, an explanation of why cities consistently affect military operations in the way that they do is now possible. Its value here is that it confirms the evolutionary and incremental nature of change within urban operations, and emphasizes that less has changed in the post-Cold War world than might at first be assumed.

This explanation of urban operations is based on the conviction that a coherent set of facts and variables is identifiable, and that it provides insight into the function and purpose of military force in an urbanizing world. This suggests that an urban field is also identifiable, and that a set of relationships between positions characterized by their own logic and practices can be established. A strategic grammar of urban war is increasingly evident. The assumptions behind the logic include the following linked principles. City fighting is always difficult, destructive, and manpower intensive. It places a premium on military skills because not only does the terrain magnify and intensify every problem and vulnerability, but also cities often require a range of operations to be performed, sequentially or simultaneously, during a single mission. Urban war fighting also marks the regression of industrialized societies to pre-industrial styles of war. It usually results in close combat in which a soldier's experience, training, cunning, and motivation are more valuable than advanced technology or innovative doctrine. Indeed, "the greater the determination of the enemy, the greater the need for close combat" (Director of Infantry, 2000: 3); war is a clash of wills, but the best way of defeating an enemy remains killing him. And belligerents usually target civilians. This is either because they are being used as shields by the enemy, or because of ill discipline, the desire for retribution or punishment, deterrence, or as a means to a political or tactical end. Suffering and brutality are thus part of the logic of war – past, present, and future. In consequence, urban war and Western notions of humanitarian war are irreconcilable regardless of the technology used or the political rationale offered.

The great value of such axioms is that they are proven by experience across a range of operations and decades, rather than simply the most recent war. They are not present in every operation, but they represent archetypical aspects of operations. For, unlike the tactics associated with peacekeeping and humanitarian relief, the aggressive and survivalist tactics underpinning urban operations have evolved reactively or pragmatically, rather than as a result of technological or conceptual developments. Even so, the fact remains that conventional militaries probably still do not fully understand cities or the urban battlespace, and have yet to integrate either into strategy. Much is known about the tactical problems, but little is understood of cities' strategic and operational potential.

Continuity in War

Most visions of urban war in the coming decades are technologically based and distinctly futuristic. "Precision" systems and nanotechnology will, it is argued, either revolutionize operations or radically improve a soldier's lot. Predator imagery is to be fused on a JSTARS aerial surveillance platform, robotics and hunter-killer battlefield unmanned aerial vehicles (UAVs) are to mitigate casualties and enhance lethality, while nanotechnology will monitor the state of a soldier's health. For Western militaries, technological solutions to urban operations' challenges are undeniably highly desirable, and new technologies in areas such as reconnaissance undoubtedly suggest important possibilities. The American faith in technology's enhancing virtues and leverage potential is widely shared – American technological sophistication is one of the attractions of the USA as an ally. The changes associated with President Bush's election pledge to give the Pentagon the opportunity to "skip a generation" in military technology could conceivably affect the course of future urban war fighting. Or it could merely pander to the vision of war as the US would like to fight it – "controllable, quick, clean, and with victory assured" (McInnes, 2002: 136).

Recent military operations in Iraq suggest that what makes the US powerful in urban war is the technology that gives it information. But, as America (and Russia and Israel) has rediscovered, poorly armed adversaries should never be underestimated, least of all by forces whose confidence is founded primarily on technological capabilities and national power. All too often the possession of technological advantages encourages complacency. Reliance on information technology may even be inappropriate in cities, given the short-range, multidimensional challenges of urban terrain; digitalized equipment such as sensors may show units in the same location even though several dozen floors of reinforced concrete separate them. Sophisticated communications and short-range information, surveillance, and reconnaissance systems are undoubtedly significant enablers, but technology has its limits, especially in urban war; the West's technological superiority will not ensure success, because its enemies need only avoid defeat.

It is possible that tactics will change; that economic targeting and information operations, perhaps involving subtle forms of exploitation, denial, and punishment, will eventually replace more conventional forms of war. This could result from the lucrative potential of globalization – yet it is unlikely given the strategic grammar of urban war. Other types of military operations, such as peacekeeping, may be oriented towards achieving political stabilization and the defeat rather than destruction of an adversary, but the unpredictability of cities means that war fighting capabilities remain essential for urban military operations; they may be the only thing adversaries respect. And when urban war degenerates into street fighting it remains at a state that would be recognizable by the great grandfathers of today's soldiers. With the exception of Russia, however, most major states no longer have direct experience of protracted war fighting in cities. More to the point, there is no evidence that Western forces are more effective at fighting in cities than they were in 1945, constrained as they now are by international law, cultural norms, the presence of the international media, and the political imperatives shaping discretionary interventions. There is still no easy way to distinguish between combatants and non-combatants, the military significance of sewers or a warren of alleys is as important as ever, and operations continue to be exhausting. Close combat is likely to remain premodern in nature for the foreseeable future.

Urban war suggests that neither technological advances, globalization, nor political contingencies have changed the essential nature of military force or the purpose of its application. It is not accidental that Western doctrinal manuals for urban warfare continue to understand operations in cities as primarily a tactical (technical) challenge. Neither is the marked degree of consensus across armies that urban terrain complicates operations in ways that other environments do not. In other words, war fighting in cities has changed less than military operations other than war. Technology can undoubtedly offer advantages, or at least offset some of the known disadvantages of cities, but urban war remains a particularly brutal business. In consequence, a strategic grammar of urban operations is evident, in which continuity is a stronger theme than discontinuity.

Conclusion: Inherent Tensions

In the long term advanced technology may permit the development of new approaches to urban war, but there is as yet no evidence that advanced technology has or can cause a fundamental shift in the nature or conduct of urban operations. Indeed, current vulnerabilities (which includes the West's known preference for fighting from a distance) suggest that the West has still to assess realistically the conditions under which it might fight sustained operations in cities. Most of the effort and resources of Western militaries devoted to developing new technology have concentrated on materiel for personnel at the lowest levels of operations – and much of it is aspirational, rather than mature. As a result, technology runs the risk of becoming a tactical panacea or diversion, whereas it is better regarded as a support or enabler.

There is very little about urban military operations that is new. But it is precisely this fact that challenges liberal assumptions about the transformational potential of sophisticated technology. The greatest danger most Western armies face is that their politicians do not appreciate this. There is little evidence that Western politicians and publics will find it easy to accommodate the proven characteristics of urban war – the tenacity defending forces often display, the short-term advantage that accrues to the side with least regard for civilians, the increasing irrelevance of restraint in the face of heavy losses, and the difficulty of suppressing (rather than fragmenting) chronic low-level violence. Not surprisingly, strategic and operational tensions result from the changed political landscape, the technical possibilities, and the realities of urban terrain.

Part III

Exposed Cities: Urban Impacts of Terrorism and the "War on Terror"

Introduction

Cities are especially vulnerable to the stresses of conflict . . . City-dwellers are particularly at risk when their complex and sophisticated infrastructure systems are destroyed and rendered inoperable, or when they become isolated from external contacts. (Barakat, 1998: 12)

There is no technical solution to the vulnerability of modern populations to weapons of mass destruction. (Schell, 2001: 4)

Enclosed space turns out to be a trap rather than a way out. (Lütticken, 2001: 118)

Part III of this book emphasizes the inescapable fact that, in a world of intensifying globalization and urbanization, the "urban" and the "international" blur into one another. The division between "domestic" and "international" politics has now melted away. Terrorist acts, and acts of war, are simultaneously global and local events. Strategies of surveillance, militarization, terrorism, social control, and war are now constituted through transnational webs of power and technology which reconstruct "target" cities both in the advanced capitalist world and in the global South in parallel.

All of these processes provide enormous challenges to the ways in which we conceptualize, experience, and attempt to shape cities and urban life. As the crude war-mongering of fundamentalists on both sides of the current transnational struggle threatens to fatally undermine ideas of the open city, of cultural plurality, of democratic dissent, of robust citizenship before the law, and of positive cycles of immigration and urban, diasporic mixing, this part of the book seeks to begin to address these critical challenges.

The chapters in Part III demonstrate that 9/11, the "war on terror," and the intensifying social controls that are part of the "homeland security" drive must be analyzed in parallel. Chapter 13, by the architect and writer Michael Sorkin, meditates on the urban experiences of catastrophic terrorism, and state terror against cities, across the world. As a New Yorker, Sorkin writes about his own experiences of Manhattan since September 2001 and contrasts these with his experience of a visit to Ramallah in the spring of 2003. While these two cities clearly face radically different situations, Sorkin nevertheless captures similarities: the deep anxieties of urban life; the asphyxiating effects of militarized security on the daily flows of city life; the edginess and the collapsing infrastructures; the palpable fortification of urban space.

Lambasting the emerging architectures, urbanisms, and technologies of what he calls the "national security city," Sorkin ends with a warning that this rapid transformation will divert the city "from its human tasks by the architecture of manufactured fear." The challenge, to him, is for congeniality and citizenship to assert themselves against the progressive militarization and securitization of urban life.

Chapter 14 explores in much more detail the ways in which the 9/11 attacks, and the "war on terror" and "homeland security" drives which have followed, have dramatically reshaped the economic structures, political dynamics, and the treatment of urban planning problems within New York City. Here, the urbanist Peter Marcuse examines in detail how the protagonists in the war on terror – security companies, real estate companies, surveillance operations, and all those set to benefit from the homeland security drive – have sought to rework the institutional fabric of urban governance in New York to directly benefit their own interests. This is leading to an increased emphasis on the barricading and "citadelization" of strategic buildings and a reduced emphasis on public policy planning. These trends have combined with an accelerating decentralization of corporate office jobs, a collapse of tourism-related industries, a massive fiscal crisis, and a big reduction in social-welfare oriented programs. The result, Marcuse argues, is that downtown New York as a whole faces an unprecedented economic, social, and political crisis. Marcuse concludes by arguing that the strategic discussions that are ongoing about the need to rebuild and replan New York will have a critical influence in the future development of this iconic global city.

The ways in which "global" city cores are being restructured to address the real and perceived threats of terrorist attack are also the focus of chapter 15, by planning academic Jon Coaffee. He provides a detailed analysis of the ways in which London's financial district has been remodeled and remanaged since a series of spectacular terrorist attacks by the IRA devastated key parts of the City of London in 1992 and 1993. Coaffee shows how a powerful governance coalition came together after these events to construct a "ring of steel" around the strategic heart of the financial district. This combined urban design, traffic management and high-tech surveillance elements. The story of this attempt to "design out" terrorism is a complex one. It illustrates the ways in which constructions of security, in response to specific threats, invariably creep into attempts to control wider incursions and perceptions of threat (for example, anti-globalization protestors or small-scale crime). Coaffee also underlines the tensions between barricading and separating off strategic urban spaces, and the imperatives of maintaining flow, connectivity, and the appearance of "normality" in the key geo-economic enclaves of globalized capitalism. Thus, constructions of "security" are as much about image and perception as physical barricades and high-tech surveillance systems.

Coaffee's emphasis on the role of high-tech surveillance systems in urban responses to real or perceived threats of terrorist violence usefully leads into chapter 16. Here, sociologist David Lyon provides a state-of-the-art analysis of the massive "surveillance push" that is occurring in cities across the world as part of the so-called war on terrorism. Stressing the ambivalent tensions that surround the efforts to continually record, monitor, and surveille a widening portion of the day-to-day life of cities, Lyon shows how a whole suite of devices and "technical fixes" are being installed and celebrated. These cover biometric surveillance, ID cards, CCTV, face-recognition technology, and communications monitoring. As such systems become more interlinked, and more automatic, Lyon sounds a note of caution.

While Lyon argues it is unhelpful to construct sinister conspiracy theories to explain this growing urban surveillance "assemblage," he does stress that a purely technological response to the real or perceived risks of catastrophic urban terrorism is bound to fail even on its own terms. More worrying still, he shows how state power will inevitably be centralized in the process; social discrimination will increasingly be built into hidden, automated, technological systems which operate across transnational scales; and accountability for these systems will probably whither under the carefully constructed imperatives of "homeland security."

Chapter 17 attempts to balance the emphasis of preceding chapters on urban security and the war on terror in affluent, northern cities such as New York and London – placed as they are in the geostrategic capitalist heartlands of the global North. For it is crucial to remember that, as well as a creeping militarization of urban sites in North America and Europe, the war on terror has involved massive aerial and terrestrial onslaughts on the civilians of Afghanistan and Iraq (as well as many smaller scale, covert military operations elsewhere). With both countries already deeply impoverished by war or sanctions, the results of these invasions have been, and continue to be, bloody and catastrophic.

In this context, Marc Herold – a leading analyst of the history of US aerial bombing – looks in detail at how the punishment of Afghanistan by US bombers since autumn 2001 has impacted on daily urban and rural life in this extremely poor country. In particular, Herold outlines in detail the murderous impacts of the use of coercive air power on the civilians in Afghanistan's few cities. Looking beyond the thousands of dead and injured, Herold also traces the long-term devastation that these attacks – and their deadly legacies of unexploded ordinance – have wrought on already-fragile systems of infrastructure, healthcare, survival, and psychological and economic well-being.

Placing the attacks in the context of the long history of aerial US assaults in the past three decades, Herold concludes that, because they had second-degree intentionality – that is, US military planners knew very well that their attacks would kill large numbers of innocent civilians – these assaults need to be seen as acts of state terrorism. These were even more murderous and lethal than the acts of informal terrorism in the USA on September 11, 2001 that they were supposedly meant to avenge.

13

Urban Warfare: A Tour of the Battlefield

Michael Sorkin

Pregnancy

Heading uptown for a panel discussion about architecture and politics, I found myself in the back of the taxi, unprepared. Looking at the passing scene, I noticed what seemed an unusually large number of pregnant women, something I had recently observed in my building, as well. America was deep into Iraq and the rash of pregnancies was only natural: sending young people to the slaughter demanded that the species replenish.

Were pregnancies on the rise in Baghdad, too? Will GIs marry Iraqis? What were the implications for urbanism?

New Yorkers focus on the home front: more people chasing fewer rooms can only have an upward impact on prices, especially now when money is cheap. A baby boomlet would add growth pressure on schools, on recreational space, on neighborhood character and continuity. How will the relation between existing paradigms and actual uses currently being negotiated play itself out in this new growth? Will there be an adjustment in the misfit output of family homes in the suburbs for what had appeared a bygone demographic? Will we have to move to Brooklyn to make way?

Blackout

In the largest such failure in American history, a portion of the electrical grid – serving 50 million people – collapsed in summer 2003, leaving New York City in the dark for 24 hours. On television, gloating Iraqis in Baghdad cafés allowed how we'd gotten a little of our own back. Ours was just a mild version of the power outages endemic in Iraq since our occupation, but we briefly felt their pain.

I tend to the paranoid view. There had been a local harbinger of the blackout, clearly ominous. The day before the lights went out, a tremendous explosion blew manhole covers sky-high along several blocks of Hudson Street and produced an acrid smell that was unmistakably reminiscent of the odor of September 11. Firemen had been fighting a mysterious underground fire since the previous day and it seemed to be centered on a local building that is fat with communications lines, a purported high-value target, the only building in our immediate vicinity that retains its post-9/11 concrete barriers. The same building has been the object of long-standing neighborhood complaints about the constant noise of its private generators and fear of the catastrophic explosion of the large quantities of fuel-oil – which the building owner currently seeks to increase! – that is stored within, a disaster waiting to happen.

When we heard the blast we all had the same thought and rushed to the window. Sirens were already wailing and the street was preternaturally quiet: police and firemen had blocked off the street. The swarm of emergency vehicles from both city agencies and Con Ed – the electrical utility – gathered quickly and were around for days. The too familiar stillness after disaster settled over the neighborhood and small groups of people gathered on corners and at barricades to share information and establish momentary bonds.

The blackout the following day fueled even greater crisis conviviality. Since 9/11 we have a new paradigm for responding to breakdowns in the urban infrastructure and we deployed it with fine results during the power outage. Pedestrians took over the streets and sidewalks, walking home and enjoying continuous linear socializing. Outside every bar and bodega, a crowd gathered – it was almost cocktail time when the power went out, but the mood was upbeat. The timing couldn't have been better and the blackout became the Disney version of the blitz. The city was "paralyzed" but we enjoyed the opportunity to display our civil solidarity, and to use the disaster to temporarily expand the territory of public space, "appropriating" the street like a closing for a street fair.

For many, this dramatic expansion of public space is the most indelible memory of 9/11. That attack produced the most powerful set of collective emotions the city has ever known and caused, among other things, the imposition of a series of planning and traffic measures that many have dreamt of but which "realistically" never had a prayer. Suddenly, there were *severe* restrictions on motor vehicles, mandatory car-pooling, streets for pedestrians, a dramatic increase in water-born transport. The disaster opened a window for the reorganization of fundamental infrastructures, now largely reshut.

Civil disaster – particularly the relatively benign, like a snowfall or blackout – is inconvenient rather than horrible and has become a new form of civic event, one that binds the celebratory sense of New Year's Eve in Times Square with a dose of moral satisfaction. It is both a measure of our resilience as citizens and of our frustrated longing for concrete forms of the civility of the face to face. In some ways, these events parallel the rise of "reality" programming in the media, a way of authenticating our enjoyment by the inscription of a standard of cause and by a set of authentic emotional responses to events.

Reality is the postmodern sublime, a credible extremity in a culture of fakery. Just as the terror bombing of World War II was intended – according to the theories of Bomber Harris and Curtis LeMay – to break civilian morale but accomplished the opposite, the actuality of disaster has, to date, been likewise galvanizing. The question, of course, is one of limits. Disaster is obviously an inappropriate medium of urban design, but it certainly does function as a prompt. With victims rhetorically transmuted into heroes, we feel a dangerous *frisson* of moral satisfaction simply walking home when the lights go out. Good citizens.

Ramallah

During the spring of 2003 – at the time of the Aqaba summit – I lectured at Bir Zeit University in Ramallah. Getting there was largely a matter of traffic, which included congestion amplified by checkpoints and the need to switch taxis at each barrier. Door to door from my hotel in Jerusalem via three taxis was under an hour. Without the occupation apparatus, the trip might have been 30 or 40 minutes less.

After breezing through the first checkpoint on the way out, we changed taxis, and made our way through crawling traffic to a second barricade on the far side of town. This was very different from the first. Accustomed to the idea of being "controlled" by passing a needle-eyed security review, I was surprised to find a passage with virtually no soldiers in sight. Instead of inspection, this was controlled by inconvenience. Big concrete blocks placed in the roadway forced us to get out of our taxi and walk down and up a hot and dusty hillside – a kilometer – before passing through another concrete block barricade to the knot of waiting taxis.

The discipline was effective, forcing people to carry their goods out in the open over a restricting distance. For the elderly, the sick – or anyone with luggage – this forced walk was more than simply inconvenient and it had the double effect of humiliation and control. Because the gap was near the main entrance to the university, it was (as it was surely designed to be) especially annoying to students. There was a spontaneous commerce of wheelbarrow porters who carry purchases – and sometimes people – across the gap, a microscopic, adaptive, transportation system.

The return trip was considerably different. While I was lecturing, an Israeli security alert had apparently taken place, based, it seemed, on information that an attack was forthcoming somewhere. Word spread quickly and the customary cell phone cacophony took on an added urgency. One message reported that merchants were shutting their gates in anticipation of a curfew, another that the Kalandia roadblock had been closed, and another that Israeli troops were entering the city in force.

Moving quickly, we managed to work our way into the city center of Ramallah – where there were no obvious signs of crisis – and, thinking that it had been a false alarm, had tea at the house of a friend. We were in the midst of an automobile tour of new architectural projects when the cells began ringing again. Urged by various informants to skedaddle back across the border, we found a taxi and set off. Almost immediately, we came upon a group of Palestinians burning tires and throwing stones at an Israeli patrol. Our driver made a hasty u-turn, got on his phone – which remained fixed to his ear – and began racing through back streets to circumnavigate the trouble spot, a routine with which he was obviously very familiar.

And so we arrived again at the main checkpoint at Kalandia. Here was something more familiar. A seemingly endless line of cars and trucks was queued for inspection. Motors were switched off and drivers milled around waiting for movement, inured to a wait of hours. The situation for pedestrians was similar, if more compact. A huge crowd jostled to squeeze into single file for examination by Israeli troops. As at Bir Zeit, commercial activity had sprung up, but here it was contoured not to alternative movement strategies but to the exigencies of stasis. Cold drinks, ice-cream, and other merchandise were being hawked, as were cell-phone calls for those who didn't have a handset with them and a brisk business in explanations for being late was being done.

We joined the crowd and pressed our way forward. The sun was blazing and the numbers of people were far greater than the metal roofed waiting shed could accommodate and so we spilled out around it. Apparently, we were too restive, too pushy, or too disorderly and a young soldier – who was standing on the other side of a barbed wire barrier, perhaps two feet away from me – fired her gun. The flash and the huge noise momentarily confused me and, as the crowd ran, my first thought was "bomb." This was my neophyte inexperience, but harrowing nonetheless. Suddenly, what had been an almost out-of-body experience of looking on became much more intimate.

Brandishing my American passport I squeezed my way to the head of the line, filed through the narrow barrier and was confronted by a soldier in battle gear who asked sarcastically if I couldn't find a better place for a holiday and accused me of not having a proper stamp in my passport. Petty, needless harassment (accompanied by sharp and instantaneous violence), multiplied by tens of thousands every day, colors life in Palestine, shapes the character of its public spaces, and creates a beleaguered wartime sociability of suffering that I recognized.

And so it went for five hours. At the next checkpoint, another style. By now we were in a big collective taxi and the soldiers took our papers and walked slowly back to their jeep, parked 200 feet away. After a long wait, our names were slowly called out and one by one we had to clamber over each other to get out of the taxi and walk to the jeep to be handed back our identification. One boy was not so lucky and was led off by the soldiers under some unexplained suspicion.

By the next checkpoint we were by a trunk road into Jerusalem which intersected a smaller road, part of the parallel system built for quick access to and from the settlements. Seeing that the settler traffic was speeding through while we were backed up and immobilized, the cabbie veered into a little lane, a detour that brought us onto the free-flowing roadway. Here we were lucky and – to the great satisfaction of the passengers – made it through with a wave, although five minutes later we found ourselves in another line of cars and had to wait another hour to get by.

It is possible that the only answer to persistent "terror" is a police state. The two form a perfect symbiosis and it is easy to understand the utility of regular attacks to the authors of the US government's "Patriot" Act, the breeders of sniffer dogs, and the private security firms that have become such a growth industry. To produce both legibility and intimidation, the whole panoptic repertoire of spatial and social control is deployed with little objection. And the powers that be keep ratcheting up the stakes. The database that Israeli (and Palestinian) security relies on is linked to John Poindexter's data mine and produces the lists controlling who should get through "security," who should be turned back, and who should be given a hard time.

As irony would have it, the Palestinian friend who guided me through that day has recently moved temporarily to Orange County, California and has found some of the similarities to home spooky. In the numerous gated communities that surround him, he felt something familiar from the urban language of the Israeli occupation: walled settlements. But the American security fences are transcendently commodified. These are bulwarks against the danger in general, against fear itself, barricades in the absence of any actual threat. These communities are secured instead against a spectral other, pure paranoia, blossoming precisely because the threat is unknown (although people of color figure in many a fantasy).

If an effect of the Cold War – created by the perpetually invisible threat of instant annihilation – was to motivate more dispersed forms of settlement, like the suburbs in America or massive deurbanization in China (see Farish, this volume), the prospect of a perpetual state of "preventive" warfare risks extending the logic beyond a carpet of low-density enclaves to their continued fortification. The world will be divided between fortified settlements for the materially and psychically privileged and a global refugee camp in which the world's misery will simply be banked in a huge reserve army of poor-space. Palestine and Orange County (which already boasts high-priced toll bypass roads for the rich) will converge.

The Inner Checkpoint

We know that the best policeman is the one we carry inside us. Watching my Palestinian friend forbear through what is, for him, a daily experience of harassment and humiliation, I realized something about the psychic cost of this repression. If only in complicity at our own inconvenience, we are all implicated in the anti-terror network, surrendering to its demands every time we offer up credit cards or identification, every time we pass through the magnetometer in the office building lobby, every time we see a suspicious cop pulling over a truck about to cross a bridge or enter a tunnel.

In America, we have well-developed profiling skills, habits of identification and prejudice. Al-Qaeda has only increased the ambit of our gaze. Now the most likely suspect is no longer simply the African-American male but something more alien, more vague. Post-9/11, I profiled compulsively. On the subway not long ago I was sitting opposite an elderly Muslim man (bearded and traditionally dressed) who was carrying several large parcels. The well-drilled formula *Muslim plus package equals bomb* flitted through my mind even as I judged it ridiculous. How much time every day wasted with these thoughts?

The city maps fear. Added to the repertoire of dark streets, fast traffic, rapacious ghetto dwellers, and crowd-loving pickpockets is now anxiety at beards and turbans, close reading of hack licenses from the back seats of taxis, a weird vibe when reaching for the baba ghannous at the deli. The evildoers are everywhere locked in their invisible cells, ready to explode. Preemption proceeds.

Wozniak

Stephen Wozniak, Steve Jobs' old partner from Apple Computers, has a new company. After working for 18 months below the radar, Wheels of Zeus has presented its first product: WozNet. The technology enables the creation of a low-cost wireless network that – using radio signals and global-positioning satellite data – allows very larger numbers of "people, pets, or property" to be tracked from a single base station. According to a story in the *New York Times*, "the tags – expected to cost less than $25 to produce – will be able to generate alerts, notifying the owner by phone or email message when a child arrives at school, a dog leaves the yard, or a car leaves the parking lot."

Although Wozniak suggests that the networks may have unspecified other uses, the roll-out is being accompanied by a rhetoric insisting that use of the WozNet is voluntary, that encryption technologies will keep unauthorized users from piggy-backing on such ready-made domestic surveillance data. The situation is ripe for the creation of such networks of "elective" control. Persuaded that these technologies can be disciplined to confine themselves to keeping track of Fido, we invite them in.

For the city, the WozNet adds further impetus to reorganization based on non-geometrical styles or order. With the world now reproduced as an infinitely locatable collection of points, Cartesian strategies of mapping and place-based definitions of property are freed to float without losing any operational precision or utility. Indeed, security will make place itself less relevant, making the tasks of both hiding and seeking less and less physical. The button in our ear will tell us whether to turn left or right, speeding us on our way, even as we are assaulted by a variety of immaterial networks that can place us without reference to the physical qualities of the environment.

Like the satellite navigation systems installed in rental cars and SUVs, the WozNet reflects an in many ways necessary adjunct to the pattern of sprawl. The exponentially growing expanse of the interstitial city – unresponsive to landscape, ecology, or physical clarity – can increasingly only be navigated with the aid of continuous updates and electronic maps. New technology offers the sanction of convenience and a deterrent to old styles of "freedom of the city." In the grid of infinite sameness, content must be constantly added to this stem-space to give it meaning.

The unremitting psy-ops of the advertising industry constitutes a form of warfare on the consciousness of citizens everywhere, political speech unregulated by the niceties of response and equal time. New York is more and more covered by building-scaled advertising scrims, gigantic billboards harkening the inevitability – the necessity – of consumption. The ten-story high image of Kate Moss in her Calvin's is also a form of camouflage. Like more traditional strategies of disguising, the city becomes increasingly illegible in terms of its specifics of scale and location. Revisualized as a compendium of applied images, the city is remeasured in pixels or benday dots, evacuated of the particulars of place, rushing towards the condition of a pure field of top-down communication and surveillance. We eliminate our enemies by making them indistinguishable from us and, thereby, bring the entire world under suspicion.

Ground Zero

The little debate over whether or not the American government should
display the bloody images of Uday and Qusay Hussein provided an interesting measurement of the relation between warfare and its representation.
During Gulf War 2, there had been howls of protest when Al Jazeera
broadcast images of the corpses of American soldiers killed in battle.
This, the media alleged, bore witness to the barbarism of the enemy. The
networks seized the opportunity to replay over and over those awful pictures of dead GIs being dragged through the streets of Mogadishu.

During World War II, it was not until 1943 that the censors allowed
images of dead Americans to be displayed in the press. Still, it is very hard
to combat terror without a renewable supply of images of the consequences
– periodically fear of the unknown has to be topped up with palpability.
At the urban scale, this anxiety reproduces itself in arguments about
commemoration and the city's relationship to its war wounds. Dresden
attempts to reconstruct its obliterated monuments. Rotterdam renews with
a vigorously new precinct. Paris and Budapest retain the pock-marks of
bullets in historic walls. Oklahoma City clears the site and constructs a
poetic memorial. The Pentagon is carefully repaired and a monument is
commissioned for the lawn out front.

New York struggles with a meaningful commemoration at Ground Zero.
Almost entirely coopted by financial power (see Marcuse, this volume),
rebuilding proceeds with commercial space as the driver and the scheme
now likely to be built will reproduce the sum of activities previously on the
site, add more, and devote a modest residue to formalized commemoration. A remnant of the Trade Center complex – the still useful slurry wall –
will perhaps be retained as an evocatively literal presence. Throughout the
argument over reconstruction, however, the focus has been too tenaciously
on the site itself, on the insistence that the effects of the attack were limited,
that there was no collateral damage to the city as a whole.

That damage is legible not simply in the misery of survivors but in
joblessness, in relocations out of the city, in the travails of the Chinatown
economy (see Marcuse, this volume). But is it equally visible in the recod-
ing of the landscape in the language of the bomber. As high value targets are
hardened with Jersey barriers, security cameras, armed guards, identification checks, metal detectors, and other elements of the anti-terror, the city
is remapped in terms of its potential for disaster, its strategic locations
revealed as a series of target sets.

This mapping of the new landscape of fear has its effects, barely studied.
For my part, I have come to identify several Manhattan buildings as particularly sinister. One of these is a very large federal building that houses, among
other agencies, the Passport Bureau, its own documents made ambivalent by

the terror. For Americans abroad, the passport itself can function as a target marker. Equipped with a bar code scanned at the ticket counter and immigration booth, it enables our own authorities to keep track of any movements offshore. For foreign passport holders, their very foreignness restricts opportunities to visit the United States and renders their bearers suspect.

I give this building wide berth. Having identified this place as my particular target, I also invent the surrounding blocks as dangerous and am forced into inconvenient circumnavigations and alternate routes. On days when my own substrate of fear is high, I look at every parked car and truck near this building as a potential bomb. I have been certain more than once that some nondescript van is packed with explosives and moments from detonation. Self-conscious, I hasten away at an urgent pace but short of an incriminating run. The anti-terror regime forces all of us to alter our repertoire of urban dangers and make many small adjustments to the way we use the city and its streets.

Recently, I heard a colleague describe design work he had been doing in Washington, DC, to help secure that target against terrorists. Asked to provide an array of physical barriers in front of strategic buildings, he adopted a strategy that he disingenuously described as "deputizing." Quotidian objects – benches, bollards, trees, kiosks, etc. – were redesigned to withstand the rushing vehicle and explosive detonation of the suicide bomber. The point, though, was to do it without the appearance of menace, ha-ha's for the age of terror. By providing security without alteration to their benign and familiar guise, these devices permit an unaltered view of the world to abide on the surface, the elaborate stage machinery of deterrence artfully hidden from view. Everything's fine.

Baghdad on the Hudson

When Walter Winchell originated the phrase, he had another kind of sin in mind than those we've gone to war to punish. Still, there's something apposite in the comparison. Like the Iraqis, we are tyrannized by an unremitting culture of coercive images of the desirable, by relentless panic-mongering, by shrinking civil liberties under the guise of self-protection and we likewise adopt the Saddamite cultures of bellicosity and fear, not to mention his triumphalist style of architectural self-celebration.

It is now unexceptional to find gun-toting troops in battle-dress on New York streets, at transportation termini, and around other "strategic" locations. If there is a marker of the failure of the good city, it is soldiers in the street and it is a failure we New Yorkers are now obliged to share with both pre- and postwar Baghdad. Here, the troops join the other population that has come to signify the failure of our polity, the homeless. My evidence is purely anecdotal, but the number of people living in the street in New

York seems again to be growing. It oversimplifies to ascribe this to the war in Iraq, but the reduction of taxes on the privileged, the growing spasm of war-related expenditures, and a general obliviousness to the human conse-quences of policies driven by meanness, greed, and ignorance do have predictable effects.

Like Saddam, we celebrate our self-inflation with the stupidities of opulence. It continues to amaze me that what will stand as a memorial to 9/11 will be the world's tallest office building, disaster triumphalized. In building this way, we ape the luxuries of Saddam's collection of palaces and the hypertrophic crossed swords with which he celebrated his "victory" over Iran. But we run the risk, like Saddam, of creating shrines to the uninhabitable, opulence that cannot be consumed. Just as the despot was unable – for fear of bombing or assassination – to actually stay in these palaces (or anywhere else for more than 10 hours), so many will balk at being the sitting ducks of the unsustainable, in-your-face hubris of our own architectural celebrations of death.

Invisible Threats

The discovery of "white powder" in some public place has become a regular event in the life of New York. Recently, my part of town was paralyzed by an envelope of what turned out to be talcum powder on the subway. The line was shut down for several hours in the middle of the work day and the event attracted a gaggle of TV news vans to Canal Street where the discovery had been made. What would have been a meaningless event in the pre-Anthrax days was now the medium of panic and, inevitably – because of the dramatically inconvenient response – a "newsworthy" event.

Such is the style of contemporary paranoia. The flip side of crisis sociability must be the ongoing presence of some legible threat. The ad-ministration, aware that its policies cannot be sustained in the absence of fear, resorts to portentous warnings and color-coded threat assessment. Although these are much derided for the meaninglessness of their distinc-tions, even as objects of ridicule they do assure that everyday discourse is infiltrated by the subject matter of fear if not by anything to actually be afraid of. This too becomes part of the discussion, as the fact that we have not again been attacked undercuts the urgency of the build-up and the ancillary assault on civil liberties.

Although I would not advance such a cynical view of wag-the-dog causality, it is certain that there are urgent and ongoing conversations in the corridors of power about acceptable levels of American casualties. Accustomed to a threshold that is impossibly low – per the deathless intervention in Bosnia – the now daily list of Americans killed in Iraq challenges public support of warfare with an intensity no longer low. We respond with a policy of suburbanized occupation, withdrawing troops from unquiet cities into garrisons on the peripheries, abandoning the streets to local strongmen and hastily trained Iraqi police.

The initial invasion of Iraq was designed to avoid the fraught promise of urban warfare. Racing around towns to seek a classic engagement with an army in the field, we had no real idea what would happen when we took over the country's towns, which have now become the primary sites of resistance to the incivility of occupation (see Hills, this volume). Transformed overnight from liberators to policemen, the American army becomes that vanguard of the monstrous apparatus (wielded with panache by Saddam for so many years) that turns every citizen in society into a potential other, a conceptual doubling of every person on the planet into both one with a genuine identity and a potential identity that must be repeatedly disproved.

The Airport

Over a billion people a year pass through the air transport system and here we find the *locus classicus* of the globalized checkpoint. An emergency rule of law is in place: all who pass through it are presumed guilty and obliged to prove they are not. And so we sweat through screeners' questions, offer up our luggage for scanning and inspection, have our identities tracked against burgeoning databases of suspicious persons, surrender our anonymity at every stage of the journey. Yes, yes, for our own safety, but the awful calculus now playing out is one that weighs safety against freedom and imprisons us behind higher and higher walls.

I slip off my shoes and place them along with my laptop, keys, loose change, and eyeglasses in the plastic bin and send it all through the x-ray. I then pass through the magnetometer trying to look harmless, hoping to avoid any additional hassle. I watch sheepish and improbable travelers – kids, the elderly, mid-western business types – being patted down or scanned by detection wands. These unlikely candidates are inconvenienced by random checks, a marker of America's sense of fair play, our ostensible refusal to profile. Every time we detain some granny, we force her – and those watching – to question the system of control and, parenthetically, to invent the other for whose rights these "good" citizens are obliged to suffer. And we hate him all the more.

The airport is the primary training ground, the vanguard of the organization of the city as a space of heavily surveilled, highly managed flows. The airport is modernity incarnate. It models the city as a pure space of circulation and commerce, mapping the circuit of capital directly onto the circuit of bodies. As a classification engine, airport design is a distilled version of the segregated efficiencies of transportation planning in general in which the grail is the separation of means and, thereby, of people and privileges. That this is managed within a space of great crowding makes airports the premier research sites (along with places like Disneyland) for the burgeoning technologies of surveillance, data processing, perpetual motion, information management, and other top-down styles of security.

The City After Clausewitz

If there has been a change in the epistemology of warfare post-Cold War, it is in the shift to plausible, long-term styles of "engagement" (destruction). The "theory" of deterrence was not simply based on the threat of extinction, but on mutuality. Bound together by rational fear of an irrational prospect, nuclear warfare is a great equalizer, but only in circumstances in which the opponent is presumed not to be suicidal. Despite the efforts of a variety of policy crazies to find appropriate circumstances for promoting "limited" atomic warfare, some remnant of rationality kept us free of this horrific prospect. But the era of the suicide bomber is upon us.

The Cold War (which lasted through eight US presidencies and over fifty years) inured the body politic to the idea of perpetual conflict and to a titanic flow of funds in the direction of the military–industrial complex. The new "war on terror" will engorge not simply the familiar players in this sector – the Boeings and the Grummans – but will support the proliferation of an even larger complex of profit. From the architects who have become specialists in everyday fortification, to the planners for whom security will become job-one, to the Wozniak-style surveillance queens masking their efforts behind the fiction of "convenience," to the camp-following Halliburtons and Bechtels who will arrive to pick up the pieces after further acts of smart-bomb urban renewal, to the huge cadre of private security services with their armies for hire, we are moving toward a national security city, with its architecture of manufactured fear.

The basic premise of Clausewitzian strategic theory – that war was not an aberration but an activity conducted by states in pursuit of rational aims – is now obsolete. As the importance of nations and their armed forces continue in parallel decline, the political, economic, and military role of cities is likely to increase. Filled with a plethora of actors – drug entrepreneurs, jihadists, local liberation fronts, animal rights activists, abortion abolitionists, and the rest, the future will be increasingly one of sharp small conflicts in defense of positions that have only a marginal relationship to territories and boundaries. Whether the congeniality and citizenship that represents the legacy of our best urbanism can prevail against this remains to be seen.

14

The "War on Terrorism" and Life in Cities after September 11, 2001

Peter Marcuse

Introduction

Not terrorism, but what has been done under the mantel of counter-terrorism, has had a significant effect on cities since the attack on the World Trade Center on September 11, 2001. The consequences are particularly noticeable in the United States, but their repercussions will be felt throughout the global economy. They suggest, not a change in direction, but a continuation of trends already well under way before September 11, reinforced and aggravated by the cover given by the so-called "war on terrorism." The war on terrorism needs to be read always as in quotes, because it is not in any conventional sense a war – no national enemy, no troops, no territorial goal as such, no confrontation in battles – with the war on Iraq having only the most tenuous connection to actual terrorism. Nor are the policies undertaken in the name of the war on terrorism rationally related to the prevention of terrorism – they do not deal with the relations that produce terrorism, they are not proportional to the actual threats from real terrorism, they are not based on reliable information, and they serve purposes that are quite independent of any danger of terrorism, strengthening policy directions already well under way before September 11.

Hearings before the US Congress as this is being written highlight some of the irrationalities of the intelligence services dealing with actual terrorism. The repeated "orange alerts" declared by the government ("high risk," as compared to yellow alerts, which are only "elevated risks") lead to measures looking more like Ariel Sharon's reaction to Hamas than to any threats from Al-Qaeda:

> Attorney General John Ashcroft...identified "lightly secured targets" as the most vulnerable, especially hotels, shopping centers, and apartment

complexes. The increased measures are particularly visible in New York, which Ashcroft indicated was a potential target area for terrorists. Ashcroft also pointed to so-called "soft targets," which are potential targets that are a symbol of American power or prosperity, such as the Statue of Liberty or the Golden Gate Bridge. (Government Security Solutions.com, 2003)

But of course Al-Qaeda saw the commercial towers of the World Trade Center and the military bastion of the Pentagon as the symbols of American power, not the Statue of Liberty.

The prognosis of the impact of the war on terrorism is not good, for those interested in urban life and democracy. Both are threatened by actions in the market, and governmental responses are likely to aggravate problems. The war on terrorism is leading to a continued downgrading of the quality of life in US cities, visible changes in urban form, the loss of public use of public space, restriction on free movement within and to cities, particularly for members of darker-skinned groups, and the decline of open popular participation in the governmental planning and decision-making process. The planning both for the reuse of the site of the attack in New York City, for the "revitalization" of its financial district, and for measures to deal with the proclaimed threat of terrorism in the future in many other areas, suggest these developments. They are only tangentially related to a serious and rational concern with the lives of those that were actually directly affected by the terrorism of the attack.

This chapter concentrates on the impact at the level of urban form. The net result might be described as a decentralization of key business activities and their attendant services, but to very concentrated off-center locations in close proximity to the major centers – *concentrated decentralization* – with earlier tendencies to move out lower-level activities accelerated. Within both the new and the old urban concentrations, there will be an increased *barricading* within the city, a *citadelization* of new construction for major businesses and upper-class residences, and actors on the demand side in the real estate market will move in this direction, and they will influence government to assist in the process. That assistance will come both through limited public subsidies and from an abdication of independent planning and regulatory action by government in pursuit of social welfare goals: governments will be pushed to see their role as simply smoothing the way for private forces to act in the market. *Deplanning* might be a good term for much of governmental planning in this process, since what is not done is frequently accompanied by a surrender even of previously instituted procedures and an abdication of regulatory powers. Property developers and owners in the central areas, the supply side of the real estate industry, will however press to maintain earlier levels of centralization, and paradoxically they will be the ones calling for the maximum of governmental action to help them in the effort.

What follows deals first with developments in the market and in governmental policy at the urban level, then looks at the array of forces producing those developments. But before examining these issues, a look at one of the most direct consequences of the war on terrorism – the exponential growth of the security industry – is necessary to give some indication of the direction of events.

The Growth of the Security Industry

What the official war on terrorism means most directly is an enormous boon to particular sectors of industry, who have been quick to see its profit potentials. The Center for Responsive Politics has estimated that "businesses appeared to be focusing on the creation of the Homeland Security Department more than any other legislation in recent memory." And successfully: private security services, overwhelmingly in urban centers, are booming; they may well be the fastest growing sector in a sluggish economy. The figures are illuminating:

- Private security employment is already over 1.7 times the level of employment in public security agencies, and the ratio is expected to grow to 2.4 by 2010.
- Expenditures for private security in 2000 were already $103 billion, up from $20 billion in 1980 and $52 billion in 1990.
- There are now over 100,000 private security firms in business, up from less than 30,000 twenty years ago (Security Industry Association, 2003).

It is specifically public spaces in cities that are affected by this multiplication of devices of control and surveillance. In recent debates about the reconstruction of Pennsylvania Station in New York City – one of the city's two major rail and commuter terminals – Senator Schumer asked for more security. He was told security was already based on the Rail Security Program, which included increased policing, new K-9 (police dog) bomb teams, sensors to detect chemical, biological, and radioactive materials, explosive trace detection devices that scan the air for traces of bomb materials, bomb-resistant trash cans, intrusion alarms, and vehicle barricades. But he nevertheless asked for $450 million more to be spent on even further augmented "security."

The public costs incurred in the purported quest for security are substantial. A whole new bureaucracy has been created at the federal level, much of it under the new Department of Homeland Security. It includes the new Transportation Security Administration (TSA) and incorporates other agencies that formerly existed as separate government agencies:

the US Customs Service, which was previously part of the Department
of Treasury; the enforcement division of the Immigration and Naturalization Service, which was previously part of the Department of Justice;
the Federal Protective Service, which was previously part of the General
Services Administration; the Federal Law Enforcement Training Center,
which was previously part of the Department of Treasury; and the Animal
and Plant Health Inspection Service, which was previously part of the
Department of Agriculture. Altogether, over 170,000 people are employed
in this work.

And of course these expenditures are at the expense of others, and what
are particularly short-changed are programs that affect cities. Housing
subsidies are cut from a level already low by international standards, social
service programs are curtailed, public education is left so short of money
some cities are forced to close their schools early in the year to save money,
urban infrastructure is neglected, public libraries are closed early, and fire
stations are closed completely to save money.

All of this cannot be blamed on Al-Qaeda, or on any known real terrorist
organization or threat, yet it is the propaganda of the war on terrorism
that justifies it. It is part of a long-term policy approach that seeks to
minimize the public sector, privatize every possible governmental function
for private profit, and protect those people and business firms that rate the
top of the urban hierarchy from any possible diminution of their privileges,
whether it is from taxation, from internal discontent, or even from radical
criticism. The connection to the invasion of civil liberties has been
well documented elsewhere and is discussed below, but is part of the
same long-term pattern.

In this context, then, what has been the impact of the war on terrorism on
the shape of cities in the United States (Marcuse, 2002b: 591–6)?

Urban Form I: Concentrated Decentralization
in the Market

The spatial impulses that followed September 11 in New York City were
not so much a change in direction as an intensification of what has been
happening anyway, now accelerated and explained by reference to concern
over terrorism. In the market, both business patterns and residential
changes were involved. To give perspective: some 2,825 people were killed
in the attack on the World Trade Center; up to 100,000 jobs, including
those of small business persons (further breakdowns below) were directly
affected; 13.45 million square feet of office space was destroyed (Bagli,
2001), 30 percent of the Class A space in the downtown area, and 3.6
percent of all office space in Manhattan (Glaeser and Shapiro, 2001). Just

as major disasters permit reconstruction on a newer basis, that might earlier have been wished but could not be implemented, so the destruction in lower Manhattan permits a clearer view of some longer-term trends, which it in turn amplified.

Employment patterns have for some time been towards decentralization of almost all types of jobs, with only a very narrow band of activities remaining concentrated in the central business districts of major cities, and most activities focusing on less central areas of the city – the suburbs, edge cities – with a noticeable movement from primary cities to secondary and even tertiary (economically defined) cities. A number of factors came together to shape this trend: the availability of technology to make both transportation and communication easier across greater distances; the pressure on central real estate prices in a market dominated by private land ownership; the costs of congestion and environmental degradation; and, last but hardly least, the social tensions and insecurities that result from increasing polarization of the population and continuing racial division tied, both in fact and even more in perception, to life in big cities. To these negative aspects of concentration there has been counter-poised the advantages of agglomeration: the efficiencies of shared services, the importance of face-to-face meetings, in some cases the reduced friction of transportation, the desirability of a creative, diverse, lively, urban milieu.

In this balance, the fear of terrorism now added a significant weight to the side of decentralization. Over-agglomeration is equated with danger. In the more "global" cities, this balance has hitherto been more on the side of concentration than it has in other cities; that balance has now changed. The centers of global cities will no longer be exempt, even to the extent that they ever were. The pattern is already visible in New York City. The New York Stock Exchange won't build its long-planned new trading floor and 900-foot tower across the street from its current headquarters, but may build a secondary trading site outside lower Manhattan. But many say it should move to trading on an electronic network. More shares are traded on the NASDAQ stock market, which exists only on computer systems and the screens of its dealers, than on the Big Board at New York's Stock Exchange on Wall St. "With faster computers and data transmission, traders no longer have to meet in person to buy and sell shares," says the chief executive of the Cincinnati Stock Exchange:

"Outside the United States, floors are disappearing really quickly, and automated auctions are the wave of the future," Mr. Madhavan said. "The USA is the lone holdout, and it's the holdout because it has a strong group of dealers who are politically connected." Mr. Madhavan is head of ITG, which operates a computer trading system that competes with the Big Board. (*New York Times*, October 12, 2001: C4)

So one trend is for certain business activities to leave the concentrated center (s) of the city. Which activities? Those that are largely self-contained, that have internalized a large part of their externalities; and those that do not, with the use of modern communications and transportation technologies, need to be in the same physical location as the headquarters they serve. So the headquarters of major industrial firms and those directly marketing services to consumers may move out, and back offices will move out. Nothing new here. Yet the trends will accentuate, and the definition of back offices will expand. As Saskia Sassen (2002a: 24) has pointed out, the destruction in the financial district has permitted some firms that had previously massively concentrated their activities there to do what they had already begun to do, but now much more quickly: disaggregate their activities into those which really needed to stay agglomerated in a concentrated downtown, and those that could (increasingly as technology advances) be deconcentrated.

But those moving out of the concentrated center are not moving to just anywhere; they remain concentrated in specific locations away from the center, most but not all remaining within the metropolitan area. In the first place – and this is perhaps unique to New York City – there are two "downtowns," and there is a continuing competition within the real estate industry between them: Midtown and the "downtown" Financial District. (Midtown for this purpose is defined as between 34th and 59th Street, 8th Avenue to the East River, and downtown as Manhattan south of Canal Street – not the definition used by the Lower Manhattan Redevelopment Corporation, which takes in all of the area below Houston Street.) That competition has been going on for some time; estimates are that in 1950 downtown had more workers than Midtown, today Midtown has three times as many as downtown (Glaeser and Shapiro, 2001: 20). Even after the loss of space in the lower Manhattan financial district the office vacancy rate has doubled between September and January, "leaving some analysts to wondering which companies will move into the empty space, let alone any new towers that might be built" (Bagli, 2002: 1; Heschmeyer, 2001).

The hyper-concentrations of jobs in service-oriented office buildings in the Central Business Districts (CBDs) of the more globalized large cities (and both the high- and the low-paying jobs associated with them) will shrink, as multinational businesses change their spatial strategies in the search for security in more outlying areas. The focus will initially be within the same metropolitan regions (e.g., American Express, Lehman Brothers, and others, renting – on long-term leases – spaces in Jersey City, Stamford, etc.). Estimates are that, even by November 2001, 23,000 jobs had already moved to the suburbs after September 11, and another 144,000 were in jeopardy of such a move (Bagli 2002: 1).

Many major firms already had large satellite offices in fringe locations, to which they quickly moved on September 11; in some cases decisions to move more operations out of New York City to those locations were simply accelerated by the attack. The Bank of New York had 3,000 employees in its headquarters building at 1 Wall Street; they're all back at work there now. But it had 4,000 employees at 101 Barclay Street at one of its data centers; they've been moved. "[We are] just too concentrated in Manhattan" (*New York Times*, October 6, 2002: C1). Long Island City in Queens is touted, not only by self-interested developers but also by Senator Charles Schumer of New York, as "an ideal location for creating a new central business district" (*Grid Magazine*, 2001). In fact, since his speech, a $700,000,000 contract has been awarded by the city's Economic Development Corporation for the construction of a major mixed-use development there, expected to bring 7,000 jobs to this location in Queens (Globest. Com, 2001). Empire Blue Cross took temporary quarters in Melville, Long Island. It had 460,000 square feet in the World Trade Center. It is proposing to lease 300,000 at Metrotech in downtown Brooklyn, and less than 100,000 square feet at 11 West 42 Street, Times Square, where the chief executive and other top executives will stay (*New York Times*, October 12, 2001: D6). Deutsche Bank is building a backup operation in Jersey City. Marsh & McLennan, a major tenant at the World Trade Center, has taken some space in Midtown, but is moving 2,000 employees across the river to Hoboken, in New Jersey (Bagli, 2002: B2). Goldman Sachs is moving its entire equity trading department to Jersey City, across the Hudson River, to a $1 billion complex it is building there (with, incidentally, the highest skyscraper in New Jersey). According to a major real estate firm, "Goldman's decision is a significant setback because it affects the downtown core of financial services. It's not so much the number of jobs that's significant, but the kind of jobs. Equity trading is the heart and soul of any investment bank" (Bagli, 2002: B2).

The movement out will be primarily to the immediately adjacent but somewhat less dense and less expensive fringes, the outer boroughs in New York City and across the Hudson. But there will also be a lesser move to the suburbs, and beyond them to the edge cities (not just in Joel Garreau's narrow sense): Stamford, White Plains, etc. And over time the effects may lead to an even wider dispersal to other regions or urban enclaves. TIAA-CREF, the largest pension fund in the United States, now has 4,600 employees in New York City, 1,320 in Denver, and 597 in Charlotte. Their planned expansion will be overwhelmingly in Charlotte, hardly a global city (TIAA-CREF, 2001: pers. comm., October 9). Residential patterns, as well as business and commercial patterns, will change. In particular, the trend towards recreating residential housing and residential environments in central business districts will suffer, despite the efforts of CBD real estate interests, existing residential tenants, and local governments. In Washington, DC, where the major business tenant is government, there will be a continuing trend to the decentralization of government offices, but the hopes for bringing multi-family residential development to the downtown are now given little chance (www.globalst.com 2001: October 19). The trend here is longer standing, as suburbs generate more and more of the accoutrements of urbanity that used to be confined to the centers of cities: the sidewalk cafés, the art galleries, the cultural centers, the symphony orchestras, the theatres. The safety issue will accentuate the trend. As Paul Krugman, who holds himself out as a hard-headed economist and lives in the Jersey suburbs, wrote: "I felt perfectly safe on September 11; there are millions of people living and working nearby, but no obvious targets, because there's no there here." The "there" that isn't there is a traditional urban oriented form, with a centralized CBD, and fewer will want that, given the trade-offs, than even before.

Urban Form II: Citadelization, Barricading, and Governmental Deplanning

In the decentralized but concentrated locations that have been given a boost by September 11, the form of development has also been influenced by those events. Obtrusive skyscrapers lose some of their appeal. The towers in Kuala Lumpur and Frankfurt have already felt the threat, closing and evacuating the day after the World Trade Center collapse; workers in the Empire State building in New York and the Sears Tower in Chicago were reportedly afraid to go up to their offices. At Sears Tower taxis are not allowed to idle at the entrance and lunch deliveries may not be made to offices. The observation deck is closed; security in the lobby gives a feeling of martial law, and security guards greet long-time employees by name but demand to see their IDs. A consultant working on the 44th floor is quoted as saying he's considering buying a parachute, and found one on the Internet for $130 (*New York Times*, September 23, 2001: A36). Five months after September 11, a business newspaper headlines on its front page: "Empire State Emptying Out as Tenants Flee. Anxiety Lingers; Vacant Space Triples" (*Crain's New York Business*, February 2002: 1). (The story goes on to say: "Concerns about terrorism plague other trophy towers, as well. Some businesses have refused to consider sublets in the Chrysler Building since September 11 . . . Many companies seeking space are issuing a new mandate to their brokers – 'find us anonymous buildings' – in a blanket disapproval of all well-known properties.") The apparently unrelated crash of a light plane into the floors of the Pirelli tower in Milan added to the problem.

In lieu of going ostentatiously high-rise, the direction of development is towards protected, secured citadels, to internalize and shield the activities critical to the top tiers of global and national businesses. The trend towards citadelization already exists, but is modified and accentuated (see Coaffee, this volume). The new form is for citadels within buildings or fortified complexes, including more and more of the facilities necessary for daily life within the building itself. One will never have to leave the citadel for shopping, for meals, for entertainment, for personal services. The mall at the World Trade Center was a prototype of the form: commuters from New Jersey could arrive underground, find all their personal and business needs catered for entirely within the Center and its mall and protected adjacent areas, and leave again underground, without ever having to step foot in the City itself. That pattern, preexisting the attack on this particular citadel, will be strongly accentuated, but in less high-rise, less representative, less "signature" fashion, and more heavily barricaded and secured even than before.

So the new citadels will be less ostentatious externally, less ultra-high-rise signature buildings. They will be larger, more comprehensive fortified centers, with high-tech metal detectors, fingerprint card entry, etc. The barriers to easy access will increase (see below). The move of Morgan Stanley, the largest securities company in Manhattan and the largest tenant in the World Trade Center, typifies the kind of exclusive citadel that will increasingly be characteristic. The firm is buying the Westchester County former 107-acre headquarters campus complex of Texaco (symbolic!). It is not keeping the office tower it had begun in Midtown Manhattan, which it sold to Lehman Brothers, a company displaced from the World Trade Center. Most of its 14,000 employees will stay in New York City, but at least 2,000 will go to the 750,000 square foot campus in Westchester (Bagli, 2002). As the president of Global Marketing Consultants, a Canadian firm, said at an Urban Land Institute meeting:

> The high density and mass urbanization resulting from skyscrapers is not necessary or desirable . . . we will see more 24-hour, multi-use projects offering employees amenities such as full-service business centers and medical facilities, and which provide space that is communal, flexible, "media-rich," easily adaptable. (Heschmeyer, 2001)

And the polarization by income, by occupation, and by race that is an ongoing process in central cities will accentuate a further developing pattern: a barricading of segregated spaces. This will come about both as a result of residential developments and of changes in employment patterns. Those able to move out of town or to barricaded citadels will do so; those unable to do so will remain behind. The difference between the two groups will be both income and race related, with sharper dividing lines between and among groups. So segregation and quartering will increase. One can see the dynamic in miniature by looking at what was already the occupational and income distribution of those directly affected by the attack on the World Trade Center: the three largest industry groups, among the 108,500 jobs lost as a direct result of the attack are shown in table 14.1.

The difference in relative compensation is apparent from the table ("Securities" includes low-paid clerical as well as high-paid professional jobs). Lay-offs thus disproportionately affect high and low end workers; those without accumulated resources will be particularly hard hit. Those at the bottom of the economic ladder end up in the soup kitchens (Ruiz, 2001); those at the top are producing a boom in the ex-urban real estate market in Connecticut and upstate New York, and a more comprehensive form of gentrification in town.

The newly appointed deputy mayor of New York argues:

> I don't think that anyone has disputed the fact that we have to do anything we can to ensure that lower Manhattan remains the financial center of the city. But the lower Manhattan of the future also has to be a 24-hour community filled not just with financial firms, but also with residences, arts, culture, and other things. (Bagli, 2002)

Clearly, the danger here is that the entire area will become an exclusive, citadelized community for those who can afford to live there, socially if not physically barricaded off from the rest of the city (as Battery Park City, adjacent to the World Trade Center, had been).

The barricading of the city is a good shorthand term to describe what public policy is leading to. It is readily visible in public space, near public buildings, in places of public assembly and use. "Public space" will become less public; free access and free use will be severely limited. By contrast, controlled spaces, such as malls, will increase their attraction. Some public spaces, like the park at the Federal Courthouse in Boston (Bagli, 2001) or the plaza before City Hall in New York City and its adjacent recently

Table 14.1 The three largest sectoral job losses in New York City as a direct result of September 11, 2001

Industry	Employment	Compensation ($ millions)
Securities	12,200	2,577.2
Retail trade	12,200	311.1
Restaurants	11,900	241.8

Source: Fiscal Policy Institute

renovated park, will simply be barred for open use, or so tightly controlled as to inhibit activities normal to a democratic society. Mayor Guiliani had pioneered this conservative development with his restrictions on assemblies near City Hall (Davis, 2001: 43) and attempts to limit the use of streets for parades, in the name of "security". Less freely accessible public buildings and metal detectors and demands for identification are being normalized, a pattern reminiscent of Eastern European and Soviet public buildings before 1989. Many places, from railroad stations to bus terminals to public streets and squares, will be subject to pervasive surveillance. The attractiveness of guarded malls will increase (Davis, 2001: 45). That the danger is not one the war on terrorism is designed to meet is revealed by the most recent assassination in New York City, where a disgruntled would-be politician shot a member of the City Council from a balcony in its meeting room; an individual crime, not an act of terrorism.

The impact of the war on terrorism's urban policies on urban life is evident: in Los Angeles, for the Oscar ceremonies:

> Hundreds of officers from local and federal law enforcement agencies will ring central Hollywood on Sunday night, in at least three levels of security checks and keep guard on a traffic-free perimeter of nearly two square miles ... what makes the new venue a particular security concern is that it is in the middle of one of the most congested and urban neighborhoods in Southern California. We're not allowing any of these Oscar-viewing parties in the complex this year. (*New York Times*, March 23, 2003: 10; see Warren, this volume)

Or:

> The National Park service is planning to spend $2 to $3 million on closed-circuit television systems at the Washington Monument and the Lincoln, Jefferson, Franklin D. Roosevelt, Vietnam, and Korean War Memorials. (*New York Times*, March 23, 2003: 10)

This barricading will be particularly prominent whenever there are plans for any type of popular protest mobilization, rally, march, or protest (Warren, this volume). Mayor Guiliani had pioneered this with his attempts to prevent rallies such as that in Harlem that would attract a large number of African-American youth, but the courts had over-turned his refusal to give permits for such events; such a pro-democracy result is not likely to occur when restrictions are imposed in the name of preventing terrorism. Again, the trend was already visible in actions by conservative governments before September 11, and can include literal barricading. For instance, Washington DC police and Secret Service officials said there was no final design for the security barrier expected to be erected in anticipation of the

World Bank/International Monetary Fund protests in mid-September, although reports say it will be 2.5 miles of 9-feet-tall chain-link Cyclone fence. "The fence hasn't been completely set. It could be Cyclone fence, but it also could include Jersey barriers [giant cement blocks], vehicles, even bicycle racks. All those things are possible," one official is quoted as saying (Orin, 2001).

Barricading can be accomplished by social and legal measures as well as by physical ones. The passage of what is called, officially, the United States Patriot Act of 2001 (HR 3162: 2001) will extend the restrictions on customary civil liberties even further, with the federal government centrally involved but local communities and their residents directly affected. Key provisions of the legislation allow investigators to use roving wiretaps, following a suspect rather than a particular phone. It also gives the government the power to detain immigrants for up to seven days if they're suspected of involvement with terrorists, up from two days. The bill calls for tripling the number of immigration and border patrol agents along the 3,000-mile border with Canada. The new measure also provides new tools to fight money laundering by terrorists, allow government agencies to better share information about suspects and more easily track their communications, and increase penalties for terrorism-related crimes (ABC News, 2001).

Such measures will disproportionately affect immigrant communities in large cities. But they will more broadly affect the active participation in democratic debate that has been a characteristic of life in cities. "Stadt Luft macht freie" – city air produces freedom – becomes less true. Both official and unofficial government actions and statements lead in the same direction.

Senator Trent Lott has already called publicly for a reduction in the weight given to civil liberties in the interests of security (National Public Radio, 2001). Rage against those who don't follow the prevailing line on the terror attacks was seen in the recent firing of Dan Guthrie of the *Grants Pass Oregon Daily Courier*, who criticized President Bush for hiding in a shelter during the assaults in New York and Washington. When Tom Gutting wrote a column titled "Bush Has Failed to Lead the US" in the *Texas City Sun*, the newspaper terminated him and ran a front page apology. In covering a September 29 peace demonstration in Washington, DC, the *New York Times* chose this deliberately inflammatory and misleading headline: "Protesters Urge Peace With Terrorists." Comedian Bill Maher, host of television's "Politically Incorrect," lost many advertisers after he commented that the US was cowardly in "lobbing cruise missiles from 2,000 miles away." White House spokesman Ari Fleischer later denounced Maher and warned: "Americans need to watch what they say, [and] watch what they do." This comment was deleted from a White House transcript of the press conference, according to the *New York Times*.

Thus, "security" becomes the justification for measures that threaten the core of urban social and political life, from the physical barricading of space to the social barricading of democratic activity. Stephen Graham goes further, and speaks of the "accelerated militarization of urban civil society" and the concomitant "urbanization of the military" (Graham, 2001), as serious military concerns (not the Star Wars kind) focus more and more on cities, how to defend them and how to attack them (see Warren, Hillis, this volume).

Conclusion

So, some years after the event, the impact of September 11 has become clear. Very little has actually happened to counteract terrorism at its roots, and what has been done to deal with its symptoms is disproportionate to the danger, at least from all the available evidence to date. On the other hand, under the mantle of the so-called war on terrorism, a number of trends, often summarized under the heading of a neoliberal turn, have been accentuated and legitimated:

- A concentrated decentralization of business activities in cities, largely to outlying locations within their metropolitan areas, but also further abroad.
- A citadelization of major centers of business activities, incorporating more and more of daily functions within enclosed and protected spaces in large planned developments.
- A move towards barricading sections of the city from each other, particularly evident in so-called sensitive areas, with restrictions on the normal uses of public spaces.
- An increased public investment in security and surveillance and control mechanisms, together with a diminution of the public sector in its social welfare function.
- Deplanning, transfer of planning functions from public to private hands and within the public sphere, from traditional planning considerations to priority for police and security inputs.
- A disproportionate growth of those industries providing real or perceived or mandated security for daily activities.
- A narrowing of the limits of public discussion, of the rights of immigrants, and of civil liberties generally.

All justified in the name of a war on terrorism in the cities.

15

Recasting the "Ring of Steel": Designing Out Terrorism in the City of London?

Jon Coaffee

Introduction

The unprecedented physical, financial, and psychological damage of 9/11 will, many commentators have hypothesized, have a lasting impact on the way our major cities are planned, run, and function (Savitch and Ardashev, 2001; Graham, 2002c; Marcuse, this volume, 2002a, 2002b). Subsequently, commentators have posed questions about whether we should rethink urban development strategies on the basis of "worst case scenario" terrorism. For example, should we seek to generate a "bunker mentality," construct an "architecture of fear," create "exclusion zones," "*cordons sanitaires*" or modern-day "panopticons," on the basis of what might, or might not, happen? Will such security schemes, if developed, be acceptable to civil society?

Historically, responses from urban authorities to the risk of terrorism have been, in large part, just extrapolations of ongoing trends already employed to reduce crime, and, perhaps more importantly, the fear of crime (Davis, 1992; Flusty, 1994; Ellin, 1997). Studies of territoriality, popular in the 1970s, are now being increasingly applied to the current urban situation, where strategies of fortification and militarization have commonly been utilized to address issues of terrorist risk. In particular, a number of commentators have explicitly argued that technological advancement will become all-important in the battle against urban fear and terrorism (see Lyon, this volume). There is already widespread evidence that the "creep" of surveillance, and other methods of social control in Western cities in response to security concerns, is begin to "surge" in response to the new terrorist threat. In the contemporary city there are fears that the mushrooming of increasingly digitized, automated, and biometric systems (Lyon, this volume, 2002) will further erode civil liberties, as democratic and ethical accountability will be given a back seat in the new era of "anxious urbanism" which has followed 9/11 (Farish, this volume). In short, such surveillance technologies are increasingly leading to the "automatic production of space," with urban society quickly becoming a technologically managed system based on automated access and boundary control (Thrift and French, 2002). In particular, recent work has highlighted how new digitalized and algorithmic surveillance acts as a categorizing and social exclusionary device in contemporary urban areas (Graham and Wood, 2003). One of the most influential concepts in this area is the idea of Automated Socio-Technical Environments (ASTEs), developed by Lianos and Douglas (2000). They argue that such environments occur as a result of the pervasive "dangerization" of society and the generation of environments of risk leading to what Ulrick Beck termed a "protectionist reflex," where a "withdrawal into the safe haven of territoriality becomes of intense temptation" (1999: 153).

Since the early 1990s such territorial imperatives have been particularly evident within commercial urban centers. This is because there has been a growing realization by the world's terrorists that, by targeting financial centers and their commercial infrastructure, they can cause severe damage directly to valuable building structures, producing great uncertainty about future insurance coverage. Such attacks can also dent the reputation of the area through the negative media exposure that is guaranteed. As such, financial districts have often sought extra protection against possible attack.

This chapter will detail the attempts made by local state actors, the police and security professionals, to control and regulate space within the UK's financial heart – the City of London (also referred to as the Square Mile or The City) – as the threat of attack from the Provisional Irish Republican Army (henceforth Provisional IRA) and other potential terrorist groupings intensified in the 1990s and early 2000s.

Evolution of the City of London's Counter-Terrorist Response

During the early 1990s the City of London was attacked a number of times by the Provisional IRA. The initial security responses were a result of large bombs that exploded in the City in April 1992 and April 1993 (and a 1992 bomb found under the Canary Wharf Tower in the London Docklands), as well as a number of smaller detonations. Subsequently, strategies were devised for the City centered on the construction of roadblocks, the use of armed checkpoints, the development of a series of public and private CCTV networks, a number of traffic restrictions, increasingly visible policing, and a series of private initiatives to increasingly fortify individual buildings. This security operation was commonly referred to as the "ring of steel." This term was first used in the mid-1970s in Northern Ireland to refer to the high-level security measures, in particular the high steel gates, that were erected at all entrances into Belfast's city center (Brown, 1985; Jarman, 1993).

As a result of the continual terrorist threat, the ring of steel was enacted in the Square Mile and the City has increasingly separated itself from the rest of London in both physical terms (Coaffee, 2000, 2003a) and technological terms (Power, 2001; Graham and Marvin, 2001; Coaffee, 2003b). However, the extent to which the ring of steel was fully mobilized was related to the perceived threat level which ebbed and flowed through the 1990s, as well as non-terrorist events such as anti-capitalism demonstrations in 1999 and the introduction of "congestion charging" into central London in 2003. Overall, since 1990, eight distinct periods can be shown to have characterized the City of London's counter-terrorism response. This is shown in table 15.1.

Table 15.1   Stages in the evolution of the City of London's "ring of steel"

Stage	Dates	Key incidents	Main features of response
Apprehension	1990–April 1992	• Beginning of IRA mainland attacks against economic targets (Stock Exchange July 1990) • Fernival Street bomb (February 1992)	• More overt policing, especially for major events • Plans for city-wide security schemes
Containment	April 1992 – April 1993	• St Mary Axe bomb (April 1992) • Colman Street bomb (June 1992)	• Armed police checkpoints • Traffic management enhanced • CCTV adapted for counter-terrorism uses
Deterrence	April 1993 – Sept. 1994	• Bishopsgate bomb (April 1993) • Business lobbying for enhanced security • Wormwood Street bomb find (August 1993)	• Security checkpoints introduced • Advanced police-operated CCTV and alert systems • Private CCTV schemes • Increased no-parking areas

(Continues)

Table 15.1 (*Continued*)

Stage	Dates	Key incidents	Main features of response
Optimism	Sept. 1994 –Feb. 1996	• Provisional IRA ceasefire	• Downgrading of visible police presence • Checkpoints become permanent • Updated police-operated CCTV
Reactivation	Feb. 1996– Feb. 1997	• Docklands bomb (February 1996) • Subsequent attacks in London and Manchester	• Large increase in visible policing • Increased frequency of roving checkpoints • Use of legislation to increase stop and search
Extension	Feb. 1997– June 1999	• Decision to extend the ring of steel westwards	• Expansion of ring of steel coverage • Advanced CCTV employed • Environmental improvements highlighted
Reappropriation	June 1999– Sept. 2001	• May Day/anti-capitalism riots (June 1999) • Subsequent anti-capitalist demonstrations • Threats from dissident Irish republican terrorists	• Proactive enhancement of private building security • Better liaison between city police and other forces • New anti-terrorism legislation
Reappraisal	Sept. 2001 –present	• 9/11 and fear of further attacks • Anniversary of 9/11	• Reexamination of counter-terrorism procedures • Increased uptake of alert systems • High state of alert, especially on "key dates"

Apprehension and containment

The Provisional IRA's bombing campaign in the 1990s aimed at economic targets in London and sought to "bring terror to the heart of London with a ferocity never before experienced in the capital" (Dillon, 1996: 265). This strategy began with an attack on the Stock Exchange in the City in 1990. During 1991, perhaps aware of the state of the developing recession in Britain, and the pressure on government finances, the Provisional IRA began to appreciate the value of inflicting massive economic damage on Britain, through attacking the City. In his Annual Report for 1991, the Commissioner of the City Police referred to the question of likely terrorist attacks by the Provisional IRA in the City, particularly its transport infrastructure, in light of attacks elsewhere in London. The police significantly enhanced security arrangements for major events in the City. As a result of such high profile policing, a 10 percent reduction in recorded crime occurred. However, it was not until February 1992, when a small terrorist bomb exploded in Fernival Street in the northeast of the City, that ideas for greater and more formalized anti-terrorist security for the City began. As such, the approach adopted by the police was very much reactive rather than proactive. Such ideas were dramatically enhanced in April 1992 in the aftermath of the IRA bombing of the Baltic Exchange at St. Mary Axe, in the heart of the City.

The St. Mary Axe bomb led to emergency plans being devised to try to prevent further attacks. As this was the first major bomb in the City, the Corporation of London, the Local Authority for the City, took the view that an increased police presence was going to be an appropriate response. The police, using existing legislation to its limit, instigated a number of "roving police checkpoints" on the major road entrances into the City.

At this time the Corporation, in line with local planning guidelines, had been working on an environment and movement policy called "Key to the Future." This planned to restrict access to certain roads in the City and alter traffic signaling on others, to improve traffic flow and reduce atmospheric pollution. After the St. Mary Axe bomb, with the support of the Commissioner of Police, some traffic management measures, in line with these proposals, were introduced on an experimental basis on a number of City roads, especially those in the vicinity of prominent City buildings. Furthermore, traffic management CCTV was extended and adapted to focus on incoming traffic, and private businesses were encouraged by the police to install CCTV cameras.

The City Police at this time wanted to set up permanent vehicle checkpoints on all entrances into the City, but a combination of legal and financial restrictions and public opinion made this unrealistic. A minor explosion in June 1992 in Coleman Street in the center of the Square

Mile further enhanced the perceived need for improved anti-terrorism measures. However, there was a feeling that a permanent security cordon would be "an over-reaction, would make the City look like Belfast, [and] give a propaganda coup to the IRA" (Kelly, 1994).

Deterrence

The worst fears of the police were realized on April 24, 1993, when a Provisional IRA bomb exploded in Bishopsgate in the east of the City. In the immediate aftermath, the media and sections of the business community began to suggest that drastic changes should be made to City security. This view was backed up by leading City figures, who indicated that a Belfast-style scheme should be implemented:

> The City should be turned into a medieval-style walled enclave to prevent terrorist attacks . . . In private there is talk about a "walled city" approach to security with access through a number of small "gates" and controlled by security discs. (Cited by Sivell, 1993)

Initially, the leaders of the Corporation were skeptical about implementing such drastic proposals. However, in May 1993, given the heightened risk of further attack, the police confirmed that they were considering radical plans in the form of a security cordon. In August 1993, shortly after the implementation of the ring of steel, the Corporation issued two draft consultation papers asking City businesses for their comments about the "experimental traffic scheme" (i.e., ring of steel) and security initiatives relating to spot checks, CCTV technology, and the use of pagers for anti-terrorism purposes. Widespread support for all the suggested initiatives was obtained, with over 80 percent of respondents agreeing with the measures proposed (see Corporation of London, 1993a, 1993b).

Such traffic modifications were criticized by those who felt that they would cause traffic chaos at the boundaries of the City because vehicles would increasingly be pushed into neighboring areas. There were also fears that such a radical scheme could geographically displace the risk of terrorist attack to other areas. There was vocal opposition to such measures from several adjoining boroughs, as well as civil liberty groups concerned about the increased use of camera surveillance and police "stop and search" procedures (Ford, 1993; Smith, 1993; Wadham, 1994; Coaffee, 2000). The home secretary at that time summed up the situation facing the City: "There is a balance to be struck between having roadblocks which will frustrate what the terrorists can do," he said, "and creating enormous traffic jams which would disrupt the life out of the City" (cited in Garvey, 1993).

Eventually, on the weekend of July 3–4, 1993, a full "Belfast-style" ring of steel was set up in the City securing all entrances. The main access restrictions imposed are shown in figure 15.1. This shows that most routes were closed or made exit-only, leaving seven routes (plus one bus route) through which the City could be entered. On these routes into the City road-checks manned by armed police were set up.

Locally, the ring of steel was often referred to as the "ring of plastic," as the temporary access restrictions were based primarily on the funneling of traffic through rows of plastic traffic cones (plate 15.1). Officially, it was called the Experimental Traffic Scheme, in an attempt to remove references to terrorism.

The ring of steel did not provide full security coverage to the Square Mile, as much of the western side of the City remained outside the cordon. Initially, the Police Commissioner wanted to make sure that all of the key financial targets were included in an "inner cordon." The ring of steel also had to be developed so that traffic flow through the City was not disrupted. Throwing a cordon around the entire City would have led to all traffic being diverted to neighboring boroughs. As such, the original placement of the cordon was, according to computer modeling, to have a relatively minor impact on traffic flows outside the City. Finally, by setting up the cordon, the police could minimize the number of entry points into the secure zone. This aided security, as well as minimizing the police manpower needed to run the scheme effectively.

In addition to access restrictions the City began to enhance its electronic surveillance capabilities, which led to the development of three separate, but interdependent, camera systems. In addition to traffic management CCTV, police-operated security cameras were erected to constantly monitor the entrances into the Square Mile so that every vehicle entering the security cordon was recorded. From November 1993 there were two cameras at each entry point – one that read the vehicle number plate, and the other that scanned the front profile of the driver and passenger.

By the summer of 1993 there were more than seventy police-controlled cameras covering the City. But the police felt that there was still inadequate coverage of many public areas due to lack of private cameras. Subsequently, a scheme called Camera Watch was launched by the police in September 1993. This encouraged the police, the Corporation, and City organizations to cooperate on camera surveillance, thereby creating an effective, and highly visible, camera network for the City which could be used for crime prevention and anti-terrorist activity. Nine months after Camera Watch was launched, only 12.5 percent of buildings had camera systems, leaving a very large proportion of public areas without the security of constant CCTV coverage. However, this situation improved and, by 1996, well over 1,000 private security cameras, in over 376 separate camera systems, were

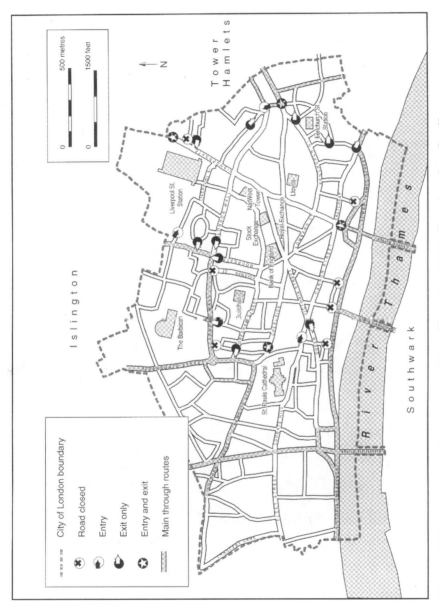

Figure 15.1 Access restrictions in the City of London, 1993. Drawing: Jon Coaffee.

Plate 15.1 Entrance into the City of London's "ring of plastic," 1996. Photograph: Jon Coaffee.

operational in the City. It was also suggested that in the future it might be possible for these private systems to be linked into the police camera systems when the need arose (Kelly, 1994).

The Corporation's response to terrorism after the Bishopsgate bomb was a result of severe pressure from the business community, especially the foreign institutions, to improve security. The Bishopsgate attack was widely seen as an attempt to undermine confidence in the reputation of the City as a financial center. However, others saw the ring of steel as predominantly a public relations exercise. As the Commissioner of Police noted:

> Some ill-informed people think that all we are doing is protecting those "fat cats" in the City. The reality is that if the City of London is brought down economically, perhaps never to be recovered, then all of us...will be the losers from the damage done to the nation's economy...It would be difficult to overstate the importance of securing the City against that threat. Of course, the terrorists, too, see the potential results of their activities and that makes the City their most desirable target. (Police Committee, November 24, 1993)

Optimism

Immediately after a Provisional IRA ceasefire was called on August 31, 1994, there were suggestions in the media that the ring of steel should be scaled down. Subsequently, this was done, with permanent armed guards being taken off most of the checkpoints, and a less visible police presence on the streets. However, this downgrading of security had a noticeable influence on recorded crime levels, which began to increase steadily.

The ring of steel, although less visible, still offered a framework through which to launch a security operation if required. Indeed, throughout the ceasefire, permanent bollards began replacing temporary traffic cones. As the ceasefire progressed, further moves to scale down security were suggested, as many began to feel that the threat level was in decline. In particular, there was an attempt, on behalf of a number of prominent business organizations around Christmas 1995, to persuade the Corporation to disband the security cordon completely.

The situation going into 1996 was one of optimism that the cessation of violence would continue. Despite this, the police camera network had been continually upgraded to meet perceptions of the terrorist threat. In the early months of 1995, new high-resolution cameras for the traffic system were installed and 13 further cameras were added to monitor the cars exiting the City. Before this date security cameras only focused on cars entering the cordon. Exit cameras were particularly important, as police could now monitor traffic into the City and, if needed, track suspect vehicles across the City.

Reactivation and extension

In February 1996 a large bomb was detonated in the London Docklands, an area seen as a symbolic extension of the City of London. Immediately, the fortress mentality returned to the City and the full pre-ceasefire ring of steel was reactivated and operational within a number of hours, as there were fears that the City would be attacked. Initially, there was a large increase in high visibility policing at the entry points and the City streets in general, and an increased frequency of roving checkpoints.

Further suggestions to increase security in the Square Mile were also made. Such suggestions centered on a proposed westward extension of the ring of steel that was initially mooted in February 1995, to bring about environmental improvements and to complement the existing traffic and environment zone. The proposed extension sought to bring over 75 percent of the Square Mile within the "secure zone." The Commissioner of the City's police was in strong support of the proposals, despite downplaying its anti-terrorist importance, believing that:

> An extended zone [would] be of considerable benefit to the traffic and environmental conditions in the City...A byproduct of an enhanced traffic zone would be the opportunity to introduce security measures (as necessary) in a manner similar to that currently attaching to the present traffic zone. (Engineer's Report, September 26, 1996)

Subsequently, the proposal for a western extension was implemented in January 1997, for an initial period of six months (see figure 15.2).

As well as the extension to the ring of steel, the police were again extending their electronic surveillance capabilities. In particular, the installation of an advanced CCTV system, which began in early 1995 covering the entry points, was completed. This automated system, linked to national police databases, allowed almost immediate detection of vehicles illegally entering the zone. The digital and automatic number plate recognition (ANPR) system allowed the information to be processed and gave a warning to the operator within four seconds (Coaffee, 2000; Power, 2001). Camera technology was perhaps the single most important factor in the City of London Police's counter-terrorist campaign. This was highlighted during the trial of eight suspected Provisional IRA terrorists in London in 1997, who had been involved in a plot to blow up various electricity substations in and around the capital in the early months of 1996. At the subsequent trial one of the accused gave the immobilization of the ring of steel as one of the key aims of this attack: "If the IRA were capable of closing down all electricity in London without going into London, it would make the ring of steel null and void" (*Electronic Telegraph*, 1997).

By implication, this meant that the IRA could then have more easily planted a bomb in the City without being detected, as it would have taken hours (if not days) to restore power to many parts of London. Surveillance-

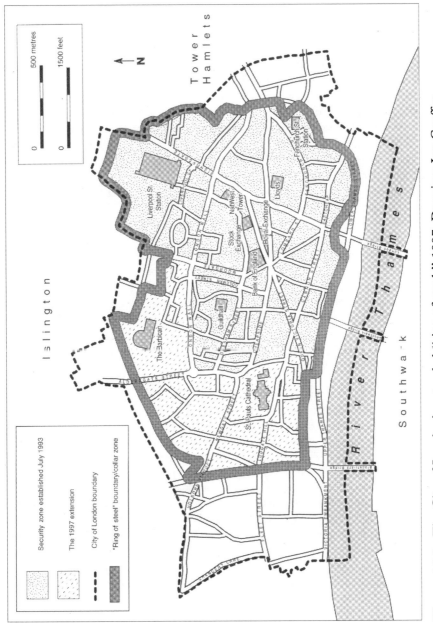

Figure 15.2 The City of London's extended "ring of steel," 1997. Drawing: Jon Coaffee.

wise, the City of London became the most intensely monitored area in the UK. For example, at the end of 1996, Camera Watch had 1,250 private cameras and the police controlled 8 permanent entry point cameras, 13 exit cameras, and 47 area traffic control cameras.

In April 1996 the ring of steel was given yet another layer of protection by new legislation relating to the new Prevention of Terrorism Act. This allowed the City Police to search pedestrians randomly, as well as cars, in and around the Square Mile.

As the 1990s drew to an end the ring of steel became a permanent part of the landscape in the City. The counter-terrorist security arrangements that were put in place served to protect the general interests of the City as a financial center, and to reassure business, especially foreign institutions, that the Corporation of London was doing all it could to prevent further bombings.

Since the ring of steel's implementation there have, to date, been no further bombs in the City, and a number of other benefits have emerged, such as a reduction in recorded crime, pollution, and traffic accidents. Indeed, the landscape changes that have occurred in the City are highlighted as improving the quality of life and business confidence in promotional material. In this the City is now portrayed as a safe area in which to conduct business. However, other commentators have been more skeptical, suggesting that the ring of steel might actually have increased the likelihood of further terrorist attack. For, as *The Times* newspaper indicated:

> The ring of steel increases the risk to the City in two ways. It increases the incentive to the IRA to strike, because of the propaganda value to be derived from penetrating that loudly trumpeted ring. The other way in which the charade increases the risk to the city is that it diminishes manpower available to counter the IRA threat. Fixed roadblocks need a lot of trained manpower. (O'Brien, cited in Dillon, 1996: 292–3)

Generally, though, two main criticisms were made about the development of the ring of steel. First, it was alleged that it gave the Provisional IRA a propaganda coup. The police countered this criticism, indicating that publicity would have been magnified many times if the City was bombed for a third time. Second, it was argued that the ring of steel displaced the risk of terrorist attack to other areas. Lessons from Belfast indicted that, when faced with such a cordon, car bombers had targeted areas just outside the cordon or had moved on to alternative, "softer," and less prestigious targets (Coaffee, 2000). In particular, within the City, certain businesses located on the edges of the Square Mile were beginning to get concerned that bombs could be planted at the edge of the newly constructed security cordon. The City Police and the Corporation were well aware of this Provisional IRA tactic and set up a so-called "collar-zone" around the ring of steel with extra police patrols, including roving checkpoints, to attempt to alleviate the fears of businesses within this area (see plate 15.2).

Reappropriation

Towards the end of the 1990s, with paramilitary ceasefires and a reduced state of terrorist alert in the Square Mile, the full ring of steel became relatively dormant. However, the City, like a number of other strategic urban sites in "global" cities, came under threat from anti-capitalist protesters (see Warren, this volume). Initially, a large-scale demonstration was to have been held in the City in May 1998, but access restrictions and the blanket CCTV coverage of the ring of steel, and the fact that the planned event was going to be held during the weekend (meaning the City would be empty of office workers), meant that it wasn't a feasible option (Do or Die, 1999).

A year later, on Friday June 18, 1999 – this time a work day in the Square Mile – between 6–10,000 demonstrators under the collective banner of J18 assembled in the City for a worldwide "Carnival against Capitalism" to coincide with a G8 economic summit in Cologne. This led to a massive

Plate 15.2 The "mainstreaming" of anti-terrorist number plate recognition in the central London congestion charge system which started operation in February 2003. Photograph: Jon Coaffee.

mobilization of police drawn from the City as well as the British Transport and Metropolitan forces. As a result of subsequent rioting, damage was put at £2 million, with many landmark buildings attacked and over forty people injured.

During the demonstrations the ring of steel entry points were manned by police who monitored the flow of people into the Square Mile. Although the anti-terrorist cordon could do little in preventive and legal terms to stop the vast number of people entering the City, it could use its extensive camera systems to monitor the event and subsequently pinpoint those involved in the worst of the violence. To an extent this was nullified by a number of cameras being immobilized by spray painting or being covered by plastic bags.

Despite the focus shifting to thwarting anti-capitalist demonstrators, counter-terrorism was still at the forefront of the City Police's thoughts. During 1998, 1999, and into the new millennium, the terrorist threat was still being seriously considered. During 2000 and 2001 the threat against the City of London was further increased by the bombing campaign of a dissident Irish republican group, the Real IRA, who were responsible for bomb or rocket grenade attacks against a number of prominent landmark buildings in Central London, such as the BBC and MI6. As a senior City Police officer indicated:

> There is a clear and credible threat from Dissident Irish Republican Terror-
> ists, particularly the Real IRA . . . The Greater London area will always be
> seen as the most attractive target as it will raise their profile in the media. We
> all need to be vigilant at this time and remember that they pose a *high* threat to
> the UK mainland. (*City Security*, 2001: 4; original emphasis)

Reappraisal

The unprecedented events of 9/11 led to an instant counter-response from the City of London Police. Just as with the immediate aftermath of the Docklands bomb in 1996, the ring of steel swung back into full-scale operation. This was part of a coordinated London-wide operation which saw over 1,500 extra police patrolling the streets of the capital. In the Square Mile the police also liaised with American firms to improve their security through extra patrols, as well as instigating a far greater number of stop and search checkpoints. The Corporation of London also examined its own emergency procedures through liaison with senior businesses and security professionals, as well as recommending to all businesses that they reassess their contingency plans with the help of City Police (Mayhew, 2001). The initial approach adopted, drawing on the previous experiences of terrorist attack, was very much "business as usual" and "vigilant but calm." As a Corporation of London press release noted the day after 9/11:

> The City is carrying on with business as usual. The City of London has had robust security measures in place for many years to deal with any terrorist threat and these are in operation now, as they are 365 days a year... These security arrangements are regularly reviewed and will again be examined in the light of yesterday's events.

As further noted by a senior police officer:

> Those who live in the Square Mile have... had to live with the threat of terrorist attack for more than three decades. The positive aspect of that experience is that it makes us uniquely prepared to confront the new threats posed by global terrorism. (*City Security*, 2001: 4)

The subsequent response involved not just the City Police but also Scotland Yard's anti-terrorist branch and the Metropolitan Police, who jointly reviewed and reappraised the counter-terrorist strategy in place around the Square Mile. In the aftermath of 9/11, subscriptions to the City Police's Pager Alert and E-Alert emergency communication systems increased by 44 percent and 139 percent, respectively (City of London Police, 2002a). Subsequently, the success of the City Police's Pager Alert in effectively sending out early warning messages to businesses has meant the scheme is now being rolled out on a London-wide basis with the help of the Metropolitan Police, and potentially to other UK cities.

The City Police also moved quickly to relay messages that they were prepared for attacks from both conventional weapons and unconventional biological and chemical agents, although on the latter the risk was considered slight. Echoing similar messages relayed in the aftermath of attacks against the City in the 1990s, public vigilance was seen as "the most formidable weapon we can deploy against terrorism" (City of London Police, 2002a). In short, balancing security needs with realistic threat assessments was seen as paramount. As one senior source highlighted:

> There is a debate between some people who think we should throw everything at guarding buildings and others who want to respond to a specific threat... At the moment there is no specific threat. But there was no intelligence before the World Trade Center, so do we assume the worst and expect the possibility of suicide bombers and throw everything into protecting London now or do we react when there is intelligence. It is a dilemma. (*Evening Standard online*, October 8, 2001)

9/11 has refocused the City police's minds on counter-terrorism, especially on the threat of potential attacks by dissident Irish republican groups.

However, 9/11 added a new dimension to defending the City, as the potential attacks are operationally very different to the tactics employed by the IRA. In short, as the Commissioner of Police noted:

> They are unlikely to be deterred by the high levels of technical surveillance we have successfully used against domestic terrorists who seek to avoid identification, arrest, and prosecution as part of their operating methods. (City of London Police, 2002a)

Although the international terrorist threat was considered high in the year following 9/11, the City quickly returned to business as normal, although security was noticeable on a higher state of alert at specific times. Most noticeably, security was stepped up on the first anniversary of 9/11, with a large and visible increase in armed police on the streets of the City, in London generally, and particularly around prominent target buildings such as US-owned banks. The possibility of attack from dissident Irish republican terrorists was also deemed high given problems with the peace process in Northern Ireland.

More recently, the Automatic Number Plate Recognition (ANPR) technology developed throughout the City's attempts to deter Provisional IRA terrorists has been "rolled out" across central London for use in traffic "congestion charging." This system became operational in February 2003. Such a scheme is intended to significantly reduce congestion (by 10 percent), as it was regarded as a major negative feature for international businesses locating in Central London. This was part of a wider integrated transport strategy (Greater London Assembly, 2000). The congestion charging scheme uses 450 cameras in 230 different positions. All number plate images are captured by ANPR technology when entering the zone and automatically matched against a database of those registered to pay or have exemption. A 90 percent accuracy reading is reported. Other cameras monitor the general flow of traffic throughout the zone. There are also mobile camera patrols operating throughout the zone. The City of London is on the eastern border of the zone. In essence, Inner London will be circled by digital cameras, creating a dedicated "surveillance ring" affording not just the City Police, but also the Metropolitan Police, vast surveillance gathering capabilities for tracking the movement of traffic and people, and by inference highlighting potential terrorist threats.

Not surprisingly, such an anti-terrorist function for the new congestion zone has been largely absent from information and promotional material circulated about the scheme which can, in essence, be considered a full-scale extension to the City of London's ring of steel. As noted by Townsend and Harris (2003), "security cameras will be able to zoom in on the faces of drivers entering London's congestion charge zone as part of a sophisticated 'ring of steel' around the capital."

Townsend and Harris allege that "MI5, Special Branch, and the Metropolitan Police began secretly developing the system in the wake of the 11 September attacks." Thus, "the controversial charging scheme will create one of the most daunting defense systems protecting a major world city." It is also alleged that "the system also utilizes facial recognition software which automatically identifies suspects or known criminals who enter the 8-square-mile zone," although this type of technology is unlikely to be available at present. Using facial recognition technology to "snap" the driver rather than the number plate of a vehicle would also necessitate different legislation under the 1998 Data Protection Act and a rigorous code of conduct set up for operators and monitors of the system.

Not surprisingly, civil libertarians feel "misled" over this hidden use for the scheme that is promoted as an attempt to beat traffic congestion. Townsend and Harris quote Gareth Crossman, policy director of Liberty, the UK's premier civil liberties organization: "There is an issue we are concerned about which is called 'function creep.' This is where we are told that a system is being set up and used for a certain purpose and then we find out it is being used for another totally different one. It is a dangerous precedent."

Conclusion: Terrorism and the Future of Cities

Over the past decade, as a result of terrorist attack, and the risk of further bombings, a series of counter-terrorist strategies to control and regulate the space within the Square Mile has been adopted and refined. This has attempted to balance security with business continuity through the four aims of "high visibility policing, directed intelligence, technology, and partnership" (City of London Police, 2002a). In particular, it has developed through the introduction of a number of armed road checkpoints, the imposition of parking restrictions, the fortification of individual buildings, and three interrelated camera networks. The City now has well over 15,000 surveillance cameras operating in the Square Mile. Most notable are 52 high-resolution ANPR cameras, situated strategically around the area (City of London Police, 2002b). In the space of a decade the City of London has been transformed into the most surveilled space in the UK and perhaps the world.

The threat of terrorism that the City had to face in the 1990s increasingly focused attention on how the Corporation was adapting to modern conditions and maintaining its influence within global finance. The ring of steel, or "ring of confidence" (Coaffee, 2000), helped the City to create a secure platform upon which it could continue to develop and adapt its role as the financial heart of a "world city." The City embraced inclusion in the economic globalization process, while at the same time excluding itself from the rest of central London through its territorial boundedness, surveillance, and fortification strategies. The situation that developed in the City can therefore be seen in terms of a condition of global connection and local disconnection. As a result of terrorism, such a condition continues to characterize the dislocated nature of the City's relationship with the rest of London, both physically (Coaffee, 2000, 2003b; Graham and Marvin, 2001) and technologically, through surveillance (Power, 2001; Norris and Armstrong, 1999).

For the majority of occupiers in the City the counter-terrorist strategy has been viewed positively, not only as an effective security approach but also as a traffic management measure and a beneficial environmental policy. However, statistically, the ring of steel appears to be more about crime prevention. For example, Rosen (2002) highlights that the CCTV operation in the City has never in fact caught a single terrorist and in fact operators "spend most of their time following car thieves and traffic offenders." For instance, by 1998, 340 arrests and 359 stolen vehicles had been triggered by the ANPR CCTV system, all non-terrorist related (Graham and Marvin, 2001). Similarly, figures for 2001/2 highlighted that over 12,000 offenses were detected using this system, with over 6,000 prosecutions made.

In Western cities in general, in the aftermath of 9/11, the commodification of ever more technological surveillance and social control devices has "surged," in particular around ideas of using biometric/facial recognition software (Lyon, this volume). Stanley and Steihardt (2002), for example, highlight that facial recognition software is being used in surveillance systems at a number of major airports in America, as well as at prominent sporting fixtures such as the Super Bowl. However, other commentators report that, at present, such technology is highly inaccurate and unlikely to be of any practical use until refined (Meek, 2002; National Institute of Standards and Technology, 2003). Furthermore, Rosen notes that the City of London is thinking about using a biometric database for face recognition, which would not only include terrorists but also "all British citizens whose faces are registered with the national driving license bureau." This has severe civil liberty implications: "biometrics is a feel-good technology that is being marketed based on a false promise – that the database will be limited to suspected terrorists" (Rosen, 2001: 6, 7).

The expanding surveillance web, as described above, is akin to Lianos and Douglas's (2000) concept of Automated Socio-technical Environments (ASTEs). Such environments are seen as high-tech risk management devices that radically change the social infrastructure of cities as they become reconfigured according to ever-changing management priorities, distinguishing and discriminating only on the ground of "quality of user." As technology develops it is likely that urban areas will see ever increasing numbers of ASTEs with security concerns being integrated into the automated environment with a "a massive deployment of digital technology" (Huber and Mills, 2002), most notably with CCTV technology (Graham, 2002c; Graham and Wood, 2003).

The ANPR system, used by the City of London Police since 1997, provides a perfect example of an ASTE. More recently, the Greater London Authority has further extended the geographical boundaries of the automatic surveillance network, which is ringed with similar automated "congestion charging" devices that "double-up" as counter-terrorism systems (Coaffee, 2003b). These systems are certainly ones that the agencies of security, most notably the police and insurers, will endorse fully, as they are constructed as a means to promote safety and retain movement while meeting commercial imperatives (Lianos and Douglas, 2000: 270).

These wider applications of the ring of steel mean that the measures in place will remain a concrete part of the contemporary urban landscape in the Square Mile for the foreseeable future. Just as importantly from a public and social policy viewpoint, the ring of steel is now seen by business coalitions, motoring organizations, commuters, residents, and neighboring local authorities as part of London's daily life.

A research report published in April 2003 highlighted that terrorism is still perceived as a significant threat by those who work in the City, with almost one in ten considering the threat of terrorism on a daily basis (City of London Police, 2003). In the City, much attention is given by the police to maintaining the culture of security and vigilance with a belief that "communities defeat terrorism" (City of London Police, 2003). This echoes national UK guidelines and rhetoric which seeks to provide a balance between democracy and appropriate risk and security management responses:

> We are mindful of the desire and the need of people in a vibrant democracy like ours to live normal lives without a sense of constant fear. We also know that in part because the terrorists want us to live in fear, and want to damage our economy, and the well-being of our people, that they are capable of feeding false information to us in the hope that we over-react ... Getting the balance right is not easy. ("Counter Terrorist action Since September 11, 2001": A report to the UK parliament, September 9, 2002)

In the City of London the threat of terrorism, and subsequent policy responses, have, to date, succeeded in creating an environment where the needs of safety and security sit side by side with business vibrancy. This has been done without the need to develop an overt fortressing approach to security that other urban areas have adopted in response to the threat of terrorism. Ultimately, as Swanstrom (2002: 135) notes, "the main threat to cities comes not from terrorism but from the policy responses to terrorism that could undermine the freedom of thought and movement that are the lifeblood of cities."

16

Technology vs. "Terrorism": Circuits of City Surveillance Since September 11, 2001

David Lyon

Introduction

I had no more than a slight feeling of apprehension when the pilot of the plane on which I was flying said we were obliged to make an unscheduled landing, under direction from the airline. I had never before heard of such an order but I assumed, like everyone else, that some simple explanation would be forthcoming when we landed. But I did fear that I might miss my connection to Singapore from Vancouver. It was the morning of September 11, 2001 and as yet no symbolic charge was attached to that date.

As soon as we landed, it became clear that a world event was unfolding. Strangers swapped stories of spectacular attacks on the heart of US global commerce and media in New York, and of the military power at the Pentagon. Soon we were in sight of TV screens that told the same unbelievable story. Even for someone aware of the power of some Islamic varieties of fundamentalism (Lyon, 2001a) and of their anti-American animus, sheer incredulity needed some hours to settle down. It also took a while to come to terms with the fact that I was not going to Singapore after all, and that getting home again, several days later, would involve running the gauntlet of armed security guards and waiting in lengthy security lines.

I tell the personal story because this is how we experience such events, and also because I should be perfectly clear that, like most other sane people, I want to have some assurances that I am safe when I fly. Indeed, it goes without saying that governments and airlines have a responsibility to make every effort to ensure public safety. But the personal trouble rapidly turned out to be a public issue, which is where sociology comes in (Mills, 1967). Security measures introduced since September 11 include prominently a number of surveillance devices and systems. They are intended to increase safety and allay fears primarily by predicting and preempting danger and by restricting access to a given country or site to eligible persons only.

The focus of what follows is not primarily the threat of "terrorism" or the meanings of the spectacular attacks on the World Trade Center and the Pentagon, though these cannot be ignored and are widely discussed elsewhere in this volume. Nor do I dwell on the "anti-terrorism" laws passed in the wake of 9/11, except insofar as they authorized the use of expanded surveillance techniques. I am interested in exploring rather the character and the meanings of the surveillance systems being mounted and reinforced in response to 9/11. Which devices are being promoted (and by whom) as the keys to security? What does this mean in terms of the already existing developments in surveillance at the turn of the twenty-first century? And what are the likely consequences of installing these new systems in what appears to be a new global alliance of surveillance states?

In short, I argue firstly that the devices promoted are precisely those that are already on hand, and already utilized in some (usually more limited) contexts. What transpired after 9/11 is that companies and government departments that already had an interest in such surveillance systems now had a rationale – and public support – for installing them. Technological fixes are the common currency of crisis in late modern societies.

Secondly, this represents a continuation, albeit at an accelerated pace, of trends that were already strongly present in all advanced industrial (or "informational") societies. "Surveillance society" (see Lyon, 2001c) describes well the personal and population data-processing aspect of the "network society" (Castells, 1996). One trend is accented, however: an unprecedented convergence between state and commercial surveillance (Lyon, 2001b).

Thirdly, the consequences are mixed. Success with the intended consequences of increased security is hard to discover. Indeed, most systems retain embarrassing limitations and flaws as far as their overt rationale is concerned. The unintended consequences are a widening of the surveillance web (see Cohen, 1985; McCahill, 2002) and an enhanced exposure to monitoring of ordinary people in their everyday lives (Lyon, 2002a). In comparison, non- or low-technological approaches to security receive little discussion.

Fourthly, the larger perspective is that "technology" is still seen as a savior, as the first resort of "advanced" societies. This is nothing new, but the quest for technologies, geared to guaranteed security, has been gathering pace especially since World War II. Technological solutions are invoked before other more labor-intensive and human-oriented surveillance methods (which, ironically, are in fact more likely to succeed), let alone efforts aimed at mutual understanding and the reduction of Western threats to Islamic countries.

Surveillance Technologies

Four main means of improving technological surveillance have been proposed since 9/11. They are: biometrics, the use of data extracted from the body, such as an iris scan, digital image, or fingerprint; identification (ID) cards with embedded programmable chips ("smart cards"); closed circuit television (CCTV), often enhanced by facial recognition software; and communicational measures, such as wiretaps and other message interception methods, including Web-based surveillance. In some places, several of these measures are now in place, while others had to await legal change and are now being implemented.

Biometrics has to do with the verification of identities, on the assumption that truly unique identifiers are found in the body. These may be used in smart cards, and are implicated in CCTV facial recognition systems as well. Smart cards, similarly, are intended to ensure a one-to-one fit between the identity of the cardholder and the unique card and thus to prevent unauthorized use or access. CCTV systems may be used "live" to monitor persons in transit for risky behaviors (for example, at airports), but also may be enhanced using databases of facial images or other biometrics such as retinal scans. Communicational surveillance is intended to check for potentially dangerous messages passing between suspect persons and groups.

Communicational surveillance is concerned primarily with *monitoring* behaviors, as is "live" CCTV. All the others, including facial recognition, are more concerned with *identifying* individuals. But these two are linked. The Echelon system of international intelligence monitors *in order to* identify messages, and their senders, that seem risky. Surprise was expressed after 9/11 that the monitoring technologies did not seem to have provided warnings (although it now appeared that, rather, the warnings given were not heeded in a coordinated fashion; see Rich, 2002). As we shall see, the trend is towards the use of more identifying technologies, and this has important consequences.

Biometrics

Recent advances in biometrics have made the use of physical attributes – body parts, if you will – popular candidates for identification systems. Some means are sought of verifying claims to identity and privilege, and unique physical attributes such as fingerprints, irises, retinas, hand geometry, vein patterns, voices, and faces are good tokens. Of course, these are never fully permanent tokens, so one can only ever claim a "probable" match. Such systems are most reliable when used in conjunction with others. If someone makes a claim at a bank with a name, and that is supported by a biometric identifier, the probability of error is low. Errors are much more likely when the system has to identify an individual on its own.

The system must acquire an image, using an appropriate scanner, before localizing it for processing. The image must be cleaned by removing extraneous information, and the remaining minutiae turned into a template for eventual comparison with attributes stored in the database. The "minutiae" are the uniquely distinguishing features of the image – the whorl on the fingerprint or the mole on the face scan – for which matches are then sought on the database. Of course, DNA is reliable in this context, too, but because it is invasive and requires special expertise, it is unlikely to be used for more than forensic purposes in the near future. The others have been seeking mass-market acceptance for the past few years.

Biometrics, then, is a more general term than the others, and indeed may be implicated in ID cards or CCTV systems. Biometrics relies on having access to some physical characteristic, and then on algorithms that enable the verification process to be automated. An example is iris scanners, installed at Schiphol Airport in Amsterdam in October 2001. (At Schiphol, and at Heathrow, London, iris scanning systems were planned well before 9/11. See, for example, Greenman, 2001.) The "Privium" system is intended to fast track passengers carrying the iris data-embedded smart card through passport control and customs. This system does not use a database; the scanner simply checks the eyes to see if they match the ones recorded on the card. In 2003 the Dutch government planned to seal the bearer's iris code into passports (Simons, 2001). In Canada, before 9/11, iris scans were mainly associated with bank machine tests (Pearsall, 1998).

Other systems use, or in the case of Canada plan to use, fingerprint scanners to enhance security. Canadian airports, ship-ports, and border crossings will have equipment linked to FBI and RCMP databases, to identify terrorists whose fingerprints are on file (CBC, 2001). While international airline authorities have applauded the relatively reliable eye-based scanners, Japanese researcher Tsutomu Matsumoto recently tested several fingerprint scanners, fooling them with his gelatin-based fake finger. He also lifted latent prints from glass and used his Photoshop to enhance them to make yet more "fingers" (Costello, 2002).

ID cards

Various kinds of biometric identifiers may also be used to authenticate ID cards, the second major surveillance technology proposed to deal with "terrorism." The government of Peru, for example, issues photo ID cards with an embedded face recognition chip for residents (Francis, 2000).

DNA patterns have been proposed for ID cards in the USA (Marx, 1998), and ID implants are also likely to be marketed soon (Reuters, 2001). Since 9/11, "smart" ID cards have been consistently touted as a key means of enhancing security – a way of being sure that people are who they say they are and that they have a right or a reason to be where they are.

Other "crises" have sparked similar calls for new ID card systems over the past few decades. During the twentieth century, world wars were a major impetus to the widespread and routine use of identification documents. In some countries the cards remained in place after the war was over, in others, such as the UK, the ID card system was dismantled following the "warfare state" – if only to be replaced by the ID documents of the welfare state (Lyon, 1991; Agar, 2001). Calls for ID cards were repeated during the worst IRA attacks in the UK in the mid-1990s, and soon afterwards in Spain, in response to the ETA (Basque separatist) attacks.

It is highly likely that several of the schemes proposed after 9/11 will be implemented, though not necessarily in the original form proposed. Larry Ellison, CEO of the world's largest database software company, Oracle, was quick to offer the US government free software for a national ID system. There is little doubt that the offer was serious or that Oracle could have backed it up. The idea of using "smart" cards on a very large scale for ID purposes has been projected in commercial and administrative schemes for several years, not least because it represents a technological "next step" from less complex and comprehensive systems. Multi-purpose commercial smart cards (such as Mondex; see Stalder, 1999) were tested during the 1990s. And some countries, such as Malaysia, Thailand, China, and Hong Kong (Chen, 2003), have already started to implement similar cards as national IDs. But others, such as the USA, the UK, and Canada, have held back – or at least they did until September 11, 2001.

The apparent threat of terrorism to national security helped to put electronic ID cards back on national agendas and several proposals were made in the aftermath of the September 11 attacks, no doubt to test the waters of public opinion. While Larry Ellison's offer was turned down, the US nevertheless embarked on a process that could well culminate in the use of enhanced drivers' license cards (and their surrogates) acting as national IDs. Although part of the justification for these schemes is the knowledge that several of the 19 hijackers of September 11 were using assumed IDs, it is not clear that the American public will agree to universal identifiers. Opinion polls show a declining acceptance of such schemes, and in particular, doubt about the competence of drivers' license authorities to have charge of them.

Other countries, such as Germany and the UK, have also looked at new national ID systems in order to strengthen security in the wake of September 11. Although the official position is that it does not relate to

9/11, the British "entitlement card" is being phased in as a smart card with biometrics identifiers, building on the already introduced Applicant Registration Cards which are designed to help cope with asylum seekers. In the German case, machine-readable cards, introduced after a political tussle in 1987, will be upgraded using hologram technology following the 9/11 attacks. Yet other countries, such as Malaysia and Spain, have claimed that the systems already being implemented in those countries will have the effect of reducing terrorist threats. Countries are also looking to each other to provide models, guidance, or warnings about potential failure, abuse, or other unintended consequences (for further details, see Stalder and Lyon, 2002).

In Southeast Asia, China, Malaysia, and Hong Kong are in the process of introducing national smart card IDs, following Thailand's adoption of a Sun Microsystems ID backbone within its National Registration System. Malaysia's "Mykad" is currently optional, and contains a drivers' license and passport information. In Europe, Spain is introducing a national smart card ID as well, partly in an attempt to demonstrate its leadership in European high technology developments. In each of these cases, change was well underway before 9/11. These initiatives are not unopposed, however. In the early months of 2002, for instance, considerable controversy was evident in Hong Kong over the new capabilities of the smart card, designed primarily to reduce illegal Chinese immigration. In 2003, however, resistance seemed to have evaporated.

In countries such as France, Japan, and Canada, much interest has been shown in the possibility of introducing new ID systems, including the use of smart card technologies. If adopted, they are likely to be built onto existing systems. In Canada, for example, since 2001, public hearings have been held in Quebec regarding the Telehealth smart card project, which, if implemented as planned, will confirm admissibility to services, create statements of services used by patients, produce data on insured services, access to a provincial patient index, and so on. Such a system would offer useful lessons for smart card use and acceptability. And in a federal program, new immigrants are issued a card with a photo and biometrics measures, a move prompted by the attacks of 9/11. In August 2003 official calls were still being made for a national debate on smart ID cards in Canada.

There are several difficulties with the new "smart" ID cards, however. For one thing, they are usually only as reliable as the other documents they are based on. This is often, ultimately, the birth certificate, a document that is notoriously easy to falsify if one has a mind to do it. Secondly, if central databases are used, these become very vulnerable to attack. But thirdly, assuming these problems are overcome, there is still the difficulty that, to put it simply, suicide bombers do not strike twice. It is unlikely that the kinds of terrorists to whom the ID cards are an answer will ever find their way onto suspect lists.

On another level, it has to be said that the new generation of smart ID cards has, even more prominently than in earlier systems, the task of classifying and discriminating between different groups of persons. They are intended to check for illegal immigrants or other persons in transit who have inadequate documentation. This is obvious to any observer, but what may be less than obvious is the negatively discriminatory practices that can easily accompany the use of such identifiers. The history of the twentieth century is replete with such, not only in Hitler's Germany, South Africa under apartheid, or contemporary Israel, but also in countries such as the USA and Canada, who mistreated persons of Japanese origin (using the census for ID) during World War II. Even now, following 9/11, there is evidence that some "Arab" and "Muslim" people in the USA have been singled out for very negative treatment, including lengthy detention without charge or trial (Burkeman, 2002; see Introduction).

CCTV and Face Recognition

As we have seen, biometrics is also implicated in new generation CCTV systems, where face recognition is involved. Airports including Pearson International in Toronto had a system limited to a RCMP search of suspects already in place, when Keflavik in Iceland announced in September 2001 that all visitors' faces would be screened. During October 2001 American airports were quick to respond with announcements that face-recognition technology would be installed. Oakland International laid claim to being first in the USA, using the system to check on passengers detained under suspicion (policing authorities determine who they are) (Fernandez, 2001), but a much broader system was announced at Boston Logan Airport, which uses Visionics "Face It" technology at an undisclosed checkpoint to compare facial characteristics of all travelers, airport employees, and flight crews with those of suspected terrorists (PR Newswire, 2001).

In this field, airport security systems are most closely associated with urban CCTV systems. An ordinary crowd of Superbowl fans in Tampa, Florida was scanned using Visage equipment in January 2001 (and of the 100,000 about nineteen petty criminals were recognized), but similar equipment has been used for some time with 300 cameras on public streets in the Newham district of east London, UK. This was mainly in response to the IRA threats of the 1990s (see Coaffee, this volume), but street camera systems in the UK got their biggest single boost from the James Bulger case – the toddler murdered by teenagers who were caught on camera in 1993

(Norris and Armstrong, 1999). Britain is easily world leader in using CCTV in public places, but the face recognition aspect is only in some very limited sites. It is unclear whether face recognition systems work for cases of street crime in public places (despite the claims of their promoters), let alone whether their limited successes there can be reapplied to cases of international terrorism (Wood, C. 2001: 97).

It is clear that there was mounting pressure – for instance from the US Defense Department as well as from a number of major companies, and think-tanks such as the RAND Organization – before 9/11 to develop and to install face-recognition CCTV systems (O'Harrow, 2001; Greene, 2001). The Defense Advanced Research Projects Agency had anti-terrorism in mind, but private corporations sought customers from banks, motor vehicle officials, and others as customers. Imagis, a Vancouver-based company, has been vigorously promoting its products before and after 9/11. It sells to casinos and also to the RCMP (the Pearson airport system) and the FBI. It markets its software through Groupe Bull in France, and Fujitsu and NTT in Japan. The Peruvian ID system is based on Imagis technology, too (Francis, 2000).

But while many promises are made for face-recognition CCTV, the reality is that, like the other biometric technologies, it has only limited uses and reliability. Some airports are using it to scan airport employees such as maintenance workers and baggage handlers. When there is a known database for employee identification, the two checks (biometric and ID) can work together satisfactorily. But picking terrorists out of crowds is a quite different issue –the question is, "does this biometric match anyone in the crowd?" (Schneier, 2001). Terrorists do not pose for photos (and are likely to use evasive techniques and disguises), but even if one had some good images, the so-called base rate fallacy means that the chances of false alarms would be very high indeed (9,999 for one terrorist – which means a full alert each time).

It is also argued that face-recognition systems, while they may not work for their ostensible purposes, would end up being used for finding petty criminals. These people will already have images in the database, and thus will stand more chance of being "seen" by the camera. But there are further arguments raised against face recognition. The potential for abuse – such as tracking individuals – is huge, and data are easily combined with those from other systems such as location systems of the E-911 type. There could also be "premature disclosure" as Philip Agre calls it – similar to that offered by call display telephones, but based on the passing face image. Informed and meaningful consent is almost impossible to obtain, and the chances are also high that civil liberties will be overridden in places where systems are established – especially if there is a weak tradition of appeal to them (Agre, 2001).

Communications monitoring

As with other forms of surveillance, 9/11 did not prompt the introduction of communications monitoring. Intercepting communications is one of the oldest methods of surveillance, which has a long history of use for law enforcement and military intelligence in particular. During the twentieth century, these were increasingly rationalized, and eventually enhanced by computerization. Indeed, many of the surveillance technologies that are now visible in policing and even in marketing found their origin in military intelligence systems. Policing has in this way as in others become increasingly militarized (Haggerty and Ericson, 2001), and it must be said that the language of "strategy" and "targeting" is not absent from marketing either (Lyon, 1994).

Computerization made possible the narrowing of searches for delinquent communications and, combined with satellite tracking stations and then Internet surveillance, created a situation in which massive power is vested in "intelligence" services – of all kinds. The searchable database is key to this, and the well-known search engine, Google, demonstrates the ease with which, given a few clues, numerous likely "hits" can be made very quickly. It also shows how effective – at least in principle – the Internet and World Wide Web are in facilitating remote searches.

After 9/11 many mass media outlets drew attention to the existence of Carnivore, the Internet surveillance system already used by the FBI, and to Echelon, the far larger system for international monitoring of all communications – fax, telephone, telex, and email. It came as a surprise to many that such sophisticated search engines already existed, powered by huge "dictionaries" that check messages for key words and contexts in quest of suspicious or risky communications. These are used not only for military or terrorist threats. Increasingly, they may be used by police departments trying to prepare for protests such as those by anti-globalization groups, and also as a means of technological and commercial intelligence, to raise the stakes of economic competition (Lyon, 2001a).

One might justifiably ask how the attacks of 9/11 were not detected, given the huge intelligence infrastructure that was in place. FBI assistant director Ron Dick noted that the hijackers had used the Net well (Campbell, 2001: 3). Internet Service Providers (ISPs) handed over records of hundreds of messages sent from PCs and public sites such as libraries, in the USA and internationally. They were unencrypted and used simple open codes. The National Security Agency response to growing Internet traffic has been to multiply the power of its storage and search facilities, from a petrabyte (roughly eight times the information in the Library of Congress) to a petraplex (20 million gigabytes) system. But it is not clear that this will work any better than what was in place before 9/11, because the problem of correlating diverse information rises exponentially as ever more communications are intercepted.

Several other interesting issues are raised by the rise in communications interception, and particularly Internet surveillance, following 9/11. It demonstrates, firstly, the ways in which national governments and corporations are working together more closely, such that companies may do "police" work, both on their own account and for the authorities. Law enforcers have increased by five times their demands for information from email providers and ISPs in the USA (CNN.com, 2002). Concerns about "privacy" in this area, which were growing before 9/11, seem to have been exchanged for a new willingness of companies to cooperate in the "war against terror." Companies start to comply with requests for data even before the warrant has been issued, which suggests that an ongoing state of "emergency" has been accepted (CNN.com, 2002). Under the US Patriot Act, customer payment records can be subpoenaed to find the ID behind an email address, clickstreams can be monitored, and messages can be read or listened to in real time. Similar provisions are in force elsewhere (Mathieson, 2001).

Secondly, the US government in particular has taken on a stronger policing role in other countries. Foreign hackers can be prosecuted by the USA under the Patriot Act, when computers in the USA or abroad are attacked. A large volume of global Internet traffic flows through the USA (80 percent of Asian, African, and South American access points, for example; Associated Press, 2001). Such traffic can, thus, be criminalized under US law.

Thirdly, the upshot of post-9/11 surveillance is that more and more mundane transactions and conversations of everyday life are under scrutiny as never before. The new provisions may not catch terrorists, but they could complicate life for others, especially as they are monitored, classified, and evaluated. In the UK, for example, where the Regulation of Investigatory Powers Act already had sweeping capacities to obtain communications data without a court order, anti-terrorist legislation allows these to be retained for longer (Millar, 2001). When one considers that the meaning of a website or of search words is different from, say, a phone number (which gives little away in itself), it is clear that captured communicational data is also more and more detailed.

Needless to say, these conclusions about the growing range of surveillance technologies are not uncontroversial. The ever-optimistic *Wired Magazine* still believes that "Little Brothers" will answer back, that ordinary people will empower themselves with their own technologies, that the US Constitution still stands as a bulwark of liberty, and that the sheer volume of new gadgets will countervail against government power

(Penenberg, 2001). But the larger sociological context must also be borne in mind before such sanguine conclusions can be confirmed.

Theorizing Surveillance After 9/11

The surveillance measures introduced after 9/11 are not new. They are all devices and systems with a track record. By and large they extend, enhance, or place in an unfamiliar context technologies whose promise has been advertised for some time or whose use has been proven in some other context. For many readers of newspapers and TV news watchers, words like "biometrics," for example, appeared to be novelties in the last part of 2001. But for a number of years biometric devices have been tested in several contexts, from retinal scans at bank machines to digital records of fingerprints in police databases.

Technologically, what these surveillance systems have in common is a reliance on searchable databases (see Lessig, 1999). This does not hold in the case of ordinary, "live" CCTV monitoring by a human operator, but it is true of the commonly advanced proposal for facial recognition facilities with CCTV. This means that they are "algorithmic" – mathematically coded for computers to make "decisions" as to what behavior, signal, word, or image fits in which category (Wood, D., 2001; Graham and Wood, 2003). Their key feature is thus that they are automated, dispensing as far as possible with human operatives (Norris, Moran, and Armstrong, 1998).

In order to understand how these systems developed and became central to surveillance in the last part of the twentieth century, one has to examine in brief the history of surveillance in modern times.

It is important to note from the outset that surveillance is practiced with a view to enhancing efficiency, productivity, participation, welfare, health, or safety. Sheer social control is seldom a motivation for installing surveillance systems, even though that may be an unintended or secondary consequence of their deployment. From the earliest days of state surveillance in sixteenth-century England, for example, the aim was to consolidate state power against others, and to maintain the position of elites, rather than use raw informational power to keep subjects in line (Higgs, 2001).

Surveillance in capitalist workplace settings developed as an intrinsic element of this mode of production (Webster and Robins, 1986), and is related in particular to what James Beniger (1986) calls the control revolution. It is not doomed by this fact to produce only further exploitation – it can make for more fairness in some cases – but by and large employees have had to struggle against the potentially oppressive aspects of workplace surveillance. It should also be noted that surveillance in the capitalist workplace is not paradigmatic for surveillance in other contexts. There is a surveillance spectrum, from hard, centralized, panoptic control to soft, dispersed, persuasion and influence. Workplace surveillance lies somewhere between the categorical suspicion of policing and the categorical seduction of consumption.

The computerization of administrative tasks and systems that took place from the 1960s had the effect of reducing the burdens of cumbersome bureaucracies, but with the frequent side-effect of increasing dramatically the visibility of all citizens, workers, and, before long, consumers, through routine surveillance checks. By the 1980s and 1990s, however, this was also tied into the general economic restructuring that dismantled state welfare and radically individualized risks. Rising affluence and mobility also increased opportunities for crime and deviance, which in turn fostered an emerging "culture of control" (Garland, 2001). It is important to put these matters in their broad social context, rather than viewing them as some kind of conspiracy of the powerful.

Much of the mushrooming growth of surveillance in twentieth-century administration and commerce may be related to "disappearing bodies." Rising rates of mobility, coupled with the stretching of social relationships enabled by new technologies of travel and communications, meant that fewer and fewer transactions and interactions are based on face-to-face relationships. This produces a quest for means of compensation with what can be called "tokens of trust" (Giddens, 1990; Lyon, 2001c). Hence the Personal Identification Numbers (PINs), bar codes, signatures, and eventually photo IDs and biometrics that lace the cards we carry. Human beings, embodied persons, are thus abstracted from place and are siphoned as data into flows, to be reconstituted as "data images" in surveillance systems. Multifarious systems developed from the 1960s to the 1980s, some of which had links but in general (and partly due to legal constraint) few opportunities to trace across databases without specific cause. Is this "Orwellian?"

Theoretically, what George Orwell feared was a state-organized central surveillance apparatus, a pyramid of power in which ruler and ruled were transparent to each other. As electronic forms of surveillance became more widely distributed, however, many turned to Foucault's treatment of Bentham's panopticon as a means of considering ubiquitous power based on continuous observation. It is partly a centralized scheme, though there is scope for its localization into the "capillary" levels in the minutiae of everyday life. Such centralized surveillance always brings with it the risk of totalitarianism (as Giddens 1985a, b, argues) but checks and balances, and vigilance of privacy lobbies, labor unions, civil rights movements, and consumer groups has traditionally proved quite effective in curbing it, especially in the West.

In recent years, interest in the surveillant *apparatus* has been depleted somewhat as the notion of a surveillant *assemblage* has attracted some sociological attention. The latter idea originates in the fertile imagination of Gilles Deleuze (Deleuze and Guatarri, 1987), and has been pursued fruitfully by a number of sociologists (see Haggerty and Ericson, 2000). The assemblage, in this context, is a set of loosely linked systems, to be distinguished from the operation of government, at least as classically understood by political scientists. It is emergent and unstable. It operates across state institutions and others that have nothing (directly) to do with the state. Examples of this might be insurance categories used by police to determine risk. The assemblage is all about linking, cross-referencing, pulling threads together that previously were separate. And this also hints at its mode of growth – like the weed "Creeping Charlie" that sends out horizontal shoots which in turn become new nodes in a constantly growing network. Deleuze and Guatarri think of this as "rhizomatic" development.

From what we have seen of surveillance after 9/11, however, it is a mistake to imagine that the loosely networked assemblage simply supplants the centralized apparatus. The rising tide of risk management techniques has indeed flooded over old distinctions between different institutional areas, but instability is endemic. Outcomes are impossible to predict. True, "organized risk management" was somewhat eclipsed by "disorganized" and "disorderly" systems in the last part of the twentieth century (Crook, 1995). But statist forms have by no means disappeared, and a world event like 9/11 has shown that they have both power and influence when perceived threats are of a sufficient magnitude. The assemblage and the apparatus are overlapping, even superimposed systems, and the assemblage can still be appropriated by the apparatus.

The key effect of 9/11, then, is to bring the apparatus and the assemblage into closer coordination with each other (Lyon, 2001b) within a larger frame of governance. As we have seen, the rhizomatic operation of consumer surveillance can be raided by police and intelligence services, when required to do so. The longer-term consequences of this are as yet unclear. But one thing that is clear is that "privacy" and even "data protection" are inadequate as means of limiting today's newly augmented surveillance power. While there is an important "care" motif (see Lyon, 1994: 211–17) in the post-9/11 measures, the balance seems to be tipping in favor of heightened "control." This is neither inevitable nor irrevocable, but it is a trend which, if unchecked, could become a serious threat to human rights.

I say "human rights" because the effect of increased algorithmic surveillance is to deepen the process of social sorting, of categorization for various purposes. It is a means of inclusion and exclusion, of acceptance and rejection, of worthiness and unworthiness. What may be called "digital discrimination" is the ways in which the flows of personal data – abstracted information – are sifted and channeled in the process of risk assessment, to privilege some and disadvantage others, to accept some as legitimately present and to reject others. The language of privacy is indeed of decreasing salience to the emerging situation of rhizomatic, algorithmic, assemblage-type surveillance. But this does not mean either that some notions lying behind privacy concerns are irrelevant, or that a fresh vocabulary for mobilizing dissent is superfluous. To the contrary, without it, some very regressive tendencies appearing since 9/11 will simply be reinforced.

Conclusions: Consequences and Critique

It will be clear by now that I have no quarrel with the idea that serious measures should be taken to prevent repetition of the horrendous events of September 11, 2001. But the problem is that merely "technological" solutions are in themselves inadequate to the threat, and simultaneously dangerous to democratic polity. They are "dangerous" because of three key trends, illustrated in the foregoing discussion: (1) the effective recentralization of state power; (2) the increased capacity to discriminate between different classes of persons, using algorithmic surveillance; and (3) the relative lack of accountability of these systems, paralleled by the willingness of populations to accept them as the "price of security."

The problem with the last point about security is of course that the intended consequences of the technologies we have considered are unlikely to be realized. The evidence from biometrics, ID cards, facial recognition associated with CCTV, and communications monitoring is that as tools for an anti-terrorist campaign they are flawed. The automated, algorithmic systems are poorly equipped, by and large, for the task of identifying or monitoring the actions or messages of previously unknown potential terrorists. Moreover, to the extent that surveillance depends on information technologies, the easier it will be for persons who wish to evade detection to do so, just because human beings are more flexible and imaginative than technologies. Any technology can be outwitted, given time and ingenuity.

Of course, many unintended consequences follow from the tightening of security by surveillance. There will be closer monitoring of all who are in fact "clean" (and have a data image to "prove" it). The culture of control will colonize more areas of life, with our permission or without, because of the understandable desire for security, combined with the pressure to adopt particular kinds of systems. Ordinary inhabitants of urban spaces, citizens, workers, and consumers – that is, people with no terrorist ambitions what-soever – will find that their life-chances are more circumscribed by the categories into which they fall. For some, those categories are particularly prejudicial, restricting them from consumer choices because of credit ratings, or, more insidiously, relegating them to second-class status because of their color or ethnic background. It's an old story in high-tech guise.

The alternatives to high-tech monitoring and identification methods seem to receive little attention. The labor-intensive intelligence gathering, the physical checking at airports, the use of security personnel to screen travelers – all these seem to have a low premium compared with extending the surveillance system with a new biometric or search device. Actually mounting programs to try to understand the reasons why certain countries, religious adherents, or political groups would have serious enough misgivings about and mistrust of the Western world to sacrifice their lives in order to destroy it seems well beyond the pale. This is not only labor intensive. It would also involve slow learning processes and cultural contacts of apparently very unwelcome kinds (see Downey and Murdock, 2003).

Much better, it appears, to fall back on the technological fix, just as has been done for over thirty years, since the first hijackings prompted technical modifications to aircraft and airport facilities (Lyon, 2002b). There is tremendous commercial pressure to purchase new surveillance equipment; the current situation is seen as an unprecedented business opportunity by some who have seen their share prices rise several-fold since 9/11. American security companies in particular are hawking their wares around the world in hope of taking advantage of the political climate of anti-terrorist activity (Marcuse, this volume). Chief executive officers (CEOs) such as Larry Ellison are still arguing that the interests of Oracle and the USA are virtually identical and that they lie in integrated ID systems (Rosen, 2002).

Political (and public) fears continue to produce panic regimes (that seem like earlier moral panics on a larger scale). Safety and security are good things to desire, but the means are highly dubious, and spring from other sources (Stuart, 2001). So why the fixation on technology (which is even shared, sometimes, by groups such as the American Civil Liberties Union, who warn that the technologies are not *yet* good enough to serve the purposes claimed for them)? I suggest that this is articulated with one of the deepest currents of (late) modernity – the deep-seated belief in the power of technology to protect and to guarantee progress. "In technique we trust" is the slogan about which Jacques Ellul, Ursula Franklin, and David Noble have warned us repeatedly. Whatever one makes of their particular perspectives, they are surely right to say – as I do in relation to "technology vs. terrorism" – that technology won't save us.

17

Urban Dimensions of the Punishment of Afghanistan by US Bombs

Marc W. Herold

Air bombardment is the terrorism of the rich. (Lummis, 1994: 304)

Fixed fortifications are monuments to man's stupidity. (General George S. Patton)

Afghanistan was a show of retaliative firepower. (Jenkins, 2002)

Introduction

Few large urban agglomerations exist in Afghanistan. Afghan cities have grown from the twin processes of economic and military interventions during the last half of the twentieth century (aggravated in recent years by drought). The commercialization of agriculture played an important part in this process.

The village remains the urban epicenter of Afghanistan. It represents the urban form in the Afghan sea of tribal-peasant society. A couple of cities – Herat and Kandahar – emerged centuries ago as vibrant commercial centers at oases located along the trade caravan routes (Curzon, 1999). During the years of the Zahir monarchy, Kabul gradually became a city, accounting for close to half the country's urban population by 2000. While a modest urbanization took place over the past fifty years, the poor rural-based village neighborhood has simply reappeared in cities. Only the minuscule, urban upper middle class lives in the world of the Western, individualistic, consumption-centered urban middle class.

Modernist economic interventions during the last half of the twentieth century sought to create a "modern" Afghanistan as facsimiles of the Soviet or American landscapes – whether the huge Soviet-built bread factory in Kabul or the enormous, integrated, Tennessee Valley Authority-like Helmand Valley Authority in Kandahar. With these interventions, naturally, new social strata emerged as proselytizers of those largely urban visions. After all, postwar economic development has been characterized by a powerful "urban bias" (Lipton, 1977).

However, traditional peasants and nomads stood arrayed against such projects of social engineering. These groups had internalized neither the social rhythms of modernist, linear time nor the drive to accumulate. Historically, Afghanistan's rural areas had fiercely resisted the encroachment of the urban-based modern state, correctly seeing it as a looming predator. No centralized system of national taxation existed, neither then nor today.

The mujahideen of the 1980s and the Taliban of the 1990s expressed in their own different ways the realities of rural Afghanistan. The anti-Soviet war of the 1980s and the intra-mujahideen fighting of the 1990s destroyed the meager urban infrastructure of Afghanistan. The US finished off what was left. In the words of the *Toronto Star*'s Kathleen Kenna, "much of Kandahar was bombed into rubble by US-led air strikes that began October 7th" (Kenna, 2001). Kandahar, as seat of the Taliban, was especially hard hit.

The Taliban, more visibly, represented the forceful imposition upon the city of distorted traditional, decentralized, rural values and lifestyles. The Taliban came mostly from the lower rungs of society (Baldauf, 2001). Many poor, hungry, often orphan Pashtun youths found their way to the frontier madrassas, becoming militants for Islamic Deobandi fundamentalism and serving the interests of Pakistan (Makhmalbaf, 2001). One might say it was a revenge of the poor countryside against the city. During the later 1990s, the descendents of the Soviets' Afghan allies – grouped in the United Front and later Northern Alliance – battled the black-turbaned Taliban villagers and village clerics. These latter had little experience of the mujahideen struggles of the 1980s, representing instead elements schooled in madrassas of the border regions.

The reality of a world system comprised of states with their typical institutions nonetheless compelled the Taliban to construct a skeletal state in urban spaces – a minimal bureaucracy comprised of the "new Taliban" (neither mullahs nor black-robed troops) of the past – whether civilian or military. The old Afghan Army and Soviet barracks, government buildings, and airports located in urban areas became the bases for the new Taliban militia.

The actual control of the Taliban across Afghanistan remained relatively limited to some provinces in the south and the east, and even there mostly in the urban centers (e.g., Jalalabad, Khost, Ghazni, Tirin Kot, Kandahar, Herat). Strict Taliban social mores were brutally enforced upon the urban proselytizers and wannabees of Western modernity. In rural areas, life simply went on as it had for centuries, permeated by cyclical time and centered upon family and mosque.

Given such a context, the first aim of this chapter is to analyze the ways in which the aerial bombing of Afghanistan – starting in the early autumn of 2001 and continuing to the publication of this book – has impacted upon the social, economic, and urban life in the country. In analyzing these devastating impacts on an already war-torn and deeply impoverished country, the chapter aims, secondly, to look beyond the sanitizing rhetoric of the US and UK military and politicians. It does this by collecting, and piecing together, detailed information on the situation "on the ground." This helps to redress the overwhelming absence of the voices of bombed Afghani civilians in mainstream Western media accounts of this first so-called "war on terrorism." Finally, the chapter seeks to compare the bombing and its impacts with previous US-led aerial attacks in Asia and the Middle East over the last forty years or so.

The Destruction of Urban Spaces in Afghanistan

When the US political and military elite decided to attack and dislodge the Taliban in Afghanistan, it faced a physical and cultural reality very different from that in say, Indochina of the 1950s, Iraq of 1991, or Yugoslavia of the latter 1990s (see table 17.1).

Other parameters also influenced the implementation and execution of the US aggression. For one, world public opinion has been increasingly averse to large numbers of innocent, civilian casualties. Secondly, the

Table 17.1   Urbanization levels in three countries bombed by the United States since 1991

	1980	2000
Urban population (millions)		
Afghanistan	2.5	5.8
Fed. Yugoslavia	4.5	5.6
Iraq	8.5	17.9
Urban as % total population		
Afghanistan	16	22
Fed. Yugoslavia	46	52
Iraq	66	77
Population of largest city as % of total population		
Afghanistan	39	45
Fed. Yugoslavia	24	27
Iraq	39	27

Source: Table 3.10, World Bank, *World Development Indicators 2002*, at: http://www.worldbank.org/data/wdi2002/pdfs/table%203-10.pdf

technology of communication had progressed tremendously, permitting the nearly instant transmission of battle scenes into the living rooms of San Francisco, London, Sydney, Cairo, or Delhi. Thirdly, the American public was averse to US military casualties.

The American elite decided to use air power as a form of coercive foreign policy (Horowitz and Reiter, 2001). US air power did not succeed in delivering Osama bin Laden, though it did eliminate the Taliban from government. In the model of Horowitz and Reiter, US coercive air power, as applied in Afghanistan, resulted in failure because the Taliban never conceded, and an ongoing guerrilla war continued throughout 2003 and beyond (see Herold, 2003a). One recalls that after some days of bombing, the Bush administration offered to halt the bombing if the Taliban delivered Mr. Bin Laden.

The Pentagon's course of action, aided immensely by a pliant corporate media, was to loudly celebrate the advent of air-delivered "Precision" Guided Munitions (PGMs), which would be employed in much greater numbers than in the previous conflicts of Yugoslavia and the first Gulf War. Innocent Afghan civilians would be spared and US casualties would be minimized by using proxy mercenary forces. But the employment of proxy Afghan and Pakistani forces, in turn, reduced the likelihood of capturing bin Laden and his top associates. Apparently, sparing US military personnel was more important than capturing those individuals.

The fact that the Taliban was not a state, but rather a religious-ideological movement, had major implications. This meant that, after the first week, the US bombing campaign was heavily directed at the villages of Afghanistan where the movement derived its strength. The only real exception to this was the spiritual heart of the Taliban – Kandahar – which was bombed throughout the campaign. The unstructured and decentralized nature of the Taliban – in contrast to Saddam Hussein's Iraq – has offset the two key US military assets, namely overwhelming air power and rapid mobility.

The Ultimate "Asymmetric" War: Civilian Impacts

What needs to be emphasized here is that the United States deployed the world's greatest military arsenal upon one of the world's weakest militaries – comprised of religiously trained or conscripted youths, devoid of post-1965 technologies (e.g., a handful of aging MIG-21s, some T-55 and T-62 Soviet tanks, and a couple hundred Soviet and Stinger missiles which are ineffective above 15,000 feet), and whose main striking forces were a sort of mechanized cavalry on four wheels (Toyota pick-up trucks often "tricked-out, hip-hop ghetto rigs"; Sifton, 2001). Yet it took more than two months for the US–UK militaries and their purchased Northern Alliance proxies to win on the conventional military battlefield. The low-intensity conflict rages on.

In addition, the US military campaign was characterized by numerous equipment failures (most of the unmanned aerial vehicles crashed, a B1–B fell into the Indian Ocean on December 12, a tanker craft flew into a mountain in Pakistan); a bungled Special Forces operation in Kandahar on October 19; high numbers of friendly-fire deaths; reliance, as proxies, upon the very thugs who devastated Afghanistan between 1990–6; and, most importantly, a bombing campaign that was, to innocent civilians, the most deadly in recent times (see table 17.2).

The air attack on Kabul began at 8.57 p.m. local time, October 7. On that Sunday night, US and British missiles and strike aircraft hit thirty sites across Afghanistan, including seven in urban areas (three in Kabul).

Twelve-year-old Haziza lived with her father, mother, and four brothers and sisters in a poor neighborhood next to Kabul's airport. Her father ran a

Table 17.2 A history of US bombing campaigns and resulting civilian deaths

Bombed region	Date	Tonnage dropped	Reported civilian deaths	Ratio of civilians killed per 10,000 tons of bombs
Vietnam, Rolling Thunder campaign	1964–7	650,000	52,000 North Vietnamese	800
Laos	1965–73	2,000,000*	350–500,000	1,750–2,500
Cambodia, Arclight campaign	1969–73	540,000	50–150,000	926–2,778
Christmas bombing of Hanoi–Haiphong	1972	20,000	1,600	800
Iraq Gulf War	1991	88,000	2,500–3,200	284–363
NATO bombing of Yugoslavia	1999	13,000	500–1,200– 2,000	385–923–1,538
US Afghan War	2001	14,000	3,100–3,600	2,214–2,571
Iraq War, March 20–April 5 only	2003	6,350	940–1,112	1,480–1,752

*The US bombing of Laos involved a planeload of bombs being dropped on the tiny country every eight minutes for nine years. See Jenkins (2001) and "American genocide of the Laotian people, 1965–1973," at free.freespeech.org/americanstateterrorism/Laos.html.
Sources: available upon request

small grocery business there, selling chewing gum and cigarettes. A refugee in the Tajabad locality of western Peshawar, leading a miserable life in one of the city's many squatter colonies, Haziza recalled the first night of US attacks:

> I, along with my father and three brothers, was in my grandfather's house when the first batch of thundering war planes started pounding Kabul on October 7 last, whereas my mother and a 2-month old brother stayed back in our home . . . It was really very terrifying as there were explosions one after the other. (Amir, 2001)

Upon returning to their home they found it in ruins and her mother and baby brother buried in the wreckage. Rescue workers were desperately lighting pieces of paper, one after another, trying to burn away small patches of Kabul's night, as electricity had been cut (Lamb, 2001). Her father fled Kabul for Pakistan. Haziza washed clothes there to earn a few rupees, one of 20 persons living with her aunt.

That same morning of October 8, 34-year-old Abdul Bashir agonized over losing his beloved 5-year old daughter, Zaniulla, who was killed when a US "precision" bomb, aimed at a Taliban tank post on a nearby hill, fell instead in front of the apartment block in northern Kabul. The London *Observer* (October 14, 2001) reported:

> Around the city, other anti-aircraft installations and barracks used by the Taliban were hit too. There were misses as well. One bomb hit a family house close to a gun position in the west of the city, killing and injuring several more civilians. (Ahmed et al., 2001)

Mirza Jan, selling fruit in the market, admitted having feared the US bombing:

> That will add to our pains. We have already suffered enough . . . I have not told Osama bin Laden to come to Afghanistan. I have not chosen the Taliban to reign over us. If they do something wrong, why should I pay for that? (Harding and McCarthy, 2001)

The sentiment expressed was that innocents would pay and few would care.

How did these worries pan out? Table 17.3 summarizes the Afghan civilian casualties caused by US bombing or by ground force attacks.

Analysis of civilian casualty data reveals two important characteristics of the US air war:

1 Most civilian deaths were registered in regions of high population density (Herold, 2002b).

Table 17.3 Civilian casualties of the US air and ground campaign in Afghanistan*

Time period	Low estimate	High estimate
October	931	1,148
November	961	1,073
December–present	995	1,190
No date available	186	186
Total	3,073	3,597

* Includes only impact deaths. The data are derived from my "Appendix 4: Daily casualty count" at http://pubpages.unh.edu/~mwherold and reflects numbers through May 31, 2003.

2   The high number of civilian deaths is the result of a very large number of small death tolls in many bombing attacks. This fits well with the fact that most fighter planes were carrying out three or four bombing attacks per sortie. The US bombing campaign in Afghanistan was certainly not an example of "area or carpet bombing" (Hewitt, 1983).

Phases of the Air Attack

The US air war in Afghanistan was played out in five phases, though without any overall grand plan. The air war was adjusted to the shifting realities on the ground. The five sequential phases were:

1   The bombing of perceived military facilities in urban areas, airports and 23 outlying training camps (October 7–20) (Mateen, 2001).
2   The battle for the central plains area, the Shomali Plain campaign, and the carpet bombing around Kunduz, Khanabad, and Mazar (October 21–November 25).
3   The bombing campaign around Kandahar and the southern provinces, including Nangarhar (November 15–December 10).
4   The Tora Bora campaign (November 27–December 17).
5   The bombing of selected sites believed to harbor Al-Qaeda or Taliban leadership (December 20–present), mostly in Paktia, Paktika, Kunar, Helmand, and Uruzgan provinces.

During the first two or three weeks, US planes followed the classic twentieth-century doctrine of "strategic bombing" – seeking to weaken an enemy's military force indirectly, by destroying its underpinnings (radar sites, airfields, command posts, arms and armor depots, etc.), rather than attacking the force itself (Fallows, 2002). The US hoped that the ferocity of its air campaign would sap the will to fight and lead to splits within the Taliban. This initial phase was counter-productive from the US standpoint because the Taliban/Al-Qaeda proved to be elusive and the bombing was causing visible civilian casualties in cities.

The US air campaign then shifted towards "close air support" for proxy forces' ground operations. By late October what came to be called the Afghan Model for US campaigns came together (Hendren, 2002; Biddle, 2002). This model comprises three highly interacting components: special forces spotter teams, "precision" guided munitions, and local proxy armies. Its direct advantages to the US are minimal US casualties and a lower US politico-military profile on the ground, which serves to accommodate historic Afghan hatred of outside occupying forces.

The Taliban's facilities were widely dispersed, reflecting the decentralization so typical of Afghanistan. Besides the camps located in remote regions, US planes targeted ammunition and fuel storage areas, government buildings, anti-aircraft emplacements, Taliban barracks, concentrations of armored vehicles, etc. Scores of innocent civilians died from exploding munitions when US bombs hit ammunition depots in the Qargha (Kabul) and Tapai Muhaimat (Kandahar) areas in October 2001 (Herold, 2003b).

Endless examples exist of the official US and mainstream corporate press lying about the US military campaign in Afghanistan. The pattern of deception involves minimizing the destruction wrought upon average Afghans while exaggerating the influence of Al-Qaeda. For example, the US bombing in mid-October 2001 of the old army base at Rishkor was presented as having destroyed the facility and killed many Al-Qaeda members (Makler, 2001). In fact, the Rishkor facility, while having once served as an Al-Qaeda training camp from 1997–2000, in particular for Osama's 55th Brigade, had been abandoned by all fighters in June 2000 (Clark, 2000).

The accuracy and ferocity of US bombing surprised the Taliban and Al-Qaeda. The military facilities around major cities (and adjoining poor neighborhoods) were quickly reduced to rubble, thereby making the few regular Taliban forces homeless – the Central Army Corps (Kabul), the 2nd Army Corps (Kandahar), the 3rd Army Corps (Paktia), the 4th Army Corps (Herat), the 5th Army Corps (Mazar), the 1st Army Corps, and the 81st Brigade in Jalalabad. The surviving regular troops joined the decentralized Taliban militia, first in the positional warfare in the Shomali Plains. The obvious futility of this tactic led the Taliban to seek refuge in the non-Pashtun cities of the north, where US bombs pursued them, but also killed hundreds of terrorized civilians in the Khanabad–Kunduz area. US military officials admitted that bombing focused upon Taliban units defending cities in November (Cushman, 2001). As of the second week of November 2001, a full-scale, disorganized retreat into the eastern mountains and the Kandahar area took place.

The US Afghanistan Air Assault in Context

As table 17.2 indicates, the past seven major US bombing campaigns fall into three clusters in terms of resulting civilian deaths. The first Iraq Gulf War of 1991 has the lowest ratio of civilians killed per tonnage dropped – although I am not suggesting by any means that it was a "clean" air war (Lopez, 1991). This is followed by the Vietnam and Serbian bombing campaigns and a third group comprising Cambodia, Laos, and Afghanistan (which killed over 2,000 civilians for every 10,000 tons of bombs dropped).

The Afghan air war was particularly destructive in terms of civilian impact deaths compared with previous aerial bombing campaigns, contrary to what some have claimed (e.g., O'Hanlon, 2002). In an article in the *Boston Globe*, Fred Kaplan argued that the so-called "kill ratio" in Serbia was about the same as in the Vietnam Rolling Thunder campaign – about 1 civilian killed for every 10 tons of bombs dropped. In the Iraq war, it was reportedly one-half of that figure, although this seems to be a serious underestimation (Kaplan, 1999). The index is, of course, at best suggestive, since civilian casualties will reflect the type of ordnance used, local demographic factors, topography, and emplacement of military facilities, etc.

After surveying innumerable reports on civilian impact deaths caused by bombing, I estimate the following total numbers for civilians killed in each war: Cambodia, 100,000; Iraq, 3,200; Serbia, 1,200; Afghanistan, 3,100. These translate into respective "kill ratios" (civilians killed per 10,000 tons of bombs) of: Afghanistan, 2,214; Cambodia, 1,852; Serbia, 522; and the first Iraq Gulf War, 363.

The US air war upon Afghanistan is best described as being of low bombing intensity but with a high civilian casualty intensity – precisely the opposite of the air war carried out in Iraq a decade ago. The American bombing was carried out from altitudes far beyond the reach of Taliban anti-aircraft fire and relied heavily upon sophisticated targeting technology. But this technology could not prevent the inevitable killing of thousands of innocent Afghan civilians. The effects of technology, as anyone familiar with the process of economic development knows, are heavily determined by context. To talk about "precision" guided munitions outside of context is rather meaningless.

Afghan civilians in proximity to alleged military installations will die, and must die, as "collateral damage" of US air attacks aiming to destroy these installations, in order to make future military operations from the sky or on the ground less likely to result in US military casualties. The military facilities of the Taliban were mostly inherited from the Soviet-supported government of the 1980s, which had concentrated its military infrastructure in cities, which could be better defended against the rural insurgency of the mujahideen. This reality is compounded insofar as the Taliban maintained dispersed facilities: smaller units, spread out. US military strategists and their bombers thus engaged in very widespread high intensity bombing. Such intense urban bombing causes high levels of civilian casualties. From the point of view of US policy-makers and their mainstream media boosters, the "cost" of a dead Afghan civilian is zero, as long as these civilian deaths can be hidden from the general US public's view. In this, the US corporate media has done the Pentagon's bidding – with a few notable exceptions (like Barry Bearak and Carlotta Gall of the *New York Times*, John Donnelly of the *Boston Globe*, and Philip Smucker of the *Christian Science Monitor*).

The "benefits" of saving future lives of US military personnel are enormous, given the US public's post-Vietnam aversion to returning body bags. In effect, the US military has made a trade-off: dead Afghan civilians today versus possible US military casualties in the future.

The absolute imperative to avoid US military casualties meant flying high up in the sky, increasing the probability of killing civilians:

> Better stand clear and fire away. Given this implicit decision, the slaughter of innocent people, as a statistical eventuality is not an accident but a priority – in which Afghan civilian casualties are substituted for American military casualties. (Gray, 2001)

The documented Afghan civilians killed were not participating in war-related activities (e.g., working in munitions factories) and therefore had not forfeited their right to immunity from attack (Wheeler, 2001: 5). In effect, as an astute scholar has noted, I am turning Michael Walzer's (1977) notion of "due care" upside down: that is, far from acknowledging a positive responsibility to protect innocent Afghans from the misery of war, US military strategists chose to impose extreme levels of harm upon innocent Afghan civilians to reduce present and possible future dangers faced by US forces.

Much of what was capable of being bombed in Afghanistan – schools, houses, factories, bridges, hospitals, power plants and lines, infrastructure – had already been destroyed in 22 years of civil war. New bombs would just make more dust.

Deadly Legacies: Cluster Bombs and Unexploded Munitions

And, crucially, the destruction continued after the bombs fell from the sky. The typical urban areas of Afghanistan – the small villages and neighborhoods on city perimeters – were often the recipients of US cluster bombs – the CBU-87 or CBU-103 made by Alliant Techsystems. The outskirts of Herat, close to the facilities of the 4th Armored Brigade, were heavily cluster-bombed in October, as were villages in the Shomali Plain, and the Kunduz and Kandahar areas. The CBU-87 leaves a "footprint" of 458 square meters and each of its 202 bomblets injures or kills anyone within a 152-meter radius. The new wind-corrected version of the CBU-87, called CBU-103, was used for the first time by F-16s on November 13, 2001 "near Jalalabad" (Thibodeau, 2002). Reports from the ground confirm heavy attacks that night upon installations, 4 kilometers south of Jalalabad, of the Taliban's 81st Brigade. A canal in western Jalalabad was hit, leading to flooding, and four civilians died in the Jalalabad region (*Pakistan Observer*, November 15, 2001).

The Herat area where the Taliban had concentrations of armor, anti-aircraft equipment, and troops was particularly hard hit by cluster bombs during the two weeks beginning on October 20, 2001. Shawn Moorehouse, working for Swiss Mine Action, said he found unexploded cluster bombs far from military targets:

> They've been dropped in houses, in the gardens, in fields, in vineyards. People couldn't cultivate the fields because of them. They couldn't actually live in the houses because of them. (Moorehouse, 2002)

Moorehouse even discovered one unexploded American 2,000 lb. bomb which had burrowed more than 15 feet underground in Herat. In January 2002 Suzanne Goldenberg of the *Guardian* reported:

> At least 41 people have been killed and 46 injured in Herat and nearby villages by cluster bombs which did not immediately explode when they were unleashed by the US bombers. (Goldenberg, 2002)

Figure 17.1 points out some of the connected deadly legacies of the US air war upon Afghanistan, many of which I have addressed elsewhere.

The Human Costs: Death, Immiseration, and Infrastructural Collapse

An examination of the first twenty weeks of US bombing of Afghanistan reveals the following human costs of the attack. Between 3,100 and 3,600 civilians were killed at the point of impact of bombs and missiles. Between 4,000 and 6,500 civilians were injured, many requiring artificial limbs. I estimate that there were between 8,000 and 10,000 dead Taliban and allies. An additional 19,000–43,000 Afghan refugees died of hunger, dis-

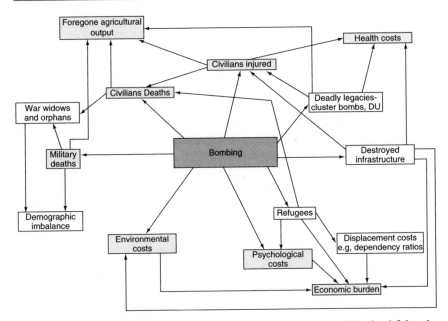

Figure 17.1   Map of the human costs of the US air campaign in Afghanistan. Drawing: Marc Herold.

ease, and cold in camps as a result of US bombing (Steele, 2002). An additional estimated 5,000 war widows and thousands of orphans resulted from Operation Enduring Freedom. Widespread destruction of livestock and animals took place. Approximately 49,000 BLU-97 cluster bomblets, more deadly than land mines, were scattered across Afghanistan (Herold, 2002c). Serious long-term health effects from using munitions containing depleted uranium have been noted. The already damaged infrastructure was further destroyed – bridges, power plants, water supplies, roads, communication systems, hundreds of incinerated trucks, burned fuel storage facilities, etc. Environmental costs (in addition to the aforementioned unexploded ordnance), which cause loss of agricultural land and human injuries, included massive forest fires in Tora Bora, and killed wildlife, altered migratory patterns, etc. Lastly, the bombing had psychological costs: post-traumatic stress disorders, anxiety, irritability, loss of appetite, and depression. According to Dr. Ghulam Rasool, a psychiatrist treating Afghan refugees in Quetta, there "is a real feeling of loss – loss of body, loss of money, loss of friends and family" (Parry, 2001).

A report by the World Health Organization estimated that mental illness is serious for one in five Afghans as a result of 23 years of war (Hanley, 2002a, b). A recent account detailed the forms of mental disorders:

A 4-year-old boy named Hasib grimaces like an animal and repeatedly butts his head on the floor. A young man named Fawad says his father startles awake, terrified, in the middle of every night. A man, Mohammad, averts his eyes from the rubble of his village; when he looks, he is overwhelmed by a flashback vision of dismembered bodies. (Hanley, 2002a)

The widely touted "just war" doctrine used to excuse the killing of civilians has nothing to say about those who die in the wake of a bombing campaign – from diseases caused by destruction of water treatment and sewage facilities, from the consequences of depleted uranium, and from fields and neighborhoods littered with cluster bombs (Lopez, 2002). Yet all these innocent civilians must also be entered in any "counting of the dead."

The severity of the US bombing of cities can be indirectly gauged insofar as, within a month, cities like Kabul, Kandahar, Jalalabad, etc. were three-quarters empty – and this of a population used to 20 years of war.

The bombing campaign also took a very heavy toll upon urban infra-structure, destroying buildings, bridges, airports, clinics, communication systems, water and electricity supplies, and fuel storage depots, and the cratering of innumerable roads. Afghan fuel trucks became a favored target (Gannon, 2002). US "precision" bombs hit the warehouses of the Inter-national Red Cross in Kabul twice, the CNN office in Kandahar, the UN's World Food Program buildings in Kandahar, and scored a direct hit on the Al Jazeera residence in Kabul and UN de-mining agency buildings in both Kabul and Kandahar (killing two trained dogs), etc.

A neglected feature of the US bombing campaign in urban areas was its class bias. US projectiles invariably fell close to or into poor neighborhoods adjacent to what US military planners (and pilots) perceived as military targets. Examples include airports and hills upon which the Taliban had placed anti-aircraft batteries. Moreover, the well-to-do left the cities long before the US bombing began. It is the civilian "urban" poor, whether in the poor neighborhoods of large cities, or in the villages of Afghanistan – places like Karam, Chowkar Karez, Kama Ado, Shah Aga, or Kakarak – which have been wiped off the map by US "precision" bombs.

Even before the US bombing campaign began, Afghanistan's urban infra-structure was heavily damaged from two decades of civil war. Nonetheless, US planes, in deja vu performances of the 1991 Iraq and 1999 Yugoslav campaigns, proceeded to bomb electrical power facilities (Everest, 2002). Proponents of bombing usually justify bombing electricity and communi-cation facilities because of their "dual-use" nature. The most severe conse-quence was cutting off power to hospitals and clinics, which were compelled to use diesel generators.

The functioning of hospitals was impaired in three ways: being bombed outright; having vital supplies reduced (whether medicines or electricity);

and by having their staff simply flee for fear of being bombed. At 4.30 a.m. on October 31, 2001, a Navy F/A-18 dropped a 2,000 lb. bomb on the Wazir clinic in the Dand district, west of Kandahar City. The clinic and two adjoining houses were flattened and between 11 and 15 civilians were killed. Doctor Obeidallah Hadid, injured, said 15 died. An AFP reporter said the small medical facility was in ruins. Two ambulances and two pickup trucks were also destroyed.

Numerous reports exist of the deplorable conditions in hospitals – lack of supplies, staff which fled, operating on the injured without anesthetics, cramped facilities, etc. Hospitals resorted to diesel-powered generators, but diesel fuel became very scarce once US planes targeted privately owned fuel trucks. The Afghan hospital system had collapsed by late October under the bombing onslaught as hospital staff fled for safety (Pakistan News Service, 2001). Those wounded who were able, headed off to clinics in Pakistan, while "those too wounded or poor to make the journey have been left to die in their homes in Kandahar" (ibid). The *Guardian*'s Rory Carroll reported about Kandahar: "parents with mutilated children have been turned away and told to hire smugglers to take them across the border to Quetta, Pakistan" (Carroll, 2001). In early November, the doctors at Kandahar's Chinese-built Mir Wais said the hospital was receiving 10–20 new victims of US bombing each day, but on average three died daily. Medicine supplies were inadequate, most trained doctors and nurses had fled in fear, there was no electricity except for a generator, since US planes hit the city's main power supply unit (ibid). Another report cited 300 people a day being treated at Mira Wais hospital during the height of the US bombing campaign around Kandahar, many of them victims of US bombs, with 10–15 percent of them dying. In Kabul's 300-bed children's hospital, supplies ran out and most of the staff fled (*Frontier Post*, 2001). By early November, doctors in the only government hospital in Jalalabad were operating without anesthetics, and yet the hospital was receiving 30 injured people daily, of whom at least five were in serious condition (Out There News, 2001a).

During the last two weeks of October, US warplanes made a concerted effort to hit Afghanistan's meager electricity generating capacity. The first such attack took place 8 kilometers outside Kandahar on October 22, destroying three trucks and incinerating at least five drivers. The Kandahar-based reporter for Al Jazeera broadcast footage shortly after the US strike. The destruction of electrical power supplies also hampered operation of Afghanistan's meager clean water treatment and sewage treatment plant.

The Afghan power system consisted largely of isolated regional networks supplied by small power and diesel facilities. The two exceptions were Kabul, supplied by the Soviet-built 100 MW Naghlu dam on the Kabul River, and Kandahar, fed by the large American-built Kajakai 33-megawatt hydroelectric facility in Helmand province. My database lists five or six attacks upon Afghanistan's power systems, including on October 10, when US planes hit a "small hydro-electric dam" outside Jalalabad (Cody, 2001: 21). This was probably the Darunta dam adjacent to bin Laden's empty Darunta camp, which was hit on October 10/11, resulting in two or three civilian deaths (Parry, 2001).

On October 14, US planes also hit high-power tension lines near Kandahar. The following day, US planes hit the large Naghlu power station northeast of Kabul, which is the main supplier to Kabul. US planes bombed the Jalalabad power system, probably again with bombs aimed at the Darunta camp (Out There News, 2001). On October 19, US bombs damaged an electrical distribution plant in Kandahar (Parry, 2001). And on October 31, a major bombing attack hit the Kajakai power station supplying the cities of Lashkargah and Kandahar, probably undertaken either to cut off power supplies in the south as the Taliban hold on the north weakened, or to hit a nearby alleged Al-Qaeda military post (Parry, 2001). A report from US energy research group Frost and Sullivan noted that "this has led to major health and sanitation concerns as cities require electricity to pump water (Thayer, 2001).

On December 3, US planes bombed two bridges leading out of Kandahar, no doubt seeking to thwart a Taliban escape from the surrounded city.

US warplanes also bombed vehicles on roads and highways, creating thousands more craters and rendering the roads virtually impassable. The highways are so badly damaged that it takes two or three times as long to travel between cities as it once did, crippling commerce in a land of traders (Baker and Glasser, 2002). As a result, transportation costs soared and the bombing campaign aggravated an already dire refugee crisis by idling trucks laden with relief supplies (Birch, 2002).

US bombs destroyed fuel depots, the downtown Kabul telephone exchange (the only international fixed wire telecommunications link), and radio stations. Two Chinese companies had been involved since 1999 in installing a telephone switching network in downtown Kabul (Geertz, 2001). The Chinese also assisted in adding 16.5 MW capacity to the Kajakai dam in Helmand in early 2001, but the dam area was bombed by the US before the work could be completed (Pomfret, 2001). The Kabul telephone exchange was bombed on October 13, resulting in at least some injured persons and on the following day the US hit Kabul's main power station northeast of the city. The Taliban's Abdul Hanan Hemat argued that "targeting electricity supply and international telephone lines is against international law. This can only hurt ordinary people – it is really contemptible" (Agence France-Presse, 2001).

In both Serbia and then Afghanistan, US warplanes attacked national media outlets. NATO forces bombed Belgrade's leading TV station, Radio

Television Serbia, early on April 23, 1999, killing 16 civilian employees (Holland, n.d.). On the night of October 8, 2001, US warplanes bombed the Taliban radio station, Voice of Shariat, with a tower located on a hill in eastern Kabul and offices in downtown Kabul, killing civilians. Some days later, the US bombed a small 1-kilowatt mobile radio transmitter station that the Taliban had set up in Kabul (Salahuddin, 2001).

Violations of International and Humanitarian Law

US bombing of Afghanistan, as we document, consistently and egregiously violated the tenets of international humanitarian law. US planes targeted, and sought to silence, Afghan media as of the first night of bombing. Reporters Without Borders (Reporteurs Sans Frontieres – RSF) described this action:

> According to information obtained by RSF, the US forces struck the radio and television in Kabul, Kandahar [south of the country], Jalalabad [east], and Puli Khomri [north of Kabul] during the first days of the military operation "Enduring Freedom" against the Taliban regime. On the first night of the strikes, the building and antennae of the official station Radio Shariat in Kabul were targeted and the programs were cut off . . . the television installations, banned from broadcasting since 1996 by the Taliban, were also targeted. Following the strikes, programs were suspended for more than three weeks. On October 24 the radio station that broadcasts mostly the Taliban authorities' press releases and religious prayers, started to broadcast again for no more than two hours per day. The Taliban used a mobile transmitter, but on the night of 25 October the air strikes destroyed this installation. (Reporters Without Borders, 2001)

But US bombs also hit the infrastructure of the Afghan mind. Between October 10 and December 20, US bombs and missiles fell very close to twelve different mosques in Afghanistan, killing at least 100 innocent civilians. Mosques were hit in the provinces of Nangarhar, Kunduz, Herat, Kandahar, and Paktia (Herold, 2002a).

During late November and early December, venturing out in any vehicle on the highways and roads of the provinces of Kandahar, Helmand, Zabul, and Ghazni meant risking death. Ferocious US air attacks during the last week of November and the first week of December upon any moving vehicles severely disrupted food deliveries to Kandahar.

US military strategists made a concerted effort to deny modern sources of power to Afghanistan. Fuel depots and fuel trucks were savagely attacked, as were the country's few hydro-electric facilities. A Canadian reporter working for the AP, Kathy Gannon, wrote about life on the highway stretching 300 miles from Kandahar to Kabul. The gutted road was Kabul's lifeline for diesel fuel:

> All along the 300-mile road are bitter reminders of the war that drove the Taliban to abandon the country's cities. About 60 miles outside Kandahar lies a heap of charred and crumpled oil tankers, the remains of a convoy blasted by US-led air strikes. Iftikar Ali leaned against the side of one of the hulks, held his head in his hand and lamented the fate of a relative who was driving one of the trucks. "All his life he worked to build something," said Ali. "There were no Taliban or al-Qaida with this tanker, just my relative bringing fuel from the Iranian border to Jalalabad, in eastern Afghanistan. (Gannon, 2002)

Three months later on April 2, Haji Zaman, 55, a retired Afghan truck driver, stood outside the new US Embassy compound in Kabul, part of a group seeking to draw attention to their claims for compensation from the US government. Zaman said his 25-year-old son was killed when a US bomb struck his fuel tanker on the road from Kabul to Kandahar. He can't sleep for worry over how he will support his ten family members. Zaman sold everything so his son could buy the tanker, but now: "I've lost my land, my property, and my son as well" (Lakshamann, 2002).

In a widely circulated article, *Boston Globe* journalist John Donnelly (2002) reported on what was already well known two months previously: systematic US targeting of vehicles in an arc from Herat in the west to Qalat in the east, as well as southern routes leading from Iran and Pakistan. Citing UN data, Donnelly said that in just two days in late November, US planes destroyed some 160 Afghan fuel tanker trucks along with 210 cars.

The strikes against vehicles continued after the Taliban had surrendered Kandahar. Leslie Oqvist, the UN regional coordinator in southern Afghanistan, recalled that he had "been in meetings here where 'Americans' have justified everything on the 3,000-plus killed in New York" (Donnelly, 2002).

Conclusions

This chapter has not argued, in a strict sense, that US military planners intentionally targeted civilians in the Afghanistan bombing campaign. This was not, after all, a *strategic* bombing campaign (Hewitt, 1983). However, I believe the attack was a case of second-degree intentionality. A 1,000-pound satellite-guided bomb, dropped upon a residence, or upon a tank parked in a residential area, will necessarily kill people in proximity. And all the more so, since most of the US bombing attacks were carried out at night when people were in their homes. Moreover, most Afghan homes, whether in urban neighborhoods or mountain or plains villages, are made out of mud bricks. To this one should add the many instances where US bombs simply landed way off target. Sean Moorehouse, a de-mining expert working with the UN's World Food Program, compared the target coordinates provided by the US military with where the bombs fell and found that "the accuracy of the US figures is pretty doubtful," differing by as much as 4 miles on occasion (Struck, 2002b).

Military planners know ahead of time about the high probability of civilian casualties when bombing takes place near civilians. Vijay Prashad argues the salient point well:

> To say that the civilian deaths from aerial bombardment are unintentional is sophistry, because if there is a probability that the bombs will hit civilian targets, then *ipso facto* the civilian deaths are not unintentional... aerial bombardment always already intends to kill civilians, despite the best intentions of military planners. (Prashad, 2001)

Paraphrasing Amyreh (2002), the US bombing campaign in Afghanistan has been about "killing deliberately by mistake." A foreign state terrorized an innocent civilian population by such killing, injuring, and uprooting, destroying the fabric of life (Herman, 2002).

Precisely killing Afghanistan's civilian, urban (and rural) poor, these acts were state aggression and terrorism. That is, the sovereign state of the USA engaged in actions which reasonably can be expected to, and did, harm large numbers of innocent Afghan civilians, both by killing them directly and indirectly by destroying vital infrastructure. All this was done under the convenient soporific of "precision" guided munitions:

> Really large-scale killing and torture to terrorize – "wholesale" terrorism – has been implemented by states, not by non-state terrorists. The reason people aren't aware of this is that states define terrorism and identify the terrorists, and they naturally exempt themselves as always "retaliating" and engaging in "counter-terror" even when their own actions are an exact fit to their own definitions. And their mainstream media always follow the official lead. (Herman and Peterson, 2002)

Epilogue

Stephen Graham

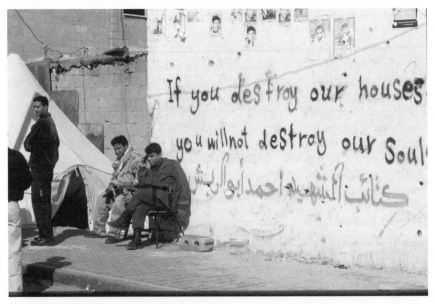

Plate Epilogue.1 Palestinians sitting by protest graffiti after the Israeli Defense Force demolished the centre of the Jenin refugee camp, April 2002. Photograph: Susan Brannon, used with permission.

It is a lot easier to destroy than it is to create. (Nijman, 2001)

Cities are long-lived artifacts. Their tendency is to continue. (Kostof, 1992: 250)

Wounded cities, like all cities, are dynamic entities, replete with the potential to recuperate loss and reconstruct anew for the future. (Susser and Schneider, 2003: 1)

The city is a kind of collective immortality – we may die, but the forms and structures of our city live on . . . The ordeal of having to learn to see and to speak all over again – to look at the world from inside the ruins, to communicate by signaling through the flames – has often enlarged the people who could survive . . . Forced to live amongst these gigantic broken forms, we can learn what is worth putting together and what must never be allowed to come together. (Berman, 1996: 175–84)

You can destroy our city, but never our soul. (Hrasnica, 1993)

Editing this book has, I must admit, been a sobering and disturbing experience. As it has evolved, and its unprecedented breadth of perspectives has started to outline what an urban geopolitics might actually be, so acts of urban terrorism and state violence against cities and their inhabitants seemed to erupt daily before my eyes. There has been a palpable sense of catastrophic violence against cities (once again) running out of control.

This makes it all the more important, at the end of this book, to stress one thing: if any single characteristic defines cities, it is their *resilience*. Above all, cities have a propensity to *survive*. Cities *endure*. They *recover*. The very dynamism that makes cities grow, function, and flourish also drives them to outlast even the most extreme violence pitted against them (witness the extraordinary resurgence of Hiroshima, Nagasaki, Hamburg, Dresden, Rotterdam, Coventry, and Tokyo since 1945). "The processes at work during and after disasters are the same as those that account for concentrated social and economic development in less stressful times," writes Josef Konvitz. "Yet the myth of terrible urban vulnerability endures" (1990: 62).

In many ways cities are always "hyperactive sites of creative destruction" (Harvey, 2003b: 25). The destruction and violence wrought by terror and war often mimic, and accentuate, the wider processes of destruction and creation forged through acts of planning, modernization, civil reconstruction, tides of hyperactive speculation, urban investment (and disinvestment), innovation, and technological development that characterize capitalist urban change.

While it is beyond the scope of this book, and rather neglected by urban social science, the history of urban reconstruction, and the phoenix-like resurgence of urban civil societies after periods of urban war and terror, is an inspiring one (see, for example, Schneider and Susser, 2003; Bollens, 1999, 2000; Barakat, 2003; Rowe and Sarkis, 1998; Ockman, 2002; Van Allen Institute, 2002; Schneider and Susser, 2003; Sorkin and Zukin, 2002; Chickering and Funk, 2004; Woods, 2001). This work demonstrates very clearly that urbicide or place annihilation is not so simple after all. The (attempted) annihilation of urban places is, itself, a contingent event which tends to pass as better times emerge. In most cases, urban war, and terrorist outrage, tend, mercifully, to be ultimately transient.

Very often, the physical, social, economic, and cultural dynamics of cities recover remarkably quickly once the mass violence stops. In fact, if one looks over the *long durée*, the astonishing *continuity* of cities demonstrates that, these days, very few cities ever actually truly die as a result of even the most savage violence or cataclysm of war (see Calvani, 1976). "Only in the far distant past did cities crumble into dust and not rise again," writes David Harvey. "In recent times, the extraordinary growth of cities throughout the world seems set to override catastrophes, losses, indignities, and woundings, no matter whether externally visited or self-inflicted" (Harvey, 2003b: 25).

This does not mean, of course, that the painful legacies and traumas that follow attacks against cities and their residents – psychological, physical, cultural, economic, and social – are not profound or long lasting. Acts of rebuilding are always contested (see Guy, this volume). This is especially so in the contemporary period because, in the context of a hegemonic, neo-liberal capitalism, urban reconstruction tends to pander to the often exploitative dynamics of global finance, inward investment, and international tourism. In fact, "large-scale corporate developers target damaged locations" (Harvey, 2003b: 25).

As I write this epilogue, US corporate capital (linked intimately to the Bush regime) is systematically stripping Iraq of its assets, backed up by US military control. Emerging here is a form of twenty-first century colonialism by invasion and privatization (Ali, 2003; Harvey, 2003a). Such neoliberal reconstruction and restructuring can itself create "new waves of trauma and suffering" because local civil societies, and especially poorer communities, tend to be marginalized physically, economically, and geographically by such patterns of activity (Schneider and Susser, 2003: 316).

Sometimes, however, urban reconstruction does manage to connect creatively with indigenous capabilities and social movements, while also bringing in required external investment. Sometimes, long-term healing and accommodation between conflicting social groups does occur. In such circumstances, postwar, or post-trauma, rebuilding can even have cathartic power. It can create new spaces of real social, economic, or political potential and a new, sustainable, collective mentality of city life. Cities can thus reemerge as new "bodies politic" (Schneider and Susser, 2003: 317) – critical spaces of heterogeneity and mixing in which the crises of war, conflict, and violence are gradually overcome. Such transformations can galvanize conflict-torn societies to creatively overwhelm the traumas of the past. In so doing, they can also demonstrate how to cope with the inevitably multicultural and "mongrel" futures of cities in our urbanizing world (Sandercock, 2003).

This is why it is so crucial that cities are not abandoned, or dramatically reshaped, to address the purported risks of war or terror, as so many commentators have naively urged since 9/11. "The city has been shaken again," wrote Tom Vanderbilt (2002: 209) after those attacks. "Architecture has provided an uncertain shelter. [But] the same impulses [of the Cold War that have been] reborn – to leave the city, to construct buildings capable of withstanding attacks – are ultimately just as untenable now as they were fifty years ago." "What," asks Vanderbilt, "would life be without cities and without architecture and without the positive values of civic life?"

As a global polarization threatens to occur between those who are pro-"Western" and those who are pro-"radical Islam" – stoked by sickening and self-perpetuating cycles of informal and state terror and fundamentalist, essentialist, propaganda – one thing is sure. Normatively, cities must be seen as key sites, perhaps *the* key sites, for nurturing the tolerances, diasporic mixings, and multicultural spaces that will push fundamentalist fantasies of all sorts to the lunatic fringes where they belong.

Whether we like it or not, our world is moving headlong towards an urban, transnational, diasporic future (see Sandercock, 2003) Rather than being perceived as the targets of Al-Qaeda suicide attacks, or US or Israeli F-16 bombings, cities need to be constructed, discursively and physically, as critical sites where justice and tolerance can be built out of the dreams and drive of those who live there. This needs to be done – somehow – without annihilating the biospheres on which we all depend. Simply put, our planet faces no bigger challenge.

The first part of this challenge, of course, is to forcibly reject *both* of the racist, masculinist fundamentalisms that are currently being mobilized to try to force the world to polarize between what Rosalind Petchesky has called "the permanent war machine (or permanent security state) and the reign of holy terror" (cited in Joseph and Sharma, 2003: xxi). Untrammeled, the self-perpetuating cycles of atrocity between terror and counter-terror that these discourses legitimize and sustain offer up an extremely bleak urban future indeed: perhaps the ultimate urban dystopia.

The purpose of this book has been to demonstrate that a creative dialogue is long overdue between those concerned with the critical analysis of cities and those concerned with the critical analysis of political violence and international relations. My hope is that this collection will help this process along. Such a dialogue, however, will only succeed if it looks beyond "urbicide," "place annihilation," the urbanization of war, and the nature of cities as targets or strategic, geopolitical sites. Such a dialogue can only bring positive benefits by seeing beyond the roles of cities in war, terror, and the terrors of the "war on terror." Above all, the focus must fall on creatively fostering civil societies – transnational and urban at the same time – which make the hatreds which fuel urbicide, terrorism, and urban war less likely to emerge in the first place.

After two million grieving people mingled on the streets of Madrid on March 11, 2004, to express their revulsion after the horrific train bombs that killed nearly 200 people in the city the day before, Madeleine Bunting reflected on the trauma. "Cities have become our battlegrounds," she concluded:

> Where once they were places of safety to which country folk retreated in times of war, they are now where the war in conducted. [After these attacks] fear could empty the city and cauterize the mass transit systems that are its lifeblood. One is haunted by the image of shut-down tube stations, of empty streets where weeds break the Tarmac and everyone retreats to their laptop, and we look back on the conviviality of the era before mass terrorism with nostalgic disbelief . . . Over half the world's population now lives in cities and the images we have seen over the past few days offer two alternatives of what the city might mean in the twenty-first century: a place of terror where the stranger is to be feared and distrusted, or the determined solidarity of strangers – a sea of hands waving hastily scribbled messages with the one word that says everything: "No!" (Bunting, 2004)

Bibliography

Aaronovitch, D. (2003) "One law for the west," *Observer*, November 30, 27.

ABC News (2001) Online. October 26, 2003. abcnews.go.com.

Abdelhadi, M. (2003) "Iraq rumour mill grinds on," *BBC News*, Middle East, July 6. www.bbc.co.uk.

Abrahamian, E. (2003) "The US media, Huntingdon and September 11," *Third World Quarterly*, 24 (3), 529–44.

Adams N. (1993) "Architecture as the target," *Journal of the Society of Architectural Historians*, 52, 389–90.

Agamben, G. (1998) *Homo Sacer: Sovereign Power and Bare Life*, Stanford, CA: Stanford University Press.

Agamben, G. (2002) "Security and terror," *Theory and Event*, 5 (4), 1–2.

Agar, J. (2001) "Modern horrors: British identity and identity cards." In J. Caplan and J. Torpey (eds.) *Documenting Individual Identity: The Development of State Practices in the Modern World*. Princeton NJ: Princeton University Press, 101–20.

Agence France-Presse (2001) "Kabul power supply cut after US bombing: Taliban," October 16.

Agger, B. (1989) *Fast Capitalism*. Urbana: University of Illinois Press.

Agier, M. (2002) "Between war and the city: Towards an urban anthropology of refugee camps," *Ethnography*, 3 (3), 317–41.

Agnew, J. (1998) *Geopolitics: Re-Visioning World Politics*. London: Routledge.

Agnew, J. and Corbridge, S. (1995) *Mastering Space*. London: Routledge.

Agre, P. (2001) "Your face is not a bar code," September 2003. http://dlis.gseis.ucla.edu/pagre/bar-code.html.

Ahmed, K., Vulliamy, E., Burke, J., Beaumont, P., and Salahuddin, S. (2001) "The gamble," *Observer*, October 14.

Aidi, H. (2002) "Jihadis in the hood: Race, urban Islam and the war on terror," *Middle East Report*, 224, 36–43.

Ali, T. (2003) *Bush in Baghdad: The Recolonization of Iraq*. London: Verso.

Aly, G. and Heim, S. (2002) *Architects of Annihilation: Auschwitz and the Logic of Destruction*. Wiedenfeld and Nicolson: London.

Amir, I. (2001) "Afghan children – a ray of hope for their country," *Dawn*, November 4.

Amyreh, K. (2002) "Killing deliberately 'by mistake'," *Palestine Chronicle*, September 4.

An Architektur (2003) "Extra-territorial spaces and camps in the 'War on Terrorism'." In A. Franke (ed.) *Territories*. KW Institute for Contemporary Art: Berlin, 20–9.

Anderson, J. (2002) "Borders after 11 September 2001," *Space and Polity*, 6 (2), 227–32.

Andreas, P. (2003) "A tale of two borders: The US–Canada and US–Mexico lines after 9/11." In P. Andreas and T. Biersteker (eds.) *The Rebordering of North America*. New York: Routledge, 1–23.

Andreas, P. and Biersteker, T. (eds.) (2003) *The Rebordering of North America*. New York: Routledge.

Andreopoulos G. (ed.) (1984) *Genocide: Conceptual and Historical Dimensions*. Philadelphia: University of Pennsylvania Press.

Andreu, P. (1997) "Borders and borderers," *Architecture of the Borderlands*. London: Wiley/Architectural Design, 57–61.

Appadurai, A. (1996) *Modernity at Large: Cultural Dimensions of Globalization*. Minneapolis: University of Minnesota Press.

Arabic News (2001) "Israeli official calls for striking Palestinian infrastructure," *ArabicNews.Com*, May 6. www.arabicnews.com/ansub/Daily/Day/010605/2001060505/html; accessed April 10, 2002.

Aretxaga, B. (2003) "Terror as thrill: First thoughts on the 'war on terrorism'." Mimeo.

Armando (1996) *From Berlin*. London: Reaction Books.

Ashworth, G. (1991) *War and the City*. New York: Routledge.

Associated Press (2000) "ACLU sues Seattle for imposing no-protest zone during world trade talks." 8 March.

Associated Press (2001) "Internet takes on police role world-wide," *South China Morning Post*, November 23. http://technology.scmp.com/cgi-bin/gxcgi/AppLogic+FTContentServer?pagename = S ... _23/11/01.

Augé, M. (1995) *Non-Places: Introduction to an Anthropology of Supermodernity*. London: Verso.

Augur, T. (1946) "Planning cities for the atomic age," *American City*, 6 (8), 75–6.

Augur, T. (1949) "Decentralization can't wait," *Appraisal Journal*, 17 (1), 107–13.

Avidor, G. (2002) "The battle of Jenin: April 2002," *Urban Operations Journal*. http://www.orbanoperations.com/jenin.htm; accessed July 24, 2002.

Azoulay, A. and Ophir, A. (2002) *Bad Days*. Tel Aviv: Resling Press.

Bagli, C. (2001) "For downtown: Vacant offices and lost vigor," *New York Times*, November 19.

Bagli, C. (2002) "Seeking safety, downtown firms are scattering," *New York Times*, January 29.

Bailey, E. (2002) *Marlene Dietrich Lived Here*. London: Black Swan.

Bailey, E. and Rubin, J. (2003) "10 protesters arrested as agriculture meeting winds down in Sacramento," *Los Angeles Times*, June 25, Part 2, 6.

Baker, F. (2003) "The Berlin wall: Production, preservation and consumption of a twentieth-century monument," *Antiquity*, 67, 709–33.

Baker, P. and Glasser, S. (2002) "Miles to go before Kabul can be left behind," *Washington Post*, June 9, B1.

Bakhtin, M. (1968) *Rabelais and His World*. Cambridge, MA: MIT Press (translation of the Russian publication of 1965).

Bakic-Hayden, M. and R. Hayden (1992) "Orientalist variations on the theme 'Balkans': Symbolic geography in recent Yugoslav politics," *Slavic Review*, 51 (1), 1–15.

Baldauf, S. (2001) "Life under the Taliban cuts two ways," *Christian Science Monitor*, September 20.

Baldwin, H. (1947) *The Price of Power*. New York: Harper and Brothers.

Barakat, S. (1998) "City war zones," *Urban Age*, spring, 11–19.

Barakat, S. (ed.) (2003) *Reconstructing War-Torn Societies: Afghanistan*. London: Palgrave-Macmillan.

Barber, B. (1995) *Jihad vs. McWorld*. New York: Times Books.

Barghouti, M. (2003) "Verbicide," *New Internationalist*, 359, 34–359.

Barnett, A. and Bright, M. (2003) "Innocent victims of Britain's fight against terrorism," *Observer*, 7 December, 11.

Baroud, R. (2002) *Searching Jenin: Eyewitness Accounts of the Israeli Invasion*. Seattle: Cune Press.

Bartter, M. (1986) "Nuclear holocaust as urban renewal," *Science-Fiction Studies*, 13 (2), 148–58.

Bauman, Z. (1989) *Modernity and the Holocaust*. Cambrige: Polity Press.

Bauman, Z. (2001) "Cities of fears, city of hopes." Mimeo.

Baxandall, R., and Ewen, E. (2000), *Picture Windows: How the Suburbs Happened*. New York: Basic Books.

BBC News (1998) "Clashes in summit city," May 17. http://news.bbc.co.uk/1/hi/special_report/1998/05/98/g8/95114.stm; accessed July 17, 2003.

BBC News (2001) "Who are the Genoa protesters?" July 20. http://news.bbc.co.uk/hi/english/world/Europe/newsid_1435000/1435610.stm; accessed July 20, 2001.

BBC News (2003a) "France rings G8 town with steel," May 29. http://newsvote.bc.co.uk/1/hi/world/Europe/2947154.stm; accessed June 3, 2003.

BBC News (2003b) "Britons injured in G8 protests," June 2. http://news.bbc.co.uk/1/hi/world/Europe/2954964.stm; accessed June 3, 2003.

Beauregard, R. (1993) *Voices of Decline: The Postwar Fate of US Cities*, 1st edn. Oxford: Blackwell.

Beauregard, R. (2003) *Voices of Decline: The Postwar Fate of US Cities*, 2nd edn. New York: Routledge.

Beck, U. (1986) *Risikogesellschaft: Auf dem Weg in Eine Andere Moderne*. Frankfurt: Suhrkamp.

Beck, U. (1992) *The Risk Society: Towards a New Modernity*. London: Sage.

Beck, U. (1999) *World Risk Society*. Cambridge: Polity Press.

Becker, J. (1996) *Hungry Ghosts: China's Secret Famine*. London, John Murray.

Bedell, G. (2003) "Dispatches," *Observer Magazine*, June 15, 36–41.

Beevor, A. (2002) *Berlin: The Downfall 1945*, London: Viking.

Bellamy, C. (2003) "If the cities do not fall to the Allies, there may be no alternative to siege warfare," *Independent*, 28 March 28, 3.

Belson, K. (2002) "Japan and South Korea brace for World Cup," *New York Times*, May 22, C17, C20.

Beniger, J. (1986) *The Control Revolution: The Social and Economic Origins of the Information Society*. Cambridge, MA: Harvard University Press.

Bennet, J. (2003) "Israeli missiles kill 7, including a Hamas leader, in Gaza City," *New York Times*, April 9, A9.

Bentz, R. (1956) *Some Civil Defense Problems in the Nation's Capital Following Widespread Thermonuclear Attack*. Baltimore, MD: Operations Research Office, Johns Hopkins University.

Berman, M. (1996) "Falling towers: City life after urbicide." In D. Crow (ed.) *Geography and Identity*. Washington, DC: Maisonneuve Press, 172–92.

Berman, M. (1982) *All That's Solid Melts Into Air*. London: Verso.

Bevanger, L. (2001) "Genoa 'war zone' angers residents," *BBCNews*, July 19. http://news.Bbc.co.uk/hi/English/world/Europe/newsid_14470000/1447878.stm; accessed July 20, 2001.

Biddle, S. (2002) *Afghanistan and the Future of Warfare: Implications for Army and Defense Policy*. Carlisle, PA: Strategic Studies Institute of the US Army War College, October 20.

Birch, D. (2002) "Afghanistan's lost highways," *Baltimore Sun*, April 29, A8.

Bishop, R., Phillips, J., and Wei Wei, Y. (eds.) (2003) *Postcolonial Urbanism: Southeast Asian Cities and Global Processes*. London: Routledge.

Bishop, R., Phillips, J., and Wei Wei, Y. (eds.) (2004) *Beyond Description: Space, Historicity, Singapore*. London: Routledge.

Blanche, E. (2003) "West Bank east: Americans in Iraq make war the Israeli way," *Beirut Daily Star*, December 6. www.dailystar.com.lb/opinion/06_12_03e.asp.

Bleecker, J. (1994) "Urban crisis: Past, present and virtual," *Socialist Review*, 24, 189–221.

Blomley, N. (2003) "Law, property, and the geography of violence: The frontier, the survey, and the grid," *Annals of the Association of American Geographers*, 93 (1), 121–41.

Body-Gendrot, S. (2000) *The Social Control of Cities? A Comparative Perspective*. Oxford: Blackwell.

Boeri, S. (2003) "Border syndrome." In A. Franke, E. Weizman, S. Boeri, and R. Segal (eds.) *Territories*. Berlin: KW and Walther Keoing.

Bollens, S. (1999) *Urban Peace-Building in Divided Societies: Belfast and Johannesburg*. New York: Westview Press.

Bollens, S. (2000) *On Narrow Ground: Urban Policy and Ethnic Conflict in Jerusalem and Belfast*. New York: State University of New York Press.

Bollens, S. (2001) "City and soul: Sarajevo, Johannesburg, Jerusalem, Nicosia," *City*, 5 (2), 169–87.

Booth, B. and Dunne, T. (eds.) (2002) *Worlds in Collision: Terror and the Future of Global Order*. London: Macmillan Palgrave.

Borger, J. (2003) "Israel trains US assassination squads in Iraq," *Guardian*, December 9, 1.

Borin, E. (2002) "Non-lethal weapons shoot to hurt," *Wired News*, 30 September. http://www.wired.com/news/prints/0,1294,55337,00.html; accessed October 1, 2002.

Bourdieu, P. (1998) *Acts of Resistance: Against the Tyranny of the Market*. New York: New Press.

Bowden, M. (2000) *Black Hawk Down: A Story of Modern War*. New York: Penguin Books.

Braudel, F. (1973) *Capitalism and Material Life*. New York: Harper and Row.

Brennan, T. (2003) *Globalization and its Terrors: Daily Life in the West*. London: Routledge.

Brenner, N. and Theodore, N. (eds.) (2002) *Spaces of Neoliberalism*. Oxford: Blackwell.

Bright, M. (2003) "Under siege on all sides, Muslims plead for peace," *Observer*, December 7, 10–11.

Bringa T. (1995) *Being Muslim the Bosnian Way: Identity and Community in a Central Bosnian Village*. Princeton, NJ: Princeton University Press.

Brown, S. (1985). "Central Belfast's security segment: An urban phenomenon," *Area*, 17 (1), 1–8.

Buckley, E. (2000) "Annex 1: The active Army component and the 1992 Los Angeles Riots." In R. Glenn (ed.) *The City's Many Faces*. Santa Monica, CA: RAND, 333–45.

Buck-Morss, S. (2000) *Dreamworld and Catastrophe: The Passing of Mass Utopia in East and West*. Cambridge, MA: MIT Press.

Buck-Morss, S. (2003) *Thinking Past Terror: Islamicism and Critical Theory on the Left*. London: Verso.

Bugeaud, M. (1997) *La Guerre des rues et des maisons*. Paris: Jean-Paul Rocher.

Bumiller, E. (2003) "Who's cool at G8 meetings? It's all in Bush's gestures," *New York Times*, June 2, A8.

Bunting, M. (2004) "Listen to the silent crowds," *Guardian*, March 13, 21.

Bunyan, T. (2002) "The war on freedom and democracy," *Statewatch News* online, September 9. http://www.statewach.org/news/2002/sep/analysis13.htm; accessed November 21, 2002.

Burger, K. and Koch, A. (2002) "Afghanistan: The key lessons," *Jane's Defence Weekly*, January 2, 20–7.

Burke J. (2001) "Homes razed in new Israeli attack," *Observer*, April 15.

Burkeman, O. (2002) "Visa detainees allege beatings," *Guardian*, May 23.

Burnett, W. (1984) *The Asphalt Jungle*. London: Zomba Books.

Calhoun, C., Price, P., and Timmer, A. (eds.) (2002) *Understanding September 11*. New York: New Press.

Calvan, B. C. (2003) "Protesters to converge on agricultural conference in Sacramento," *Boston Globe*, June 16, A3.

Calvani, V. (1976) *Lost Cities*. Geneva: Minerva.

Campbell, D. (1992). *Writing Security*, 1st edn. Minneapolis: University of Minnesota Press.

Campbell, D. (1998a) *National Deconstruction: Violence, Identity and Justice in Bosnia*. Minneapolis: University of Minnesota Press.

Campbell, D. (1998b) *Writing Security*, 2nd edn. Minneapolis: University of Minnesota Press.

Campbell, D. (2001) "How the plotters slipped US net," *Guardian Online*, September 27, 1–3.

Campbell D. (2002) "Atrocity, memory, photography: Imaging the concentration camps of Bosnia – the case of ITN versus *Living Marxism*, Part 2," *Journal of Human Rights*, 1 (2), 143–72.

Careless, J. (2003) "Digital eye in the sky," *Government Video*, 14, 44–6.

Carey, R. (2001) *The New Intifada: Resisting Israel's Apartheid*. London: Verso.

Carroll, R. (2001) "Wounded forced to flee as Afghan hospital system collapses," *Guardian*, October 27.

Castells, M. (1989) *The Informational City* Oxford: Blackwell.

Castells, M. (1996) *The Rise of the Network Society*. Oxford: Blackwell.

Castells, M. (1997) *The Power of Identity*, 1st edn. Oxford: Blackwell.

Castells, M. (1998) *The End of Millennium*. Oxford: Blackwell.

Castells, M. (2004) *The Power of Identity*, 2nd edn. Oxford: Blackwell.

CBC (2001) "Fingerprint scans part of new airport security," CBC news, October 11. http://cbc.ca/cgi-bin/news 2001/10/11/airport_security.011011.

Che Café Collective (c.a. 1999) "Nagasaki nightmare," BURN! Project. http://burn.ucsd.edu/atomic.htm.

Chen, D. (2003) "China to introduce super ID card," *New York Times*, August 20.

Chickering, R. and Funk, M. (2004) *Endangered Cities*. Boston, MA: Brill.

Chiumento Consultancy (2003) *Facing the Future in the City*. April.

Chomsky, N. (2003) *Hegemony or Survival? America's Quest for Global Dominance*. London: Hamish Hamilton.

City of London Police (2002a) *Annual Report for 2001/2*. London: City of London Police.

City of London Police (2002b) *Crime and Disorder Strategy 2002–5*. London: City of London Police.

City of London Police (2003) *Crime – Terrorism*. http://www.cityoflondon.police.uk/crime/terrorism.htm; accessed January 13, 2003.

City Security (2000). April edition.

City Security (2001). September edition.

Clancey, G. (2002) "Science in Eurasia: Meiji seismology as cultural critique." In A. Chan, G. Clancey, and L. Hui Chieh (eds.) *Historical Perspectives on East Asian Science, Technology, and Medicine*. Singapore: Singapore University Press and World Scientific Publishing.

Clancey, G. (2003) "Toward a spatial history of emergency: Notes from Singapore." In R. Bishop, J. Phillips, and Y. Wei Wei (eds.) *Beyond Description: Space, Historicity, Singapore*. London: Routledge.

Clancey, J. (2003) "Goodbye Berlin," *Guardian*, May 12.

Clark, K. (2000) "Afghan militant camp disbands," *BBC News*, June 23.

Clark, K. (2004) Untitled article, *Adbusters*, 12 (1), 16.

CNN.com (1999) "Troops sent to Seattle as part of terrorism contingency plan," December 2. http://www.cnn.com/1999/US/12/02/wto.05; accessed August 3, 2003.

CNN.com (2001) "Plot to assassinate Bush – reports." July 9. http://addition.cnn.com/2001/WORLD/Europe/06/20/Russia.binladen/index.html; accessed August 1, 2003.

CNN.com (2002) "Net effect: anti-terror eavesdropping ." http://www.cnn.com/2002/TECH/internet/05/27/terror.surveillance.ap/index.html.

Coaffee, J. (2000) "Fortification, fragmentation and the threat of terrorism in the City of London in the 1990s." In J. Gold and G. Revill (eds.) *Landscapes of Defence*. London: Prentice-Hall, 114–29.

Coaffee, J. (2003a) "Morphing the counter-terrorist response: Beating the bombers in London's financial heart." *Knowledge, Technology and Policy*, 16 (2), 63–83.

Coaffee, J. (2003b) *Terrorism, Risk and the City*. Aldershot: Ashgate.

Coale, A. (1947) *The Problem of Reducing Vulnerability to Atomic Bombs*. Princeton, NJ: Princeton University Press.

Cockburn, A. and St. Clair, J. (2000) *Five Days That Shook the World: The Battle for Seattle and Beyond*. London: Verso.

Cody, E. (2001) "Life inside Afghanistan: Chaos, fear and refugees," *Washington Post*, October 14.

Cohen, N. (2003) "Guantamono UK," *Observer*, December 14, 29.

Cohen, S. (1985) *Visions of Social Control*. Cambridge: Polity Press.

Cole, T. (2003) *Holocaust City: The Making of a Jewish Ghetto*. London: Routledge.

Collins, J. (2002) "Terrorism." In J. Collins and R. Glover (eds.), *Collateral Language: A User's Guide to America's New War*. New York: New York University Press, 155–74.

Collins, J. and Glover, R. (eds.) (2002) *Collateral Language: A User's Guide to America's New War*. New York: New York University Press.

Collins, J. and Horowitz, M. (2000) *Homeland Defense: A Strategic Approach*. Washington, DC: Center for Strategic and International Studies.

Confuris, G. (2000) "Attempts at a new national beginning." In T. Scheer, J. Kleihuis, and P. Kahlfeldt (eds.) *City of Architecture: Architecture of the City – Berlin 1900–2000*. Berlin: Nicolai, 215–27.

Connolly W. (1991) *Identity/Difference: Democratic Negotiations of Political Paradox*. Ithaca, NY: Cornell University Press.

Conquest, R. (1986) *The Harvest of Sorrow: Soviet Collectivization and the Terror Famine*. London: Weidenfeld and Nicolson.

Conrad, P. (1994) *The Art of the City: Views and Versions of New York*. New York: Oxford University Press.

Cooley, J. (2000) *Unholy Wars: Afghanistan, America, and International Terrorism*, 2nd edn. Cherndon, VA: Pluto Press.

Cordesman, A. (2003) *The "Instant Lessons" of the Iraq War: Main Report*, working draft. Washington, DC: Center for Strategic and International Studies, April 28.

Corera, G. (2002) "The British in Jenin." www.bbc.couk/radion4/today/reports/international/jenin.shtml; accessed September 2003.

Corfis I. and Wolfe, M. (1995) *The Medieval City Under Siege*. Woodbridge: Boydell.

Cornwell, R. (2002) "Analysis of the G8 summit: Another year, another G8 summit. But do they achieve anything?" *Independent*, June 27, 11.

Corporation of London (1993a) *The Way Ahead: Traffic and the Environment*. Draft Consultation Paper. London.

Corporation of London (1993b) *Security Initiatives*. Draft Consultation Paper. London.

Corporation of London (2001) Press release, November 14.

Costello, S. (2002) "Japanese researcher gums up biometrics scanners," *Infoworld*, May 16. http://staging.infoworld.com/articles/hn/xml/02/05/16/020516hngumsxml?T.

Council of Europe (1993) *Information Report on War Damage to the Cultural Heritage in Croatia and Bosnia-Herzegovina*. Council of Europe, Doc. no. 6756. http://assembly.coe.int/Main.asp?link = http://3A/2F/2Fassembly.coe.int/2Fdocuments/2Fworkingdocs/2Fdoc93/2Fedoc6756.htm.

Council of Europe (1994) *Fourth Information Report on War Damage to the Cultural Heritage in Croatia and Bosnia-Herzegovina*. Council of Europe Doc. no. 6999. http://assembly.coe.int/Main.asp?link = http://3A/2F/2Fassembly.coe.int/2Fdocuments/2Fworkingdocs/2Fdoc93/2Fedoc6999.htm.

Coward, M. (2002) "Community as heterogeneous ensemble: Mostar and multiculturalism," *Alternatives*, 27, 29–66.

Crook, S. (1995) "Ordering risks." In D. Lupton (ed.) *Risk and Sociocultural Theory*. Cambridge: Cambridge University Press.

Culler, J. (1986) *Saussure*, revd. edn. London: Fontana.

Curzon, G. (1999) "British and Russian commercial competition in central Asia (1859–1925)," *Asiatic Quarterly Review*, 8, July–August.

Cutter, S., Richardson, D., and Wilbanks, T. (eds.) (2003) *The Geographical Dimensions of Terrorism*. New York: Routledge.

Cushman, J. (2001) "US says bombing focuses upon Taliban defending cities," *New York Times*, November 4.

Daily Telegraph (2002) "Tanks open fire, then troops pour in," March 30.

Dalby, S. (2000). "A critical geopolitics of global governance." www.ciaonet.org/isa/das01/; accessed September 2003.

Dao, J. (2001) "Looking ahead to the Winter Olympics, a terrorist response team trains," *New York Times*, April 11, A14.

Daskalakis, G., Waldheim, C., and Tound, J. (eds.) (2001) *Stalking Detroit*. Barcelona: Actar.

Davis, M. (1990) *City of Quartz*. New York: Verso.

Davis, M. (1992). *Beyond Blade Runner: Urban Control – the Ecology of Fear*. Westfield, NJ: Open Magazine Pamphlet Series.

Davis, M. (1998) *The Ecology of Fear: Los Angeles and the Imagination of Disaster*. New York: Metropolitan Books.

Davis, M. (2001) "The flames of New York," *New Left Review*, 12, November/December.

Davis, M. (2002) *Dead Cities*. New York: New Press.

De Cauter, L. (2004) "The capsule and the network: Notes toward a general theory." In S. Graham (ed.) *The Cybercities Reader*. London: Routledge, 94–7.

Debray, R. (1967) *Revolution in the Revolution*. London: Monthly Review Press.

Debrix, F. (1999) *Re-Envisioning Peacekeeping*. Minneapolis: University of Minnesota Press.

Deleuze, G. and Guatarri, F. (1987) *A Thousand Plateaus*. Minneapolis: University of Minnesota Press.

DeMause, N. (2000) "Pepper spray gets in their eyes," *Fairness and Accuracy in Reporting*, March/April. http://www.fair.org/extra/0003/pepper-spray.html; accessed May 6, 2002.

Department of the Army (1979) *Military Operations on Urbanized Terrain. FM 90-10*. Washington, DC: US Government Printing Office.

Department of the Army (2002) *Combined Arms Operations in Urban Terrain. FM 3-06.11*. Washington, DC: http://155.217.58.58/cgi-bin/atdl.dll/fm/3-06.11/toc.htm; accessed May 12, 2002.

Der Derian, J. (1992) *Antidiplomacy: Spies, Terror, Speed, and War*. Oxford: Blackwell.

Der Derian, J. (1998) "Is the author dead? An interview with Paul Virilio." In J. der Derian (ed.) *The Virilio Reader*. Oxford: Blackwell.

Der Derian, J. (2001) *Virtuous War: Mapping the Military–Industrial–Media–Entertainment Complex*. Boulder, CO: Westview Press.

Der Derian, J. (2002) "Cyberspace as battlespace: The new virtual alliance of the military, the media and the entertainment industries." In J. Armitage and J. Roberts (eds.) *Living With Cyberspace*. London: Continuum, 61–71.

Derrida, J. (1992) "Force of Law: The 'mystical foundation of authority'." In D. Cornell, M. Rosenfeld, and D. Gray Carlson (eds.) *Deconstruction and the Possibility of Justice*. London: Routledge, 3–67.

Desch, M. C. (2001) "Why MOUT now?" In M. C. Desch (ed.), *Soldiers in Cities: Military Operations on Urban Terrain*. Carlisle, PA: Strategic Studies Institute, US Army War College, 1–15.

Diebert, R. (1997) *Parchment, Printing and Hypermedia: Communication in World Order Transformation*. New York: Columbia University Press.

Diefendorf, J. (1993) *In the Wake of War: The Reconstruction of German Cities After World War II*. Oxford: Oxford University Press.

Diken, B. and Laustsen, C. (2002) "Security, terror, and bare life," *Space and Culture*, 5 (3), 290–307.

Diken, B. and Laustsen, C. (2003) "Camping as a contemporary strategy: From refugee camps to gated communities." AMID Working Paper Series, 32, Aalborg University.

Dillon, M. (1996). *25 Years of Terror – The IRA's War Against the British*. London: Bantam Books.

Dillon, M. (2002) "Network society, network-centric warfare and the state of emergency," *Theory, Culture and Society*, 19 (4), 71–9.

Dimendberg, E. (1997) "From Berlin to Bunker Hill: Urban space, late modernity, and film noir in Fritz Lang's and Joseph Losey's *M*," *Wide Angle*, 19 (4), 62–93.

Director of Infantry (2000) "Future infantry...the route to 2020." No place, no publisher.

Do or Die (1999) Number 8 – *The Special Pre-Millennium Tension Issues*.

Donnelly, J. (2002) "US targeting of vehicles as detailed airstrikes hit some civilians on roadways," *Boston Globe*, February 19.

Doty, R. (1996) *Imperial Encounters*. Minneapolis: University of Minnesota Press.

Douglass, W. and Zulaika, J. (1998). "On terrorism discourse: Reply to Greenwood," *Current Anthropology*, 39 (2), 65–6.

Dower, J. (1993) "Japanese artists and the atomic bomb." In J. Dower, *Japan in War and Peace*. New York: New Press.

Dower, J. and Junkerman, J. (1986) *The Hiroshima Murals: The Art of Iri Muraki and Toshi Muraki*. New York: Kodansha International.

Dower, N. (2002) "Against war as a response to terrorism," *Philosophy and Geography*, 5 (1), 29–34.

Downey, J. and Murdock, G. (2003) "The counter-revolution in military affairs: The globalization of guerilla warfare." In D. Thussu and D. Freedman (eds.) *War and the Media: Reporting Conflict*. London: Sage, 70–86.

Dows, M. (2003) "A cold, clammy hand," *Guardian*, November 25, 24.

Driver, F. and Gilbert, D. (eds.) (2003) *Imperial Cities*. Manchester: Manchester University Press.

Durkheim, E. (1933) *The Division of Labour in Society*. New York: Free Press.

Dyer, G. (2003) "Reborn yesterday," *Wallpaper*, October, 227–34.

Dyer-Witheford, N. (1999) *Cyber-Marx: Cycles and Circuits of Struggle in High-Technology Capitalism*. Chicago: University of Illinois Press.

Dzirkals, L., Kellen, K., and Mendershausen, H. (1976) *Military Operations in Built-Up Areas: Essays on Some Past, Present, and Future Aspects*. Santa Monica, CA: RAND.

Easterling, K. (2002) "Enduring innocence." In M. Sorkin and S. Zukin (eds.) *After the World Trade Center*. New York: Routledge, 189–96.

Eco, U. (2003) "Give peace a chance," *Guardian Review*, February 1, 7.

Edoin, H. (1987) *The Night Tokyo Burned*. New York: St. Martin's Press.

Edwards, S. (2000) *Mars Unmasked: The Changing Face of Military Operations*. Santa Monica, CA: RAND.

Efrat, Z. (2002) *Borderline Disorder*. Tel Aviv and Jerusalem: Israeli Ministry of Education and Israeli Ministry of Foreign Affairs.

Efrat, Z. (2003) "The plan." In R. Segal and E. Weizman (eds.) *A Civilian Occupation*. Tel Aviv: Babel Press; London: Verso.

Eitam, E. (2002) "The future of land warfare." Presentation at the conference *The City in the Twenty-First Century and War*, Haifa University, February 12.

El-Affendi, A. (2003) "Orientalism is alive and well – in Iraq," *Beirut Daily Star*, October 20, 6.

Electronic Telegraph (1997) "IRA plotted hoax bomb campaign to cripple City," June 5.

Ellin, N. (ed.) (1997) *Architecture of Fear*. New York: Princeton Architectural Press.

Ellin, N. (ed.) (1999) *Postmodern Urbanism*, 2nd edn. New York: Princeton Architectural Press.

Enkoji, M. S. (2003) "Police brace for protests at ag. expo," *Sacramento Bee*, June 12.

Etkes, D. (2003) *Settlement Watch, Peace Now*. http://www.peacenow.org.il/English; accessed October 2003.

Everest, L. (2002) *Iraq and Afghanistan: Deja Vu All Over Again*. Zmag.org, no date. http://www.zmag.org/everest.htm

Fairness and Accuracy in Reporting (1999) "WTO coverage: Prattle in Seattle," December 7. http://www.globalpolicy.org/socecon/bwi-wto/media.htm; accessed August 3, 2003.

Fairness and Accuracy in Reporting (2002) "NYC newspapers smear activists ahead of WEF protests," January 28. http://www.fair.org/press-releases/pre-wef.html; accessed August 3, 2002.

Fairness and Accuracy in Reporting (2003) "Media missing new evidence about Genoa violence 10 January." http://www.fair.org/activism/genoa-update.html; accessed March 24, 2003.

Falk, R. (1999) *Predatory Globalization: A Critique*. Cambridge: Polity Press.

Falk, R. (2003) "Resisting the global domination project," *Frontline*, 20 (8), April, 12–25.

Fallows, J. (2002) "Behavior modification: soon after the Afghan war began, the Air Force dramatically altered its tactics," *Atlantic Monthly*, April.

Fargues, P. (2000) "Fertility as a political weapon in the Palestinian–Israeli conflict," *Population and Development Review*, 26 (3).

Farish, M. (2003) "Disaster and decentralization: American cities and the Cold War," *Cultural Geographies*, 10, 125–48.

Federal Civil Defense Administration (1953a) *Civil Defense Urban Analysis*, July. Washington, DC: US Government Printing Office.

Federal Civil Defense Administration (1953b) *Home Protection Exercises*. Washington, DC: US Government Printing Office.

Federal Civil Defense Administration (1957) *Battleground USA: An Operations Plan for the Civil Defense of a Metropolitan Target Area*. Washington, DC: US Government Printing Office.

FEMA (2002) Personal correspondence, January 27.

Fenton, B. and Smith, M. (2001) "US admits dropping 1,000 bomb on old people's home," *Daily Telegraph*, October 24.

Fernandez, L. (2001) "Oakland to be first US airport to use face-recognition ID system." www.siliconvalley.com/docs/hottopics/attack/image101801.htm.

Feversham, P. and Schmidt, L. (1999) *The Berlin Wall Today*. Berlin: Verlag Baumesen.

Filkins, D. (2003) "Tough new tactics by US. Tighten grip on Iraqi towns," *New York Times*, December 7. www.nytimes.com; accessed December 10, 2003.

Financial Times (2002) "Technology brings power with few constraints," *Financial Times*, February 18.

Finch, P. (1996) "The fortress city is not an option," *Architects' Journal*, February 15, 25.

Fiscal Policy Institute (2002) *Economic Impact of the September 11 World Trade Center Attack*. Preliminary report prepared for the New York City Central Labor Council and the Consortium for Worker Education.

Fischer, H. (1999) "Collateral damage." In R. Gutman and D. Rieff (eds.) *Crimes of War: What the Public Should Know*. New York: Norton. See also http://www.crimesofwar.org/thebook/collateral-damage.html.

Flusty, S. (1994) *Building Paranoia: The Proliferation of Interdictory Space and the Erosion of Spatial Justice*. Los Angeles Forum for Architecture and Urban Design, 11.

Flusty, S. (1997) "Building paranoia." In N. Ellin (ed.) *Architecture of Fear*. New York: Princeton Architectural Press, 47–60.

Ford, R. (1993) "Police resist demands for City ring of steel," *The Times*, April 27, 3.

Foster, N. (2000) "Preface." In B. Schulz (ed.) *The Reichstag*. Munich: Prestal, 9–16.

Foucault, M. (1982) "Afterword: The subject and power." In H. Dreyfus and P. Rabinow (eds.) *Michel Foucualt: Beyond Structuralism and Hermeneutics*. Brighton: Harvester Press.

Foucault, M. (1991) *The Foucault Effect: Studies in Governmentality*, ed. G. Burchell, C. Gordon, and P. Miller. Chicago, IL: University of Chicago Press.

Francis, D. (2000) "Canadians master matching mug shots," *Financial Post*, October 19, C3.

Franklin, H. (1988) *War Stars: The Superweapon and the American Imagination*. New York: Oxford University Press.

Friedmann, J. (2002) "City of fear or open city?" *American Planning Association Journal*, 68 (3), 237–44.

Friedrich, J. (2003) *Brandstätten: Der Anblick des Bombenkriegs*. Propyläen: Munich.

Fritzsche, P. (1996) *Reading Berlin 1900*. London: Harvard University Press.

Frontier Post (2001) "War sharpens suffering in Kabul." October 30.

Furedi, F. (1997) *Culture of Fear*. Washington, DC: Cassell.

G8 Summit Security (2002) "Security area outlined for Kananaskis Country, 21 May." http://www.g8summitsecurity.ca/g8/news/nr-02–02.htm; accessed May 26 2002.

Galeano, E. (2001) "The theatre of good and evil," *La Jornada* [Mexico City], September 21, 4.

Galison, P. (2001) "War against the center," *Gray Room*, summer, 6–33.

Gannon, K. (2002) "Many Pashtuns bitter about Taliban, new Afghan regime," *Associated Press*, January 12.

Garland, D. (2001) *The Culture of Control: Crime and Social Order in Contemporary Society*. Chicago, IL: University of Chicago Press.

Garner, A. (2000) "Portable civilizations and urban assault vehicles," *Techné: Journal of the Society for Philosophy and Technology*, 5 (2), 1–7.

Garvey, G. (1993) "City security boosted in war on terrorism," *Evening Standard*, April 29, 5.

Geertz, B. (2001) "Chinese firms helping put phone system in Kabul," *Washington Times*, September 28, 2001.

Gerstell, R. (1950). *How to Survive an Atomic Bomb*. New York: Bantam.

Giacaman, R. and Husseini, A. (2002) "Life and health during the Israeli invasion of the West Bank: The town of Jenin," *Indymedia Israel*. www.indymedia.org.il; accessed May 29, 2002.

Gibson J. (1986) *The Perfect War: Technowar in Vietnam*. New York: Atlantic Monthly Press.

Giddens, A. (1985a) *A Contemporary Critique of Historical Materialism, Vol. 2: The Nation-State and Capitalism.* Cambridge: Polity Press.

Giddens, A. (1985b) *The Nation-State and Violence.* Cambridge: Polity Press.

Giddens, A. (1990) *The Consequences of Modernity.* Cambridge: Polity Press.

Gideon, S. (1941) *Space, Time and Architecture.* Cambridge, MA: Harvard University Press.

Gilloch, G. (1996) *Myths and Metropolis: Walter Benjamin and the City.* Cambridge: Polity Press.

Ginbar, Y. (1997) "Demolishing peace: Israel's policy of mass demolition of Palestinian houses in the West Bank," *B'tselem Information Sheet.* http://www.btselem.org/Download/DemoPeace.rtf.

Girard, D. (2002a) "G-8 site 'a war zone' amid security fears," *Toronto Star,* June22, A1.

Girard, D. (2002b) "G-8 protest planned for a street near you," *Toronto Star,* June 25, H2.

Giroux, H. (2003) *Public Spaces, Private Lives: Democracy Beyond 9/11.* Oxford: Rowman and Littlefield.

Glaeser, E. and Shapiro, J. (2001) "Cities and warfare: The impact of terrorism on urban form," *Harvard Institute of Economic Research,* December. Also available at http://www.globest.com; accessed October 19, 2001.

Glaeser, E. and Shapiro, J. (2002) "Cities and warfare: The impact of terrorism on urban form," *Journal of Urban Economics,* 51, 205–24.

Glenn, R. (1996) *Combat in Hell: A Consideration of Constrained Urban Warfare.* Santa Monica, CA: RAND.

Glenn, R. (ed.) (2000) *The City's Many Faces.* Santa Monica, CA: RAND.

Glenn, R. (ed.) (2001) *Capital Preservation.* Santa Monica, CA: RAND

Glenn, R. (2002) "Cleanse the polluted urban seas." www.rand.org; accessed June 2003.

Glenn, R. et al. (1998) *Denying the Widow-Maker.* Santa Monica, CA: RAND.

Glenn, R. Steeb, R., and Matsumura, J. (2001) *Corralling the Trojan Horse: A Proposal for Improving US Urban Operations Preparedness in the Period 2000–2025.* Santa Monica, CA: RAND Arroyo Center.

Globest.Com (2001) "City picks developer for $700 Mil. Queens Project." www.Globest.com; accessed October 26, 2003.

Gold, J. and Revill, G. (eds.) (2000) *Landscapes of Defence.* London: Prentice-Hall.

Goldenberg, S. (2002) "Long after the raids, bomblets bring more death," *Guardian,* January 28.

Goodman, J. (1972) *After the Planners.* New York: Basic Books.

Goodman, J. (2000) "'German village' at Dugway far from WWII horrors," *Salt Lake Tribune,* June 25, 8.

Gordon, N. (2002) "The caterpillar effect," *Indymedia Israel,* June 13. Also available at www.indymedia.org.il; accessed 29 July 29, 2002.

Gourevitch, P. (1999) *Tomorrow We Wish to Inform You That We Will Be Killed With Our Families: Stories from Rwanda.* New York: Picador.

Government Security Solutions.com (2003) "A clockwork response to orange alert." http://govtsecurity.securitysolutions.com/ar/security_clockwork_response_orange/; accessed June 2003.

Graham, P. (2003) "Americans sow the seeds of hatred," *Observer*, November 9, 21.

Graham, S. (2002a) "Bombs and bulldozers: The latest Palestinian–Israeli conflict as asymmetric urbicide," *Antipode*, 34 (4), 642–9.

Graham, S. (2002b) "In a moment: On glocal mobilities and the terrorized city," *City*, 5 (3), 411–15.

Graham, S. (2002c) "Special collection: Reflections on Cities, September 11 and the 'war on terrorism' – one year on," *International Journal of Urban and Regional Research*, 26 (3), 589–90.

Graham, S. (2002d) "Urbicide on the West Bank," www.opendemocracy.net.

Graham, S. (2003) "Lessons in urbicide," *New Left Review*, 19, January/February, 63–78.

Graham, S. (2004) "Vertical geopolitics: Baghdad and after," *Antipode* 36 (1), 12–19.

Graham, S. and Marvin, S. (2001) *Splintering Urbanism: Networked Infrastructure, Technological Mobilities and the Urban Condition*. London: Routledge.

Graham, S. and Wood, D. (2003) "Digitizing surveillance: categorization, space, inequality," *Critical Social Policy*, 23 (2), 227–48.

Gravett, C. (1990) *Medieval Siege Warfare*. Oxford: Osprey.

Gray, C. (1997) *Postmodern War: The New Politics of Conflict*. London: Routedge.

Gray, J. (2001) "The terrible downside of 'working the dark side'," *Toronto Globe & Mail*, October 31.

Greater London Assembly (2000) *Scrutiny of the Mayor's Proposals for Congestion Charging – Report of Findings*. London.

Greene, T. C. (2001) "Think-tank urges face-scanning of the masses," *Register*, August 20. www.theregister.co.uk/content/6/20966.html.

Greenman, C. (2001) "In the airport fast lane with your eyes as a passport," *New York Times*, August 2.

Gregory, D. (2003) "Defiled cities," *Singapore Journal of Tropical Geography*, 24 (3), 307–26.

Gregory, D. (2004a) "Spaces of exception and the 'war on terror'." Paper available from the author at gregory@geog.ubc.ca.

Gregory, D. (2004b) *The Colonial Present*. Oxford: Blackwell.

Gregory, D. (1994c) *Geographical Imaginations*. Oxford: Blackwell.

Gregory, D. and Pred, A. (2003) Call for a conference session on "Other Terrorisms, Other Geographies," Association of American Geographers Conference, Philadelphia, February 2004. Mimeo.

Griffin, M. (2001) *Reaping the Whirlwind: The Taliban Movement in Afghanistan*. Herndon, VA: Pluto Press.

Grossman, A. (2001) *Neither Dead Nor Red: Civilian Defense and American Political Development During the Early Cold War*. New York: Routledge.

Grossman, L. (2002) "Beyond the rubber bullet," *Time*, July 21. http://www.time.com/time/nation/printout/0,8816,322588,00.html; accessed September 21, 2003.

Guardian (2002) "How the press saw the resumption of Israeli raids," Saturday, October 12, 6.

Guardian Unlimited (2001) "Italian police admit excess," August 8. http://www.guardian.co.uk/Archive/Article/0,4273,4236019,00.html; accessed April 23, 2002.

Guardian Unlimited (2002) "The EU Barcelona summit," March 15. http://www.Guardian.co.uk/theissues/article/0,6512,667862,00.html; accessed August 8, 2003.

Habegger, L. and O'Reilly, J. (2002) "Tight security at Alberta summit," *Cleveland Plain Dealer*, June 23, K2.

Hage, G. (2003) " 'Comes a time we are enthusiasm'': Understanding Palestinian suicide bombers in times of Exigophobia," *Public Culture*, 15 (1), 65–89.

Haggerty, K. and Ericson, R. (2000) "The surveillant assemblage," *British Journal of Sociology*, 51 (4), 605–22.

Haggerty, K. and Ericson, R. (2001) "The militarization of policing in an information age," *Journal of Political and Military Sociology*, 27, 233–55.

Halberstam, D. (2001) *War in a Time of Peace: Bush, Clinton, and the Generals*. New York: Scribner.

Halevi, J. and Varoufakis, Y. (2003) "The global minotaur," *Monthy Review*, July–August, 57–75.

Hall, P. (1988) *Cities of Tomorrow*. Oxford: Blackwell.

Hall, R. (2003) "A note on September eleventh: The Arabization of terrorism," *Social Science Journal*, 40, 459–64.

Halper, J. (2001) *The Matrix of Control*. Available at http://www.icahd.org/eng/ ; accessed October 2003.

Hambling, D. (2003) "Electric shock weapons could go wireless," *NewScientist.com*, May 21. http://www.newscientist.com/news/print.jsp?id = ns99993749; accessed May 21, 2003.

Hammond, A. (1984) "Rescripting the nuclear threat in 1953: *The Beast from 20,000 Fathoms*," *Northwest Review*, 22 (1/2), 181–94.

Hamzah, M. and May, T. (eds.) (2003) *Operation Defensive Shield: Witnesses to Israeli War Crimes*. London: Pluto Press.

Hanley, C. (2002a) "A generation of war leaves many Afghans with mental disorders," *Associated Press*, May 5.

Hanley, C. (2002b) "Unseen battle scars: millions of Afghans suffering mentally," *Associated Press*, May 15.

Harding, L. and McCarthy, R. (2001) "War-weary Afghans flee in fear," *Observer*, September 16.

Hardt, M. and Negri, A. (2000) *Empire*. Cambridge, MA: Harvard University Press.

Harel, A. (2000) "This time, the chief of staff keeps his lips sealed," *Ha'aretz*, December 28, 3.

Harris, J. (2003) "Dreams of global hegemony and the technology of war," *Race and Class*, 45 (2), 54–67.

Hart, J. (2004) Untitled. *Adbusters*, 51, January/February, 16.

Harvey, D. (1989) *The Condition of Postmodernity*. Oxford: Blackwell.

Harvey, D. (2003a) *The New Imperialism*. Oxford: Oxford University Press.

Harvey, D. (2003b) "The city as a body politic." In J. Schneider and I. Susser (eds.) *Wounded Cities: Destruction and Reconstruction in a Globalized World.* London: Berg, 25–46.

Harwit, M. (1996) *An Exhibit Denied: Lobbying the History of Enola Gay.* New York: Copernicus.

Hasen, O. (2002) "Dear god, this is Effi," *Ha'aretz*, April 24, 6.

Hass, A. (2002) "What kind of war is this?" *Ha'aretz*, April 24, 3.

Hass, A. and Harel, A. (2001) "IDF digs trench to keep 65,000 villagers out of Ramallah," *Ha'aretz*, March 8.

Hatton, B. (1999) "Berlin 1999: Phantoms and formulae." In R. Moore (ed.) *Vertigo: The Strange New World of the Contemporary City.* London: Laurence King, 74–89.

Hayden, R. (1996) "Imagined communities and real victims: Self-determination and ethnic-cleansing in Yugoslavia," *American Ethnologist*, 23 (4), 783–801.

Hecht, J. (2001) "Microwave beam weapon to disperse crowds," *NewScientist.com*, October 29. http://www.newscientist.com/news/print.jsp?id = ns99991470; accessed July 12, 2003.

Hendren, J. (2002) "Afghanistan yields lessons for Pentagon's next targets," *Associated Press*, January 21.

Herman, E. S. (2002) " 'Tragic errors' in US military policy," *Z Magazine* 19 (9): 27–32.

Herman, E. S. and Peterson, D. (2002) "The threat of global state terrorism: Retail vs. wholesale terror," *Z Magazine*, January.

Herod, A., Ó Tuathail, G., and Roberts, S. (eds.) (1998) *Unruly World? Globalization, Governance, and Geography.* London: Routledge.

Herold, M. (2002a) *The US Bombing of Afghan Mosques*, April 1. http://www.cursor.org/stories/helltopray.htm.

Herold, M. (2002b) "Appendix 5. The spatial distribution of Afghan civilian casualties caused by the US air war." In M. W. Herold (ed.) *A Dossier on Civilian Victims of United States' Aerial Bombing of Afghanistan: A Comprehensive Accounting*, March. http://www.cursor.org/stories/civilian_deaths.htm.

Herold, M. (2002c) *Above the Law and Below Morality: Data on 11 Weeks of US Cluster-Bombing of Afghanistan*, February 1. http://www.cursor.org/stories/above-thelaw.htm.

Herold, M. (2003a) "A 'killing failure': 25 months of immiserating revenge – an Afghan balance sheet." http://traprockpeace.org/chicago_talk3_9nov03.pdf

Herold, M. (2003b) *Blown Away: Myth and Reality of Precision Bombing in Afghanistan.* Monroe, ME: Common Courage Press.

Heschmeyer, M. (2001) "Attack magnified existing New York City office trends." www.costargroup.com; accessed October 16, 2001.

Hewitt, K. (1983) "Place annihilation: Area bombing and the fate of urban places," *Annals of the Association of American Geographers*, 73 (2), 257–84.

Hewitt, K. (1987) "The social space of terror: Towards a civil interpretation of total war," *Environment and Planning D: Society and Space*, 5, 445–74.

Hewitt, K. (2003) "The security syndrome: Vulnerable citizens, 'first responders' and the terror connection." Mimeo.

Higgins, A. G. (2003) "France to get glory of hosting G8 summit," *FindLaw*, May 24. http://news.findlaw.com/scripts/printer_friendly.pl?page = /ap_stories/i/1103/5-24-2003/20030524134501_5.html; accessed June 3, 2003.

Higgs, E. (2001) "The rise of the information state: The development of central state surveillance of the citizen in England 1500–2000," *Journal of Historical Sociology*, 14 (2), 175–97.

Hillier, T. (1994) "Bomb attacks in city centers." http://www.emergency.com/carbomb.htm; accessed April 31, 2000.

Hirschkop, K. (1997) "Fear and democracy: An essay on Bakhtin's theory of carnival," *Associations*, 1, 209–34.

Hobsbawm, E. (2002) *Interesting Times: A Twentieth Century Life*. London: Abacus.

Hogan, M. (ed.) (1996) *Hiroshima in History and Memory*. Cambridge: Cambridge University Press.

Holland, C. (n.d.) *Chapter 10. Destruction of the Yugoslav Media*. http://www.iacenter.org/warcrime/10_media.htm.

Hoogvelt, A. (1997) *Globalization and the Postcolonial World*. Basingstoke: Macmillan.

Hookway, B. (ed.) (1999) *Pandemonium: The Rise of Predatory Locales in the Postwar World*. New York: Princeton Architectural Press.

Hooper, B. (2000) "Bodies, cities, texts: The case of citizen Rodney King." In E. Soja (ed.) *Postmetropolis: Critical Studies of Cities and Regions*. Oxford: Blackwell, 359–71.

Horowitz, M. and Reiter, D. (2001) "When does aerial bombing work? Quantitative tests, 1917–1999," *Journal of Conflict Resolution*, 45, April 2.

Howell, S. and Shryock, A. (2003) "Cracking down on diaspora. Arab Detroit and America's 'War on Terror'," *Project Muse*. http://muse.jhu.edu.

HR 3162 (2001) *Uniting and Strengthening America by Providing Appropriate Tools Required to Intercept and Obstruct Terrorism* (United States Patriot Act).

Hrasnica, M. (1993) "You can destroy our city, but never our soul." www.dosnet.org/bosnia/literature/books/urbicide/destroy.html; accessed November 2003.

Huber, P. and Mills M. (2002) "How technology will defeat terrorism," *City Journal*, 12 (1), 24–34.

Hugler, J. (2003) "Israelis trained US troops in Jenin-style urban warfare," *Independent*, March 29, 1.

Human Rights Watch (2002a) *Erased in a Moment: Suicide Bombing Attacks Against Israeli Civilians*. http://www.hrw.org; accessed October 2003.

Human Rights Watch (2002b) "Israel, the occupied West Bank and Gaza Strip, and the Palestinian Authority territories; Jenin IDF military operations," May, Vol. 14, No. 3.

Human Rights Watch (2003) *Hearts and Minds: Post-War Civilian Deaths in Baghdad Caused by US Forces*. Human Rights Watch: Washington. Also available at http://www.hrw.org/reports/2003/iraq1003/; accessed November 2003.

Humphrey, C. (2003) "Rethinking infrastructure: Siberian cities and the great freeze of January 2001." In J. Schneider and I. Susser (eds.) *Wounded Cities: Destruction and Reconstruction in a Globalized World*. London: Berg, 91–110.

Huntington, S. (1968) "The bases of accommodation," *Foreign Affairs*, 46, July.

Huntingdon, S. (1993) *The Clash of Civilizations and the Remaking of World Order*. New York: Simon and Schuster.

Huntington, S. (1998) *The Clash of Civilizations and the Remaking of World Order*, new edn. New York: Simon and Schuster.

Hyndman, J. (2003) "Beyond either/or: A feminist analysis of September 11th," *ACME: An International E-Journal for Critical Geographies*. www.acme-journal.org; accessed October 2003.

Ignatieff, M. (2003) *Empire Lite*. New York: Minerva.

Iklé, F. (1958) *The Social Impact of Bomb Destruction*. Norman: University of Oklahoma Press.

Iklé, F. C (1999) "Defending the US homeland: Strategic and legal issues for DOD and the Armed Services." Washington, DC: Center for Strategic and International Studies.

Independent Catholic News (2003) "Archbishop Vincent Nichols on world debt day," May 16. http://www.indcatholicnews.com/videbt.html; accessed July 17, 2003.

International Crisis Group (1997) "House burnings: Obstruction of the right to return to Drvar," *ICG Bosnia Report No. 24*. London: ICG.

Jackson, K. (1985) *Crabgrass Frontier: The Suburbanization of the United States*. New York: Oxford University Press.

Jameson, F (1984), "Postmodernism or the cultural logic of late capitalism," *New Left Review*, 146.

Jameson, F. (1992) *Postmodernism, or the Cultural Logic of Late Capitalism*. Durham, NC: Duke University Press.

Janis, I. (1951) *Air War and Emotional Stress: Psychological Studies of Bombing and Civilian Defense*. New York: McGraw-Hill.

Jansen, M. (2001) "The bulldozer baron," *Al-Ahram Weekly On-Line*, February 8–14, 2001. www.ahram.org.eg/weekly; accessed May 15, 2002.

Japan National Broadcasting Corporation (ed.) (1981) *Unforgettable Fire: Pictures Drawn by Atomic Bomb Survivors*. New York: Pantheon.

Jarman, N. (1993) "Intersecting Belfast." In B. Bender (ed.) *Landscape: Politics and Perspectives*. Oxford: Berg, 107–38.

Jayasuriya, K. (2002) "September 11, security, fear and the new postliberal politics of fear." In E. Hershberg and K. Moore (eds.) *Critical Views of September 11: Analyses From Around the World*. New York: New Press, 131–50.

Jenkins, H. (2003) "A war of words over Iraqi video games," *Guardian*, November 13, 18.

Jenkins, S. (2001) "Bombs that turn leaders into butchers," *The Times*, January 17.

Jenkins, S. (2002) "The Bali bombing must kill off war with Iraq," *The Times*, October 16.

Johnson, C. (1999) "In search of a new Cold War," *Bulletin of the Atomic Scientists*, 55 (5), 44–51.

Johnson, J. K. (2003) "Guest editorial," *306090: The Journal of Emergent Architecture*, 4 (3), 7.

Joint Staff (2002) "Joint Publication (JP) 3-06: *Doctrine for Joint Urban Operations*." Washington, DC.

Joseph, A. and Sharma, K. (2003) *Terror and Counter-terror: Women Speak Out.* London: Zed Books.

Kaldor, M. (1999) *New and Old Wars: Organized Violence in a Global Era.* Cambridge: Cambridge University Press.

Kaplan, A. (2003) "Homeland insecurities: Reflections on language and space," *Radical History Review*, 85, 82–93.

Kaplan, F. (1999) "Bombs killing more civilians than expected," *Boston Globe*, May 30.

Kaplan, R. (1996) *The Ends of the Earth: A Journey at the Dawn of the Twenty-First Century.* New York: Random House.

Karkouti, M. (2002) "Comment: Israel pulls the wool over world's eyes," *GulfNews Online*, June 11. www.gulf-news.com; accessed October 29, 2002.

Karp, D., Stone, G., and Yoels, W. (1991) *Being Urban: A Sociology of City Life*, 2nd edn. London: Praeger.

Katz, C. (2004) "Banal terrorism." Paper available from the author ckatz@gc.cuny.edu

Kelly, O. (1994) "By all means necessary," *Police Review*, April 15, 14–16.

Kemp, A. (2000) "Border space and national identity in Israel." In Y. Shenhav (ed.) *Theory and Criticism: Space, Land, Home.* Jerusalem and Tel Aviv: Van Leer Jerusalem Institute and Hakibbutz Hameuchad Publishing House (Hebrew).

Kendig, T. (2001) "Non-lethal weapons testing proves very inaccurate," *Penn State Inter-Com*, May 24. http://www.psu.edu/ut/archieves/intercom_2001/May24/weapons.html; accessed September 7, 2003.

Kenna, K. (2001) "Rebuilding a country," *Toronto Star*, December 22.

Kennedy, P. (1992) *Preparing for the Twenty-First Century.* New York: Random House.

Keohane, R. (2002) *Institutions, Law and Governance in a Partially Globalized World.* London: Routledge.

Kern, P. (1990) *Ancient Siege Warfare.* Bloomington: Indiana University Press.

Kerr, E. (1991) *Flames Over Tokyo: The US Army Air Forces' Incendiary Campaign Against Japan 1944–1945.* New York: Donald I. Fine.

Kiernan, B. (1996) *The Pol Pot Regime: Race, Power and Genocide in Cambodia Under the Khmer Rouge, 1975–79.* Cambridge, MA: Yale University Press.

Kimmerling, B. (2003) *Politicide: Ariel Sharon's War Against the Palestinians.* London: Verso.

Kitfield, J. (1998) "War in the urban jungles," *Air Force Magazine*, 81(12), 1–8.

Klaidman, D., Hosenball, M., Isikoff, M., and Thomas, E. (2002) "Al-Qaeda in America: The enemy within," *Newsweek*, June 23, 4–8.

Klein, N. (2002) *Fences and Windows.* New York: Picador.

Klein, N. (2003) "Iraq is not America's to sell," *Guardian*, November 7, 27.

Kleveman, L. (2003) "The new Great Game," *Guardian*, October 20, 17.

Koch, A. (2003) "When this war is over, the battleplan inquest will begin," *Jane's Defence Weekly*, April 9, 6.

Konstantin, H. and Hornig, F. (2001) "Die echtzeit-katastrophe," *Der Spiegel*, September 15, 126.

Konvitz, J. (1990) "Why cities don't die," *American Heritage of Invention and Technology*, winter, 58–63.

Kostof, S. (1992) *The City Assembled: The Elements of Urban Form Through History*. London: Thames and Hudson.

Kraska, P. (2001) *Militarizing the American Criminal Justice System: The Changing Roles of the Armed Forces and the Police*. Boston, MA: Northeastern University Press.

Kundera, M. (1980) *The Book of Laughter and Forgetting*. Harmondsworth: Penguin Books.

Kuper, A. (1981) *Genocide*. Harmondsworth: Penguin Books.

Kusno, A. (2000) *Behind the Postcolonial: Architecture, Urban Space, and Political Architectures in Indonesia*. London: Routledge.

Ladd, B. (1998) *The Ghosts of Berlin: Confronting German History in the Urban Landscape*. Chicago: University of Chicago Press.

Laguerre, M. (2003) *Urban Multiculturalism and Globalization in New York City*. London: Palgrave Macmillan.

Lakshamann, I. (2002) "Afghans call for compensation for US strikes," *Boston Globe*, April 2.

Lamb, C. (2001) "After the bombs, tales of horror and misery," *The Age*, October 22.

Lang, P. (ed.) (1996) *Mortal City*. New York: Princeton Architectural Press.

Lapp, R. (1948) "Atomic bomb explosions – Effects on an American city," *Bulletin of the Atomic* Scientists, 4 (2), 49–54.

Le Corbusier (1933) *Aircraft*. Milan: Abitaire Segesta.

Le Corbusier (1935) *La Ville radieuse, elements d'une doctrine d'urbanisme pour l'equipement de la civilization machiniste*. Boulogne: Editions De L'Architecture D'Aujourd'Hui.

LeBillon, P. (2001) "The political ecology of war: Natural resources and armed conflicts," *Political Geography*, 20, 561–84.

Lefebvre, H. (1991) *The Production of Space*. Oxford: Blackwell.

Legault, R. (2000) "The urban battlefield and the army: Challenges and doc-trines," *Canadian Military Journal*, 1. http://www.journal.dnd.ca/vol1/no3_e/history_e/hist1_e.html; accessed 20 February 2002.

Lehmann, M. (2003) "War clouds darken Oscars: Security tights as Academy tones down the glitz," *New York Post*, March 24, 21.

Lein, Y. (2003) *Behind the Barrier*. Jerusalem: B'tselem. Also available at http://www.btselem.org/Download/2003_Behind_The_Barrier_Eng.doc; accessed October 2003.

Lein, Y. and Weizman, E. (2002) *Land Grab*. Jerusalem: B'tselem. Also available at http://www.btselem.org/English/Publications/Summaries/Land_Grab_Map.asp; accessed October 2003.

Leiser, K. (2002) "Security challenges range from pickpockets to terrorists; pro-spective protesters criticize restrictions," *St. Louis Post-Dispatch*, February 5, A1.

Lemkin, R. (1944) *Axis Rule in Occupied Europe: Laws of Occupation; Analysis of Government; Proposals for Redress*. Washington, DC: Carnegie Endowment for International Peace, Division of International Law.

Leonard, J. (2002) " 'Nonlethal' beanbags can sometimes kill, police say." latimes. com 3 June, http://www.latimes.com/news/local/la-060302nonlethal.story?null; accessed 3 June 3, 2002.

Lessig, L. (1999) *Code and Other Laws of Cyberspace*. New York: Basic Books.

Lianos, M. and Douglas, M. (2000) "Dangerization and the end of deviance: The institutional environment," *British Journal of Criminology*, 40, 261–78.

Lifton, R. and Mitchell, G. (1995) *Hiroshima in America: Fifty Years of Denial*. New York: G. P. Putnam and Sons.

Light, J. (2002) "Urban security: From warfare to welfare," *International Journal of Urban and Regional Research*, 26 (3), 561–84.

Lilenthal, E. and Engelhardt, T. (eds.) (1996) *History Wars: The Enola Gay and Other Battles for the American Past*. New York: Henry Hold.

Lindee, S. (1994) *Suffering Made Real: American Science and the Survivors at Hiroshima*. Chicago, IL: University of Chicago Press.

Lindqvist, S. (2001) *A History of Bombing*. New York: New Press.

Lipton, K. (1977) *Why Poor People Stay Poor: Urban Bias in World Development*. Cambridge, MA: Harvard University Press.

Littauer, R. and Uphoff, N. (eds.) (1972) *The Air War in Indochina*. Boston, MA: Beacon Press.

Loeb, V. (2003) "National defense with Vernon Loeb and Dana Priest," *Washington Post Live Online*, March 21.

Lomnitz, C. (2003) "The depreciation of life during Mexico City's transition into the 'crisis'." In J. Schneider and I. Susser (eds.) *Wounded Cities: Destruction and Reconstruction in a Globalized World*. London: Berg, 47–70.

Lopez, G. (1991) "The Gulf War: Not so clean," *Bulletin of Atomic Scientists*, 47, September 7.

Lopez, G. (2002) "Iraq and just-war thinking: The presumption against the use of force," *Commonweal*, September 27.

Lowe, C. (2002) "US, Israeli armed forces trade urban-warfare tips," *ArmyTimes. Com*, May 31. www.armytimes.com; accessed October 29, 2002.

Luckham, R. (1984) "Of arms and culture," *Current Research on Peace and Violence*, 7 (1), 1–64.

Luke, T. (1993) "Discourses of disintegration, texts of transformation: Rereading realism in the new world order," *Alternatives*, 18, 229–58.

Luke, T. (1996) "Governmentality and contra-governmentality: Rethinking sovereignty and territoriality after the Cold War," *Political Geography*, 15 (6/7), 491–507.

Luke, T. (1999) *Capitalism, Democracy, and Ecology: Departing from Marx*. Urbana: University of Illinois Press.

Luke, T. and Ó Tuathail, G. (1997) "On videocameralistics: The geopolitics of failed states, the CNN International, and (UN) governmentality," *Review of International Political Economy*, 4: 709–33.

Lummis, D. (1994) "Times to watch the watchers," *Nation*, September 26, 302–4.

Lütticken, S. (2001) "Park life," *New Left Review*, July–August, 111–18.

Lyman, R. (2002) "Security-prone Oscar ceremony a blight on business," *New York Times*, March 23, A10.

Lyon, D. (1991) "British identity cards: The unpalatable logic of European membership?" *Political Quarterly*, 62 (3), 377–85.

Lyon, D. (1994) *The Electronic Eye: The Rise of Surveillance Society*. Cambridge: Polity Press.

Lyon, D. (2001a) "Fundamentalisms: paradoxical products of postmodernity." In C. Partridge (ed.) *Fundamentalisms*. Carlisle: Paternoster Press.

Lyon, D. (2001b) "Surveillance after September 11," *Sociological Research Online*, 6 (3). www.socresonline.org.uk/6/3/lyon.

Lyon, D. (2001c) *Surveillance Society: Monitoring Everyday Life*. Buckingham: Open University Press.

Lyon, D. (2002a) "Everyday surveillance: Personal data and social classification," *Information, Communication, and Society*, 5 (1), 1–17.

Lyon, D. (2002b) "Security and surveillance at airports since September 11," unpublished paper, The Surveillance Project, Queen's University.

Lyon, D. (ed.) (2002c) *Surveillance as Social Sorting: Privacy, Risk, and Digital Discrimination*. New York: Routledge.

Lyon, D. (2003) *Surveillance after September 11*. Cambridge: Polity Press.

Lyotard, J.-F. (1984) *The Postmodern Condition: A Report on Knowledge*. Minneapolis: University of Minnesota Press.

MacAskill, E. (2003) "Jihad has worked: The world is split in two," *Guardian*, December 8, 18.

McCahill, M. (2002) *The Surveillance Web: The Rise of Visual Surveillance in an English City*. Cullompton: Willan Publishing.

McCamley, N. (1998) *Secret Underground Cities*. Barnsley: Leo Cooper.

MacCannell, D. (1984) "Baltimore in the morning . . . after: On the forms of post-nuclear leadership," *Diacritics*, 14 (2), 33–46.

McCulloch, J. (2003) " 'Counter terrorism,' human security and globalization: From welfare to warfare state?" Conference paper, " 'Tough on Crime' . . . Tough on Freedoms? From Community to Global Interventions." Center for Studies in Crime and Social Justice, Chester, April 22–4.

McEnaney, L. (2000) *Civil Defense Begins at Home: Militarization Meets Everyday Life in the Fifties*. Princeton, NJ: Princeton University Press.

McGreal, C. (2002) "Israeli retaliation targets olive harvest and waterholes," *Guardian*, October 23, 15.

McGreal, C. (2003) "Army chief warns Sharon: We are on the verge of catastrophe, *Guardian*, October 31, 1.

McGregor, D. (2003) "The new enemy within," *The Times*, December 6, 3.

McInnes, C. (2002) *Spectator-Sport War: The West and Contemporary Conflict*. Boulder, CO: Lynne Rienner.

MacKenzie, D. (2002) "US non-lethal weapon reports suppressed," *NewScientist. com*, May 9, http://www.newscientist.com/news/print.jsp?id = ns44442254; accessed July 12, 2003.

Maher, K. (2002) "Back with a bang," *Observer*, June 30, www.guardian.co.yj; accessed September 2003.

Makhmalbaf, M. (2001) "Limbs of no body: Indifference to the Afghan tragedy," *Monthly Review*, November.

Makler, I. (2001) "Guided tour: Bombed ruins of Al-Qaeda's main military base," *VOA News*, December 3.

Mann, M. (1988) *States, War and Capitalism.* Oxford: Blackwell.

Mann, M. (2004) *Murderous Ethnic Cleansing.* Cambridge: Cambridge University Press.

Mansour, C. (2001) "Israel's colonial impasse," *Journal of Palestinian Studies*, 30 (4), 83–7.

Marcuse, P. (1998) "Reflections on Berlin: The meaning of construction and the construction of meaning," *International Journal of Urban and Regional Research*, 22 (2), 331–8.

Marcuse, P. (2002a) "Afterword. " In P. Marcuse and R. van Kempton (2002) *Of States and Cities: The Partitioning of Urban Space.* Oxford: Oxford University Press, 69–82.

Marcuse, P. (2002b) "Urban form and globalization after September 11th: The View from New York," *International Journal of Urban and Regional Research*, Vol. 26 (3), 596–606.

Markou, E. (2002) "Militariers et urbanistes durant les années trente," *Les Annales de la Recherche Urbaine*, 91, 18–27.

Markusen, N. and Kopf, D. (1985) *The Holocaust and Strategic Bombing: Genocide and Total War in the Twentieth Century.* Boulder, CO: Westview Press.

Markusen, A., Hall, P., Campbell, S., and Deitrick, S. (1991) *The Rise of the Gunbelt: Military Remapping of Industrial America.* Oxford: Oxford University Press.

Marsden, C. (2003) "US army bulldozes Iraqi farms," *World Socialist Web Site*, www.wsws.org; accessed December 10, 2003.

Martin, H. and Schumann, H. (1998) *The Global Trap: Globalization and the Assault on Democracy and Prosperity.* London: Zed Books.

Marx, G. T. (1998) "DNA 'fingerprints' may one day be our national ID card," *Wall Street Journal*, April 20.

Mateen, A. (2001) "US targets 23 training camps in Afghanistan," *The News-Jang*, October 4.

Mathieson, S. A. (2001) "The net's eyes are watching," *Guardian*, November 15. Also available at www.guardian.co.uk/0,3858,4298,894,00.html.

Mayhew, J. (2001) *Address on Management.* Presentation at Cambridge University, November 15.

Mbembe, A. (2003) "Necropolitics," *Public Culture*, 15 (1), 11–40.

Mechling, E. and Mechling, J. (1994) "The campaign for civil defense and the struggle to naturalize the bomb." In W. Nothstine, C. Blair, and G. Copeland (eds.) *Critical Questions: Invention, Creativity, and the Criticism of Discourse and Media.* New York: St. Martin's Press, 125–54.

Medact (2003) *Continuing Collateral Damage: The Health and Environmental Costs of War on Iraq 2003.* London. Available at www.medact.org; accessed November 2003.

Meek, J. (2002) "Robo-Co," *Guardian Online*, June 30.

Meek, J. (2003) "People the law forgot," *Guardian*, 2, 2–17.

Mendieta, E. (2001) "The space of terror, the utopian city: On the attack on the World Trade Center," *City*, 5 (3), 397–406.

Mepham, D. (2002) "Tackling the root causes of terrorism," *New Economy*, 9 (4), 16–24.

Merari, A. (1993) "Terrorism as a strategy of insurgency," *Terrorism and Political Violence*, 5 (4), 213–51.

Miladi, N. (2003) "Mapping the Al-Jazeera phenomenon." In D. Thussu and D. Freedman (eds.) *War and the Media*. London: Sage, 149–60.

Millar, S. (2001) "Police get sweeping access to net data," *Guardian*, November 7. Also available at www.guardian.co.uk/0,3058,4293489,00.html.

Miller, J. N. (2001) "Concluding remarks." In R. Glenn (ed.) *Capital Preservation*. Santa Monica, CA: RAND, 575–97.

Mills, C. W. (1959) *The Sociological Imagination*, 1st edn. Oxford: Oxford University Press.

Mills, C. W. (1967) *The Sociological Imagination*, 2nd edn. New York: Oxford University Press.

Ministry of Agriculture and the Settlement Division of the World Zionist Organization (1983) *Masterplan for Jewish Settlements in the West Bank through the Year 2010*. Jerusalem.

Ministry of Agriculture and the Settlement Division of the World Zionist Organization (1983) *Masterplan for Settlement for Judea and Samaria, Development Plan for the Region for 1983–1986*. Jerusalem.

Ministry of Defence (2003) *Operations in Iraq: First Reflections*. London: Ministry of Defence.

Misselwitz, P. and Weizman, E. (2003) "Military operations as urban planning." In A. Franke (ed.) *Territories*. Berlin: KW Institute for Contemporary Art, 272–85.

Mitchell, D. (1948) "Social aspects of decentralization," *Mechanical Engineering*, 70, 532–4.

Molotch, H. and McClain, N. (2003) "Dealing with urban terror: Heritages of control, varieties of intervention, strategies of research," *International Journal of Urban and Regional Research*, 27 (3), 679–98.

Monbiot, G. (2003) "Bottom of the barrel," *Guardian*, December 2, 25.

Monchuk, J. and Graveland, B. (2002) "Calgary isn't laying out the welcome mat for the G8: An hour's drive from the remote summit site, police are battening down the hatches in the city where the protesters are expected to converge," *Ottawa Citizen*, June 23, A5.

Monninger, M. (1991) "Growing together again." In V. M. Lampugnani (ed.) *Berlin Tomorrow: International Architectural Visions*. London: Architectural Design, 17–19.

Monson, D. and Monson, A. (1950, 1951) "How can we disperse our large cities?" *American City*, 65 (12) (1950), 90–2; 66 (1) (1951), 107–11.

Moorehouse, S. (2002) "Interview on *Morning Edition*," *NPR Radio*, January 30.

Morales, F. (2001) "Welcome to the free world," *Covert Action*, 70, 6–13.

Moskos, C., Williams, J., and Segal, D. (eds.) (2000) *The Postmodern Military: Armed Forces after the Cold War*. New York: Oxford University Press.

Mostar '92 – Urbicid (1992) Mostar: Hravatsko vijece obrane opcine Mostar.

"Mostar '92 – Urbicid" (1993) [extracts from *Mostar '92 – Urbicid*, 1992] *Spazio e Società/Space and Society*, 16 (62), 8–25.

Muhs, A. and Wefing, H. (1998) *Der Neue Potsdamer Platz*. Berlin: Verlag.

Muir, H. (2003) "Mosques launch protests over 'terror' arrests," *Guardian*, December 13, 7.

Mullings, L. (2003) "After the drugs and the 'war on drugs': Reclaiming the power to make history in Harlem, New York." In J. Schneider and I. Susser (eds.) *Wounded Cities: Destruction and Reconstruction in a Globalized World*. London: Berg, 173–202.

Mullins, J. (2002) "Moscow drama spurs hunt for 'non-lethals'." *New Scientist*, 21/28.

Mumford, L. (1961) *The City in History: Its Origins, Its Transformations, and Its Prospects*. New York: Harcourt, Brace and World.

Muschamp, H. (1995) "Things generally wrong in the universe." In P. Lang (ed.) *Mortal City*. New York: Princeton Architectural Press, 102–7.

Myre, G. (2003a) "Israeli helicopters attack and kill a Hamas leader in Gaza," *New York Times*, May 9, A5.

Myre, G. (2003b) "Israeli assault on Hamas leaves 7 more dead," *New York Times*, June 13, A1.

Nachtwey, J. (2002) "The battle of Jenin," *Israel IndyMedia Center*, May 8. Available at http://www.indymedia.org.il; accessed June 24, 2002.

Nash, E. (2002) "Spain's fighters and warships protect EU summit," *Independent. co.uk*, March 26. http://www.independent.co.uk/story.jsp?story = 274171; accessed March 26, 2002.

National Institute of Standards and Technology (USA) (2003) *Face Recognition Vendor Test 2002*. Evaluation Report. Washington, DC.

National Public Radio (2001) "All things considered," September 12 or 19.

NATO (1999) "Press conference by NATO spokesman Jamie Shea and Air Commodore David Wilby, SHAPE, NATO HQ, 6 April." http://www.nato.int/kosovo/press/p990406a.htm.

Naumann, M. (2003) "War in the ruins of law." OpenDemocracy.Net/themes/articles-3–1125.jsp; accessed September 2003.

Negri, A. (ed.) (2002) *On Fire: The Battle of Genoa and the Anti-Capitalist Movement*. London: AK Press.

New Internationalist (2002a) "Effi Eitam," June, 29.

New Internationalist (2002b) "War on terror – or on human rights ?" 346, 6–10.

Newman, R. (2003) "The joystick war," *US News*, May 19. www.usnews.com; accessed June 2003.

News (2003) October 30. http://www.nydailynews.com/2001-10-30/News_and_Views/City_Beat/a-130299.asp; accessed October 5, 2003.

Nijman, J. (2001) "New York City and the geopolitical transition," *Arab World Geographer*. http://users.fmg.uva.nl/vmamadouh/awg/forum2/nijman.html; accessed November 2003.

Nobile, P. (ed.) (1995) *Judgement at the Smithsonian*. New York: Marlowe.

Norris, C. and Armstrong, G. (1999). *The Maximum Surveillance Society: The Rise of CCTV*. Oxford: Berg.

Norris, C., Moran, J., and Armstrong, G. (1998) "Algorithmic surveillance: The future of automated visual surveillance." In C. Norris and G. Armstrong (eds.) *Surveillance, Closed Circuit Television, and Social Control*. Aldershot: Ashgate.

Notes from Nowhere (ed.) (2003) *We Are Everywhere: The Irresistible Rise of Global Anti-Capitalism*. NewYork: Verso.

Nunn, S. (2001) "Cities, space and the new world of law enforcement technologies," *Journal of Urban Affairs*, 23 (3/4), 259–78.

Ó Tuathail, G. (1999) *Critical Geopolitics*. Minneapolis: University of Minnesota Press.

Ó Tuathail, G. and Dalby, S. (1998) *Rethinking Geopolitics*. London: Routledge.

O'Hagan, S. (2004) "Recruitment hard drive," *Guardian Guide*, June 19–25, 12–13.

O'Harrow, R. (2001) "Matching faces with mug shots," *Washington Post*, August 1, A01.

Oakes, G. (1994). *The Imaginary War: Civil Defense and American Cold War Culture*. New York: Oxford University Press.

Oakley, R. (2001) "The urban area during support missions case study: Mogadishu." In R. Glenn (ed.) *Capital Preservation*. Santa Monica, CA: RAND, 309–54.

Ockman, J. (ed.) (2002) *Out of Ground Zero: Case Studies in Urban Reinvention*. New York: Prestel.

Office of the High Representative (1998) *RRTF Report March 1998: An Action Plan in Support of the Return of Refugees and Displaced Persons in Bosnia and Herzegovina*. http://www.ohr.int/ohr-dept/rrtf/key-docs/reports/default.asp?content_id = 5612.

Office of Public Affairs, 509th Bomb Wing, United States Air Force (1999) "Fact sheet: History of the 509th Bomb Wing." http://www.whiteman.af.mil/news/509BWhistory.htm.

O'Hanlon, M. (2002) "A flawed masterpiece," *Foreign Affairs*, 81, 3, May–June.

Olalquiaga, C. (1995) "Paradise lost." In S. Allen (ed.) *Sites and Stations: Provisional Utopias*. New York: Lusitiania, 43–50.

Opel, A. and Pompper, D. (eds.) (2003) *Representing Resistance: Media, Civil Disobedience, and the Global Justice Movement*. Westport, CT: Greenwood Press.

Orentlicher, D . (1999) "Genocide." In R. Gutman and D. Rieff (eds.) *Crimes of War: What the Public Should Know*. New York: Norton. See also http://www.crimesofwar.org/thebook/genocide.html.

Orin, D. (2001) *New York Post*, August 31.

Osborne, T. and Rose, N. (1999) "Governing cities: Notes on the spatialization of virtue," *Environment and Planning D: Society and Space*, 17, 737–60.

Out There News (2001a) "Doctors in Jalalabad operating without anesthetics," November 7.

Out There News (2001b) "Taliban accuses US of deliberately targeting civilians," October 18.

Pakistan News Service (2001) "Afghan hospital system collapses: Injured civilians forced to cross border," October 28.

Parry, M. (2001) "Mounting concern over the human cost of war in Afghanistan," *Agence France-Presse*, November 16.

Parry, R. (2001a) "Witnesses confirm that dozens were killed in bombing," *Independent*, October 13.

Parry, R. (2001b) "UN fears 'disaster' over strikes near huge dam,' *Independent*, November 8.

Partridge, C. H. (ed.) *Fundamentalisms*. Carlisle: Paternoster Press.

Passavant, P. and Dean, J. (2002) "Representation and the event," *Theory and Event*, 5 (4). Also available at http:/muse.jhu.edu/journals/theory_and_event/voo5/5.4passavant.html.

Patel, S., D'Cruz, C., and Burra, S. (2002) "Beyond evictions in a global city: People-managed resettlement in Mumbai," *Environment and Urbanization*, 14 (1), 159–72.

Pearsall, K. (1998) "This technology is eye-catching," *Computing Canada*, 24 (2), 11–12.

Penenberg, A. L. (2001) "Surveillance society," *Wired*, December, 157–60.

Peters, R. (1996) "Our soldiers, their cities," *Parameters*, spring, 1–7.

Peters, R. (1997) "The future of armored warfare," *Parameters*, autumn, 1–9.

Peterson, C. (2002) " 'Smarter' bombs still hit civilians," *Christian Science Monitor*, October 22.

Peterson, E. (ed.) *Cities are Abnormal*. Norman: University of Oklahoma Press.

Pieterse, J. (2002) "Globalization, kitsch and conflict: Technologies of work, war and politics," *Review of International Political Economy*, 9 (1), 1–36.

Plunz, R., Baratloo, M., and Conrad, M. (eds.) (1998) *New Urbanism: Mostar: Bosnia and Herzegovina*. Studio Works 6/MSAUD New Urbanisms Series. New York: Columbia Books of Architecture.

Pomfret, J. (2001) "China strengthens ties with Taliban by signing economic deal," *Washington Post*, September 13.

Porteous, J. and Smith, S. (2001) *Domicide: The Global Destruction of Home*. Montreal and Kingston: McGill–Queen's University Press.

Poster, M. (1995) *The Second Media Age*. Cambridge: Polity Press.

Power, M. (2001) "Technology and the structuring of the financial district of London." In S. Brunn and S. Leinbach (eds.) *The Worlds of Electronic Commerce*. Chichester: Wiley.

PR Newswire (2001) "Boston Logan airport chooses south Florida security company," October 31. http://ir.shareholder.com/vsnx/ReleaseDetail.cfm?ReleaseID = 63478.

Prashad, V. (2001) "Aerial bombardment in the racist contemporary," *Little India*, November. http://littleindia.com/India/nov2001/aerial.htm .

Press, D. G. (1999) "Urban warfare: Options, problems and the future." http://web.mit.edu/ssp/Publications/confseries/urbanwarfare/urbanwarfare.html; accessed 17 May 17, 2001.

Problems of Air Defense: Final Report of Project Charles (1951). Cambridge, MA: MIT.

Prodanovic, M. (2002) "Urbicide and the chances for reconstruction of Balkan cities." In J. Ockman (ed.) *Out of Ground Zero: Case Studies in Urban Reinvention*. Berlin: Prestel Verlag, 138–49.

Project for the New American Century (2000) *Rebuilding America's Defenses*. Washington, DC.

Rabinovitz, D. (2002) "Oriental othering and national identity: A review of early Israel anthropological studies of Palestinians," *Identities: Global Studies of Culture and Power*, 9, 305–24.

Rabinovitz, G. (2003) "Israel to raze Palestinian homes with robot bulldozers," *USA Today*, November 19, 6.

Rainham, M. (2003) *Myths of Homeland Security*. London: Wiley.

Rampton, S. and Stauber, J. (2003) *Weapons of Mass Deception: The Uses of Propaganda in Bush's War on Iraq*. London: Robinson.

Rashbaum, W. K. (2003) "Woman dies after officers mistakenly raid her home," *New York Times*, May 19, A17.

Rashid, A. (2000) *Taliban: Militant Islam, Oil and Fundamentalism in Central Asia*. New Haven, CT: Yale University Press.

Reeves, P. (2000) "Israelis bulldoze homes, orange groves and cattle," *Independent*, December 7, 17.

Reich, R. (1991) *The Work of Nations: Preparing Ourselves for Twenty-First Century Capitalism*. New York: Knopf.

Reinhart, T. (2002) *Israel/Palestine: How to End the War of 1948*. New York: Seven Stories Press.

Remers, W. (2000) *Chemists at War*. Tucson, AZ: Clarice Publishers.

Report of the Project East River (1952) New York: Associated Universities.

Reporters Without Borders (2001) "War coverage in Afghanistan: RSF asks the US army not to take Afghan media as military targets," November 9.

Reporters Without Borders (2003) *Israel/Palestine: The Black Book*. London: Pluto Press.

Reuters (2001) "Microchips under the skin offer ID, raise questions," *New York Times*, December 22. Also available at www.nytimes.com/reuters/technology/tech-bizchips.html.

Reuveney, R. (2003) "Fundamentalist colonialism: The geopolitics of Israeli–Palestinian conflict," *Political Geography*, 22, 347–80.

Rheingold, H. (2002) *Smart Mobs*. Cambridge, MA: Perseus Publishing.

Rich, F. (2002) "Thanks for the heads-up," *New York Times*, op-ed May 25. Also available at www.nytimes.com/2002/05/opinion/25RICH.html.

Richison, R. (2002) *Berlin: The War, The Wall*. Berlin: Jaron Verlag.

Riedlmayer, A. (1994) "The war on people and the war on culture," *New Combat*, autumn, 16–19.

Riedlmayer, A. (1995) "Killing memory: The targeting of Bosnia's cultural heritage." Testimony presented at a hearing of the Commission on Security and Cooperation in Europe, US Congress, April 4, 1995. http://www.haverford.edu/relg/sells/killing.html.

Riedlmayer, A. (2002) *Destruction of Cultural Heritage in Bosnia-Herzegovina 1992–1996: A Post-War Survey of Selected Municipalities*. Expert report prepared for the International Criminal Tribunal for the Former Yugoslavia (ICTY), the Hague. Available online as part of the Milosevic Trial Public Archive, Human Rights Program, Bard College, http://hague.bard.edu/reports/BosHeritageReport-AR.pdf.

Roberts A. and Guelff, R. (eds.) (2000) *Documents on the Laws of War*, 3rd edn. Oxford: Oxford University Press.

Roberts, J. (1982) *Walter Benjamin*. London: Macmillan.

Rodrik, D. (1997) *Has Globalization Gone Too Far?* Washington, DC: Institute for International Economics.

Rogers, A. (1996) *Law on the Battlefield*. Manchester: Manchester University Press.

Roldàn, M. (2003) "Wounded Medellin: Narcotics traffic against a background of industrial decline." In J. Schneider and I. Susser (eds.) *Wounded Cities: Destruction and Reconstruction in a Globalized World*. London: Berg, 129–48.

Roost, F. (1988) "Recreating the city as entertainment center: The media industry's role in transforming Potsdamer Platz and Times Square," *Journal of Urban Technology*, 5 (3), 1–21.

Rose, M. (1990) *Interstate: Express Highway Politics, 1939–1989*. Knoxville: University of Tennessee Press.

Rosen, B. (2001) "A cautionary tale for a new age of surveillance," *New York Times (online)*, October 7.

Rosen, J. (2002) "Silicon Valley's spy game," *New York Times*, April 14. Also available at www.nytimes.com/2002/04/14/magazine/14TECHNO.html.

Rosenau, J. (1990) *Turbulence in World Politics: A Theory of Change and Continuity*. Princeton, NJ: Princeton University Press.

Rosenau, W. (1997) "Every room is a new battle: The lessons of modern urban warfare," *Studies in Conflict and Terrorism*, 20 (4), 371–94.

Rössler, M. (1989) "Applied geography and area research in Nazi society: Central place theory and planning, 1933–1945," *Environment and Planning D: Society and Space*, 7, 419–31.

Rotbard, S. (2003a) "Tower and stockade." In R. Segal and E. Weizman (eds.) *A Civilian Occupation*. Tel Aviv: Babel Press; London: Verso.

Rotbard, S. (2003b) "White lies, white city." In Witte de With Center for Contemporary Art, *Territories: Builders, Warriors and Other Mythologies*. Rotterdam, 27–40.

Rowe, P. and Sarkis, H. (1998) (eds.) *Projecting Beirut: Episodes in the Construction and Reconstruction of a Modern City*. London: Prestel.

Rubinstein, D. (2002) "Canada preps for G8 summit," *AlterNet.org* June 24. http://www.Alternet.org/print.html?Story1D = 13446; accessed June 24, 2002.

Ruiz, A. (2001) "Soup kitchen lines longer since tragedy," *New York Daily News*, October 30.

Rummel, R. (1997) *Death by Government*. New York: Transaction.

Rumsfeld, D. (2001) "DOD acquisition and logistics excellence week kickoff–bureaucracy to battlefield," *Defense Link*, US Department of Defense, September 10, 2001. http://www.defenselink.mil/speeches/2001/s20010910–secdef.html.

Safier, M. (2001) "Confronting 'urbicide': Crimes against humanity, civility and diversity and the case for a civic-cosmopolitan response to the attack on New York," *City*, 5 (3), 416–29.

Said, E. (2003) *Orientalism*. Harmondsworth: Penguin Books.

Salahuddin, S. (2001) "Bombs leave Afghan children in shock," *Reuters*, October 26.

Sales, F. (2003) "Guerro contra el suelo que pisan," *El Pais*, October 19, 8.

Salmon, C. (2002) "Sabreen, or patience." www.autodafe.org; accessed April 18, 2002.

Sandercock, L. (ed.) (1998) *Making the Invisible Visible: A Multicultural Planning History.* Berkeley, University of California Press.

Sandercock, L. (2003) *Cosmopolis II: Mongrel Cities in the Twenty-First Century.* London: Athlone Press.

Sanger, D. E. (2002) "Summit leaves protesters stuck at base camp," *New York Times,* June 27, A13.

Sassen, S. (2002a) "Correspondence with Saskia Sassen," *Quaderns d'arguitectura I Urbanisme,* January.

Sassen, S. (2002b) "Governance hotspots: Challenges we must confront in the post September 11th world." In K. Booth and T. Dunne (eds.) *Worlds in Collision: Terror and the Future of Global Order.* London: Macmillan Palgrave, 313–24.

Savitch, H. and Ardashev, G. (2001) "Does terror have an urban future?" *Urban Studies,* 38 (13), 2515–33.

Schabas, W. (2000) *Genocide in International Law.* Cambridge: Cambridge University Press.

Scheer, T. (2000) "Where diversity rules cities: Architecture and urban design in Berlin between 1900 and 2000." In T. Scheer, J. P. Kleihuis, and P. Kahlfeldt (eds.) *City of Architecture: Architecture of the City – Berlin 1900–2000.* Berlin: Nicolai, 11–25.

Scheer, T., Kleihuis, J. P., and Kahlfeldt, P. (2000) *City of Architecture: Architecture of the City – Berlin 1900–2000.* Berlin: Nicolai.

Schell, J. (2001) "A hole in the world," *Nation,* October 1, 4.

Schemann, S. (2002) "Attacks turn Palestinian plans into bent metal and piles of dust," *New York Times,* April 11.

Scheper-Hughes, N. and Bourgois, S. (eds.) (2003) *Violence in War and Peace: An Anthology.* Oxford: Blackwell.

Schmitt, C. (1996) *The Concept of the Political.* Chicago, IL: University of Chicago Press.

Schneider, J. and Susser, I. (eds.) (2003) *Wounded Cities: Destruction and Reconstruction in a Globalized World.* London: Berg.

Schneider, W. (1963) *Uberall ist Babylon [Babylon is Everywhere],* trans. I. Sammet and J. Oldenberg. New York: McGraw-Hill.

Schneier, B. (2001) "Biometrics in airports." www.extremetech.com/ 0,3428,a%253D15070,00.asp.

SchNEWS (2003a) "After eights," May 23, Issue 407. http://schnews.org.uk/ archive/News405.htm; accessed May 23, 2003.

SchNEWS (2003b) "Mod's 'N' wreckers," September 5, Issue 421. http:// www.schnews.org.uk/archieve/news421.htm; accessed September 7, 2003.

Schulz, B. (2000) *The Reichstag,* Munich: Prestal.

Sciolino, E. (2003) "Scores of thousands protest conference, some violently," *New York Times,* June 2, A9.

Sebald, W. G. (2003) *On the Natural History of Destruction.* London: Hamish Hamilton.

Security Industry Association (2003) http://www.siaonline.org.

Segal, R. and Weizman, E. (2003) "The mountain." In R. Segal and E. Weizman (eds.) *A Civilian Occupation*. Tel Aviv: Babel Press; London: Verso.

Sells, M. (1996) *The Bridge Betrayed: Religion and Genocide in Bosnia*. Berkeley: University of California Press.

Selwyn, T. (2001) "Landscapes of separation: Reflections on the symbolism of by-pass roads in Palestine." In B. Bender and M. Winer (eds.) *Contested Landscapes: Movement, Exile and Place*. Oxford: Berg, 225–40.

Shane, D. (1995) "Balkanization and the postmodern city." In P. Lang (ed.) *Mortal City*. New York: Princeton Architectural Press, 54–70.

Sharma, S. and Kumar, S. (2003) "The military backbone of globalization," *Race and Class*, 44 (3), 23–39.

Sharon, A. and Chanoff, D. (2001) *Warrior: The Autobiography of Ariel Sharon*. New York: Simon and Schuster.

Sharp, J. (2000) *Condensing the Cold War: Reader's Digest and American Identity*. Minneapolis: University of Minnesota Press.

Shaw, M. (1991) *Post-Military Society*. Cambridge: Polity Press.

Shaw, M. (1996) *Civil Society and Media in Global Crises: Representing Distant Violence*. London: Pinter.

Shaw, M. (2001) "New wars of the city." Unpublished manuscript. Available at http://www.martinshaw.org/.

Shaw, M. (2003) *War and Genocide*. Cambridge: Polity Press.

Shemann, S. (2002) "Attacks turn Palestinian plans into bent metal and piles of dust," *New York Times*, April 11.

Shepherd, N. (2003) "Watchful eyes keep Sydney from harm: Celebrating 2003," *Daily Telegraph* (Sydney) January 1, 5.

Shveet, A. (2002) "War for the peace of the moment," *Ha'aretz*, March 10, 1

Sifton, J. (2001) "A last road trip through premodern, postmodern Afghanistan," *New York Times*, September 30.

Silber, L. and Little, A. (1995) *The Death of Yugoslavia*. London: Penguin/BBC Books.

Simmons, C. (2001) "Urbicide and the myth of Sarajevo," *Partisan Review*, 68 (4), 624–30.

Simon, R. (2002) " 'Transferring' the Arabs ?" *CBSnews.com*, April 9. Accessed May 29, 2002.

Simons, G. (1994) *Iraq: From Sumar to Saddam*. London: Macmillan.

Simons, M. (2001) "Security on the brain, solutions in the eyes," *New York Times*, October 25. Also available at www.nytimes.com/2001/10/25/international/europe/25AMST.html.

Sinnreich, R. (2002) "A hard look at Jenin," *Washington Post*, May 7, A21.

Sivell, G. (1993) "Walled city mooted to thwart the terrorists," *The Times*, April 27.

Smith, C. (2001) "Under the guise of security: House demolitions in Gaza," *Middle East Report Press Information*, Note 63. Available at www.merip.org/pins/pin63.html.

Smith, G. (2003) "The electrocuting water cannon," *Village Voice*, January 29–February 4. http://www.villagevoice.com/issues/0305/smith.php; accessed January 28, 2003.

Smith, H. (1993) "Checkpoints mark fortress London," *Evening Standard*, June 7, 6.

Smith J. (1998) *The Linebacker Raids: The Bombing of North Vietnam, 1972*. London: Wellington House.

Smith, T. (2002) "The new law of war: Legitimizing hi-tech and infrastructural violence," *International Studies Quarterly*, 46, 355–74.

Soffer, A. (2001) *Israel, Demography 2000–2020: Dangers and Opportunities*. Haifa: University of Haifa Press.

Soja, E. (2000) *Postmetropolis: Critical Studies of Cities and Regions*. Oxford: Blackwell.

Sontag, S. (1966) "The imagination of disaster." In S. Sontag, *Against Interpretation*. New York: Dell, 203–18.

Sontag, S. (2003) "The telling shot," *Guardian Review*, February 1, 4–8.

Sorkin, M. and Zukin, S. (2002) *After the World Trade Center*. New York: Routledge.

Spiller, R. (2000) *Sharp Corners: Urban Operations at Century's End*. Fort Leavonsworth, KS: Staff College Press.

Sponster, C. (1992) "Beyond the ruins: The geopolitics of urban decay and cybernetic play," *Science Fiction Studies*, 20 (2), 251–65.

Squatriglia, C. (2002) "Winter games security – swifter, higher, stronger," *San Francisco Chronicle*, January 20. http://www.globalsecurity.org/org/news/2002/020120–attack01.htm; accessed January 25, 2002.

Stalder, F. (1999) "Exploring political issues of electronic cash," *Canadian Journal of Communication*, 24 (2).

Stalder, F. and Lyon, D. (2002) "ID cards and social classification." In D. Lyon (ed.) *Surveillance as Social Sorting: Privacy, Risk, and Digital Discrimination*. New York: Routledge.

Stanley, J. and Steihardt, B. (2002) *Drawing a Black: The Failure of Facial Recognition in Tampa, Florida*. Washington, DC: ACLU.

Statewatch News online (2002) "NATO security conference protests quashed by police," March 1. http://www.statewatch.org/news/2002/mar/01munich.htm; accessed March 25, 2002.

Statewatch News online (2003) "Anti-terrorist law used against arms fair protesters," September 5. http://www.statewatch.org/news/2003/sep/05DSEi.htm; accessed September 7, 2003.

Steele, J. (2002) "Forgotten victims: The full human cost of US air strikes will never be known, but many more died than those killed directly by bombs," *Guardian*, May 20.

Stein, R. (2003) "Israeli leisure, 'Palestinian terror,' and the question of Palestine (again)," *Theory and Event*, 6 (3), 1–13.

Stein, Y. (2002) *Policy of Destruction: House Demolitions and Destruction of Agricultural Land in the Gaza Strip*. Report by B'tselem–Israeli Information Center for Human Rights in the Occupied Territories, February. Available at www.btselem.org.

Struck, D. (2002a) "At World Cup, terrorism is biggest foe," *Washington Post*, May 31, A1.

Struck, D. (2002b) "Danger looms in collecting a war's explosive residue: US bombing adds to task of clearing mines, ordnance," *Washington Post*, February 3.

Stuart, D. (2001) "The dangers of quick-fix law and order legislation in the criminal law: Despite recent government amendments the Anti-Terrorism Bill C-36 should be withdrawn." Paper given at a Surveillance Project seminar, Queen's University, November 15.

Sun Tzu (1963) *The Art of War*, trans. S. B. Griffith. Oxford: Oxford University Press.

Susser, I. and Schneider, J. (2003) "Wounded cities: Destruction and reconstruction in a globalized world." In J. Schneider and I. Susser (eds.) *Wounded Cities: Destruction and Reconstruction in a Globalized World*. London: Berg, 1–24.

Swanstrom, T. (2002) "Are fear and urbanism at war?" *Urban Affairs Review*, 38 (1), 135–40.

Tamari, D. (2001) "Military operations in urban environments: The case of Lebanon 1982." In M. Desch (ed.) *Soldiers in Cities: Military Operations on Urban Terrain*. Carlisle, PA: Strategic Studies Institute.

Taylor, P. (1996) *The Way the Modern World Works*. New York: Wiley.

Thayer, H. (2001) *Afghanistan Power: Infrastructure Requirements at the End of the Conflict*. London: Frost and Sullivan.

Thibodeau, Capt. K. (2002) "389th T-Bolts first F-16s to use new bombs," *Gunfighter*, 15, February 5, 8.

Thierae, W. (2000) "Foreword." In B. Schulz, *The Reichstag*. Munich: Prestal, 7–8.

Thomas, T. (1999) "The battle of Grozny: Deadly classroom for urban combat," *Parameters*, 29, 87–102.

Thompson, E. (1982) "Notes on exterminism: The last stage of civilization." In New Left Review (ed.) *Exterminism and Cold War*. London: Verso.

Thompson, W. S. (1946) "The atomic threat." In E. T. Peterson (ed.) *Cities Are Abnormal*. Norman: University of Oklahoma Press, 226–38.

Thornton, K. (2003) "Security for game is tighter than '98: Military jets, no fly zone among the precautions," *San Diego Union-Tribune*, January 19, A1.

Thornton, W. (2003) "Cold War II: Islamic terrorism as power politics," *Antipode*, 35 (2), 205–11.

Thrift, N. (1998). "The rise of soft capitalism." In A. Herod, G. Ó Tuathail, and S. Roberts (eds.) *Unruly World? Globalization, Governance and Geography*. London: Routledge.

Thrift, N. and French, S. (2002) "The automatic production of space," *Transactions of the Institute of British Geographers*, 27 (4), 309–35.

Thussu, D. and Freedman, D. (eds.) (2003) *War and the Media*. London: Sage.

Tibbets, P. (n.d.) "The official website of Brig. Gen. Paul W. Tibbets (USAF Ret.)." http://www.theenolagay.com.

Tiratsoo, N., Hasegawa, J., Mason, T., and Matsumura, T. (eds.) (2002) *Urban Reconstruction in Britain and Japan, 1945–1955: Dreams, Plans and Realities*. Luton: University of Luton Press.

Tisdall, S. (2003) "Resist the official pol-speak of Bush's 'war on terror'," *Guardian*, November 4, 24.

Todorova, M. (1997) *Imagining the Balkans*. Oxford: Oxford University Press.

Toolis, K. (2003) "The revenger's tragedy: Why women turn to suicide bombing," *Observer*, October 12, 22.

Townsend, M. and Harris, P. (2003) "Security role for traffic cameras," *Observer*, February 9.

Traynor, I. (1999) "MPs pick holes in the new Reichstag," *Guardian*, July 3.

Tuastad, D. (2003) "Neo-Orientalism and the new barbarism thesis: Aspects of symbolic violence in the Middle East conflict(s)," *Third World Quarterly*, 24 (4), 571–88.

Turse, N. (2003) "Bringing the war home: The new military–industrial–entertainment complex at war and play." www.ccmep.org/2003_articles/Gerenal/101703_bringing_the_war_home.htm; accessed November 2003.

Turton, D. (2002) *War and Ethnicity: Global Connections and Local Violence*. London: Routledge.

United Nations (2002) *Report of the Secretary-General Prepared Pursuant to General Assembly Resolution ES-10/10*. New York: United Nations.

Urquhart, C. (2003) "Israel's hard men fight for peace," *Observer*, November 30, 22.

Van Allen Institute (eds.) (2002) *How Cities Renew, Rebuild, and Remember*. New York: Van Allen Institute.

Van Tijen, Tjeffe (n.d.) "Unbombing the world, 1911–2001." http://people.-a2000.nl/ttijen/ubw/ubw01a.html.

Vanderbilt, T. (2002) *Survival City: Adventures Among the Ruins of Atomic America*. Princeton, NJ: Princeton University Press.

Vecsey, G. (2003) "Athens puts its game face on," *New York Times*, June 17, C15.

Vergara, C. (1997) *The New American Ghetto*. New Brunswick, NJ: Rutgers University Press.

Vergara, C. (1999) *American Ruins*. New York: Monacelli.

Victor, B. (2003) *Army of Roses: Inside the World of Palestinian Women Suicide Bombers*. New York: Rodale.

Vidal, G. (2002) *Dreaming War*. London: Clairview.

Vidal, J. (2003) "Forced to slum it," *Guardian*, October 10, 27.

Vidler, A. (2001) "Photourbanism: Planning the city from above and below." In G. Bridge and S. Watson (eds.) *A Companion to the City*. Oxford: Blackwell, 35–45.

Virilio, P. (1977) *Speed and Politics*, 1st edn. New York: Semiotext(e).

Virilio, P. (1986) *Speed and Politics*, 2nd edn. New York: Semiotext(e).

Virilio, P. (1987) "The overexposed city," *Zone*, 1 (2).

Virilio, P. (1995) *The Art of the Motor*. Minneapolis: University of Minnesota Press.

Virilio, P. (1996) *Bunker Archeology*. New York: Princeton Architectural Press.

Virilio, P. (1997) *Open Sky*, trans. J. Rose. London: Verso.

Virilio, P. (2002) *Desert Screen: War at the Speed of Light*. London: Continuum.

Wadham, J. (1994). Letter to the *Times (Internet Edition)*, April 4.

Walker, R. (1993) *Inside/Outside: International Relations as Political Theory*. Cambridge: Cambridge University Press.

Walzer, M. (1977) *Just and Unjust Wars: A Moral Argument with Historical Illustrations*, 1st edn. London: Allen Lane.

Walzer, M. (1992) *Just and Unjust Wars: A Moral Argument with Historical Illustrations*, 2nd edn. New York: Basic Books.

Warchitecture (1993) *Urbicide – Sarajevo/Sarajevo, une ville blessee*. Exhibition catalogue, Warchitecture/Association of Architects DAS – SABIH and Arc en Rêve Center D'Architecture/Center Georges Pompidou, Paris.

Warn, K. (2002) "No protesters around to disturb fireside chat," *Financial Times*, June 28, 10.

Warren, R. (2002) "Situating the city after September 11: Military urban doctrine, 'pop-up' armies and spatial chess," *International Journal of Urban and Regional Research*, 26, 614–19.

Watson, T. (2003) "Introduction: Critical infrastructures after 9/11," *Postcolonial Studies*, 6 (1), 109–11.

Weart, S. (1988) *Nuclear Fear: A History of Images*. Cambridge, MA: Harvard University Press.

Weber, M. (1958) *The City*. Glencoe, IL: Free Press.

Webster, F. and Robins, K. (1986) *Information Technology: A Luddite Analysis*. Norwood, NJ: Ablex.

Weizman, E. (2002) *The Politics of Verticality*. Available at www.opendemocracy.net.

Werrell, K. (1996) *Blankets of Fire: US Bombers Over Japan During World War II*. Washington, DC: Smithsonian Institution Press.

Weston, G. (2002) "Kananaskis? Film at 11; Because that's the only way for most media to report on the G8," *Toronto Star*, June 26, 15.

Wheeler, N. (2001) *Protecting Afghan Civilians From the Hell of War*. Viewpoint Essay 9, December. New York: Social Science Research Center.

Whitaker, B. (2002) "UN to feed 500,000 needy Palestinians," *Guardian*, May 22, 5.

White, E. (1948) *Essays of E. B. White*. New York: Harper.

White, E. (1949) *Here is New York*. New York: Harper.

Wight, M. (2003) *You Back the Attack! We'll Bomb Who We Want!* New York: Seven Stories.

Willis, S. (2003) "Empire's shadow," *New Left Review*, July–August, 59–70.

Wilson, A. (2003) "Bangkok: The bubble city." In J. Schneider and I. Susser (eds.) *Wounded Cities: Destruction and Reconstruction in a Globalized World*. London: Berg, 203–26.

Wirth, L. (1946) "Does the atomic bomb doom the modern city?" *New Jersey Municipalities*, April, 25–9.

Wirth, L. (1996) "Urbanism as a way of life." In R. LeGates and F. Stout (eds.) *The City Reader*. London: Routledge, 189–97.

Wise, M. (1998) *Capital Dilemma: Germany's Search for a New Architecture of Democracy*. Princeton, NJ: Princeton University Press.

Wolfendale, S. (2003) *Berlin: The Reich Comes Home*. http://www.travelintelligence.net/wsd/articles/art_340.html; accessed October 6, 2003.

Wood, C. (2001) "The electronic eye view," *Mclean's*, November 19, 94–7.

Wood, D. (2001) "Algorithmic surveillance and social exclusion: An agenda for research." Paper given at New Technologies and Social Welfare conference, University of Nottingham, December 17.

Woods, L. (1995) "Everyday war." In P. Lang (ed.) *Mortal City*. New York: Princeton Architectural Press, 46–53.

Woods, L. (2001) *Radical Reconstruction*. Princeton, NJ: Princeton University Press.

Woodward, C. (2001) *In Ruins*. London: Chatto and Windus.

Wright, G. and Rabinow, P. (1982) "Spatialization of power, a discussion of the work of Michel Foucault," *Skyline*, March: 14.

Wright, M. (2003) *Back the Attack! Remixed War Propaganda*. New York: Seven Stories.

Wright, S. (1999) "Hypocrisy of 'non-lethal' arms," *Le Monde diplomatique*, December. http://mondediplo.com/1999/12/09wright; accessed March 7, 2003.

Yeheskeli, Y. (2002) "Jenin bulldozer driver speaks," *Yideot Aharonot*, June 13, 2002. Also available at www.indymedia.org.il.

Yeoh, B. (1996) *Contesting Space: Power Relations and the Urban Built Environment in Colonial Singapore*. Kuala Lumpur: Oxford University Press.

Yiftachel, O. (1995) "The dark side of modernism: Planning as control of an ethnic minority." In S. Watson and K. Gibson (eds.) *Postmodern Cities and Spaces*. Oxford: Blackwell, 216–42.

Young, J. (1999) *The Exclusive Society*. London: Sage.

Zarlengo, K. (1999) "Civilian threat, the suburban citadel, and atomic age American women," *Signs: Journal of Women in Culture and Society*, 24 (4), 925–58.

Zeitoun, M. (2002) "IDF infrastructure destruction by bulldozer," *Electronic Intifada*. www.electronicintifada.net; accessed October 14, 2002.

Zizek, S. (2003) *Welcome to the Desert of the Real!* London: Verso.

Zulaika, J. (2003) "The self-fulfilling prophecies of counterterrorism, *Radical History Review*, 85, 191–9.

Zulaika, J. and Douglass, W. (1996). *Terror and Taboo: The Follies, Fables and Faces of Terrorism*. New York: Routledge.

Zunes, S. (2002) *Tinderbox: US Foreign Policy and the Roots of Terrorism*. London: Zed Books.

Zureik, E. (2003) "Demography and transfer: Israel's road to nowhere," *Third World Quarterly*, 24 (4), 619–30.

Index

STUDIES IN URBAN AND SOCIAL CHANGE BOOK SERIES

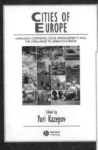

Cities of Europe
Changing Contexts, Local Arrangements and the Challenge to Urban Cohesion

Edited by YURI KAZEPOV

Cities of Europe is a unique combination of book and CD-ROM examining the effects of changing contexts on the spatial and political arrangements of western European cities.

336 pages / 1-4051-2133-5 HB / 1-4051-2132-7 PB / **November 2004**

Cities, War, and Terrorism
Towards an Urban Geopolitics

Edited by STEPHEN GRAHAM

Cities, War and Terrorism is the first book to look critically at the ways in which warfare, terrorism and counter-terrorism policies intersect in cities in the post Cold-War period. The book brings together new writing by the world's leading analysts of urban space and military and terrorist violence.

384 pages / 1-4051-1574-2 HB / 1-4051-1575-0 PB / **October 2004**

Cities and Visitors
Regulating People, Markets and City Space

Edited by LILY M. HOFFMAN, SUSAN S. FAINSTEIN & DENNIS R. JUDD

▪ Provides an analytic framework for the study of urban tourism.

▪ Brings urban tourism into focus as an important political, economic, and cultural phenomenon.

▪ Original essays by established scholars, including studies of Venice, Mexico, Montreal, New York, and London.

280 pages / 1-4051-0058-3 HB / 1-4051-0059-1 PB / **September 2003**

Visit the book series page on www.blackwellpublishing.com for more details and to find out about other books in the series.

Understanding the City Edited by JOHN EADE & CHRISTOPHER MELE

The New Chinese City Edited by JOHN R. LOGAN

Cinema and the City Edited by MARK SHIEL & TONY FITZMAURICE

Globalizing Cities Edited by PETER MARCUSE & RONALD VAN KEMPEN

The Social Control of Cities? SOPHIE BODY-GENDROT

Contemporary Urban Japan JOHN CLAMMER

Capital Culture: Gender at Work in the City LINDA MCDOWELL

Urban Poverty and the Underclass ENZO MINGIONE

Cities After Socialism MICHAEL HARLOE, IVAN SZELENYI & GREGORY ANDRUSZ

Post-Fordism ASH AMIN

Free Markets and Food Riots JOHN WALTON & DAVID SEDDON

The SUSC Editors are always interested in proposals for new books in the series. Please send details to Harvey Molotch, **molotch@aol.com**, Linda McDowell, **l.mcdowell@ucl.ac.uk**, Margit Mayer, **mayer@zedat.fu-berlin.de** and Chris Pickvance, **C.G.Pickvance@kent.ac.uk**

Blackwell
Publishing

www.blackwellpublishing.com